Study Guide

Cost Accounting
Foundations & Evolutions
SIXTH EDITION

Michael R. Kinney
Texas A & M University

Jenice Prather-Kinsey
University of Missouri – Columbia

Cecily A. Raiborn
Loyola University – New Orleans

Prepared by

Sharie T. Dow

Australia · Canada · Mexico · Singapore · Spain · United Kingdom · United States

SOUTH-WESTERN

Study Guide to accompany Cost Accounting: Foundations and Evolutions, Sixth Edition
Michael R. Kinney, Jenice Prather-Kinsey, & Cecily A. Raiborn

VP/Editorial Director:
Jack W. Calhoun

Publisher:
Rob Dewey

Senior Acquisitions Editor:
Sharon Oblinger

Developmental Editor:
Carol Bennet

Marketing Manager:
Keith Chasse

Production Editor:
Margaret M. Bril

Manager of Technology, Editorial:
Vicky True

Technology Project Editor:
Robin Browning

Manufacturing Coordinator:
Doug Wilke

Printer:
Globus
Minster, OH

Art Director:
Michelle Kunkler

Internal Designer:
Ann Small Design

Cover Designer:
Ann Small Design

Cover Images:
© Getty Images

Photography Manager:
John Hill

Photo Researcher:
Stuart Kunkler

COPYRIGHT © 2006
Thomson South-Western, a part of The Thomson Corporation. Thomson, the Star logo, and South-Western are trademarks used herein under license.

Printed in the United States of America
1 2 3 4 5 07 06 05 04

ISBN 0-324-31788-3

ALL RIGHTS RESERVED.
No part of this work covered by the copyright hereon may be reproduced or used in any form or by any means—graphic, electronic, or mechanical, including photocopying, recording, taping, Web distribution or information storage and retrieval systems, or in any other manner—without the written permission of the publisher.

For permission to use material from this text or product, submit a request online at http://www.thomsonrights.com.

For more information about our products, contact us at:

Thomson Learning Academic Resource Center

1-800-423-0563

Thomson Higher Education
5191 Natorp Boulevard
Mason, OH 45040
USA

Asia (including India)
Thomson Learning
5 Shenton Way
#01-01 UIC Building
Singapore 068808

Australia/New Zealand
Thomson Learning Australia
102 Dodds Street
Southbank, Victoria 3006
Australia

Canada
Thomson Nelson
1120 Birchmount Road
Toronto, Ontario
M1K 5G4
Canada

Latin America
Thomson Learning
Seneca, 53
Colonia Polanco
11560 Mexico
D.F. Mexico

UK/Europe/Middle East/Africa
Thomson Learning
High Holborn House
50/51 Bedford Row
London WC1R 4LR
United Kingdom

Spain (including Portugal)
Thomson Paraninfo
Calle Magallanes, 25
28015 Madrid, Spain

CONTENTS

Preface		V
Chapter 1:	Introduction to Cost Accounting	1
Chapter 2:	Cost Terminology and Cost Behaviors	23
Chapter 3:	Predetermined Overhead Rates, Flexible Budgets and Absorption/Variable Costing	49
Chapter 4:	Job Order Costing	75
Chapter 5:	Activity-Based Management and Activity-Based Costing	97
Chapter 6:	Process Costing	123
Chapter 7:	Standard Costing and Variance Analysis	155
Chapter 8:	The Master Budget	187
Chapter 9:	Break-Even-Point and Cost-Volume-Profit Analysis	215
Chapter 10:	Relevant Information for Decision Making	239
Chapter 11:	Allocation of Joint Productions and Allocation of By-Products	267
Chapter 12:	Introduction to Cost Management Systems	289
Chapter 13:	Responsibility Accounting and Transfer Pricing in Decentralized Organizations	313
Chapter 14:	Capital Budgeting	337
Chapter 15:	Managing Costs and Uncertainty	363
Chapter 16:	Implementing Quality Concepts	385
Chapter 17:	Inventory and Production Management	409
Chapter 18:	Emerging Management Practices	435
Chapter 19:	Performance Measurement, Balanced Scorecards, and Performance Rewards	457

PREFACE

This study guide accompanies the textbook entitled Cost Accounting: Foundations and Evolutions, Sixth Edition, by Kinney, Prather-Kinsey, & Raiborn. For each of the 19 chapters in the textbook, this study guide has a corresponding chapter.

Each chapter in this study guide has three separate sections. The first section is the CHAPTER OVERVIEW. This section describes the highlights of the chapter. The second section is the CHAPTER STUDY GUIDE. This section contains a detailed summary of the key issues and concepts in the corresponding chapter of the accompanying textbook. The last section is the SELF TEST. This section contains questions and answers on the material in the chapter in three formats: true/false, multiple choice, and essay questions and problems. Each chapter has 15 true/false questions, 30 multiple choice questions, and 15 essay questions and problems. The answers for each type of question appear at the end of each chapter.

This study guide separates material from an appendix or appendices at the end of a chapter from the CHAPTER STUDY GUIDE. In addition, the study guide clearly identifies questions from material in an appendix or appendices, whether they are true/false questions, multiple choice questions, or essay questions and problems. This separation will allow you to skip the material from an appendix if your instructor chooses not to cover it. On the other hand, if you need to pay careful attention to the material in an appendix, you can locate it easily.

This study guide can provide you with enhanced understanding of the material presented in the textbook. However, you should read the chapter in the textbook first. This study guide serves as a supplement to the textbook. In particular, the textbook has many helpful examples that this study guide does not discuss. The CHAPTER STUDY GUIDE refers to most of the exhibits in the textbook. You should review the exhibits carefully.

The questions and problems in this study guide can help you to evaluate your understanding of the material. By using the study guide in this manner, you can identify the areas in which you are competent and discover areas that you want to study further. To receive the most benefit from the questions and problems, you should work them yourself before looking at the answers. You can then return to the textbook to review the areas that need further study. For example, you might not understand why the answer shown in the study guide is correct. By returning to the textbook, you will usually understand why the answer is correct. You might also want to ask your instructor to clarify any issues or answers to questions that you still do not understand.

You might want to return to the study guide as you prepare for exams. The CHAPTER STUDY GUIDE section can provide you with a good review of the main points in each chapter. In addition, you can review the questions and problems that were difficult for you the first time.

Any errors in this edition are the responsibility of the preparer. Please send any comments on this study guide by e-mail to shariedow@yahoo.com.

CHAPTER 1

INTRODUCTION TO COST ACCOUNTING

CHAPTER OVERVIEW

This chapter contains an overview of cost accounting and describes the legal and ethical considerations applicable to management accounting and cost accounting. It discusses the relationships among financial accounting, management accounting, and cost accounting. This chapter also explains the significance of organizational strategy and describes how an organization's strategy relates to the cost accounting system. This chapter describes the importance of the value chain in strategic management and how organizations use the balances scorecard to measure performance in several dimensions important for achieving the organization's strategic goals. This chapter explains why accountants must understand an organization's structure to perform their jobs effectively. This chapter concludes with a discussion of cost accounting standards.

CHAPTER STUDY GUIDE

Accounting is often called the language of business. Accounting is also an information system designed to provide useful information to decision makers. Accounting has several different areas of practice, including financial accounting, management accounting, and cost accounting.

Financial accounting focuses on providing information to external users such as creditors and investors. The primary outputs of financial accounting are the financial statements, which include the income statement, the statement of changes in stockholders' equity, the balance sheet, and the statement of cash flows. Accountants must prepare these financial statements in accordance with generally accepted accounting principles, which are often called by their acronym of GAAP. The primary sources of generally accepted accounting principles are the Financial Accounting Standards Board (FASB) and the Securities and Exchange Commission. Publicly held companies must have their financial statements audited by an independent auditing firm. Financial accounting information is historical, quantitative, monetary, and verifiable. Financial accounting emphasizes the activities of the organization as a whole.

Chapter 1: Introduction To Cost Accounting

In the early 1900s, financial accounting dominated management accounting. The growth in the number of publicly held companies drove the demand for audited financial statements. Because technology was limited, generating accounting information was expensive. Companies extracted any desired management accounting information from the financial accounting system. Companies often relied on return on investment (ROI) calculations to allocate resources and evaluate divisional performance. Because ROI is equal to net income divided by total assets, the financial accounting system provided the necessary information. Using a single performance measure, such as ROI, was suitable for a company that operated in only one country, was primarily labor intensive, and owned and managed by a small number of owners who were familiar with the company's processes.

Management accounting focuses on providing information to managers to help them fulfill their functions of planning, controlling, performance evaluation, and decision making. For example, managers are concerned with achieving corporate goals, communicating and implementing strategy, producing and marketing products, and managing business segments. By the mid 1900s, adapting management accounting information from the financial accounting system often led to dysfunctional behavior. Companies had begun to operate in many countries, had a broader product line, and manufactured products by relying on a greater use of machines. As information technology improved, the cost of generating management accounting information decreased, which allowed the management accounting system to evolve independently of the financial accounting system. Exhibit 1-1 lists some of the key differences between financial accounting and management accounting.

Cost accounting overlaps financial accounting and management accounting. Exhibit 1-2 illustrates to the relationships among financial accounting, management accounting, and cost accounting. Cost accounting provides the product cost information for external parties to help them make investment and credit decisions. Cost accounting also provides information to managers for internal purposes.

Management uses cost accounting information to prepare budgets, to evaluate performance, to make pricing decisions, and to make investment decisions. Product cost includes the costs incurred in a factory to make one unit of a product. Managers need to add upstream costs and downstream costs to product costs. Upstream costs include research, development, and product design. Downstream costs include marketing, distribution, and customer service. Exhibit 1-3 illustrates the various types of costs associated with products.

Closely related to cost accounting is cost management. Cost management refers to the objective of reducing costs continually while improving customer satisfaction.

The cost accountant provides information needed by financial accountants and management accountants. Management accounting is flexible rather than being subject to generally accepted accounting principles. Managers need information to help them develop the organization's mission statement, implement strategy, measure and control the value chain and managerial performance, and in setting balanced scorecard goals, objectives, and targets.

Chapter 1: Introduction To Cost Accounting

Managers must consider the organization's mission and the underlying strategy that links the mission to its activities in meeting the challenges of globalization. An organization's mission statement shows the purpose for the organization's existence. An organization uses its mission statement to develop its strategy. The organization should modify its mission statement over time as the business environment changes.

A company develops a strategy to achieve a competitive advantage. Strategy is the plan that shows how the organization will achieve its goals and objectives by using its resources to create value for customers and shareholders. A strategic focus directs a company and its segments toward the company's mission. The subunits of large organizations should have their own strategies aligned with the company's overall strategy.

While managers are responsible for formulating strategy, cost accountants provide management with useful information so that management can assess progress toward the achievement of strategic goals. Exhibit 1-4 illustrates nonfinancial information that managers might use in formulating strategy.

Most companies adopt either a cost leadership or product differentiation strategy. Cost leadership means that a company plans to maintain its competitive advantage by reducing prices below those of competitors. Product differentiation means offering higher quality products or more unique services than do competitors. Some companies follow both strategies at the same time.

Cost accountants provide managers with financial and nonfinancial information to help managers achieve their strategic goals and objectives. Exhibit 1-5 provides a checklist of questions that an organization should answer to have a comprehensive strategy.

An organization's core competencies affect its strategy. A core competency is any critical function or activity for which the organization wants to be more proficient than its competitors. An organization's core competencies may change over time.

The foundation of strategic management is the value chain. The value chain is the set of processes that change inputs into products and services for the company's customers. Exhibit 1-6 shows the major value chain functions. The value chain helps managers emphasize activities that add value and reduce or eliminate activities that do not add value. To be successful, companies must gain the cooperation of everyone in the value chain.

Managers must communicate the company's strategy to everyone in the value chain so that the company can implement the strategy effectively. Cost accountants provide input in the design of the communications network by integrating the information needs of managers of each value chain function.

Managers measure the dimensions of performance relevant to accomplishing strategic goals using accounting information. Traditionally, management simply analyzed historical financial data to assess organizational strategic effectiveness. Generally, historical financial data reflects lag indicators or outcomes that have resulted from past actions. Currently, management may also use lead indicators. Lead indicators reflect future and nonfinancial outcomes including opportunity and problems and thereby helping assess strategic progress and guiding decision making before lag indicators are known. Management can develop lag and lead indicators for many dimensions of performance. Management often uses both lead and lag indicators in a balanced scorecard to assess strategy congruence.

The balance scorecard (BSC) developed by Robert Kaplan of Harvard University and David Norton of Renaissance Solutions Inc is a framework that restates an organizational strategy into clear and objective performance measures focused on customers, internal business processes, employees and shareholders. The BSC includes both long-term and short-term, internal and external, financial and nonfinancial measures to balance management's view and execution of strategy.

The simplified balanced scorecard in Exhibit 1-7 has four perspectives with unique goals and measures: 1) learning and growth, 2) internal business, 3) customer value, and 4) financial performance. The learning and growth perspective focuses on using the organization's intellectual capital to adapt to changing customer service needs and expectations through product or service innovations. The internal business perspective addresses those things that the organization needs to do well to meet customer needs and expectations. The customer value perspective addresses how well the organization is doing relative to important customer criteria such as speed (lead time), quality, service, and price (both purchase and after purchase). Finally the financial perspective addresses the concerns of stockholders and other stakeholders about profitability and organizational growth. Exhibit 1-8 illustrates a more complicated and realistic scorecard than Exhibit 1-7.

The global economy includes international trade, international movement of labor, and international movements of capital and information. Improved methods of communication and technology have made the world smaller. Trade agreements that encourage the international movement of goods and services among countries have contributed to the growth in the global economy. Managers of multinational corporations must develop the strategies for their companies and achieve their organizational goals and objectives within a global structure and under international regulations. Managers should also adhere to high ethical standards. One of the most important responsibilities of top managers in operating in the global economy is the assignment of authority and responsibilities to make decisions.

The organizational structure consists of people, other resources, and commitments acquired and arranged to achieve the organization's strategic goals. The organizational structure indicates the degree to which the organization distributes authority and responsibility. Authority is the right to use resources to accomplish a task or achieve an objective. Responsibility is the obligation to accomplish a task or achieve an objective.

Every organization has line managers and staff employees. Line managers work directly toward the achievement of organizational goals. Exhibit 1-9 illustrates key line managers in an organizational chart. Staff employees give assistance and advice to line managers. Two key staff

Chapter 1: Introduction To Cost Accounting

positions are the treasurer and the controller. The treasurer is responsible for achieving financing, investing, and cash management goals. The controller is responsible for delivering financial statements to management. Cost accountants usually work under the controller.

Managers might be tempted to manipulate the information investors and creditors use to measure the organization's performance. Adherence to high ethical standards can reduce deceptive manipulation of information.

Recently, executives at companies such as WorldCom (now MCI), Enron, and ImClone have been found guilty of crimes related to improper accounting practices. Congress passed the Sarbanes-Oxley Act of 2002 to curb the abuses. This law holds CEOs and CFOs personally accountable for the accuracy of their organization's financial reporting.

The accounting profession promotes high ethical standards for accountants through its professional organizations. The professional organization for management accountants, financial managers, academics, and others is the Institute of Management Accountants (IMA). The IMA also awards the Certified Management Accountant (CMA) and Certified in Financial Management (CFM) designations to its members who pass a comprehensive examination and meet the additional requirements of experience and continuing education. Exhibit 1-10 shows the *Standards of Ethical Conduct for Management Accountants*, published by the IMA. The members of the IMA must follow these standards, which focus on competence, confidentiality, integrity, and objectivity.

Many organizations are becoming more active in promoting responsible behavior because irresponsible behavior often results in more laws and government regulations. For example, after many American companies gave bribes to obtain business in foreign countries, Congress passed the Foreign Corrupt Practices Act (FCPA) in 1977. This law prohibits bribes, kickbacks, and other improper payments to officials of foreign countries to influence them or cause them to use their influence to obtain or retain business. Additionally, in February 1999, the Organization of Economic Cooperation and Development (OECD) issued a document to make it a crime to offer, promise or give a bribe to a foreign public official in order to obtain or retain international business deals. 35 countries had signed this document by the end of 2003 as illustrated in Exhibit 1-11. The United States has modified several provisions of the Foreign Corrupt Practices Act to align with the OEDC document.

The IMA issues directives on management accounting practices called *Statements on Management Accounting* (SMAs). Congress established the Cost Accounting Standards Board (CASB) in 1970 to issue uniform cost accounting standards for defense contractors and federal agencies. The CASB ceased to exist in 1980, but it was recreated in 1988 as an independent board of the Office of Federal Procurement Policy. The CASB's objectives are to increase the uniformity and consistency in government contracting.

The IMA, the CASB, and the Society of Management Accountants of Canada have helped to develop management accounting and cost accounting standards. However, much of the commonly used management accounting and cost accounting practices are based on industry practice and economic and finance theory.

In The Society of Management Accountants in Canada issues *Management Accounting Guidelines* (MAGs). Unlike the statements of the CASB, the *Statements on Management Accounting* and the *Management Accounting Guidelines* are not legally binding.

Chapter 1: Introduction To Cost Accounting

SELF TEST

TRUE/FALSE

1. T F Management accounting focuses on the needs of external users such as investors and creditors.

2. T F Financial accounting focuses primarily on providing information to managers to help them carry out their functions of planning, controlling, performance evaluation, and decision-making.

3. T F Financial perspective addresses the concerns of stockholders and other stakeholders about profitability or organizational growth.

4. T F Access to international markets creates additional opportunities with no additional risks.

5. T F Integrity means that individuals actively participate in activities that would discredit their company or profession.

6. T F Competition is now more between value chains than between individual companies.

7. T F Management accounting does NOT have to follow generally accepted accounting principles.

8. T F The Foreign Corrupt Practices Act prohibits bribes, kickbacks, and other improper payments to officials of foreign governments to obtain or retain business in foreign countries.

9. T F Cost accounting information is a part of management accounting, but companies also use cost accounting in the preparation of financial statements.

10. T F The internal business perspective addresses things that organizations need to do well to meet customer needs and expectations.

11. T F The organizational culture indicates the degree to which the organization distributes authority and responsibility.

12. T F Outcomes that have resulted from past actions are known as lag indicators.

13. T F Lead indicators do not help to asses strategic progress.

14. T F The learning and growth perspective focuses on using the organization's intellectual capital to adapt to changing customer needs.

Chapter 1: Introduction To Cost Accounting

15. T F Line managers work directly towards attaining organizational goals.

MULTIPLE CHOICE

1. Individuals that provide full and fair disclosure of all relevant information demonstrate:

    A. confidentiality.
    B. competence.
    C. integrity.
    D. objectivity.

2. Research, development and product design costs are examples of:

    A. GAAP
    B. downstream costs.
    C. ROI
    D. upstream costs.

3. What indicates the degree to which the organization distributes authority and responsibility?

    A. organizational structure
    B. organizational culture
    C. product life cycle
    D. organizational mission

4. In a company, the position of treasurer and controller are considered:

    A. line managers.
    B. staff employee.
    C. authorities.
    D. line employees.

5. The act of offering superior quality products or more unique services than competitors is known as:

    A. cost leadership.
    B. product differentiation.
    C. competitive leverage.
    D. the value chain.

Chapter 1: Introduction To Cost Accounting 9

6. Net income divided by total assets is also referred to as:

   A. downstream cost.
   B. upstream cost.
   C. product cost.
   D. return on investment.

7. Deciding on a strategy is often a difficult and controversial process that should reflect the company's:

   A. core values.
   B. organizational mission.
   C. core competencies.
   D. organizational perspective.

8. Who publishes the *Standards of Ethical Conduct for Management Accountants?*

   A. American Accounting Association
   B. Institute of Management Accountants
   C. Financial Planning Association
   D. Financial Executives Institute

9. Compared to financial accounting, management accounting is:

   A. more concerned with the segments of the business.
   B. more concerned with historical information.
   C. more concerned with adherence to generally accepted accounting principles.
   D. more concerned with Return on Investments.

10. Which of the following is not an objective of the Cost Accounting Standards Board (CASB)?
    A. increase the uniformity in cost accounting practices among government contractors
    B. establish consistency in cost accounting practices by each particular contractor over time
    C. require contractors to disclose their cost accounting practices
    D. prescribe methods for preparing client financial statements.

11. Any critical function or activity for which the organization wants to be more proficient than its competitors is a:

    A. core competency.
    B. mission.
    C. constraint.
    D. benchmark.

Chapter 1: Introduction To Cost Accounting

12. The financial accounting system:

    A. produces mostly forecasts and budgets.
    B. must use generally accepted accounting principles.
    C. emphasizes the relevance of information over its reliability.
    D. produces information primarily for managers.

13. Companies do not use cost accounting information in:

    A. preparing their financial statements.
    B. preparing plans.
    C. making managerial decisions.
    D. developing mission statements

14. The main aspect of a cost accounting system is the:

    A. preparation of budgets.
    B. preparation of financial statements.
    C. process of tracing input costs to outputs.
    D. evaluation of performance.

15. In responding to globalization challenges, managers must consider the underlying strategy that identifies how a company intends to achieve its

    A. mission.
    B. strategy.
    C. budgets.
    D. constraints.

16. The long-term dynamic plan that shows how the organization will achieve its goals and objectives by satisfying its customers' needs and wants is called:

    A. evaluation.
    B. tactics.
    C. goals.
    D. strategy.

17. A means by which actual business outcomes can be evaluated against performance targets is:

    A. learning and growth prospective
    B. balanced scorecard
    C. financial performance perspective
    D. customer value perspective

Chapter 1: Introduction To Cost Accounting 11

18. _____ addresses how well the organization is doing relative to important customer criteria such as speed, quality service and price.

    A. Learning and growth perspective
    B. Financial performance perspective
    C. Internal business perspective
    D. Customer value perspective

19. Individuals that develop and maintain the skills needed to practice their profession demonstrate:

    A. objectivity
    B. ethics
    C. competence
    D. values

20. Who issues directives on the practice of management and cost accounting called *Statements on Management Accounting?*

    A. Institute of Financial Executives
    B. Institute of American Accounting
    C. Institute of Management Accountants.
    D. Institute of Financial Planning

21. Who is responsible for providing management with necessary information to assess progression towards strategic achievement?

    A. Line managers
    B. Line Supervisors.
    C. Accountants.
    D. Chief Executive Officers.

22. Which organization awards the Certified Management Accountant (CMA) designation?

    A. American Institute of Certified Public Accountants
    B. Institute of Management Accountants
    C. Cost Accounting Standards Board
    D. American Accounting Association

Chapter 1: Introduction To Cost Accounting

23. In the United States, which organization establishes financial accounting standards?

   A. FASB and the SEC
   B. IMA
   C. AAA
   D. CASB

24. Which of the following is not addressed by the IMA's Standards of Ethical Conduct for Management Accountants?

   A. independence
   B. integrity
   C. competence
   D. confidentiality

25. Management's concern for continually reducing costs while concurrently improving customer satisfaction is reflected in:

   A. product cost
   B. cost accounting
   C. customer value perspective
   D. cost management

26. Which organization has issued nonbinding guidelines concerning cost and management accounting called *Statements on Management Accounting*?

   A. Cost Accounting Standards Board
   B. American Institute of Certified Public Accountants
   C. Society of Management Accountants of Canada
   D. Institute of Management Accountants

27. The obligation to accomplish a task or achieve an objective is:

   A. authority.
   B. responsibility.
   C. strategy.
   D. a core competency.

28. Technological innovation, engineering, and product development are all examples of:

   A. core competencies.
   B. cost leadership
   C. distribution indicators.
   D. differentiation strategies.

Chapter 1: Introduction To Cost Accounting

29. The foundation of strategic management is the:

    A. mission statement.
    B. product life cycle.
    C. value chain.
    D. business intelligence system.

30. Differentiation is not related to:

    A. the product itself.
    B. the service itself.
    C. a premium price.
    D. undercutting a competitor's price.

QUESTIONS AND PROBLEMS

1. How do financial accounting and management accounting differ? How does cost accounting relate to financial accounting and management accounting?

2. What are the purposes of cost accounting? What is the most important aspect of a cost accounting system?

3. What is a balanced scorecard? What are the aspects of a balanced scorecard?

4. What are the three competence standards of ethical conduct of the IMA?

5. What is organizational structure? What is the difference between authority and responsibility?

Chapter 1: Introduction To Cost Accounting

6. What should an organization's mission statement include? What purpose does the mission statement serve?

7. What are the confidentiality standards of ethical conduct of the IMA?

8. What are the seven integrity standards of ethical conduct of the IMA?

Chapter 1:   Introduction To Cost Accounting   16

9. List the objectivity standards of ethical conduct of the IMA.

10. What are the objectives of the Cost Accounting Standards Board?

11. List the standards of ethical conduct of the IMA.

Chapter 1: Introduction To Cost Accounting

12. What should an accountant do when confronted with ethical issues?

13. What are some of the governing authorities against unethical accounting practices?

14. Who are the OECD? What role do they play on a global scale?

15. What is the value chain? Why is the value chain important in competing in a global business environment?

Chapter 1: Introduction To Cost Accounting

SELF TEST ANSWERS

TRUE/FALSE

1.	F	4.	F	7.	T	10.	T	13.	F
2.	F	5.	F	8.	T	11.	F	14.	T
3.	T	6.	T	9.	T	12.	T	15.	T

MULTIPLE CHOICE

1.	D	7.	C	13.	D	19.	C	25.	D
2.	D	8.	B	14.	C	20.	C	26.	D
3.	A	9.	A	15.	A	21.	C	27.	B
4.	B	10.	D	16.	D	22.	B	28.	A
5.	B	11.	A	17.	B	23.	A	29.	C
6.	D	12.	B	18.	D	24.	A	30.	D

QUESTIONS AND PROBLEMS

1. Financial accounting focuses on the needs of external users such as creditors and stockholders. Management accounting provides information to managers to assist them in carrying out their functions of planning, controlling, performance evaluation, and decision-making. Financial accounting must comply with generally accepted accounting principles. Management accounting does not have to comply with generally accepted accounting principles. Financial accounting uses primarily historical information expressed in monetary terms. Management accounting uses historical information and future estimates. Management accounting information includes nonmonetary information and monetary information. Financial accounting is mainly concerned with the organization as a whole, but management accounting focuses on the segments of an organization. Financial accounting emphasizes the verifiability and reliability of the accounting information with a lesser emphasis on relevance. Reliability is important in management accounting, but the relevance of the information is more important.

2. One purpose of cost accounting is to provide the cost of inventories for the balance sheet and the cost of goods sold for the income statement. Another purpose of cost accounting is to provide cost information to managers for their use in planning, controlling, performance evaluation, and decision-making. The most important aspect of a cost accounting system is to trace the cost of inputs to an organization's outputs of goods and services.

3. A balanced scorecard is a four-perspective measure of critical goals and targets needed to operationalize strategy. It looks at success factors for learning and growth, internal business, customer satisfaction, and stockholder value. A balanced scorecard includes financial and non financial, internal and external, long-term and short-term, and lead and lag indicators.

4. Practitioners of management accounting and financial management have responsibility to maintain an appropriate level of professional competence by ongoing development of their knowledge and skill. Practitioners have a responsibility to perform their duties in accordance with applicable laws, regulations, and technical standards. They also have responsibility to prepare complete and clear reports and recommendations after appropriate analysis of relevant and reliable information.

5. Organizational structure is the degree to which an organization distributes authority and responsibility. A continuum of various organizational structures exists. At the extreme of centralization, top management exercises all authority. At the other extreme of decentralization, many people in the organization have the authority for making decisions. Most companies have organizational structures that are not at the extreme points on the continuum. Authority is the right to use resources to accomplish a task or achieve an objective. Responsibility is the obligation to accomplish a task or achieve an objective.

6. An organization's mission statement should include what the organization wants to accomplish and how the organization will uniquely meet its customers' needs with its products and services. A mission statement serves as a road map for the organization. The organization should modify its mission statement over time as the business environment changes.

7. Practitioners of management accounting and financial management have responsibility to refrain from disclosing confidential information acquired in the course of their work except when authorized, unless legally obligated to do so. Practitioners have responsibility to inform subordinates as appropriate regarding the confidentiality of information acquired in the course of their work and monitor their activities to assure the maintenance of that confidentiality. Also practitioners have responsibility to refrain from using or appearing to use the confidential information acquired in the course of their work for unethical or illegal advantage either personally or through third parties.

8. Practitioners of management accounting and financial management have responsibility to avoid actual or apparent conflicts of interest and advise all appropriate parties of any potential conflict. Practitioners have responsibility to refrain from engaging in any activity prejudice their ability to carry out their duties ethically. Practitioners have responsibility to refuse any gift, favor, or hospitality that would influence or would appear to influence their actions. Practitioners have responsibility to refrain from either actively or passively subverting the attainment of the organization's legitimate and ethical objectives. Practitioners have responsibility to recognize and communicate professional limitations or other constraints that would preclude responsible judgment or successful performance of an activity. Practitioners have responsibility to communicate unfavorable as well as favorable information and professional judgments or opinions. Practitioners also have responsibility to refrain from engaging in or supporting any activity that would discredit the profession.

Chapter 1: Introduction To Cost Accounting

9. Practitioners of management accounting and financial management have responsibility to communicate information fairly and objectively. Practitioners also have responsibility to disclose fully all information that could reasonably be expected to influence an intended user's understanding of the reports, comments, and recommendations presented.

10. The objectives of the Cost Accounting Standards Board (CASB) are to increase uniformity in cost accounting practices among government contractors, increase consistency in cost accounting practices by the same contractor over time, and require disclosure of contractors' cost accounting practices. Congress created the CASB in 1970 to establish uniform cost accounting standards for defense contractors and federal agencies. The CASB ceased to exist in 1980, but it reemerged in 1988 as an independent board in the Office of Federal Procurement Policy.

11. The standards of conduct of the IMA include competence, confidentiality, integrity and objectivity. Competence means the individuals will develop and maintain the skills needed to practice their profession. Confidentiality means that individuals will refrain from disclosing company information to inappropriate parties. Integrity means that individuals will not participate in activities that will discredit their company or profession. Objectivity means that individuals will provide full and fair disclosure of all relevant information.

12. Accountants should document what regulations have been violated, research and record the appropriate actions that should have been taken, and provide evidence of violations of such actions. This information should be kept confidential and reported and discussed with a superior who is not involved in the situation – meaning it could be necessary to communicate up the corporate ladder, even as far as the audit committee. It is important to document each communication and finding in the process. If accountants cannot resolve the matter, their only recourse could be to resign and consult a legal adviser before reporting the matter to regulatory authorities.

13. Known authorities governing unethical accounting practices include The Institute of Management Accountants (IMA), which provides the Code of Ethical Conduct. The IMA also issues directives on the practice of management and cost accounting called *Statements on Management Accounting*. SMA's while not legally binding, are commonly accepted. The Cost Accounting Standards Board was established in 1970 to issue uniform cost accounting standards to defense contractors and federal agencies. The CASB constructed 20 cost accounting standards (one of which has been withdrawn) from its inception. In 1988 it was recreated as an independent board of The Office of Federal Procurement Policy to help ensure uniformity and consistency in government contracting. Compliance is required for companies bidding on or pricing cost-related contracts to the federal government. CASB standards are legally binding. Federal laws, such as the Sarbanes- Oxley Act, provide for legal protection for "whistle blowers." The False Claims Act allows whistle-blowers to receive 15 to 20 percent of any settlement proceeds resulting form the identification of such activities.

14. OECD stands for Organization of Economic Cooperation and Development formed to combat bribery in the global accounting system. OECD is an alliance of 35 nations. These nations have signed a document "making it a crime to offer, promise or give a bribe to a foreign public official to obtain or retain international business deals.

15. The value chain is a set of value-adding functions or processes that convert inputs into products and services for company customers, and organizations add value through the value chain functions of research and development, product design, supply, production, marketing, distribution and customer service. The value chain includes the processes of suppliers as well as the company's internal processes. The value chain helps managers to emphasize activities that add value and reduce or eliminate activities that do not add value. To be successful, companies must gain the cooperation of everyone in the value chain.

CHAPTER 2

COST TERMINOLOGY AND COST BEHAVIORS

CHAPTER OVERVIEW

Accountants must understand different types of costs, how to compute these costs, and how to communicate cost information effectively. This chapter describes cost terminology necessary to understand and communicate cost and management accounting information. This chapter also illustrates the flow of costs and cost accumulation.

How cost accountants classify costs, the assumptions cost accountants make to estimate production cost, the differences in the conversion process between manufacturing, service, and retail industries, the categories of product cost, and the cost of goods manufactured are introduced in this chapter.

CHAPTER STUDY GUIDE

Cost is the monetary measure of the resources given up to acquire a good or service. Different types of cost exist for different purposes. An adjective usually precedes the word cost to identify the type of cost being described. A cost that appears as an asset on the balance sheet is an unexpired cost. The business shows the cost of the asset consumed or used during a period as an expense or expired cost on the income statement.

A set of formal methods developed for planning and controlling a company's cost-generating activities relative to its strategy, goals, and objectives is a cost management system. Managers receive information about all value chain functions about product costs, product profitability, cost management, strategy implementation, and management performance. Some of the terms and concepts used to facilitate this exchange of information are illustrated in Exhibit 2-1.

Accountants often classify costs according to three categories: (1) association with the cost object, (2) reaction to changes in activity, and (3) classification on the financial statements. These categories are not mutually exclusive.

Chapter 2: Cost Terminology and Cost Behaviors

A cost object is anything to which management attaches costs or directly relates costs. Product or service costs are costs related to the making of a product or delivery of a service. Costs that are conveniently and economically traceable to a cost object are called direct costs. Indirect costs are costs that are not conveniently or economically traceable to a cost object. Accountants allocate indirect costs to cost objects. Classification of a cost as direct or indirect depends on its relationship with the chosen cost object.

Accountants also classify costs based on cost behavior. Cost behavior is how total costs change in reaction to a change in a related activity measure. Examples of activity measures include sales, production, machine hours, and number of purchase orders. Every cost will change given enough time or a large enough change in the activity level. Thus, for managers to analyze cost behavior properly, they must specify a time frame and an activity level.

The assumed level of activity that reflects the normal operating range is called the relevant range. Within the relevant range, the two most common cost behaviors are variable and fixed. Costs that change in total in direct proportion to a change in the activity level are called variable costs. Variable costs remain constant on a per-unit basis when the activity level changes. Although accountants treat variable costs as linear, economists view variable costs as curvilinear as shown in Exhibit 2-2. Although the curvilinear model is more accurate, the linear model is easier to use and is approximately correct within the relevant range.

Fixed costs are costs that remain constant in total when the activity level changes. Fixed costs decrease on a per-unit basis when the activity level increases because more units are available to absorb a constant amount of fixed costs. When the activity level decreases, fixed costs increase on a per-unit basis because fewer units are available to absorb a constant amount of fixed costs. Exhibit 2-3 provides definitions of variable cost and fixed cost. The classification of fixed and variable costs is valid only within the relevant range of activity. In the long run, all costs are variable.

Mixed costs are costs that have a fixed component and a variable component. If the activity level increases, mixed costs will increase in total because of the variable cost component and decrease on a per-unit basis because of the fixed cost component. The cost of electricity is a common example of a mixed cost. Electricity cost normally includes a fixed cost per month and a variable cost based on kilowatt-hours. Exhibit 2-4 illustrates electricity cost graphically.

Step costs are costs that change by a certain interval or step when the activity level changes. Step costs can be variable or fixed. Step costs with small steps are step variable costs, and step costs with large steps are step fixed costs.

For cost accountants to make valid estimates of total costs at various levels of activity, they must understand the types of cost behavior. Managers usually separate mixed costs into their fixed and variable components. Accountants must choose a specific relevant range of activity to allow step variable costs to be treated as variable and step fixed costs to be treated as fixed.

Chapter 2: Cost Terminology and Cost Behaviors

Accountants disregard economic reality by separating mixed costs into their fixed and variable components and by specifying the relevant range for step costs. They assume that variable costs are fixed on a per-unit basis within the relevant range and that fixed costs remain constant in total within the relevant range. Two justifications exist for these assumptions. First, the assumed conditions approximate economic reality within the relevant range. Second, the assumptions provide a convenient, stable measurement for use in planning, controlling, and decision-making.

Accountants often use predictors and cost drivers to estimate how changes in the activity level will affect costs. A predictor is a variable that has a consistent relationship with a cost. The predictor may not have a direct cause-effect relationship with the change in the cost. A third variable might be affecting the predictor and the cost in the same way.

A cost driver is an activity or occurrence that has a direct cause-effect relationship to a cost. A change in the cost driver will cause a change in the cost. For example, production volume will drive total production cost as illustrated in Exhibit 2-5. Traditionally, accountants have used one cost driver to predict all types of costs. Now, accountants are learning that using only one driver may not lead to the most accurate cost predictions. This knowledge has led to the use of activity-based costing. Under activity-based costing, accountants use many cost drivers to predict different types of costs.

Unexpired costs that will provide the company with future benefits are called assets and appear on the balance sheet. Expired costs include expenses and losses and appear on the income statement. A company incurs expenses intentionally in the process of generating revenues. A company may incur losses in business operations, but a company does not do so intentionally.

Product costs, also called inventoriable costs, are costs related to the manufacture or purchase of products or the providing of services that generate revenue. Period costs relate to selling and administrative activities.

The three broad classes of product costs are (1) direct material, (2) direct labor, and (3) overhead. Direct material includes the major raw materials, *purchased components* and manufactured subassemblies used in making a product. Direct labor is the cost incurred for individuals who work specifically on making a product or performing a service. Overhead includes all production costs that are indirect to a product or service. Conversion cost is the sum of direct labor and overhead costs.

Period costs are associated with time periods rather than with making or purchasing a product or performing a service. Period costs that have future benefits are assets, and period costs with no future benefit are expenses.

One particular type of period cost is distribution cost. Any cost incurred to warehouse, transport, or deliver a product or service is a distribution cost. A company must charge distribution costs to expense as incurred. However, managers should remember that these costs are directly related to products and services. Managers must include distribution costs in their planning and control efforts.

A company incurs product costs in the production or conversion area and period costs in all nonproduction or nonconversion areas. All organizations are involved in converting inputs into outputs in the form of goods and services. Exhibit 2-6 compares the conversion activities of different types of companies.

Companies that perform low or moderate degrees of conversion usually charge insignificant costs of labor and overhead to expense as the costs are incurred. The clerical savings from doing so are greater than any benefit of slightly better information. However, companies that perform high degrees of conversion must accumulate product costs in inventory accounts until they sell the related products. Exhibit 2-7 illustrates the significance of accumulating certain types of costs.

A manufacturing company or manufacturer is defined for this textbook as any company engaged in a high degree of conversion of raw material input into a tangible output. A service company is a firm engaged in a high to moderate degree of conversion using a significant amount of labor to produce a tangible or intangible output that normally cannot be inspected prior to use. A firm engaging in low or moderate degrees of conversion usually has only one inventory account known as merchandise inventory and is commonly known as a retail (merchandising) company.

A retail company usually has only one inventory account (Merchandise Inventory). A manufacturing company has three inventory accounts: (1) Raw Material Inventory, (2) Work in Process Inventory, and (3) Finished Goods Inventory. Both merchandising companies and manufacturing companies charge product costs to cost of goods sold upon the sale of the goods. Service companies will have an inventory account for supplies and may have a Work in Process Inventory account. Because services cannot be stored, service companies do not have a Finished Goods Inventory account. Exhibit 2-8 compares the input-output relationships of a retail company with those of a manufacturing company or service company.

Although differences exist in the accounts used by retailers, manufacturers, and service firms, each type of company can use cost and management accounting concepts and techniques. All companies can use management accounting because managers in all companies engage in planning, controlling, evaluating performance, and making decisions. Cost accounting is imperative for all companies engaged in significant conversion activities. Managers in all companies can use cost accounting and management accounting in cost reduction efforts.

The production or conversion process has three stages: (1) work not started, (2) work in process, and (3) finished work. Each stage has its associated costs. Exhibit 2-9 illustrates production stages in a manufacturing firm and some costs associated with each stage. In the first stage, the manufacturer incurs raw materials and supplies costs. In the second stage, the company accumulates direct labor and overhead costs related to the conversion of the raw materials. The total costs incurred in the first two stages equal the cost of finished goods in the third stage. Cost accounting uses the three inventory accounts (Raw Material Inventory, Work in

Chapter 2: Cost Terminology and Cost Behaviors

Process Inventory, and Finished Goods Inventory) to accumulate the production costs and assign them to the goods produced. These three inventory accounts form a common database for cost accounting, management accounting, and financial accounting.

For a service firm, the work not started stage consists of the cost of supplies needed to perform the services. A service firm accumulates the cost of supplies in the Supplies Inventory account. When a service firm begins a job, it transfers the cost of supplies used to Work in Process Inventory. The firm also charges the cost of labor and overhead to Work in Process Inventory.

Direct material is any readily identifiable part of a product or service. Management may decide, however, that the additional clerical cost of treating an insignificant cost as direct is greater than the benefit. If materials can be directly traced to a product, but the cost of such materials is insignificant, the cost of such materials will usually be considered as an indirect cost and thus a part of overhead. Direct materials are often insignificant or not easily traceable in a service business.

Direct labor cost consists of the wages or salaries and related costs paid to people who work specifically on manufacturing a product or providing a service. Direct labor cost is traceable to a cost object. However, for a cost to be considered direct, rather than as a part of overhead, the company must be able to trace the cost conveniently and economically to the product or service. Management treats some direct labor costs as indirect costs for two reasons: (1) tracing direct labor cost to products may be cost inefficient and (2) erroneous information about product or service costs might result from treating direct labor as a direct cost.

A good example of the second reason is the treatment of the overtime premium paid when employees work more than 40 hours a week. If management treats the overtime premium as a direct cost, the products made during a week that includes overtime would cost more than products made in other weeks. Because scheduling is often a random process, products made during weeks in which employees work overtime should not have to bear the cost of the overtime premium. The overtime premium is more appropriately considered a part of factory overhead. Thus, all products made during the year would bear a small part of the cost of the overtime premium. An exception would be if a customer demands a product so quickly that employees must work overtime to satisfy that customer. Such an order should bear the entire overtime premium.

Overhead includes any indirect production cost incurred in manufacturing a product or providing a service. Indirect material and indirect labor are a part of overhead. Direct labor cost has been declining while overhead costs have been increasing. At many manufacturing companies, direct labor accounts for only 10 to 15 percent of the cost of production. This trend is due to the increased used of automation.

Overhead costs can be fixed or variable. In manufacturing firms, variable overhead costs include indirect material, lubricants for machinery, and the variable portion of electricity. Indirect labor paid on an hourly basis is a variable overhead cost. Depreciation using the units-

Chapter 2:   Cost Terminology and Cost Behaviors   28

of-production method or service-life method is another example of a variable overhead cost. Fixed overhead costs include straight-line depreciation on factory equipment, factory license fees, and factory insurance and property taxes. Indirect labor paid on a salary basis is a fixed overhead cost. The fixed portion of mixed overhead costs such as maintenance is also included in fixed overhead costs.

Quality costs are an important category of overhead costs. Managers are concerned about quality at two levels. First, they are concerned about the customer's perception of quality. Second, managers are concerned about the quality of the production process.

Two major categories of quality costs are (1) the cost of control and (2) the cost of failure to control. The cost to control includes prevention costs and appraisal costs. The cost of failure to control includes internal failure costs and external failure costs.

Prevention costs include employee training, improved production equipment, and researching customers' needs. Appraisal costs are the costs of inspection and monitoring. Internal failure costs include the costs of scrap and rework. External failure costs include handling customers' returns due to poor quality, warranty costs, and handling customers' complaints. Quality costs can be variable, step fixed, or fixed.

A company must accumulate overhead costs over a period and allocate the overhead costs to the products manufactured or services rendered during the period. Cost allocation is assigning indirect costs to one or more cost objects using some reasonable basis. Cost allocations are involved in a number of accounting procedures. In cost accounting, the accountant must allocate overhead costs to products using predictors or cost drivers. This process reflects the cost principle, which requires that all production costs attach to the products manufactured.

Three primary reasons for allocating overhead costs to products are as follows: (1) to calculate a full cost of the product, (2) to motivate the manager to manage costs efficiently, and (3) to analyze alternative courses of action for planning, controlling, and decision making. The first reason relates to financial accounting standards that require that full cost must include the indirect costs of production. Nonfactory overhead costs are not usually allocated to products under generally accepted accounting principles. The other two reasons for overhead allocation relate to internal purposes. A company may use different methods to allocate overhead for different purposes.

Companies can use either an actual cost system or a normal cost system to allocate overhead costs to production. In an actual cost system all production costs are actual costs. An actual cost system does not provide actual overhead costs until the end of the period. Managers need timely cost information to make good operating decisions. Therefore, many companies use a normal cost system. A normal cost system uses actual costs for direct material and direct labor and a predetermined overhead rate for overhead costs.

A company can accumulate its product costs using a perpetual inventory system or periodic inventory system. In a perpetual inventory system, product costs flow through Work in

Chapter 2: Cost Terminology and Cost Behaviors

Process Inventory to Finished Goods Inventory and then to Cost of Goods Sold upon sale. A perpetual inventory system provides updated information continually for financial statement purposes and for inventory and cost control. Exhibit 2-10 shows the path in the T-accounts. Technological advances such as computers and bar coding have reduced the cost of maintaining a perpetual inventory system significantly. Therefore, the textbook will assume that all companies use a perpetual inventory system. Exhibit 2-11 illustrates the journal entries used to record the flow of costs through the accounts for a company that uses a perpetual inventory system. Exhibit 2-12 shows the resulting balances in T-accounts for selected accounts.

A manufacturing company must compute its cost of goods manufactured before it can compute its cost of goods sold. The cost of goods manufactured corresponds to the net purchases amount for a merchandising company. The cost of goods manufactured also represents the total production cost of the completed goods transferred to the Finished Goods Inventory account during the period. Exhibit 2-13 illustrates a schedule of cost of goods manufactured and a schedule of cost of goods sold. Exhibit 2-14 shows a streamlined schedule of cost of goods manufactured and schedule of cost of goods sold for a company using normal costing and a perpetual inventory system.

Chapter 2: Cost Terminology and Cost Behaviors

SELF TEST

TRUE/FALSE

1. T F A cost reflects a monetary measure of the resources given up to acquire a good or service.

2. T F Costs that vary in total in direct proportion to changes in activity are known as variable costs.

3. T F The period most commonly used to compute the overhead rate is one month.

4. T F Overhead costs may be fixed or variable.

5. T F Per-unit fixed costs decrease when the activity level increases.

6. T F A mixed cost has a variable component and a fixed component.

7. T F Cost drivers have a direct cause-effect relationship to a cost.

8. T F Costs incurred in the manufacture of inventory are known as product costs.

9. T F Step costs are always variable.

10. T F Internal failure costs include the costs of scrap and rework.

11. T F Appraisal costs include warranty costs.

12. T F Overhead costs include the cost of indirect materials and indirect labor.

13. T F Quality costs are always fixed.

14. T F The cost of goods manufactured includes the cost of ending work in process.

15. T F In a service company, direct materials are often insignificant or not easily traceable.

MULTIPLE CHOICE

1. Inspection and monitoring costs are included in which category of quality costs?

    A. prevention
    B. appraisal
    C. internal failure
    D. external failure

Chapter 2: Cost Terminology and Cost Behaviors 31

2. The sum of direct labor cost and overhead cost is called:

    A. period cost.
    B. prime cost.
    C. conversion cost.
    D. quality cost.

3. The cost of scrap and rework are included in which category of quality costs?

    A. prevention
    B. appraisal
    C. internal failure
    D. external failure

4. On a per-unit basis variable costs are:

    A. zero.
    B. variable.
    C. mixed.
    D. constant.

5. What are the three categories of product costs?

    A. direct material, overhead, and work in process
    B. direct material, direct labor, and overhead
    C. direct material, direct labor, and work in process
    D. work not started, work in process, and finished work

6. What are the three inventories of a manufacturing company?

    A. raw materials, work in process, and overhead
    B. raw materials, work in process, and finished goods
    C. raw materials, direct labor, and overhead
    D. overhead, work in process, and finished goods

7. A variable that has a consistent relationship with a cost is a(n):

    A. predictor.
    B. cost driver.
    C. dependent variable.
    D. consistent variable.

Chapter 2: Cost Terminology and Cost Behaviors

8. Period costs that have been incurred and have future benefits are classified as:

    A. assets.
    B. expenses.
    C. inventory.
    D. cost of goods manufactured.

9. On a per-unit basis, fixed costs _____ as the activity level increases.

    A. decrease
    B. increase
    C. remain constant
    D. may increase or decrease

10. How does a company charge overhead to production in a normal costing system?

    A. predetermined rate times the actual activity
    B. predetermined rate times the estimated activity
    C. predetermined rate times the standard activity
    D. actual rate times the actual activity

11. A set of formal methods developed for planning and controlling a company's cost-generating activities relative to its strategy, goals, and objectives is a :

    A. quality control method.
    B. activity-based driver.
    C. cost management system.
    D. cost of quality.

12. A measure of activity that is believed to have a direct cause-effect relationship to a cost is known as a:

    A. loss.
    B. cost object.
    C. relevant range.
    D. cost driver.

13. Costs associated with making or acquiring inventory are known as:

    A. period costs.
    B. product costs.
    C. distribution costs.
    D. cost drivers.

Chapter 2: Cost Terminology and Cost Behaviors   33

14. Total mixed costs:

    A. do not change when the activity level changes.
    B. increase when the activity level decreases.
    C. decrease when the activity level increases.
    D. increase when the activity level increases.

15. For cost accountants to make valid estimates of total costs at various levels of activity, they must understand the types of:

    A. overhead.
    B. direct costs.
    C. indirect costs.
    D. cost behavior.

16. Anything to which costs attach or are directly related is a:
    A. predictor.
    B. cost driver.
    C. cost object.
    D. step cost.

17. The cost of returned products due to poor quality is an example of which category of quality cost?
    A. prevention
    B. appraisal
    C. internal failure
    D. external failure

18. On a per-unit basis, mixed costs _____ as the activity level increases.

    A. increase
    B. decrease
    C. remain constant
    D. may increase or decrease

19. Beginning work in process plus total current period manufacturing costs less ending work in process equals:

    A. cost of goods sold.
    B. cost of goods manufactured.
    C. total overhead costs.
    D. cost of goods available for sale.

20. Depreciation on factory equipment calculated using the units-of-production method is a:

    A. variable overhead cost.
    B. fixed overhead cost.
    C. variable period cost.
    D. fixed period cost.

21. What does the company add to the beginning balance of finished goods to determine the cost of goods available for sale?

    A. ending work in process
    B. beginning work in process
    C. cost of goods manufactured
    D. total current period manufacturing costs

22. A cost management system is a set of:

    A. informal statements about costs.
    B. informal methods relating to strategies and goals.
    C. formal methods developed for controlling employees.
    D. formal methods for planning and controlling activities.

23. Eaton Company uses glue to manufacture its line of toy trains. The glue would be considered part of overhead if:

    A. the amount of glue used is large.
    B. the cost of the glue is insignificant compared to the cost required to record it.
    C. the glue is water soluble.
    D. the glue becomes a permanent part of the toy.

24. Accountants do NOT assume _____ to estimate production cost within the relevant range.

    A. variable costs are constant per unit with changes in activity
    B. fixed costs are constant in total with changes in activity
    C. step cost are fixed in proportion to the size of changes in activity
    D. mixed costs fluctuate in total with changes in activity

25. In relation to cost objects, a cost cannot be both classified as being:

    A. direct and variable.
    B. direct and indirect.
    C. variable and expired.
    D. inventoriable and unexpired.

Chapter 2: Cost Terminology and Cost Behaviors 35

26. A firm engaged in a high or moderate degree of conversion using a significant amount of labor is a:

   A. service company.
   B. retail company.
   C. merchandising company.
   D. manufacturing company.

27. Taken from Ruiz Manufacturing's accounting records: Total current period manufacturing costs = $700,000, Ending work in process = $55,000, Cost of goods manufactured = $742,000, Cost of goods available for sale = $912,000, Cost of goods sold = $884,000. What was Ruiz's beginning balance in work in process?

   A. $ 13,000
   B. $ 42,000
   C. $ 97,000
   D. $170,000

28. Taken from Ruiz Manufacturing's accounting records: Total current period manufacturing costs = $700,000, Ending work in process = $55,000, Cost of goods manufactured = $742,000, Cost of goods available for sale = $912,000, Cost of goods sold = $884,000. What was Ruiz's beginning balance in the finished goods inventory?

   A. $ 28,000
   B. $170,000
   C. $184,000
   D. $212,000

29. Taken from Ruiz Manufacturing's accounting records: Total current period manufacturing costs = $700,000, Ending work in process = $55,000, Cost of goods manufactured = $742,000, Cost of goods available for sale = $912,000, Cost of goods sold = $884,000. What was Ruiz's ending balance in the finished goods inventory?

   A. $ 28,000
   B. $170,000
   C. $184,000
   D. $212,000

30. Direct labor would be most likely treated as an indirect cost in a:

   A. customer service center.
   B. hair salon.
   C. computer repair shop.
   D. automobile manufacturing plant.

Chapter 2:   Cost Terminology and Cost Behaviors   36

QUESTIONS AND PROBLEMS

1. What are the differences between expired and unexpired costs? Are losses expired or unexpired costs?

2. Explain how fixed, variable, and mixed costs behave both in total and on a per-unit basis with a change in the activity level.

3. What are step costs? Are step costs fixed or variable?

Chapter 2: Cost Terminology and Cost Behaviors

4. What is the difference between a predictor and a cost driver?

5. Why does management treat some direct labor costs as indirect manufacturing costs and therefore a part of overhead?

6. What are distribution costs? Why should managers pay special attention to distribution costs?

7. How does a service firm accumulate costs?

8. Owens Company provides the following information:

   Beginning finished goods inventory $465,000
   Ending finished goods inventory $490,000
   Cost of goods available for sale $982,000

   Compute the following for Owens Company:

   (a) cost of goods manufactured

   (b) cost of goods sold

9. The following information is taken from the accounting records of Crump Company for calendar year 20XX:

	Beginning of Year	End of Year
Raw materials	$ 65,000	$ 68,000
Work in process	$ 90,000	$ 85,000

Raw materials purchases	$310,000
Direct labor cost	$220,000
Variable overhead cost	$440,000
Fixed overhead cost	$217,000

Prepare a Schedule of Cost of Goods Manufactured for Crump Company.

Chapter 2: Cost Terminology and Cost Behaviors

10. Wilder Manufacturing makes one product only. For the month of April the company made 1,000 units and incurred the following product costs:

Raw materials	$50,000
Direct labor	25,000
Variable overhead	9,000
Fixed overhead	44,000
Total product costs	$128,000

(a) Compute the variable cost per unit, the fixed cost per unit, and the total cost per unit for the month of April.

(b) Assume that Wilder plans to make 800 units in May. Estimate the total product costs that Wilder would incur. Estimate the variable cost per unit, the fixed cost per unit, and the total cost per unit.

(c) Assume that the company plans to make 1,100 units in June. Estimate the total product costs that Wilder would incur. Estimate the variable cost per unit, the fixed cost per unit, and the total cost per unit.

Chapter 2: Cost Terminology and Cost Behaviors

11. Russ Company's beginning and inventory accounts for June were as follows:

	Beginning	Ending
Raw materials	$61,000	$50,000
Work in process	100,000	94,000
Finished goods	100,000	124,000

During June, Russ Company purchased $80,000 of raw materials. All raw materials are considered direct materials. During June, Russ Company also incurred $220,000 of direct labor cost and $500,000 of overhead cost.

REQUIRED: Compute the following:

(a) conversion cost added to production in June

(b) the cost of goods manufactured in June

(c) the cost of goods sold in June

Chapter 2:   Cost Terminology and Cost Behaviors   42

12. Discuss a perpetual inventory accounting system and outline the flow of product costs.

13. For the three types of organizations, discuss the degree of conversion at which each operates.

14. What are the three reasons for allocating overhead to products or services?

Chapter 2:   Cost Terminology and Cost Behaviors   43

15.   The president of your accounting club has lined up Bill G. to talk at your next meeting. He has decided to open the presentation to the whole college and wants to charge enough admission to cover the costs plus have a $2 profit on each ticket. Bill needs $1,000 to show, and $500 for each hour he speaks. The auditorium seats 2,500 and the club pays $1 for each seat used and has been scheduled at no cost. The president estimates that 1,000 students will come.

(a) Assuming Bill talks for one hour, how much should the tickets be sold for?

(b) The tickets are sold, the auditorium is packed to capacity, what is your profit or loss?

(c) If only 500 tickets are sold, what is your profit or loss?

(d) If 1,500 tickets are sold, and Bill talks for an extra hour, what is your profit or loss?

(e) Which costs are variable, fixed, or mixed?

Chapter 2: Cost Terminology and Cost Behaviors

SELF TEST ANSWERS

TRUE/FALSE

1.	T	4.	T	7.	T	10.	T	13.	F
2.	T	5.	T	8.	T	11.	F	14.	F
3.	F	6.	T	9.	F	12.	T	15.	T

MULTIPLE CHOICE

1.	B	7.	A	13.	B	19.	B	25.	B
2.	C	8.	A	14.	D	20.	A	26.	A
3.	C	9.	A	15.	D	21.	C	27.	C
4.	D	10.	A	16.	C	22.	D	28.	B
5.	B	11.	C	17.	D	23.	B	29.	A
6.	B	12.	D	18.	B	24.	C	30.	D

QUESTIONS AND PROBLEMS

1. A cost that appears as an asset on the balance sheet is an unexpired cost. The business shows the cost of the asset consumed or used during a period as an expense or expired cost on the income statement. Unexpired costs that will provide the company with future benefits are called assets and appear on the balance sheet. Expired costs include expenses and losses and appear on the income statement. A company incurs expenses intentionally in the process of generating revenues. A company may incur losses in business operations, but a company does not do so intentionally.

2. Total fixed costs remain constant in total. On a per-unit basis fixed costs decrease with an increase in the activity level and increase with a decrease in the activity level. Total variable costs increase proportionally with an increase in the activity level and decrease proportionally with a decrease in the activity level. On a per-unit basis, variable costs remain constant whether the activity level increases or decreases. Mixed costs have a fixed cost component and a variable cost component. Total mixed costs increase with an increase in the activity level and decrease with a decrease in the activity level. The increase or decrease in total mixed costs is due to the variable cost element. However, because of the fixed cost component, the increase or decrease is not proportional to the change in the activity level. On a per-unit basis, mixed costs decrease when the activity level increases and increase when the activity level decreases. These changes are due to the fixed cost element.

3. Step costs are costs that change by a certain interval or step at a certain shift in the activity level. Step costs can be fixed or variable. Step costs that have small steps are considered variable. Step costs with large steps are considered fixed. However, one must know the relevant range to classify step costs as variable or fixed.

Chapter 2: Cost Terminology and Cost Behaviors

4. A predictor is an activity measure that when changed is accompanied by consistent, observable change in a cost. The relationship may not be a causal relationship. A cost driver has a direct cause-effect relationship to a cost.

5. Management treats some direct labor costs as indirect costs for two reasons: (1) tracing direct labor cost to products may be cost inefficient and (2) erroneous information about product or service costs might result from treating direct labor as a direct cost. A good example of the second reason is the treatment of the overtime premium paid when employees work more than 40 hours a week. Because scheduling is often random, products made during weeks in which employees work overtime should not have to bear the cost of the overtime premium. An exception would be if a customer demands a product so quickly that employees must work overtime to satisfy that customer.

6. Distribution costs are the costs a company incurs to warehouse, transport, or deliver a product or service. Managers should pay special attention to distribution costs because they relate directly to products and services. Managers may be tempted to ignore these costs because they are expensed as incurred for financial accounting purposes. However, managers must plan for these costs in relation to sales volume and carefully control them to ensure profitability.

7. A service firm accumulates the cost of supplies in the Supplies Inventory account. When a service firm begins a job, it transfers the cost of the supplies used to Work in Process Inventory. Service firms usually do not maintain an account for finished work because a firm cannot store services. When a service firm completes a job, it transfers the cost of the job to Cost of Services Rendered.

8. (a) The beginning finished goods inventory plus the cost of goods manufactured equals the cost of goods available for sale. Therefore, to determine the cost of goods manufactured, subtract the beginning finished goods inventory from the cost of goods available for sale.

Cost of goods available for sale	$982,000
Less: Beginning finished goods inventory	465,000
Cost of goods manufactured	$517,000

(b) To determine the cost of goods sold, subtract the ending finished goods inventory from the cost of goods available for sale. All of the cost of goods sold section is shown below.

Beginning finished goods inventory	$465,000
Add: Cost of goods manufactured	517,000
Cost of goods available for sale	$982,000
Less: Ending finished goods inventory	490,000
Cost of goods sold	$492,000

Chapter 2: Cost Terminology and Cost Behaviors

9.

Crump Company
Schedule of Cost of Goods Manufactured
For the Year Ended December 31, 20XX

Beginning work in process		$ 90,000
Beginning raw materials	$ 65,000	
Add: Raw materials purchases	310,000	
Raw materials available	$375,000	
Less: Ending raw materials	68,000	
Raw materials used	$307,000	
Direct labor	220,000	
Variable overhead	440,000	
Fixed overhead	217,000	
Total current period manufacturing costs		1,184,000
Total costs to account for		$1,274,000
Less: Ending work in process		85,000
Cost of goods manufactured		$1,189,000

10.

	(1) April	(2) May	(3) June
Raw materials	$50,000	$40,000	$55,000
Direct labor	25,000	20,000	27,500
Variable overhead	9,000	7,200	9,900
Total variable costs	$84,000	$67,200	$92,400
Fixed overhead	44,000	44,000	44,000
Total product costs	$128,000	$111,200	$136,400
Number of units	1,000	800	1,100
Per unit:			
Variable cost	$84	$84	$84
Fixed cost	44	55	40
Total cost	$128	$139	$124

Raw materials, direct labor, and variable overhead are the variable product costs. Fixed overhead is a fixed product cost. Variable costs are constant per unit and change in total proportionally with a change in the activity level. The variable cost per unit of $84 is determined by dividing the $84,000 total variable costs for April by the 1,000 units produced. Fixed costs remain constant in total when the activity level changes. Thus, on a per-unit basis fixed costs increase with a decrease in the activity level and decrease with an increase in the activity level. The total cost per unit changes because of the change in the per-unit fixed cost.

11. (a) Conversion costs are computed by adding direct labor cost and overhead cost.

Direct labor cost	$220,000
Overhead cost	500,000
Conversion cost	$720,000

(b)

Beginning work in process		$100,000
Beginning inventory of raw materials	$61,000	
Add: Raw materials purchased	80,000	
Raw materials available for use	$141,000	
Less: Ending inventory of raw materials	50,000	
Direct materials added to production	$91,000	
Direct labor cost	220,000	
Overhead cost	500,000	
Total manufacturing costs for June		811,000
Total costs to account for		$911,000
Less: Ending work in process		94,000
Cost of goods manufactured in June		$817,000

(c)

Beginning finished goods inventory	$100,000
Add: Cost of goods manufactured	817,000
Cost of goods available for sale	$917,000
Less: Ending finished goods inventory	124,000
Cost of goods sold in June	$793,000

12. In a perpetual inventory accounting system, all product costs flow through Work In Process Inventory to Finished Goods Inventory and, ultimately to the Cost of Goods Sold, as illustrated in Exhibit 2-10. It continuously provides current information for financial statement preparation and for inventory and cost control. Because the costs of maintaining a perpetual system have diminished significantly as computerized production, bar coding, and information processing have become more pervasive, it is a good assumption that most businesses use it.

Chapter 2:   Cost Terminology and Cost Behaviors   48

13. A manufacturing company or manufacturer is defined for this textbook as any company engaged in a high degree of conversion of raw material input into a tangible output. A service company is a firm engaged in a high to moderate degree of conversion using a significant amount of labor to produce a tangible or intangible output that normally cannot be inspected prior to use. A firm engaging in low or moderate degrees of conversion usually has only one inventory account known as merchandise inventory and is commonly known as a retail (merchandising) company.

14. Three primary reasons for allocating overhead costs to products are as follows: (1) to calculate a full cost of the product, (2) to motivate the manager to manage costs efficiently, and (3) to analyze alternative courses of action for planning, controlling, and decision making. The first reason relates to financial accounting standards that require that full cost must include the indirect costs of production. Nonfactory overhead costs are not usually allocated to products under generally accepted accounting principles. The other two reasons for overhead allocation relate to internal purposes. A company may use different methods to allocate overhead for different purposes.

15. (a) Assuming Bill talks for one hour, and 1,000 students buy tickets, the total cost for the presentation would be $2,500 ($1,000+$500+[1,000 x $1]). To get a profit of $2 per student would add ($2,000) to achieve a total revenue of $4,500. Spread across 1,000 students that equals a price of $4.50 per ticket.

(b) The auditorium is packed to capacity, 2,500 tickets sold at $4.50 would be a total revenue of $11,250 less the total cost of $4,000 ($2,500 for 2,500 seats plus $1,500 for the speaker) equals $7,250 profit.

(c) 500 sold at $4.50 would be total revenue of $2,250 less $2,000 ($500 for seats and $1,500 for the speaker) would result in a $250 profit.

(d) 1,500 tickets are sold at $4.50 resulting in a total revenue of $6,750, and Bill talks for an extra hour increasing total cost to $3,500 (1,500 seats $1,500 and speaker at $2,000), resulting in a $3,250 profit.

(e) The variable cost is the cost of seats. There are no fixed costs. And Bill Gates is a mixed cost with a fixed portion for showing up and a variable part for speaking.

CHAPTER 3

PREDETERMINED OVERHEAD RATES, FLEXIBLE BUDGETS, AND ABSORPTION/VARIABLE COSTING

CHAPTER OVERVIEW

In the business world, any cost that is not incurred for direct material or direct labor is overhead. This chapter discusses normal costing and how accountants determine product costs using predetermined overhead rates. How accountants separate mixed costs into variable and fixed elements, how accountants use flexible budgets, and various production capacity measures are also discussed in this chapter. Accountants generating external reports commonly use absorption costing. The two methods of presentation for financial statements, absorption and variable costing are illustrated as well as mathematical analysis for determining various overhead costs presented.

CHAPTER STUDY GUIDE

Normal costing is an alternative costing system to actual costing. Exhibit 3-1 shows actual versus normal costing. Normal costing assigns actual direct material and labor to products while allocating production overhead to products using a predetermined overhead rate.

Four reasons exist for using a predetermined overhead rate. First, a predetermined overhead rate allows the company to charge overhead costs to products during the period rather than at the end of the period. Second, predetermined overhead rates compensate for changes in actual overhead costs unrelated to the activity level. Third, predetermined overhead rates can overcome the problem of changes in the activity level that do not affect actual fixed overhead costs. Changes in the activity level do not affect fixed overhead costs, but changes in the activity level cause actual fixed overhead costs to vary on a per-unit basis. Using a predetermined overhead rate reduces such per-unit cost fluctuations. Lastly, predetermined overhead rates are used to permit managers to be more aware of the profitability of a product or line of product in addition to the profitability of doing business with certain customers or suppliers.

Normal cost system journal entries are the same as those made in an actual cost system except that an actual cost system transfers the total amount of actual overhead cost from the overhead account to the Work in Process Inventory. A normal cost system assigns overhead cost to Work in Process Inventory through a predetermined overhead rate.

Chapter 3:
Predetermined Overhead Rates Flexible Budgets, & Absorption/Variable Costing

The accountant computes the predetermined overhead rate by dividing the budgeted overhead costs at a specific activity level for the period by the budgeted activity level for the same period. The period generally used to determine the overhead rate is one year. The overhead charged to Work in Process Inventory is the predetermined rate multiplied by the actual activity level. This is known as the applied overhead.

The activity base the company uses to apply overhead cost should bear a logical relationship to the overhead cost incurred. Using production volume as the activity base makes sense if the company makes only one product. To allocate overhead cost to multiple products, the company must use an activity measure common to all the products. Preferably, the base should be a cost driver. Historically, many companies have used direct labor hours or direct labor cost to allocate overhead cost to production. Using direct labor to allocate overhead costs in an automated plant results in erroneously high overhead rates because costs are applied over a relatively small activity base.

Applied overhead is the amount of overhead assigned to Work in Process Inventory. Applied overhead is equal to the predetermined rate multiplied by the actual activity. The company uses a single general ledger account to record actual overhead and applied overhead, but could use two separate accounts. Additionally, the company could use separate accounts for fixed and variable overhead or multiple overhead accounts by activity or department. If the company uses separate accounts for fixed and variable overhead, the accountant must separate mixed costs. Exhibit 3-2 illustrates the different ways for recording overhead.

The general ledger would have separate variable and fixed overhead accounts if accountants use separate rates to apply variable and fixed overhead. Actual overhead is debited to the general ledger overhead account and credited to the source of the overhead cost regardless of the number of predetermined overhead rates. Overhead is applied as the designated activity or cost driver actually occurs.

A company debits Manufacturing Overhead for actual overhead costs and credits various accounts as appropriate. A company applies overhead by debiting Work in Process Inventory and crediting Manufacturing Overhead. The Manufacturing Overhead account will have a balance at the end of the period. If actual overhead is greater than the applied overhead, then overhead is underapplied and the Manufacturing Overhead account will have a debit balance. If actual overhead is less than the applied overhead, then overhead is overapplied and the Manufacturing Overhead account will have a credit balance. Underapplied overhead means that the overhead applied to Work in Progress Inventory is less than actual overhead incurred: overapplied overhead means that the overhead applied to WIP is more than actual overhead incurred. Cost differences and utilization differences are two factors that can work independently or simultaneously causing applied overhead to be different from actual overhead.

Exhibit 3-3 demonstrates the effects of underapplied and overapplied overhead. A company must close the balance in the Manufacturing Overhead account. If the balance is not material, the accountant closes it to Cost of Goods Sold. If the balance is material, the

Chapter 3:
Predetermined Overhead Rates Flexible Budgets, & Absorption/Variable Costing

accountant must allocate it pro rata among Work in Process Inventory, Finished Goods Inventory, and Cost of Goods Sold. Exhibit 3-4 gives an example of the proration and disposition of overapplied overhead.

Two causes of underapplied and overapplied overhead are (1) a difference between actual and budgeted costs and (2) a difference between actual activity and activity or capacity used to compute the fixed overhead application rate.

Measures of capacity are illustrated in Exhibit 3-5. Possible capacity measures are theoretical capacity, practical capacity, normal capacity, and expected capacity. Theoretical capacity is the maximum potential activity for a particular period assuming that everything works perfectly. Practical capacity is the production the company could achieve taking regular operating interruptions into consideration. Normal capacity is the long-run average capacity considering cyclical fluctuations. Expected capacity is the anticipated activity level for the upcoming period based on the current budget. Management often uses expected capacity in computing the predetermined overhead rate and is used in the text unless stated otherwise.

Overhead costs can be fixed or variable. Variable overhead costs include indirect material, lubricants, and the variable portion of electricity. Indirect labor paid on an hourly basis is a variable overhead cost. Depreciation using the units-of-production method or service-life method is another example of a variable overhead cost. Fixed overhead costs include straight-line depreciation on factory equipment, factory license fees, and factory insurance and property taxes. Indirect labor paid on a salary basis is a fixed overhead cost. The fixed portion of mixed overhead costs such as maintenance is also included in fixed overhead costs.

Mixed costs are costs that have a fixed component and a variable component. Managers usually separate mixed costs into their fixed and variable components. If the activity level increases, mixed costs will increase in total because of the variable cost component and decrease on a per-unit basis because of the fixed cost component. The cost of electricity is a common example of a mixed cost. Electricity cost normally includes a fixed cost per month and a variable cost based on kilowatt-hours.

Accountants consider all costs to be linear rather than curvilinear. Thus, accountants use a straight line to describe any type of cost behavior within a relevant range of activity. The formula for a straight line is $y = a + bX$ where y = total cost, a = fixed cost, b = per-unit variable cost, and X = activity base or cost driver in units of the activity base or cost driver. Management can use the formula $y = a + bX$ to predict total mixed costs and the fixed and variable elements of such mixed costs at any activity level within the relevant range.

If a cost is entirely variable, the a value in the formula is zero. If the cost is entirely fixed, the b value is zero. If the cost is mixed, it is necessary to determine formula values for both a and b. The high-low method and regression analysis are two methods of determining these values. Exhibit 3-6 provides a step-by-step illustration of the high-low method.

Chapter 3:
Predetermined Overhead Rates Flexible Budgets, & Absorption/Variable Costing

The high-low method is the simplest method of separating mixed costs. The first step in using the high-low method is to identify the high level of activity and the low level of activity. The high level and the low level must be within the relevant range. Activity levels that fall outside the relevant range are called outliers. The next step is to compute the differences in total costs and activity levels. The change in the total costs divided by the change in the activity level provides the per-unit variable cost. The reason is that fixed costs do not change when the activity level changes. Variable costs are the only costs that change. The per-unit variable cost multiplied by the number of units (either at the high or the low) equals total variable costs. Total costs minus total variable costs equals fixed costs.

A weakness of the high-low method is that the accountant may unintentionally use outliers in the calculation. Another weakness of the high-low method is that it uses only two data points. The high-low method ignores all other activity levels and corresponding costs.

Least squares regression analysis is a statistical method that analyzes the relationship between dependent (cost) and independent (activity) variables. Least squares regression analysis helps in developing an equation to predict an unknown value of a dependent variable (cost) from the known values of one or more independent variables (activities). If multiple independent variables exist, least squares regression analysis can be used to determine the independent variable that is the best predictor of the dependent variable.

Simple regression analysis uses only one independent variable to predict the dependent variable. If more than one independent variable exists, the process is called multiple regression. Simple regression uses the linear formula $y = a + bX$. Least squares regression analysis determines the fixed costs (a) and the per-unit variable cost (b). The company then uses this formula to predict total mixed costs for any activity level within the relevant range.

As illustrated in Exhibit 3-7, least squares regression analysis determines the line that best fits the data points. This line is called the regression line, which is any line that goes through the means of the independent and dependent variables in a set of observations. The regression line minimizes the sum of the squares of the deviations between the data points and the line. Accountants can use least squares regression analysis to separate mixed costs into their fixed and variable components and predict total mixed costs at a different activity level within the relevant range. The regression line of best fit is found by predicting a and b values in a straight line formula using the actual activity and cost values (y values) from the observations.

Regression analysis is based on assumptions that produce constraints on the use of the model. Three of these assumptions are: (1) for the analysis to be useful, the independent variable must be a valid predictor of the dependent variable; the relationship can be tested by determining the coefficient of correlation. (2) regression analysis should be used only within a relevant range of activity. (3) the regression model is useful only as long as the circumstances existing at the time remain constant: consequently, if significant additions are made to capacity or if there is a major change in technology usage, the regression line will no longer be valid.

Chapter 3:
Predetermined Overhead Rates Flexible Budgets, & Absorption/Variable Costing

A flexible budget is a planning document that presents expected variable and fixed overhead costs at different activity levels. These activity levels usually cover the contemplated range of activity for the upcoming period. If activity levels are within relevant range, costs at each successive level should equal the previous level plus a uniform monetary increment for each variable cost factor. The increment value is equal to variable cost per unit of activity times the quantity of additional activity. Expected cost information from the flexible budget is used for the numerator in computing the predetermined overhead rate. An example flexible budget is illustrated in Exhibit 3-8.

Some companies use a single overhead rate for the entire plant, but a single rate is often not adequate for management's needs. Departmental overhead rates usually provide better information to management because departments have different manufacturing processes and cost drivers. Some departments are more labor intensive than other departments, and some departments are more machine intensive than others. Exhibit 3-9 illustrates the differences in calculation of a single overhead rate and departmental overhead rates.

The two basic methods of cost accumulation and cost presentation are absorption costing and variable costing. Each method uses the same basic data, but organizes and processes the data differently. A company can use either method with job order costing or process costing discussed in later chapters.

The traditional product costing approach is absorption costing. Absorption costing treats direct material, direct labor, variable overhead, and fixed overhead as product or inventoriable costs. Thus, absorption costing treats all manufacturing costs as product costs. Another name for absorption costing is full costing. Exhibit 3-10 illustrates the absorption costing model.

An absorption costing income statement presents costs according to their functional classifications. A functional classification is a group of costs that a company incurs for the same basic purpose. Examples include cost of goods sold, selling expenses, and administrative expenses. An absorption costing income statement shows the difference between sales and cost of goods sold as gross margin as illustrated in Exhibit 3-10. Gross margin minus the period expenses is income before income taxes.

Variable costing treats only direct material, direct labor, and variable overhead as product costs. Variable costing considers only the variable manufacturing costs as product costs and treats fixed overhead as a period cost.

A variable costing income statement presents costs according to their behavior as variable or fixed costs and then perhaps according to functions within the behavioral classifications. Another name for variable costing is direct costing.

A difference in the cost presentation of variable costing is that expenses are categorized first by behavior and then by function. A variable costing income statement shows the variable cost of goods sold. Product contribution margin is the difference between sales and variable cost

Chapter 3:
Predetermined Overhead Rates Flexible Budgets, & Absorption/Variable Costing

of goods sold. Product contribution margin minus variable selling and administrative expenses equals total contribution margin as illustrated in Exhibit 3-11. Total contribution margin minus the sum of fixed overhead and fixed selling and administrative expenses is income before income taxes. Thus, total contribution margin is the difference between total revenues and total variable expenses. A variable costing income statement is also known a contribution income statement. Variable costing relationships are illustrated in Exhibit 3-12.

A company must use absorption costing for external financial reporting and for income tax purposes. Managers, however, may prefer variable costing to help them fulfill their managerial duties. Variable costing allows managers to see more easily the effect on costs of a change in the activity level. Thus, managers often find variable costing more helpful in making short-term decisions.

Exhibit 3-13 provides some basic data the textbook uses to illustrate absorption costing and variable costing. Exhibit 3-14 shows the differences in income before tax using absorption costing and variable costing. Income before tax is the same for either costing method in the example because units produced are equal to sold units.

A volume variance reflects the monetary impact of a difference between the budgeted capacity used to determine the fixed overhead application rate and the actual capacity at which the company operates. No volume variances are shown in variable costing because fixed manufacturing overhead is not applied to products using a budgeted capacity measure; the FOH is deducted in its entirety as a period expense.

Phantom profits are temporary absorption costing profits caused by producing more inventory than is sold. When the excess inventory is sold the phantom profits disappear. Alternatively, variable costing expenses all fixed manufacturing overhead in the year it is incurred.

An increase in inventory causes the income before tax under absorption costing to be greater than the income before tax under variable costing. The reason is that absorption costing defers some of the fixed overhead costs in ending inventory, but variable costing treats fixed overhead costs as a period expense. Thus, a company using absorption costing can increase income before tax simply by producing more units than it sells. These temporary increases in profits caused by producing more units than sold are phantom profits. On the other hand, if a company sells more units than it produces, the ending inventory will decrease. When inventory decreases, the income before tax is higher under variable costing than under absorption costing. If the units produced equal the units sold and inventory levels remain constant, the income before tax will be the same under absorption costing and variable costing. Exhibit 3-15 indicates the possible relationships between production and sales levels and the effects of these relationships on income.

Chapter 3:
Predetermined Overhead Rates Flexible Budgets, & Absorption/Variable Costing

SELF TEST

TRUE/FALSE

1. T F Overhead includes any direct production cost incurred in manufacturing a product or providing a service.

2. T F Overhead is any cost of doing business that is not incurred for direct material or direct labor.

3. T F Underapplied overhead means that the overhead applied to Work in Progress Inventory is less than actual overhead incurred.

4. T F Overhead costs may be fixed or variable.

5. T F Accountants consider all costs to be linear rather than curvilinear.

6. T F A mixed cost has a variable component and a fixed component.

7. T F One cause of underapplied and overapplied overhead is a difference between budgeted and actual costs.

8. T F Variable costing expenses only part of its fixed manufacturing overhead in the year it is incurred.

9. T F Management often uses expected capacity in computing the predetermined overhead rate.

10. T F Outliers are observations that are abnormal and not representative of the costs the company does typically incur.

11. T F The cost of electricity is a common example of a mixed cost.

12. T F Overhead costs include the cost of indirect materials and indirect labor.

13. T F The fixed portion of mixed overhead costs such as maintenance is included in product costs under variable costing.

14. T F A volume variance reflects the monetary impact of a difference between the actual capacity used to determine the fixed overhead application rate and the budgeted capacity at which the company operates.

15. T F Simple regression uses only one independent variable.

Chapter 3:
Predetermined Overhead Rates Flexible Budgets, & Absorption/Variable Costing

MULTIPLE CHOICE

1. The period generally used to determine the overhead rate is:

    A. three weeks
    B. three months
    C. one year
    D. five years

2. The maximum potential activity for a particular period assuming that everything works perfectly is:

    A. practical capacity.
    B. normal capacity.
    C. theoretical capacity.
    D. expected capacity.

3. The overhead charged to work in process is known as the:

    A. applied overhead.
    B. manufacturing overhead.
    C. underapplied overhead.
    D. overapplied overhead.

4. Which of the following is not an example of included expenses in absorption costing?

    A. personal expenses
    B. cost of goods sold
    C. selling expenses
    D. administrative expenses

5. Temporary absorption costing profits caused by producing more inventory than is sold are:

    A. budgeted profits
    B. volume variance profits
    C. articulated profits
    D. phantom profits

Chapter 3:
Predetermined Overhead Rates Flexible Budgets, & Absorption/Variable Costing

6. The production the company could achieve taking regular operating interruptions into consideration is called:

    A. normal capacity
    B. practical capacity
    C. theoretical capacity
    D. expected capacity

7. In computing the predetermined overhead rate management often uses:

    A. expected capacity.
    B. practical capacity.
    C. theoretical capacity.
    D. normal capacity.

8. Variable costing expenses all fixed manufacturing overhead :

    A. before it is incurred.
    B. in the year it is incurred.
    C. two years after it is incurred.
    D. three years after it is incurred.

9. A method for financial statement presentation commonly used for external reporting is:

    A. absorption costing.
    B. external costing.
    C. process costing.
    D. job order costing.

10. Applied overhead is equal to the predetermined rate _____ the actual activity.

    A. plus
    B. minus
    C. multiplied by
    D. divided by

11. A company usually charges a small amount of underapplied overhead at the end of the year to:

    A. work in process.
    B. finished goods.
    C. cost of goods sold.
    D. miscellaneous expense.

Chapter 3:
Predetermined Overhead Rates Flexible Budgets, & Absorption/Variable Costing

12. Observations that are abnormal and not representative of the costs typically incurs are:

    A. volume variances
    B. dependent variables
    C. outliers
    D. independent variables

13. The high-low method uses:

    A. one point.
    B. two points.
    C. three points.
    D. four points.

14. Total mixed costs:

    A. do not change when the activity level changes.
    B. increase when the activity level decreases.
    C. decrease when the activity level increases.
    D. increase when the activity level increases.

15. If the amount of underapplied or overapplied overhead is significant at the end of the accounting period, the accountant should close the balance by allocating it pro rata among:

    A. direct materials, work in process, and overhead.
    B. direct materials, work in process, and finished goods.
    C. direct materials, work in process, and cost of goods sold.
    D. work in process, finished goods, and cost of goods sold.

16. If a company sells more units than it produces, the ending inventory will

    A. decrease.
    B. increase.
    C. stay the same.
    D. radically fluctuate.

17. Which of the following is likely not an overhead cost?

    A. property taxes
    B. indirect labor paid on a salary basis
    C. factory license fees
    D. direct material

Chapter 3: 59
Predetermined Overhead Rates Flexible Budgets, & Absorption/Variable Costing

18. On a per-unit basis, mixed costs _____ as the activity level increases.

    A. increase
    B. decrease
    C. remain constant
    D. may increase or decrease

19. If a cost is entirely variable, the ____ value is zero.

    A. a
    B. b
    C. x
    D. y

20. Two factors that affect overhead application are called:

    A. cost differences and utilization differences.
    B. dependent and independent variances.
    C. variable and period cost.
    D. fixed and period cost.

21. Another name for variable costing is:

    A. process costing
    B. direct costing
    C. absorption costing
    D. job order costing

22. Roe Company had a $6,000 credit balance in its overhead account at the end of the year just before closing. Actual overhead was $300,000. Roe applies overhead at the rate of $10 per machine hour. How many machine hours did Roe Company use during the year?

    A. 28,800
    B. 29,400
    C. 30,000
    D. 30,600

Chapter 3:
Predetermined Overhead Rates Flexible Budgets, & Absorption/Variable Costing

23. Eaton Company applies overhead on the basis of machine hours. Eaton Company estimated that its total overhead costs would be $500,000 and its total machine hours would be 200,000. At the end of the year, actual overhead was $495,250 and actual machine hours were 199,200. For the year overhead was:

   A. underapplied by $2,000.
   B. overapplied by $2,750.
   C. underapplied by $2,750.
   D. underapplied by $4,750.

24. The balance in Patman Company's overhead account at the end of the year was $90,000 debit (underapplied). Patman Company considers this to be a material amount. At the end of the year the accounts shown below had the following balances:

Work in Process	$ 200,000
Finished Goods	$ 600,000
Cost of Goods Sold	$1,200,000

   After Patman Company closes its overhead account, what is the cost of goods sold?

   A. $1,110,000
   B. $1,146,000
   C. $1,254,000
   D. $1,290,000

25. Rowen Company had total maintenance costs of $9,000 in May when the company used 50,000 machine hours. In July, the total maintenance costs were $12,000 and the total machine hours were 70,000. What is Rowen Company's estimated variable maintenance cost per machine hour?

   A. $0.06
   B. $0.15
   C. $0.18
   D. $6.67

26. Rowen Company had total maintenance costs of $9,000 in May when the company used 50,000 machine hours. In July, the total maintenance costs were $12,000 and the total machine hours were 70,000. What is Rowen Company's estimated monthly fixed cost for maintenance?

   A. $ 1,500
   B. $ 3,000
   C. $ 7,500
   D. $10,500

Chapter 3:
Predetermined Overhead Rates Flexible Budgets, & Absorption/Variable Costing

27. Belanger, Inc recorded these figures for the past three periods for direct labor hours (DLH) and Utility costs (UL$): (1) DLH = 800 and UL$ = $60, (2) DLH = 400 and UL$=$40, (3) DLH = 600 and UL$ = $55. Using the high-low method, what is the variable cost element?

    A. $ 20.00/DLH
    B. $ 30.00/DLH
    C. $ 0.05/DLH
    D. $ 1.50/DLH

28. Belanger, Inc recorded these figures for the past three periods for direct labor hours (DLH) and Utility costs (UL$): (1) DLH = 800 and UL$ = $60, (2) DLH = 400 and UL$=$40, (3) DLH = 600 and UL$ = $55. Using the high-low method, what is the fixed cost element?

    A. $ 20
    B. $ 40
    C. $ 15
    D. $ 25

29. Belanger, Inc recorded these figures for the past three periods for direct labor hours (DLH) and Utility costs (UL$): (1) DLH = 800 and UL$ = $60, (2) DLH = 400 and UL$=$40, (3) DLH = 600 and UL$ = $55. Using simple regression, what is the fixed cost element?

    A. $ 20.05
    B. $ 20.10
    C. $ 20.15
    D. $ 20.20

30. Least squares regression analysis:

    A. analyzes the relationship between independent and dependent constants.
    B. determines the line that does not fit the data points.
    C. can be used to predict total fixed costs over all ranges.
    D. can determine a line that best fits the observed data points.

Chapter 3:
Predetermined Overhead Rates Flexible Budgets, & Absorption/Variable Costing

QUESTIONS AND PROBLEMS

1. What are the three primary reasons for using predetermined overhead rates rather than using actual overhead rates for product costing?

2. Explain the causes of over and underapplied overhead.

3. Briefly explain the difference between absorption and variable costing.

Chapter 3:
Predetermined Overhead Rates Flexible Budgets, & Absorption/Variable Costing

4. Why do differences between sales and production volume result in differences in income between absorption and variable costing?

5. Describe the high-low method of analyzing a mixed cost.

6. Differentiate between plantwide and departmental overhead rates. How are departmental overhead rates better?

Chapter 3:
Predetermined Overhead Rates Flexible Budgets, & Absorption/Variable Costing

7. Discuss the normal costing system.

8. How are flexible budgets used by managers to help set predetermined overhead rates?

9. What are the steps in preparing a flexible budget?

Chapter 3:
Predetermined Overhead Rates Flexible Budgets, & Absorption/Variable Costing

10. What costing method is required for preparing external financial statements? Who are the authoritative bodies governing it?

11. What are the four measures of organizational capacity? Describe each.

Chapter 3: Predetermined Overhead Rates Flexible Budgets, & Absorption/Variable Costing

12. The following are the maintenance costs and machine hours (MH) of Moseley Company for the first six months of the year:

Month	Maintenance Costs	Machine Hours
January	$5,970	9,000
February	$5,490	8,200
March	$7,467	11,100
April	$6,122	9,700
May	$7,810	12,200
June	$7,429	11,900

Use the high-low method to estimate the following:

(a) variable maintenance costs per machine hour

(b) fixed maintenance costs per month

Chapter 3:
Predetermined Overhead Rates Flexible Budgets, & Absorption/Variable Costing

13. Abel Company applies overhead on the basis of machine hours (MH). For the current year, Abel estimated that the total overhead costs would be $480,000 and that the total machine hours would be 120,000. At the end of the year Abel had incurred $486,000 in actual overhead costs and had used 123,000 machine hours.

    (a) Compute the predetermined overhead rate.

    (b) Compute the ending balance in the overhead account. Was overhead underapplied or overapplied?

    (c) Prepare the journal entry to close the overhead account. Assume that the underapplied or overapplied overhead was not material.

Chapter 3:
Predetermined Overhead Rates Flexible Budgets, & Absorption/Variable Costing

14. Outdoor Supply Company has two departments Brown and Green. The following information is provided to you:

	Brown	Green
Estimated overhead costs	$600,000	$300,000
Estimated machine hours	200,000	19,000
Estimated direct labor hours	24,000	75,000

Compute departmental overhead rates for each department using the activity with the more intensive use in each department.

Chapter 3:
Predetermined Overhead Rates Flexible Budgets, & Absorption/Variable Costing

15. Kinder Company is attempting to predict its maintenance costs more accurately. Maintenance costs are a mixed cost. Maintenance costs and machine hours for the first four months of the year are as follows:

	Maintenance Costs	Machine Hours
January	$5,860	1,000
February	5,290	900
March	6,120	1,080
April	5,270	860

Compute the a value (fixed costs per month) and the b value (variable cost per machine hour) using least squares regression analysis.

Chapter 3:
Predetermined Overhead Rates Flexible Budgets, & Absorption/Variable Costing

SELF TEST ANSWERS

TRUE/FALSE

1. F   4. T   7. T   10. T   13. F
2. T   5. T   8. F   11. T   14. F
3. T   6. T   9. T   12. T   15. T

MULTIPLE CHOICE

1. C   7. A   13. B   19. A   25. B
2. C   8. B   14. D   20. A   26. A
3. A   9. A   15. D   21. B   27. C
4. A   10. C   16. A   22. D   28. A
5. D   11. C   17. D   23. B   29. A
6. B   12. C   18. B   24. C   30. D

QUESTIONS AND PROBLEMS

1. The three primary reasons for using predetermined overhead rates are as follows: (1) A predetermined overhead rate allows overhead costs to be charged to a product or service during the period rather than at the end of the period. (2) Predetermined overhead rates compensate for fluctuations in actual overhead costs unrelated to activity levels. (3) Predetermined overhead rates compensate for changes in the activity level that do not affect total fixed overhead costs.

2. Under- or overapplication is caused by two factors that can either work independently or simultaneously. These two factors are cost differences and utilization differences. If actual fixed overhead (FOH) cost differs from expected FOH cost, a fixed manufacturing overhead spending variance is created. If actual capacity utilization differs from expected utilization, a volume variance arises. The independent effects of these differences are as follows:
   if Actual FOH cost > Expected FOH cost = Underapplied FOH
   if Actual FOH cost < Expected FOH cost = Overapplied FOH
   if Actual Utilization > Expected Utilization = Overapplied FOH
   if Actual Utilization < Expected Utilization = Underapplied FOH
   In most cases, both costs and utilization differ from estimates. When this occurs, no generalizations can be made as to whether FOH will be over or underapplied.

Chapter 3:
Predetermined Overhead Rates Flexible Budgets, & Absorption/Variable Costing

3. Two differences exist between absorption and variable costing. One relates to cost accumulation and the other relates to cost presentation. The cost accumulation difference is that absorption costing treats fixed overhead as a product cost; variable costing treats it as a period cost. Absorption costing advocates contend that products cannot be made without the production capacity provided by fixed manufacturing costs and, therefore, these costs "belong" to the product. Variable costing advocates contend that fixed manufacturing costs would be incurred whether or not any products are manufactured; thus such costs are not caused by production and cannot produce costs. The cost presentation difference is that absorption costing classifies expenses by function on the income statement and on management reports while variable costing categorizes expenses first by behavior and then, possibly by function.

4. Absorption costing requires fixed costs to be written off as a function of the number of units sold; thus, if production volume is higher than sales volume, some fixed costs will be deferred in inventory at year-end, making net income higher than under variable costing. Alternatively, if sales volume is higher than production volume, the deferred fixed costs from previous periods will be written off as part of cost of goods sold, making net income lower than under variable costing. Variable costing requires that all fixed costs are written off in the period incurred, regardless of when the related inventory is sold; thus, if production volume is higher than sales volume, all fixed manufacturing costs will be expensed in the current period and not be deferred until sold, making net income lower than under absorption costing. Conversely, if sales volume is higher than production volume, only current period fixed manufacturing costs will be expensed in the current period, making net income higher than under absorption costing.

5. The high-low method analyzes a mixed cost by first selecting the highest and the lowest levels of activity within the relevant range. Levels of activity outside the relevant range are ignored. Next, changes in activity and cost between the two points are determined. The variable unit cost is equal to the change in the total cost divided by the change in activity level. This unit cost in multiplied by the activity level at either level to determine the variable costs at that level. Lastly, the fixed costs are equal to the total cost less the variable cost at the activity level.

6. A plantwide predetermined overhead rate generally does not produce the most useful information for companies that produce many different kinds of products. A company with multiple departments that use significantly different types of work effort, different materials and require different lengths of time to convert inputs to outputs should use separate predetermined overhead rates. This provides for the derivation of the most rational product cost because homogeneity is more likely to occur at the departmental level than across all departments. Managers computing the overhead rates at the departmental level achieve more useful information and more appropriate cost drivers.

Chapter 3:
Predetermined Overhead Rates Flexible Budgets, & Absorption/Variable Costing

7. An alternative to actual costing is normal costing. Normal costing assigns actual direct material and direct labor to products but allocates production overhead to products using a predetermined overhead. A normal cost system assigns overhead to Work in Process Inventory as the activity that is used to apply overhead occurs. Overhead is first debited to the control accounts (Fixed Overhead and Variable Overhead) to record the actual overhead, the applied overhead is then debited to Work in Process Inventory and credited from the control accounts in the general ledger. If the amount left in the control is relatively small at the end of the period then it is debited to Cost of Goods Sold, otherwise it is prorated across Work in Process Inventory, Finished Goods Inventory, and Cost of Goods Sold.

8. Flexible budgets allow managers to understand manufacturing overhead costs incurred and the related cost behaviors. Flexible budgets also allow managers to separate mixed costs into their variable and mixed components. Managers utilize flexible budgets because they provide information on the budgeted costs to be incurred at various levels of activity. Also they provide a visualization of the impacts on the predetermined fixed overhead rate from changing the level of activity.

9. 1. Separate the mixed costs into ariable and mixed elements.
2. Determine the a+bX cost formula for each item on the budget category.
3. Select several potential levels of activity within the relevant range.
4. Use the cost formulas to determine the total cost expected at each of the selected levels of activity.

10. Major authoritative bodies of the accounting profession, such as the Financial Accounting Standards Board and the Securities and Exchange Commission, require the use of absorption costing for to prepare external financial statements; absorption costing is also required for filing tax returns with the Internal Revenue Service.

11. The four measures of organizational capacity are theoretical capacity, practical capacity, normal capacity, and expected capacity. Theoretical capacity is the estimated maximum potential capacity for a specified time assuming that all production process are operating perfectly. Practical capacity is theoretical capacity reduced by the ongoing, and regular operating interruptions. Normal capacity is encompasses the firm's long-run average activity by considering historical and estimated future production levels and cyclical fluctuations. Expected capacity is a short-run budget-based activity level for the upcoming period based on projected project demand.

Chapter 3:
Predetermined Overhead Rates Flexible Budgets, & Absorption/Variable Costing

12. The first step is to identify the high month and the low month. Then, compute the change in costs and the change in machine hours.

	Maintenance Costs	Machine Hours
High month: May	$7,810	12,200
Low month: February	5,490	8,200
Changes	$2,320	4,000

(a) The variable maintenance cost per machine hour is the change in costs divided by the change in machine hours.

$2,320 ÷ 4,000 machine hours = $0.58 per machine hour

(b) Compute the fixed costs per month by subtracting the total variable costs from the total costs. You can do this for the high month or the low month.

	May	February
Total maintenance costs	$7,810	$5,490
Total variable costs:		
$0.58 per MH x 12,200 MH	7,076	
$0.58 per MH x 8,200 MH		4,756
Fixed costs	$ 734	$ 734

13. (a) The predetermined overhead rate equals the estimated overhead divided by the estimated machine hours: $480,000 ÷ 120,000 MH = $4 per machine hour

(b) Actual overhead $486,000
    Less: Applied overhead:
      $4 per MH x 123,000 MH = 492,000
    Overapplied overhead $ 6,000

The ending balance in the overhead account would be a $6,000 credit balance.

(c) Manufacturing Overhead   6,000
       Cost of Goods Sold   6,000

Chapter 3:
Predetermined Overhead Rates Flexible Budgets, & Absorption/Variable Costing

APPENDIX

14. For the Brown Department machine hours is the appropriate activity, and for the Green Department direct labor hours is the appropriate activity. Divide the estimated overhead costs in each department by the expected activity level used in each department.

Brown $600,000 ÷ 200,000 machine hours = $3 per MH
Green $300,000 ÷ 75,000 direct labor hours = $4 per DLH

15.

X	Y	XY	X^2
1,000	5,860	5,860,000	1,000,000
900	5,290	4,761,000	810,000
1,080	6,120	6,609,600	1,166,400
860	5,270	4,532,200	739,600
3,840	22,540	21,762,800	3,716,000

Mean of X = 3,840 ÷ 4 = 960; Mean of Y = 22,540 ÷ 4 = 5,635

$$b = \frac{21,762,800 - 4(960)(5,635)}{3,716,000 - 4(960)(960)} = \frac{124,400}{29,600} = 4.203$$

a = 5,635 − 4.203(960) = 1,600.12

CHAPTER 4

JOB ORDER COSTING

CHAPTER OVERVIEW

A primary purpose of cost accounting is to compute the cost of a company's products or services. Different methods exist to value inventory and compute product cost for manufacturing companies and service firms. The method used depends upon a company's conversion processes and the product or service. Companies must use a cost flow assumption for costs that they cannot attach to specific units.

Manufacturing companies use either job order costing or process costing. This chapter focuses on job order costing. Job order costing is useful for companies that make a limited quantity of goods tailored to customer specifications. Many service firms also use job order costing.

In addition to a product costing system, a company needs to select a valuation method. The possible valuation methods are actual costing, normal costing, or standard costing. This chapter assumes the use of normal costing. In normal costing, a company uses actual costs for direct material and direct labor but applies overhead using a predetermined rate.

This chapter shows the journal entries in a job order costing system from the requisition of raw materials to the sale of a completed job. This chapter also briefly discusses the use of the standard costing valuation method with a job order costing system.

CHAPTER STUDY GUIDE

Before a company can compute the costs of its products, it must first decide on (1) a product costing system and (2) a valuation method. The product costing system specifies the cost object and the method for assigning costs to production. The valuation method specifies how the company will measure product costs. Exhibit 4-1 shows six possible combinations of costing systems and valuation methods.

The two main costing systems are job order costing and process costing. Job order costing is suitable for companies that make relatively small quantities or separate batches of identifiable products. Process costing is appropriate for companies that make large quantities of homogeneous products. Process costing requires a cost flow assumption such as FIFO or weighted-average cost.

Three possible valuation methods are actual, normal, and standard costing. Actual costing uses actual costs for direct material, direct labor, and overhead. Normal costing uses actual costs for direct material and direct labor but applies overhead using a predetermined rate. In standard costing, a company uses standards or benchmarks to compute the costs of products. The differences between actual costs and standard costs are variances. Companies reconcile standard costs and actual costs using the variances. This chapter addresses the combination of a job order costing system with a normal costing valuation method. This chapter also briefly discusses the combination of job order costing and standard costing.

Product costing involves (1) cost identification, (2) cost measurement, and (3) product cost assignment. Job order costing accumulates costs by job. A job is a single unit or group of the same or similar units produced to customer specifications. Each job is a separate cost object. The company keeps the costs for each job in subsidiary ledger accounts. The Work in Process Inventory control account in the general ledger maintains the costs for all jobs. Periodically, the company should reconcile the Work in Process Inventory Control account with the amounts in the subsidiary ledger accounts. Exhibit 4-2 illustrates the separate subsidiary accounts for each job and the Work in Process Inventory Control account in the general ledger.

Companies classify jobs by their stage in the production cycle. The three stages of production are (1) contracted for but not yet started, (2) in process, and (3) completed. When the company buys raw materials, it debits the cost of the materials to the Raw Material Inventory account. Some materials may be unique and designated for a particular job. The company should indicate such designations in subsidiary records.

When a company needs raw materials to start a job, it prepares a material requisition form to authorize the transfer of the materials from the warehouse to the production area. Exhibit 4-3 illustrates a material requisition form. This source document indicates the types and quantities of materials needed for production. These forms are usually prenumbered forms with multiple copies. Material requisition forms are important for the audit trail. They provide the basis for placing responsibility for material cost and for tracing the flow of materials from the warehouse to the production area. The material requisition form releases the warehouse employees from subsequent responsibility for the issued materials and assigns responsibility to the department that requisitioned them. Many companies are replacing paper material requisition forms with electronic documents.

When the warehouse issues materials, the company debits the Work in Process Inventory account for the cost of direct materials issued. For indirect materials, the company debits the Manufacturing Overhead account. The company credits the Raw Material Inventory account for the cost of direct materials and indirect materials issued.

The issuance of direct materials begins the in process stage of production. In this stage, the company must begin accumulating costs using the primary accounting document in a job

Chapter 4: Job Order Costing

order costing system. This source document is the job order cost sheet, which may exist only in electronic form in many companies. It provides the financial information about a particular job. The collection of job order cost sheets for all incomplete jobs constitutes the Work in Process Inventory subsidiary ledger. Exhibit 4-4 illustrates a job order cost sheet.

The company posts the cost of direct material issued to a particular job from the material requisition forms to the job order cost sheet. The company posts direct labor cost to the job order cost sheet from employee time sheets. Exhibit 4-5 illustrates an employee time sheet. Larger companies typically use computers to track the time employees spend on specific jobs. Employees can simply swipe their employee identification card and a job card through a card reader when they begin working on a different job. The company applies overhead to the job based on predetermined rates that may differ by department.

In the modern manufacturing environment, direct labor cost is often a small portion of total cost. In such cases, machine clocks may track machine time. Machine time would be a surrogate for operator time. Companies can also track employee time using bar codes to trace products as they flow through workstations.

Labor cost is equal to the wage rates multiplied by the employee's time spent on the job. The company debits the Work in Process Inventory account for the direct labor cost. The company charges the indirect labor cost to Manufacturing Overhead. The company credits Salaries and Wages Payable for the payroll liability for the sum of the direct labor and indirect labor cost.

The company should file and retain employee time sheets. They are useful if management wants to know why actual labor cost was different from the budgeted labor cost for a particular job. In addition, for cost-plus contracts (basis), buyers may want to inspect the number of hours worked on the job. Employee time sheets provide information on overtime hours. Under the Fair Labor Standards Act, companies must pay a nonmanagement employee at a time-and-a-half rate for overtime hours when he or she works more than 40 hours in a week.

Overhead costs are a major cost in manufacturing and service businesses. A company may use activity-based costing with job order costing to compute product costs more accurately. If a company uses a predetermined overhead rate, it debits the Manufacturing Overhead account for actual overhead costs incurred. The company then applies overhead to jobs at the earlier of the completion of production or the end of the period.

To apply overhead, the company debits the Work in Process Inventory account and credits the Manufacturing Overhead account. The company posts the overhead applied to a particular job to the job order cost sheet. At the end of the accounting period, the company closes the underapplied or overapplied overhead to Cost of Goods Sold if the amount is immaterial. The company would close the underapplied or overapplied overhead in a pro rata manner to Work in Process Inventory, Finished Goods Inventory, and Cost of Goods Sold if the amount is material.

Chapter 4: Job Order Costing

Upon the completion of production, a company using the perpetual inventory method transfers the cost of the job to Finished Goods Inventory by debiting the Finished Goods Inventory account and crediting the Work in Process Inventory account. The company also transfers the job order cost sheets from the work in process subsidiary ledger to its permanent files. The job order cost sheets for jobs the company completed and sold could be useful for bidding on future jobs and for cost control efforts.

When the company sells the job, it debits the Cost of Goods Sold account and credits the Finished Goods Inventory account. The company records a sale by debiting Accounts Receivable or Cash and crediting Sales. Managers are concerned with controlling costs in each department as well as by job. Managers compare actual costs incurred in a department with budgeted costs. Managers should investigate significant variances.

Many companies that use job order costing maintain little finished goods inventory. These companies sell the goods upon the completion of production because the company makes the products only after receiving a specific customer contract. Thus, these companies could avoid using a Finished Goods Inventory account and simply debit Cost of Goods Sold at the completion of production.

Service firms can also use job order costing. However, raw materials are an insignificant cost for most service firms. Thus, service firms may treat raw materials cost as a part of overhead. Service firms allocate overhead to jobs based on direct labor hours, direct labor cost, or other bases as appropriate.

Companies are increasingly automating the data collection and data entry functions in job order costing. Automating these functions reduces record keeping burdens and makes the data accessible for many purposes. Many companies are creating intranets to manage information about jobs. An intranet is a device that uses Web technology to share information and deliver data from corporate databases to desktop computers on a local area network (LAN). Intranets are restricted networks that can heighten communication and distribute information. Exhibit 4-6 lists the types of information that managers can access on an intranet. The data on an intranet are available to managers on a real-time basis.

Job order costing is useful to managers in carrying out their managerial functions. Knowing the cost of completed jobs can help managers set prices on future jobs. The job order cost sheets provide managers with useful information in controlling costs. Comparisons of actual costs and budgeted costs aid in performance evaluation. Exhibit 4-7 illustrates a completed job order cost sheet.

The use of actual costs for direct material and direct labor could cause the cost of similar units to vary because of changes in component costs. Using standard costing as the valuation method can minimize such fluctuations. The use of a predetermined overhead rate for applying overhead costs minimizes fluctuations in overhead costs applied to similar units.

A standard cost system uses predetermined norms or benchmarks for prices and/or

Chapter 4:   Job Order Costing

quantities of components. After the completion of production, management compares the actual prices and quantities with the standard prices and quantities. Differences between actual amounts and standard amounts are variances.

A company should use standard costing with a job order costing system only if the company frequently produces similar products. One type of standard cost system uses standards for material prices and labor rates only. This system uses actual quantities of raw materials and actual direct labor hours. Thus, it is a hybrid of normal costing and standard costing.

A company can compute variances regardless of whether it uses standards for both quantities and prices/rates or for prices/rates only. Standard costs for material and labor provide management with more timely information and comparisons against actual amounts. Predetermined overhead rates provide management with these benefits with respect to overhead costs. In fact, a predetermined overhead rate is essentially a type of standard.

Standard job order costing systems are good surrogates for actual or normal costing systems if they provide management with useful information. A cost system should be effective and efficient in meeting the unique production needs of a company. The cost of a system should also be reasonable compared to its benefits.

Job order costing is helpful to management of manufacturing companies and service firms that make customized products or provide unique services. Job order costing will become more pervasive as product variety increases and the size or production lots decreases. Tailor-made goods will become the norm rather than the exception in production environments that use flexible manufacturing systems and computer-integrated manufacturing.

Few production processes result in no loss of units. Losses from evaporation, leakage, or oxidation are inherent in the production process. These inherent losses result in shrinkage. Modifying the production process to reduce shrinkage may not be feasible or cost-effective.

In addition to shrinkage, errors in the production process can result in units that do not meet acceptable quality standards. The classification of these units as spoiled or defective depends on whether the company can economically rework the units. If the company can economically rework the unit, it is a defective unit. If the company cannot economically rework the unit, it is a spoiled unit. An inspector determines if the unit is defective or spoiled.

A normal loss of units falls within an expected tolerance level. Management creates a tolerance level based on the acceptable quality level. Any loss in excess of the acceptable quality level is an abnormal loss. The difference between a normal loss and an abnormal loss is one of degree. Accounting for these lost units depends on whether such loss is incurred for most jobs or is it specifically identified with a particular job and is the loss considered normal or abnormal.

If management expects a certain loss on all jobs, the predetermined overhead application rate should include an amount, which is net of such loss. The net cost of the loss equals the cost of the defective or spoiled work less estimated disposal value if any. The text illustrates the

Chapter 4: Job Order Costing 80

accounting and journal entries for accounting for losses generally anticipated on all jobs.

When defects or spoilage are related to specific jobs based on job related characteristics, the cost of the loss attaches to that specific job. The disposal value of the loss on the units, if any, reduces the cost of that specific job. The textbook shows the journal entry for defective work with disposal value when such loss is specifically identified with a particular job.

If management expects a certain loss on all jobs or expects no loss, the amount over the expected loss is abnormal spoilage. Abnormal spoilage should be written off as a period cost. Management should separately identify and investigate the abnormal spoilage to determine future prevention measures. The text illustrates the journal entries for accounting for losses considered both normal and abnormal.

Chapter 4: Job Order Costing

SELF TEST

<u>TRUE/FALSE</u>

1. T F Job order costing is appropriate for manufacturing companies that make large quantities of homogeneous goods.

2. T F Service firms cannot use job order costing.

3. T F Job order costing and process costing are types of valuation methods.

4. T F A normal cost system uses actual costs for direct material, direct labor, and manufacturing overhead.

5. T F The source document that provides almost all financial information about a particular job is the job order cost sheet.

6. T F Each job is treated as a unique cost object.

7. T F A company should debit the cost of indirect materials issued from the warehouse to Manufacturing Overhead.

8. T F A company should debit Wages and Salaries Expense for the direct labor cost of a job.

9. T F Bar codes are a convenient way to track employee time as products pass through individual workstations.

10. T F At the completion of production, a company usually debits Finished Goods Inventory and credits Work in Process Inventory for the cost of the completed job.

11. T F A company closes an insignificant amount of underapplied or overapplied overhead at the end of the accounting period to Finished Goods Inventory.

12. T F An intranet is a device for sharing information and delivering data from corporate databases to local area network desktop computers.

13. T F Differences between actual costs and standard costs are variances.

14. T F Because a company uses a predetermined overhead rate in normal costing, the company does not consider it as a standard.

15. T F Although some companies use standard cost systems, such systems are seldom reasonable substitutes for actual or normal costing.

Chapter 4: Job Order Costing

MULTIPLE CHOICE

1. Which types of organizations use job order costing systems?

    A. manufacturing companies only
    B. service firms only
    C. manufacturing companies and service firms
    D. not-for-profit organizations only

2. What are the three possible valuation methods?

    A. actual, normal, and standard
    B. job order, process, and standard
    C. actual, job order, and process
    D. normal, job order, and standard

3. A normal cost system uses actual costs for:

    A. direct material, direct labor, and overhead.
    B. direct material and direct labor only.
    C. direct material only.
    D. direct material and overhead only.

4. When the production department needs materials to begin a job, what document must the company prepare?

    A. job order cost sheet
    B. material requisition form
    C. employee time sheet
    D. work in process subsidiary ledger

5. When a company transfers direct material from the warehouse into production, what account does the company debit?

    A. Raw Material Inventory
    B. Manufacturing Overhead
    C. Work in Process Inventory
    D. Accounts Payable

Chapter 4: Job Order Costing

6. When a company transfers indirect material from the warehouse into production, what account does the company debit?

    A. Raw Material Inventory
    B. Supplies Expense
    C. Work in Process Inventory
    D. Manufacturing Overhead

7. What account does a company debit to record the indirect labor cost of a job?

    A. Salaries and Wages Expense
    B. Salaries and Wages Payable
    C. Work in Process Inventory
    D. Manufacturing Overhead

8. For overtime hours, what rate must a company pay nonmangement employees?

    A. a time-and-a-half rate
    B. twice their regular rate
    C. three time their regular rate
    D. the average rate paid to management employees

9. Which act mandates a higher overtime pay rate for nonmanagement employees who work over 40 hours in a week?

    A. Fair Labor Standards Act
    B. Employee Retirement and Income Security Act
    C. Sherman Act
    D. Tax Reform Act of 1986

10. The journal entry to apply overhead to production involves a credit to:

    A. Manufacturing Overhead.
    B. Work in Process Inventory.
    C. Cost of Goods Sold.
    D. Wages and Salaries Payable.

11. What is the focal point of a job order costing system?

    A. costs incurred in each department
    B. the individual job
    C. the Work in Process Inventory account
    D. the Cost of Goods Sold account

Chapter 4: Job Order Costing   84

12. The journal entry to record the completion of production involves a debit to:

    A. Finished Goods Inventory.
    B. Work in Process Inventory.
    C. Manufacturing Overhead.
    D. Cost of Goods Sold.

13. The journal entry to record the sale of a completed job involves a debit to:

    A. Cost of Goods Sold.
    B. Work in Process Inventory.
    C. Accounts Payable.
    D. Sales.

14. Managers are interested in controlling costs by:

    A. job only.
    B. department only.
    C. job and by department.
    D. the use of standard costing only.

15. If the amount of underapplied overhead is insignificant at the end of the accounting period, the company usually closes the underapplied overhead to:

    A. Work in Process Inventory.
    B. Finished Goods.
    C. Cost of Goods Sold.
    D. Work in Process, Finished Goods and costs of Goods sold on a pro rata basis.

16. What is the major difference between job order costing for a service organization and job order costing for a manufacturing company?

    A. Service organizations have little overhead.
    B. Service organizations usually incur large direct material costs.
    C. Service organizations use a small amount of direct material relative to direct labor.
    D. Service organizations usually treat direct labor as a part of overhead.

17. Job order costing usually is NOT useful to managers in their functions of:

    A. planning and controlling.
    B. decision making.
    C. performance evaluation.
    D. costing of large quantities of homogeneous products.

Chapter 4: Job Order Costing

18. Job order costing becomes more applicable for manufacturing companies as:

    A. product variety increases.
    B. the size of production lots increases.
    C. direct labor cost increases significantly in the modern environment.
    D. standard, homogeneous goods become more popular.

19. As product variety increases and the size of production lots decreases, which of the following becomes more applicable?

    A. standard costing
    B. actual costing
    C. process costing
    D. job order costing

20. In a job order costing system, the company assigns the costs incurred while a job is in process to:

    A. Work in Process Inventory.
    B. Cost of Goods Sold.
    C. Raw Material Inventory.
    D. Finished Goods Inventory.

21. In a job order costing system, when does a company apply overhead to Work in Process Inventory?

    A. at the end of the period only
    B. at the end of the job only
    C. at the end of the period or the end of the job, whichever is earlier
    D. at the end of the period or the end of the job, whichever is later

22. How many combinations of cost systems and valuation methods are possible?

    A. 2
    B. 4
    C. 6
    D. 8

23. What is a characteristic of a highly automated factory?

    A. Employee time sheets are extremely useful.
    B. Direct labor cost is a large proportion of total cost.
    C. Companies often track machine time using machine clocks or counters.
    D. Machine time cannot be equated with employee-operator time.

Chapter 4: Job Order Costing

24. An intranet is a(n):
    A. unrestricted computer network.
    B. mechanism that uses Web technology to share information and deliver data.
    C. device that results in more accurate information but decreases communication.
    D. a new computer system totally unrelated to Web technology.

25. Knowing the costs of individual jobs does NOT allow management to:

    A. estimate the costs of future jobs better.
    B. establish realistic bids for future jobs.
    C. set selling prices.
    D. charge normal spoilage to period costs.

26. For a cost system to be acceptable in practice, it usually is NOT:

    A. effective and efficient in serving the company's unique production needs.
    B. provide the information that managers desire.
    C. capable of being implemented at a reasonable cost compared to its benefits.
    D. applying abnormal spoilage costs to regular inventory.

27. A difference between the actual quantity, price, or rate and its related standard is a:

    A. difference.
    B. variance.
    C. fluctuation.
    D. deviation.

28. A company can use standards with a job order costing system only if the company:

    A. has an audit by an outside CPA firm.
    B. has prior approval from the IRS.
    C. has jobs that usually produce fairly similar products.
    D. produces large quantities of homogeneous goods in a continuous process.

29. Thomas Company used 1,080 pounds of direct material at a cost of $3.10 per pound to make 500 units of its product. The standard price for the direct material is $3.00 a pound. The standard quantity of direct material is 2 pounds per unit of product. What was Thomas Company's direct material quantity variance?

    A. $108 F
    B. $108 U
    C. $240 F
    D. $240 U

Chapter 4: Job Order Costing

30. Bartlett Company used 600 direct labor hours at a cost of $6,600 to make 100 units of a product. The standard direct labor rate is $10 per direct labor hour. The standard direct labor hours per unit of product are 5.5. What was the direct labor rate variance?

    A. $500 U
    B. $500 F
    C. $600 F
    D. $600 U

QUESTIONS AND PROBLEMS

1. For which types of companies is job order costing appropriate? Give some examples of these companies.

2. What are the three valuation methods? How do companies charge costs to production under each of the three valuation methods?

3. What constitutes the subsidiary ledger accounts for jobs in process in a job order costing system? How do these subsidiary ledger accounts relate to the Work in Process Inventory account in the general ledger?

4. What source document does the company prepare to transfer material from the warehouse to the production area? What information does this source document contain?

5. What source document provides most of the financial information about a particular job? What information does this source document contain?

Chapter 4: Job Order Costing

6. What are some alternatives to employee time sheets in the modern manufacturing environment?

7. What are the differences in a job order costing system for a service firm and a job order costing system for a manufacturing company?

8. Why are managers interested in recording costs by department as well as by job?

Chapter 4: Job Order Costing

9. What is an intranet? How are companies using intranets?

10. What are the benefits of using a standard costing valuation method?

11. Why do some companies that use job order costing not have a Finished Goods Inventory account?

Chapter 4: Job Order Costing

12. What are the criteria for a cost system to be acceptable to management?

13. Explain the accounting treatment for product and material losses in job order costing.

14. Miller Company's job order costing system uses actual quantities of direct material and actual labor hours, but standard prices and labor rates to assign costs to jobs. Prepare journal entries, in general journal form, to record the transactions below. Omit explanations.

    (a) The issuance of 600 gallons of direct material into production. The actual price was $5.25 per gallon, but the standard price is $5.20 per gallon.

    (b) Used 800 direct labor hours. The actual rate was $10.25 per hour, but the standard rate is $10.00 per hour.

Chapter 4: Job Order Costing

15. Saunders Company uses a job order costing system with a standard cost valuation method. During the month, Saunders used 680 pounds of direct material at a cost of $7.10 per pound to make 100 units. The standard for direct material is 7 pounds per unit at a cost of $6.80 per pound. Saunders also used 1,000 direct labor hours at an average cost of $11.80 per direct labor hour to make the 100 units. The standard direct labor hours are 9 hours per unit; the standard direct labor rate is $12.00 per hour. Calculate the following variances. Label each variance as favorable (F) or unfavorable (U).

(a) direct material quantity variance

(b) direct material price variance

(c) direct material total variance

(d) direct labor quantity variance

(e) direct labor rate variance

(f) direct labor total variance

Chapter 4: Job Order Costing

SELF TEST ANSWERS

TRUE/FALSE

1.	F	4.	F	7.	T	10.	T	13.	T
2.	F	5.	T	8.	F	11.	F	14.	F
3.	F	6.	T	9.	T	12.	T	15.	F

MULTIPLE CHOICE

1.	C	7.	D	13.	A	19.	D	25.	D
2.	A	8.	A	14.	C	20.	A	26.	D
3.	B	9.	A	15.	C	21.	C	27.	B
4.	B	10.	A	16.	C	22.	C	28.	C
5.	C	11.	B	17.	D	23.	C	29.	D
6.	D	12.	A	18.	A	24.	B	30.	D

QUESTIONS AND PROBLEMS

1. Job order costing is appropriate for companies that make relatively small quantities or particular batches of identifiable products. Service firms that perform small batches of distinctive services can also use job order costing. Companies that make custom cabinets, print shops, tax preparation firms, architects, and research firms are examples of companies that could use job order costing.

2. The three valuation methods are actual costing, normal costing, and standard costing. In actual costing, companies use the actual costs of direct material, direct labor, and overhead to assign costs to production. Normal costing uses actual costs for direct material and direct labor, but applies overhead to production using a predetermined rate. Standard costing uses predetermined standards or norms for the prices and/or quantities of direct material and direct labor. The overhead standard is the predetermined rate.

3. The collection of job order cost sheets for jobs in process constitutes the subsidiary ledger accounts for jobs in process. The sum of the costs on the job order cost sheets should equal the balance in the Work in Process Inventory account in the general ledger. The Work in Process Inventory account serves as a control account over the subsidiary ledger accounts.

4. The source document used to release material from the warehouse to the production area is the material requisition form. This form shows the kinds and quantities of materials to be placed into production or used to provide a service. These documents are usually prenumbered and have multiple copies. In the modern manufacturing environment, material requisition forms may exist in electronic form only.

5. The source document that contains most of the financial information about an individual job is the job order cost sheet. This document shows the job number, a brief description of the job, the customer, scheduling information, delivery instructions, and the contract price. The document will show the direct material cost, direct labor cost, and overhead charged to the job. The job order cost sheet may also show budgeted costs. In the modern manufacturing environment, job order cost sheets may exist in electronic form only.

6. Larger companies might use electronic time-keeping software. Employees swipe an identification card and a job card through a card reader when they begin working on a different job. The software accumulated labor costs by job and by department. In highly automated factories, employee time sheets may not be very useful because direct labor cost is a small portion of total product cost. Companies can track machine time with machine clocks or counters. Machine time approximates machine operator time. Another option is to use bar codes to track how long a job stays at each workstation. The company can use the time spent at each station to measure employee time on a particular job.

7. In a service firm, direct material is often an insignificant part of the total cost of providing a service. In these cases, the firm may treat direct material cost as a part of overhead and trace only direct labor cost to an individual job. The firm would allocate direct material and other overhead costs to the jobs using a predetermined rate often based on direct labor hours or direct labor cost. The firm could use other drivers to assign overhead. In some service firms, direct material cost could be significant. In these cases, the firm would trace direct material cost to a particular job.

8. Managers are interested in recording costs by department as well as by job because managers are interested in controlling costs by department as well as by job. Managers want to compare the costs incurred in each department with the budgeted costs for each department. In this way, inefficient departments cannot avoid scrutiny simply because the total costs incurred for the job were under budget. The other departments' costs may have been under budget by an amount that was more than enough to offset the costs over budget in an inefficient department.

9. An intranet is a device that uses Web technology to share information and deliver data from corporate databases to desktop computers on a local area network (LAN). Intranets are restricted networks that can heighten communication and distribute information. Companies are increasingly automating the data collection and data entry functions in job order costing. Automating these functions reduces record keeping burdens and makes the data accessible for many purposes. The data on an intranet are available to managers on a real-time basis.

10. A company that uses a standard costing valuation method records actual costs and standard costs in the accounting records. Standard costs provide benchmarks against which managers can compare actual costs. These benchmarks help managers to control costs. A standard cost system allows managers to see quickly deviations or variances from normal production costs and to correct problems resulting from excess usage or abnormal costs.

Chapter 4: Job Order Costing

11. Some companies that use job order costing do not have a Finished Goods Inventory account because they sell the goods at the completion of production. Companies that use job order costing often make custom goods under a contract that calls for the sale of the goods at the completion of production. These companies transfer the cost of the job from Work in Process Inventory directly to Cost of Goods Sold.

12. A cost system should be effective and efficient in serving the special production needs of a company. A cost system should produce the information that management wants. A company should be able to implement a cost system at a reasonable cost compared to its benefits.

13. The accounting treatment for product and material losses in job order costing is as follows: Any loss in excess of the acceptable quality level is an abnormal loss. The difference between a normal loss and an abnormal loss is one of degree. Accounting for these lost units depends on whether such loss is 1) incurred for most jobs or is specifically identified with a particular job and 2) considered normal or abnormal. If management expects a certain loss on all jobs, the predetermined overhead application rate should include an amount, which is net of such loss. The net cost of the loss equals the cost of the defective or spoiled work less estimated disposal value if any. When defects or spoilage are related to specific jobs based on job related characteristics, the cost of the loss attaches to that specific job. The disposal value of the loss on the units, if any, reduces the cost of that specific job. If management expects a certain loss on all jobs or expects no loss, the amount over the expected loss is abnormal spoilage. Abnormal spoilage should be written off as a period cost. Management should separately identify and investigate the abnormal spoilage to determine future prevention measures.

14. (a) Work in Process Inventory   3,120
        Raw Material Inventory   3,120

    (b) Work In Process Inventory   8,000
        Salaries and Wages Payable   8,000

15. (a) $6.80(680 – (7 x 100)) = $6.80(680 – 700) = $6.80(–20) = –$136.00 = $136.00 F

    (b) 680($7.10 – $6.80) = 680($0.30) = $204.00 = $204.00 U

    (c) $7.10(680) – $6.80(7 x 100) = $4,828.00 – $4,760.00 = $68.00 = $68.00 U or
        $136.00 F + $204.00 U = $68.00 U

    (d) $12.00(1,000 – (9 x 100)) = $12.00(1,000 – 900) = $12.00(100) = $1,200.00 U

    (e) 1,000($11.80 – $12.00) = 1,000(–$0.20) = –$200.00 = $200.00 F

    (f) $11.80(1,000) – $12.00(9 x 100) = $11,800.00 – $10,800.00 = $1000.00 U or
        $1,200.00 U + $200.00 F = $1,000.00 U

CHAPTER 5

ACTIVITY-BASED MANAGEMENT AND ACTIVITY-BASED COSTING

CHAPTER OVERVIEW

Accounting reports based on traditional overhead allocation systems might not provide managers with the information they need to make good business decisions. This chapter focuses on topics at the cutting edge of cost accounting. These topics result from the intensely competitive nature of the global economy. Important aspects of activity-based management are discussed.

This chapter discusses how companies can reduce costs without reducing quality by eliminating non-value-added activities. This chapter also explains why some companies are using activities to compute product costs, including cost drivers, to compute service costs, and to measure performance. Such a cost system is called activity-based costing (ABC). This chapter discusses and illustrates the basic concepts of activity-based costing.

CHAPTER STUDY GUIDE

Accurate product costs are important to all managers. Product costs affect decisions on corporate strategy, finance, and marketing. A company must keep costs under control to sell products at prices that provide acceptable value to customers and profits for the company.

Activity-based management focuses on production activities as a means to improve the value of a product in the mind of a customer and the resulting profits to the company. Exhibit 5-1 lists the components of activity-based management. The concepts of activity-based management help companies to produce more efficiently, compute more accurate product costs, and evaluate performance more effectively. Activity analysis is a major part of activity-based management. Activity analysis involves classifying activities as value-added or non-value-added and developing ways to reduce or eliminate non-value-added activities.

An activity is a repetitive action performed in a business function. A value-added activity is an activity that increases the value of a product from the perspective of a customer. A non-value-added activity increases the time spent on a product, but it does not raise its worth. Customers view non-value-added activities as unnecessary. Thus, a company can eliminate non-

Chapter 5:   Activity-Based Management and Activity-Based Costing   98

value-added activities without having an impact on the market value or quality of the product or service. However, some non-value-added activities are essential to the business though customers do not assign value to them. These activities are business-value-added activities. Examples of business-value-added activities are sending sales invoices and statements of account. Exhibit 5-2 provides classifications of activities.

The first step in activity analysis is identifying organizational processes. Typical processes include production, distribution, selling, and administration. Processes overlap different functional areas of the business. See Exhibit 5-3 for an illustration of the complexity of only part of the process flow in an organization. The company should prepare a process map for each process. The process map shows every step involved in making a product or performing a function. Companies should be careful to identify all steps involved, not just the major ones.

Next, a company should prepare a value chart that shows the stages and the time spent in each stage from the beginning of a process to its end. A company can spend time in each stage in four different ways: (1) processing, (2) inspection, (3) transfer, and (4) idle. Processing time is the actual time spent on activities necessary to make the product or provide a service. Processing time is a value-added activity. Inspection time involves performing quality control. Transfer time is the time spent in moving products or components from one place to another. Idle time includes storage time and time spent waiting at a production operation. Inspection time, transfer time, and idle time are all non-value-added activities. Cycle time is the time from the receipt of an order to the completion of a product or performance of a service. Cycle time is equal to the sum of value-added processing time and non-value-added time.

Companies cannot eliminate all non-value-added activities. However, managers should understand the non-value-added nature of quality control activities and transfer time. Managers should attempt to eliminate the activities that take the most time, add the most cost, and create the least value. Exhibit 5-4 illustrates a value chart for a chemical product.

Value-added processing time divided by cycle time equals manufacturing cycle efficiency (MCE). A company can never achieve 100 percent manufacturing cycle efficiency. Many companies have an MCE of about 10 percent. Thus, companies spend about 90 percent of cycle time performing non-value-added activities. Another term for non-value-added activities is waste. Usually, as Exhibit 5-5 illustrates, the longer the cycle time, the greater the propensity for products to pull costs to them.

A just-in-time manufacturing process endeavors to improve efficiency by making components and products exactly at the time the next production station or customer needs them. A just-in-time manufacturing process eliminates a great deal of idle time. A company can also increase its MCE by using automated production equipment.

In a retail business, cycle time is the time from ordering a product to selling it. Non-value-added activities include the transit time from suppliers, time spent counting merchandise received, and storage time between the receipt of a product and its sale. In a service firm, cycle time is the time between a service order and the completion of the service. All time spent on

Chapter 5: Activity-Based Management and Activity-Based Costing

activities not involved in the actual performance of the service are non-value-added activities.

The causes of non-value-added activities involve systemic, physical, and human factors. A company should direct its efforts in reducing non-value-added activities at all these causes. However, management should focus on the non-value-added activities that cause the most costs. Eliminating non-value-added activities should result in an increase in quality and a decrease in cycle time and cost.

All activities have cost drivers, which are the factors that have a direct cause-effect relationship to a cost. Companies should be able to identify many cost drivers for each business unit. However, management should limit the cost drivers used for cost accumulation or activity elimination to a reasonable number. Management should make sure that the cost of measuring a driver does not exceed the benefit from using it. A cost driver should be understandable, directly related to a particular activity, and suitable for performance measurement.

Traditionally, companies have accumulated factory overhead costs in one or two cost pools and used one or two drivers to assign the overhead costs to products. This cost allocation procedure is acceptable for financial reporting purposes. However, using one or two drivers may result in distorted product costs for managerial purposes.

Exhibit 5-6 shows potential cost drivers for shipping cost. Exhibit 5-7 shows how a company can manage costs by combining activity analysis with cost driver analysis. Activity analysis reveals activities that are not value-adding to target for reduction, and cost driver analysis identifies activities that cause costs.

Cost driver analysis is concerned with investigating, quantifying, and explaining the relationships of drivers and their associated costs. Companies incur costs at four different levels. A company incurs unit-level costs each time it produces or purchases a single unit of product. Batch-level costs are the costs a company incurs each time it makes a group of products. A company incurs product- or process-level costs to support a type of product. A company incurs organizational- or facility-level costs for the support of the overall production process. Traditionally, companies assigned overhead costs as though they were all unit-level costs. Exhibit 5-8 provides examples of costs at each of the four levels.

Accountants have historically assumed that costs that did not vary with changes in the number of units produced were fixed costs. However, costs at the batch level, product level, and organizational level vary with activities other than production volume. To compute more accurate product costs, companies should accumulate costs at each of the four levels. Exhibit 5-9 shows how a company can use costs collected at the unit, batch, and product or process levels to compute total product cost. Theoretically, a company should not assign organizational-level costs to products. However, many companies assign such costs to products using an arbitrary basis. Exhibit 5-10 presents a product profitability analysis for a sample manufacturing company with three product lines.

Activities consume costly resources, and products consume activities. Using traditional

Chapter 5: Activity-Based Management and Activity-Based Costing 100

volume-based measures to assign overhead costs to production understates the cost of low-volume specialty products and overstates the cost of high-volume standard products. This distortion occurs because a company assigns overhead costs of volume-based measures such as direct labor hours, and much of the costs of making specialty products are not a function of volume.

Activity-based costing (ABC) is a cost system that assigns overhead costs based on the activities that cause the costs. The three fundamental components of ABC are as follows: (1) recognizing the existence of different levels of costs, (2) accumulating costs into related cost pools, and (3) using multiple cost drivers to assign costs to products and services. Activity-based costing is a cost accounting system that focuses on assigning costs to products and services based on the activities used to produce, distribute, and support products and to perform services.

Activity-based costing is especially useful in companies that have certain characteristics. Activity-based costing is useful for a company that produces a variety of products or performs a variety of services. As a company produces more products or performs more services, the potential for cost distortion increases. If overhead costs are high and not proportional to the unit volume of individual products, a company can benefit from activity-based costing. Traditional volume-based methods of overhead allocation would lead to distorted product costs. If a company has significantly automated its production process, an activity-based cost system might be especially useful. Assigning overhead costs based on volume-based measures often leads to distorted product costs in highly automated companies. If management has difficulty in explaining profit margins, the cause might be distorted product costs. An activity-based costing system might be the solution. Finally, if products that are difficult to manufacture show large profits and products that are easy to manufacture show small profits or losses, the problem might be distorted product costs for which activity-based costing is the solution.

Activity-based costing uses a two-step cost assignment procedure. First, a company records costs in its general ledger and subsidiary ledgers. Second, the company accumulates costs in activity center cost pools. An activity center is a portion of the production or service process for which management wants a cost report. In selecting activity centers, managers should consider the following issues: (1) geographic proximity of equipment, (2) centers of managerial responsibility, (3) magnitude of product costs, and (4) manageable number of activity centers. The relationship between a cost driver and a cost pool shows that if a company can reduce or eliminate the cost driver, it can reduce or eliminate the related cost.

Accumulating costs with common cost drivers in cost pools helps managers to recognize the cross-functional activities in the company. Some companies accumulate overhead costs by department, which reflects a vertical-function approach to cost accumulation. However, production and service activities are inherently horizontal activities.

After a company accumulates costs into cost pools using cost drivers, it allocates costs to products and services using an activity driver. An activity driver measures the demands placed on activities and the resources consumed by products and services. The activity driver often reflects the activity's output. Activity drivers are often different from cost drivers because some

Chapter 5: Activity-Based Management and Activity-Based Costing

activity center costs are not traceable to lower activity levels. Exhibit 5-11 illustrates the two-step process of assigning costs using an ABC system.

A company should allocate unit-level costs using volume-based drivers. The activity drivers for batch-level and product-level costs should be volume-based measures associated with the batch of products or product line. Exhibit 5-12 lists some common activity drivers for various activity centers. Exhibit 5-13 illustrates assigning maintenance costs to a product using activity-based costing.

Differences in costs computed using traditional methods and activity-based costing are common. Activity-based costing reveals that low-volume products and complex operations consume substantial resources. The cost of high-volume products often drops 10 to 30 percent using ABC. Increases in cost for low-volume products may be several hundred percent or more. As shown in Exhibit 5-14, ABC moves a significant amount of overhead cost from standard, high-volume products to specialty, low-volume products. Activity-based costing is also applicable to service department costs.

Short-term variable costs change in direct proportion to changes in the volume of activity. Accountants have viewed costs that do not change with changes in volume as fixed costs. However, many people now view these apparently fixed costs as long-term variable costs. Long-term variable costs are not fixed costs. Rather, they vary with cost drivers not related to volume.

Two significant cost drivers of long-term variable costs are product variety and product complexity. Product variety is the number of different kinds of products made. Product complexity is the number of components in a product or the number of processes involved in manufacturing a product. These factors often occur with a need to consider an ABC system. Additions to a company's product line cause numerous overhead costs to increase.

Activity-based costing is very beneficial for many companies, but not every traditional cost system provides poor information. Managers should consider the following factors in evaluating whether ABC is appropriate: (1) the number of different products the company makes, (2) the different levels of support needed for the products, (3) the extent of common processes, (4) the effectiveness of the current cost system, and (5) the growth rate of period costs.

If management expects an ABC system to generate better information, management must have the ability to act on the information to benefit the company. The factors to consider in determining whether management will be able to make better decisions based on the information generated by an ABC system are as follows: (1) the ability to set prices, (2) strategic considerations, and (3) the climate and culture of
cost reduction. Before a company switches to an ABC system, it should make sure that is meets the following two conditions: (1) homogeneous activities drive the costs in each pool, and (2) the costs in each pool are proportional to the activity.

Some companies use flexible manufacturing systems to provide mass customization of products to customers at a low cost. However, mass customization has several potential

Chapter 5: Activity-Based Management and Activity-Based Costing

problems: (1) customers may have too many choices, (2) it creates a tremendous opportunity for errors, and (3) customers often make selections from a small percentage of the available choices. Companies may find that about 20 percent of the products account for about 80 percent of the sales. This 20:80 ratio is the Pareto principle.

Management of companies with complex products or processes might seek ways to reduce the complexity. Management can reduce product complexity by standardizing the company's products and processes. In addition, management should reduce the number of different components, tools, and processes required. Management should ask whether the company could reduce complexity, while maintaining equal quality, by using more common parts. If not, management should ask if the parts are for products purchased by important customers who are willing to pay a premium price for the products. Another issue that management should address is whether the customers would be equally happy if the company produced the products with more common parts and reduced the prices. Complexity should be acceptable to a company only if it adds value to the product from the customer's viewpoint. See an example of a problem with product complexity in Exhibit 5-15.

Process complexity can develop over time, or it might be due to inadequate planning in product development. Process complexity involves many non-value-added activities and thus increases non-value-added costs. A process is complex if it creates difficulties for the people performing production operations or using manufacturing machinery.

A company can apply simultaneous (or concurrent) engineering to reduce both product complexity and process complexity. Simultaneous engineering refers to the continuous involvement of primary functions and personnel from the beginning of a project. Design for manufacturability occurs when a multifunctional team considers customer expectations, vendor capabilities, common parts, and production process compatibility in the design of a product. Simultaneous engineering helps companies to reduce time-to-market for new products, minimize complexity, and reduce cost.

Unlike traditional cost systems, activity-based cost systems can account for the number of different parts used in making a product. Activity-based cost systems provide important information concerning cost drivers and relationships among activities to those involved in reengineering efforts. Thus, reengineering efforts can focus on the primary causes of process complexity and those activities that create the greatest amount of waste.

Another cause of significant overhead costs is a variety of support services. Examples of these support services include advertising, distribution channels, and the use of high-technology machinery.

Distortions in product costs occur when a company uses only one or two cost pools to allocate overhead costs. A company would allocate overhead costs related to a specific product among all products. This practice leads to higher costs for products not responsible for such costs. The distortion is not usually significant if production volumes for all products are similar. When production volumes are significantly different, greater cost distortion will occur.

Chapter 5:   Activity-Based Management and Activity-Based Costing

A company should consider setting up an activity-based cost system when any of the following occurs: (1) products or processes change because of automation, (2) the competitive environment changes, or (3) management strategy changes.

As a company uses more automation in production, cost systems based on direct labor become less valid. Using a cost system based on direct labor, a company would charge too little overhead to products made with automated equipment. In addition, the company would charge too much overhead to products made with a large amount of direct labor.

When competition increases, management needs accurate product costs to know whether it can adjust prices while maintaining adequate profit margins. Competition may increase because of three reasons: (1) other companies recognize the profit potential of a particular product or service; (2) the product or service has become cost effective to produce or perform; and (3) government has deregulated the industry.

Another problem with traditional cost systems is that they often ignore period costs and place too much emphasis on product costs. Activity-based costing recognizes that companies can trace some period costs to particular products.

The need for more accurate product costs might accompany changes in management strategy. Management might want to know the effects of their decisions on product costs. For example, if management wants to start new operations, the cost system needs to provide information on how costs will change. The traditional separation of costs into fixed or variable might not provide accurate information. Rather, management should view costs as short-term variable or as long-term variable.

An activity-based cost system can help in a company's goal of continuous improvement. Continuous improvement involves eliminating non-value-added activities to reduce cycle time, making products with zero defects, reducing product costs on an ongoing basis, and simplifying products and processes. An activity-based cost system shows the relationship between cost drivers and costs. Management can use this information to reduce or eliminate non-value-added activities. Reducing non-value-added activities reduces costs, eliminates waste, and increases profits.

Although activity-based costing results in more accurate product costs, it does not provide exact product costs or solve all of management's problems. In addition, several problems accompany the implementation of activity-based costing.

Activity-based costing requires a large investment in time and money. Implementation requires substantial support throughout the organization. The company must overcome individual, organizational, and environmental barriers to change for the implementation to be successful. Individual barriers often relate to (1) fear of the unknown, (2) a possible loss of status, and (3) the need to learn new skills. Organizational barriers involve territorial, hierarchical, or corporate culture issues. Employee groups such as unions, regulatory agencies,

Chapter 5: Activity-Based Management and Activity-Based Costing

or other stakeholders might raise environmental barriers.

Management must recognize the barriers, investigate their causes, and communicate information about activity-based costing to the concerned parties. Commitment to the implementation process by top management is imperative. The company must educate managers and other employees about the new terminology, concepts, and performance measures accompanying the ABC implementation. The company will need more time to analyze the activities, trace costs to those activities, and determine the cost drivers.

Another problem with activity-based costing is that it does not conform specifically to generally accepted accounting principles (GAAP). Consequently, most companies with an ABC system use it in addition to their cost systems for financial reporting purposes.

Another criticism of ABC is that it does not support total quality management (TQM) and continuous improvement. This criticism has merit only if companies view ABC as a panacea for all their problems. Companies can use ABC, however, along with total quality management, just-in-time systems, and continuous improvement. Activity-based costing and activity-based management can promote continuous improvement, reduce lead times, and enhance flexible manufacturing by helping managers do the following: (1) recognize and monitor major technology costs, (2) trace many technology costs to products, (3) increase market share, (4) identify cost drivers, (5) identify non-value-added activities and waste, (6) understand the effect of new technologies on all aspects of performance, (7) translate company goals into activity goals, (8) analyze performance of activities across business functions, (9) analyze performance problems, and (10) foster standards of excellence.

Managers use activity-based management and activity-based costing together to do "the right things; the right way." Exhibit 5-16 graphically illustrates the efficiency and effectiveness of operations. Activity-based costing is one tool that managers can use to compete successfully in the global economy.

Chapter 5: Activity-Based Management and Activity-Based Costing

SELF TEST

TRUE/FALSE

1. T F The modern manufacturing environment is highly automated with low overhead costs.

2. T F Overhead costs are often related to product variety.

3. T F Activities are repetitive actions performed to fulfill a business function.

4. T F Value-added activities increase the perceived worth of a product in the mind of the customer.

5. T F Moving products from one place to another during production is a value-added activity.

6. T F The Pareto principle refers to the 20:80 ratio.

7. T F A cost caused by the development, production, or acquisition of a type of product is a batch-level cost.

8. T F The time taken to move products or components from one place to another is called idle time.

9. T F Most traditional cost systems can easily account for how many different parts a company uses to make a product.

10. T F Costs reported under an activity-based costing system usually do not conform to generally accepted accounting principles.

11. T F Customers are willing to pay for business-value-added activities.

12. T F A company can trace some period costs to products using activity-based costing.

13. T F Mass customization involves the use of flexible manufacturing systems to produce customized products at relatively low cost.

14. T F A process map indicates every step that goes into making or doing something.

15. T F Cycle time is the time from the receipt of an order to the completion of a product or the performance of a service.

Chapter 5: Activity-Based Management and Activity-Based Costing

MULTIPLE CHOICE

1. How do traditional cost systems often distort product costs?

    A. All products are overcosted.
    B. All products are undercosted.
    C. High-volume products are undercosted, and low-volume products are overcosted.
    D. High volume products are overcosted, and low-volume products are undercosted.

2. What is the process of studying activities to classify them and to find ways to reduce or eliminate non-value-added activities?

    A. activity analysis
    B. budgeting
    C. simultaneous engineering
    D. Pareto principle

3. Which of the following is a value-added activity?

    A. inspection time
    B. processing time
    C. idle time
    D. transfer time

4. What is the time from the receipt of an order to the completion of a product or service?

    A. transfer time.
    B. processing time.
    C. cycle time.
    D. idle time.

5. Cycle time equals value-added production time:

    A. plus non-value-added time.
    B. minus non-value-added time.
    C. plus value-added time.
    D. minus value-added time.

6. Costs created by a group of things made, handled, or processed at a single time are:

    A. unit-level costs.
    B. batch-level costs.
    C. product-level costs.
    D. organizational-level costs.

Chapter 5: Activity-Based Management and Activity-Based Costing

7. In activity-based costing, after a company records costs, it then charges the costs to:

    A. products.
    B. customers.
    C. cost of goods sold.
    D. activity center cost pools.

8. In the second stage of cost allocation in activity-based costing, a company charges costs to:

    A. products and services.
    B. activity center cost pools.
    C. cost of goods sold.
    D. expense.

9. Many people have come to view fixed costs as:

    A. short-term variable costs.
    B. long-term variable costs.
    C. long-term mixed costs.
    D. not worthy of management's attention.

10. What are activities that are essential to operations but for which customers would not willingly pay?

    A. business-value-added activities
    B. value-added activities
    C. non-value-added activities
    D. essential activities

11. The use of automation:

    A. decreases direct labor cost and increases overhead cost.
    B. increases direct labor cost and increases overhead cost.
    C. decreases direct labor cost and decreases overhead cost.
    D. increases direct labor cost and decreases overhead cost.

12. Activity-based costing allows managers to recognize the _____ flow of products and services through an organization.

    A. horizontal
    B. diagonal
    C. upward
    D. downward

Chapter 5: Activity-Based Management and Activity-Based Costing

13. Companies use activity-based costing primarily for:

    A. preparing the financial statements for external users.
    B. preparing the tax return.
    C. product profitability analysis by management.
    D. preparing payroll.

14. Increased competition is less likely when:

    A. other companies recognize a product's profit potential.
    B. the product is cost-feasible to produce.
    C. the government has deregulated the industry.
    D. additional new technology and increased regulation is required.

15. Which of the following is a unit-level cost?

    A. direct material
    B. machine set up
    C. plant depreciation
    D. product design

16. A cost caused by the development, production, or acquisition of a type of product is a(n):

    A. unit-level cost.
    B. batch-level cost.
    C. product-level cost.
    D. organizational-level cost.

17. Which of the following is a batch-level cost?

    A. engineering change orders
    B. setup of production equipment
    C. plant manager's salary
    D. direct material

18. What highlights value-added and non-value-added activities and the time spent in those activities from the beginning of a process to its end?

    A. value chart
    B. process map
    C. simultaneous engineering report
    D. budgeting

Chapter 5:   Activity-Based Management and Activity-Based Costing   109

19. Management accounting information produced from the financial accounting system is often _____ for management's planning and control decisions.

    A. very relevant
    B. too distorted to be relevant
    C. too detailed to be useful
    D. very timely

20. Companies would NOT usually need product cost information to:

    A. report to external parties.
    B. help in product decisions.
    C. control operations.
    D. prepare the payroll.

21. A repetitive action performed in fulfillment of a business function is a(n):

    A. process.
    B. activity.
    C. value chart.
    D. process map.

22. Storage time is a part of:

    A. processing time.
    B. transfer time.
    C. idle time.
    D. inspection time.

23. Potential cost drivers for shipping costs would NOT likely include:

    A. truck depreciation and purchase price
    B. both length of trip and breakdowns
    C. weather and truck driver
    D. traffic and vehicle maintenance

24. Which of the following is an integrated approach that involves the continuous involvement of all the primary business functions and personnel that contribute toward a product's design and production?

    A. budgeting
    B. simultaneous engineering
    C. activity-based management (ABM)
    D. business-value-added activities

Chapter 5: Activity-Based Management and Activity-Based Costing

25. Mass customization is the production at a relatively low cost of a variety of products made to customers' specifications using:

    A. flexible manufacturing systems.
    B. just-in-time manufacturing systems.
    C. activity-based management (ABM).
    D. activity-based costing.

26. What can achieve high efficiency by making components and goods at the exact time needed by the next production station or the customer?

    A. a just-in-time manufacturing process
    B. activity-based costing (ABC)
    C. activity-based management (ABM)
    D. simultaneous engineering

27. In analyzing activities, managers should prepare a _____, which indicates the activities performed in making or doing something.

    A. cost of goods manufactured statement
    B. value chart
    C. process map
    D. product complexity report

28. One of the criticisms of activity-based costing is that it:

    A. requires a significant amount of time.
    B. results in very distorted product costs.
    C. cannot be used to assign period costs to products.
    D. is not suitable in highly automated production environments.

29. Howe Company completed production of an order for a customer five days after receiving the order. The five days consisted of the equivalent of two days of value-added production time and three days of non-value-added time. What was the manufacturing cycle efficiency for this order?

    A. 40 percent
    B. 60 percent
    C. 67 percent
    D. 250 percent

Chapter 5: Activity-Based Management and Activity-Based Costing

30. Dickey Company produced 400 units of gizmos—one of its three products. Each gizmo costs $15.00 in direct material and $6.50 in direct labor. Total setup costs for 10 setups for all three products were $2,000. Of these 10 setups, gizmos required 2 setups. Other overhead costs for all products made by Dickey Company relate to the usage of machines. The total other overhead costs were $30,000 for all three products. Dickey used 6,000 machine hours to make all three of its products. Each gizmo requires two machine hours to make. What is the per-unit cost for gizmos using activity-based costing?

   A. $21.50
   B. $27.50
   C. $32.17
   D. $32.50

QUESTIONS AND PROBLEMS

1. How does an activity-based cost system differ from a traditional cost system?

2. Define value-added activities, non-value-added activities, and business-value-added activities. Give examples of each.

Chapter 5: Activity-Based Management and Activity-Based Costing

3. To what factors can management attribute non-value-added activities? What should be the focus of reducing non-value-added activities?

4. What factors should management consider in selecting the cost drivers to use in allocating overhead in an activity-based cost system?

5. Define four different levels of costs. Give examples of each.

Chapter 5: Activity-Based Management and Activity-Based Costing   113

6. Describe some situations that indicate that a company should consider implementing an activity-based cost system.

7. Explain how activity-based costing and activity-based management can be useful for making short-term decisions.

8. How can simultaneous engineering reduce product complexity and process complexity?

Chapter 5: Activity-Based Management and Activity-Based Costing

9. What are some of the criticisms of activity-based costing (ABC)?

10. What factors should managers consider to determine whether ABC is appropriate?

11. What is a value chart?

Chapter 5: Activity-Based Management and Activity-Based Costing

12. Turner Company took 10 days from the receipt of a customer's order until Turner shipped the order. Turner Company spent these 10 days as follows:

   value-added production time: 2 days
   transfer time: 4 days
   idle time: 1.5 days
   inspection time: 2.5 days

   Calculate Turner Company's manufacturing cycle efficiency for this order.

13. Fahr Company produces two versions of its product—the regular model and the premium model. Fahr produces the regular model on a regular basis. However, Fahr produces the premium model only upon customer request. Production costs and other information are as follows:

	Regular	Premium
Direct material and direct labor:	$105,000	$20,000
Number of setups	70	50
Machine hours	25,000	5,000
Direct labor hours	5,000	600
Total number of units produced	10,000	1,000

Overhead costs:	Both Products
Machine set-up cost	$ 33,600
Machine processing costs	168,000
Total overhead costs	$201,600

If Fahr uses direct labor hours to allocate all overhead costs, what will be the total production costs charged to each product? What will be the per-unit cost for each product?

14. Fahr Company produces two versions of its product—the regular model and the premium model. Fahr produces the regular model on a regular basis. However, Fahr produces the premium model only upon customer request. Production costs and other information are as follows:

	Regular	Premium
Direct material and direct labor:	$105,000	$20,000
Number of setups	70	50
Machine hours	25,000	5,000
Direct labor hours	5,000	600
Total number of units produced	10,000	1,000

Overhead costs:	Both Products
Machine set-up cost	$ 33,600
Machine processing costs	168,000
Total overhead costs	$201,600

If Fahr uses machine hours to allocate all overhead costs, what will be the total production costs charged to each product? What will be the per-unit cost for each product?

Chapter 5: Activity-Based Management and Activity-Based Costing

15. Fahr Company produces two versions of its product—the regular model and the premium model. Fahr produces the regular model on a regular basis. However, Fahr produces the premium model only upon customer request. Production costs and other information are as follows:

	Regular	Premium
Direct material and direct labor:	$105,000	$20,000
Number of setups	70	50
Machine hours	25,000	5,000
Direct labor hours	5,000	600
Total number of units produced	10,000	1,000

Overhead costs:	Both Products
Machine set-up cost	$ 33,600
Machine processing costs	168,000
Total overhead costs	$201,600

If Fahr uses the number of setups to allocate machine set-up costs and machine hours to allocate machine processing costs, what will be the total production costs charged to each product? What will be the per-unit cost for each product?

Chapter 5: Activity-Based Management and Activity-Based Costing

SELF TEST ANSWERS

TRUE/FALSE

1.	F	4.	T	7.	F	10.	T	13.	T
2.	T	5.	F	8.	F	11.	F	14	T
3.	T	6.	T	9.	F	12.	T	15.	T

MULTIPLE CHOICE

1.	D	7.	D	13.	C	19.	B	25.	A
2.	A	8.	A	14.	D	20.	D	26.	A
3.	B	9.	B	15.	A	21.	B	27.	C
4.	C	10.	A	16.	C	22.	C	28.	A
5.	A	11.	A	17.	B	23.	A	29.	A
6.	B	12.	A	18.	A	24.	B	30.	D

QUESTIONS AND PROBLEMS

1. An activity-based cost system differs from a traditional cost system in the number of cost pools. A traditional cost system uses only one or two cost pools and one or two allocation bases to assign manufacturing overhead costs to products. If a company uses two cost pools, they are usually fixed manufacturing overhead and variable manufacturing overhead. A company can use one cost pool, which includes all manufacturing overhead costs. An activity-based cost system also differs from a traditional cost system in the way a company assigns overhead costs in the cost pools to products. The allocation bases in a traditional cost system are often volume-based measures such as direct labor hours or machine hours. An activity-based cost system uses multiple activity center cost pools to accumulate costs at four levels. An activity-based cost system assigns costs to products using multiple activity drivers. An activity-based cost system results in more accurate product costs because the activity drivers have a causal relationship to the manufacturing overhead costs incurred. A company can also use an activity-based cost system to assign some period costs to products for managerial purposes.

2. An activity is a value-added activity if it increases the worth of the product or service in the mind of the customer. Because the customer perceives the value of the activity, the customer is willing to pay for it. The time spent actually producing a product or providing a service is usually a value-added activity. Activities that do not add to the product's worth in the mind of the customer are non-value-added activities. Inspecting the product, moving it between work stations, and idle time are examples of non-value-added activities. Business-value-added activities are activities essential to the company's operations though customers are not willing to pay for the activities. An example of a business-value-added activity is the preparation of a customer's statement of account.

Chapter 5:   Activity-Based Management and Activity-Based Costing

3. Non-value-added activities are due to systemic, physical, and human factors. Systemic factors relate to the requirements of the system. Physical factors often relate to the layout of the plant. Human factors can contribute to non-value-added activities because of poor training, poor morale, or the need to be sociable. Companies should focus on the non-value-added activities that cause the greatest amount of unnecessary costs. Non-value-added activities are wasteful. Reducing waste leads to higher profits.

4. Management should keep the number of cost drivers used to a reasonable number. The cost of measuring the cost driver should be reasonable. The cost system may produce some cost driver information already. If so, these drivers might be preferable to similar cost drivers not yet produced by the accounting system. Cost drivers should be understandable, directly related to the activities they measure, and useful for performance evaluation.

5. Unit-level costs occur each time the company produces or purchases a single unit of a product. Examples are direct materials and direct labor. Batch-level costs occur when the company makes, handles, or processes a group or batch of things at the same time. Examples of batch-level costs include machine setup and movement of work in process. Product- or process-level costs occur when the company develops, produces, or acquires different items. Examples of product-level costs include engineering change orders, maintenance, and product development. Organizational-level costs result from the need to support the entire facility. Examples of organizational-level costs include the plant manager's salary and plant depreciation.

6. One situation that could warrant the implementation of an activity-based cost system is a significant change in the product line. As product variety increases, management has a greater need for accurate product cost information. Management needs a more accurate cost system when the company lacks commonality in the incidence of overhead costs. This lack of commonality might be due to process complexity or differences in support services. When competition increases, management needs more accurate product cost information to make better strategic decisions. Management may need activity-based costing to provide this information. When management changes its strategy, management may need a new cost system. Management might want to use activity-based costing to reduce non-value-added activities and to encourage continuous improvement.

7. Activity-based costing and activity-based management provide management with the cost of activities. Management can see how reducing non-value-added activities can reduce costs. Managers can implement programs to reduce or eliminate non-value-added activities and thereby reduce costs and waste.

8. Simultaneous engineering refers to the continuous involvement of primary functions and personnel from the very beginning of a project. Design for manufacturability occurs when a multifunctional team considers customer requirements, vendor capabilities, common parts, and production process compatibility in the design of a product. Simultaneous engineering helps to minimize product complexity, process complexity, and cost by assisting in the design of a product that is easier to manufacture.

Chapter 5: Activity-Based Management and Activity-Based Costing

9. Criticisms of activity-based costing include that it requires a large investment in time and money to implement. Another problem with activity-based costing is that it does not conform specifically to generally accepted accounting principles (GAAP). Another criticism of ABC is that it does not support total quality management (TQM) and continuous improvement. However, this last criticism is valid only if a company views ABC as a solution to all of its problems. Many companies can successfully use ABC along with TQM and continuous improvement.

10. Managers should consider the following factors in evaluating whether ABC is appropriate: (1) the number of different products the company makes, (2) the different levels of support needed for the products, (3) the extent of common processes, (4) the effectiveness of the current cost system, and (5) the growth rate of period costs.

11. A value chart shows the stages and time spent in each stage from the beginning of a process to the end of the process. On a value chart, a company can indicate the time spent in four ways. Processing time is the time spent in performing the tasks necessary to manufacture a product. Inspection time is the time spent in quality control efforts. Transfer time is the time spent moving components or products. Idle time includes storage time and the time spent waiting at a production operation. Only processing time is value-added.

12. Manufacturing cycle efficiency is equal to value-added production time divided by cycle time. Cycle time is the time elapsed from the receipt of an order until its shipment. Thus, the cycle time is 10 days for this order. Transfer time, idle time, and inspection time are not value added. Thus, the manufacturing cycle efficiency for Turner Company for this order was 20 percent (2 days ÷ 10 days).

13.

	Regular	Premium
Direct material and direct labor	$105,000	$20,000
Overhead costs:		
$201,600 ÷ 5,600 DLH = $36.00 per DLH		
$36.00 per DLH x 5,000 DLH	180,000	
$36.00 per DLH x 600 DLH		21,600
Total production costs	$285,000/	$41,600/
Divided by Number of units	10,000	1,000
Per-unit cost	$28.50	$41.60

14.	Regular	Premium
Direct material and direct labor	$105,000	$20,000
Overhead costs:		
$201,600 ÷ 30,000 MH = $6.72 per MH		
$6.72 per MH x 25,000 MH	168,000	
$6.72 per MH x 5,000 MH		33,600
Total production costs	$273,000/	$53,600
Divided by Number of units	10,000	1,000
Per-unit cost	$27.30	$53.60

15.	Regular	Premium
Direct material and direct labor	$105,000	$20,000
Overhead costs:		
Machine set up:		
$33,600 ÷ 120 setups = $280 per setup		
$280 per setup x 70 setups	19,600	
$280 per setup x 50 setups		14,000
Machine processing:		
$168,000 ÷ 30,000 MH = $5.60 per MH		
$5.60 per MH x 25,000 MH	140,000	
$5.60 per MH x 5,000 MH		28,000
Total production costs	$264,600/	$62,000/
Divided by Number of units	10,000	1,000
Per-unit cost	$26.46	$62.00

CHAPTER 6

PROCESS COSTING

CHAPTER OVERVIEW

Companies that make large quantities of identical products use process costing to assign costs to products. Many types of manufacturers—including manufacturers of candy, bricks, food products, gasoline, and paper—use process costing. Process costing differs in several ways from job order costing. However, both systems accumulate costs by cost component in each production department. In a job order system, a company assigns costs to specific jobs and then to units in those jobs. Process costing uses an averaging technique to assign costs directly to the units produced during the period. In both systems, a company transfers unit costs to accumulate production cost as it moves goods from one department to the next. The chapter shows how to calculate equivalent units of production (EUP).

This chapter discusses process costing procedures and illustrates the two alternative methods of computing unit costs in a process costing system. These two methods are the weighted average method and the first-in, first-out (FIFO) method. These two methods differ only in their treatment of beginning work in process inventory units and costs. After a department computes its unit costs, it assigns the production costs for the period to units transferred out and units in its ending work in process inventory. This chapter also illustrates process costing using the standard cost valuation method, which is similar to process costing using the FIFO cost flow assumption. The chapter further discusses hybrid costing systems and why a company might use a hybrid costing system. Appendix 1 presents alternative calculations under the weighted average and FIFO methods of process costing. Appendix 2 discusses how normal and abnormal spoilage losses are treated in an EUP schedule.

CHAPTER STUDY GUIDE

Assigning costs to units of production using process costing is an averaging process. A department computes its unit cost by dividing its production costs by the number of units produced. A company accumulates costs by product within each department. Companies can use different Work in Process Inventory accounts for each product and for each department involved in manufacturing the products. Another approach is to use different Work in Process

Chapter 6:   Process Costing

Inventory accounts for each department supported by subsidiary ledgers for each product.

A job order costing system and a process costing system differ in two main ways. The first difference is the quantity of production. A process costing system is appropriate for companies that produce large quantities of products. A job order costing system is appropriate for companies that make small quantities of products. The second difference is the cost object. In a process costing system, the company assigns costs to departments and then to products. In a job order costing system, the company assigns costs to specific jobs and then to products.

Exhibit 6-1 shows the source documents used to make the initial cost assignments to production departments during a period. At the end of the period, the department assigns costs to units of production. As one department transfers partially completed units to the next department, it also transfers the related departmental production costs. At the completion of production, the company transfers the costs from Work in Process Inventory to Finished Goods Inventory.

A department computes direct material cost based on the material requisition forms and determines direct labor cost from employee time sheets and wage rates. Overhead costs are indirect production costs. A company usually assigns overhead costs to production using a predetermined overhead rate. Companies may change the definition of cost pools or the basis for assigning overhead costs to compute more accurate product costs. In these respects, process costing is similar to job order costing.

To compute unit costs, the department must consider that seldom will all units be 100 percent complete at the end of a period. The department would likely have partially completed units in its beginning work in process inventory and in its ending work in process inventory. Exhibit 6-2 illustrates a two-period production sequence which shows partially completed units over more than one period. Process costing assigns costs to complete units and to partially completed units by computing the equivalent whole units.

A department incurred costs for the partially completed units in its beginning work in process inventory in the preceding period. The department will incur additional costs in the current period to complete these units. The department will likewise incur additional costs in the next period to complete the units in its ending work in process inventory. Management can estimate the degree of completion of the ending work in process inventory by physically inspecting the units.

A department usually has partially completed units in its work in process inventory at the beginning and end of a period. Departments use equivalent units of production because completed units do not clearly reflect the production achieved during a period. To compute the per-unit cost, the accountant must first compute the equivalent units of production (EUP). Equivalent units of production are an estimate of the number of whole units the department could have produced during a period based on its actual effort during that period. A department computes its equivalent units of production by multiplying partially completed units by the

Chapter 6: Process Costing

percentage of completion.

Weighted average and FIFO are the two alternative methods used to compute production costs and equivalent units of production. Using the weighted average method, a department computes an average cost per unit of the combined beginning inventory and current period production. The FIFO method, however, separates beginning inventory and current period production and their related costs to compute a current period cost per unit.

A company must introduce some direct material for production to begin. The material added at the beginning of production is 100 percent complete as to materials throughout the production process. A company can add materials at any point during the production process. Exhibit 6-3 illustrates the production flow for a manufacturing process and shows the need for separate cost accumulations for each cost element.

If the materials are at the same degree of completion, a company can make one calculation for the equivalent units of production for materials. If a company uses multiple materials and places them into production at different stages, it must make multiple equivalent units of production calculations for materials. If a company applies overhead using direct labor (or if these two elements are always at the same stage of completion) the company can make one equivalent units of production calculation for conversion cost. Otherwise, the company will make separate calculations for direct labor and overhead. More companies are using activity-based costing with multiple cost pools for overhead cost. Thus, the degree of completion for direct labor and overhead cost is likely to be different.

The calculation of the equivalent units of production requires the specification of a process cost flow method (weighted average or FIFO). The production costs divided by the equivalent units of production equals the cost per equivalent unit. Both methods usually result in approximately the same unit costs. The main difference in the two methods lies in how they treat beginning work in process inventory.

Exhibit 6-4 is an important exhibit that illustrates the six steps involved in process costing. These six steps are as follows: (1) calculate the physical units to account for, (2) calculate the physical units accounted for, (3) determine the equivalent units of production, (4) determine the total cost to account for, (5) calculate the cost per equivalent unit, and (6) assign the costs to inventories and to units transferred.

The physical units to account for are the sum of the units in the beginning work in process inventory and the units started into production. The department accounts for these units by showing them transferred to another department, transferred to finished goods, or remaining as partially completed units in the ending work in process inventory. The total units to account for must equal the total units accounted for. Exhibit 6-6 illustrates how these are separately calculated. The total cost to account for includes the costs in the beginning work in process inventory and all current period manufacturing costs. A company uses the same method (weighted average or FIFO) to compute the cost per equivalent unit as it did to compute the equivalent units of production. The department must assign the total costs to account for to another production department, to finished goods, or to the ending work in process inventory. Exhibit 6-5 provides production and cost information the textbook uses to illustrate the six steps in process costing.

The weighted average method assumes that all units in beginning work in process entered into production in the current period. This assumption simplifies the calculations. Thus, the weighted average method ignores the work done in the prior period on partially completed units. The weighted average method computes equivalent units of production as follows: units in beginning work in process + units started and completed in the current period + (units in the ending work in process inventory x percentage of completion). The production costs in the weighted average method include the beginning inventory cost and the current period's manufacturing cost. The cost per equivalent unit is equal to the sum of the cost per equivalent unit for each cost element. The cost per equivalent unit for each cost element is equal to the production costs for each cost element divided by its equivalent units of production.

Under the weighted average method, the cost per equivalent unit multiplied by the units completed equals the cost transferred to another department or to finished goods. The cost per equivalent unit multiplied by the equivalent units in the ending work in process inventory equals the cost of the ending work in process inventory. The total costs assigned must equal the total costs to account for.

The basic document in a process costing system is the cost of production report. This document shows all manufacturing quantities and costs, the computation of equivalent units of production, the cost per equivalent unit, and the assignment of the production costs. Exhibit 6-7 illustrates a cost of production report using the weighted average method.

The calculation of the total units to account for and the accounting for the physical units is the same under the FIFO method as under the weighted average method. In computing equivalent units of production, the FIFO method considers that the department worked on the partially completed units in the beginning work in process inventory during the prior period. The FIFO method does not commingle the work done in the prior period with the work done in the current period. The FIFO method calculates the equivalent units of production as follows: units in the beginning work in process inventory x (100 percent – percentage of completion at the beginning of the period) + (units completed – whole units in the beginning work in process inventory) + (units in the ending work in process inventory x percentage of completion).

The total cost to account for under the FIFO method is the same as under the weighted average method—beginning work in process inventory plus current period manufacturing cost. The only production costs included in the numerator in computing the cost per equivalent unit under FIFO are the current period's manufacturing costs. The cost per equivalent unit is equal to the sum of the cost per equivalent unit for each cost element. The cost per equivalent unit for each cost element is equal to the production costs for each cost element divided by its equivalent units of production.

Under the FIFO method, the cost assigned to the next production department or to finished goods is equal to the sum of (1) the beginning work in process inventory cost, (2) the cost incurred to complete the units in the beginning work in process inventory, and (3) the cost of units started and completed in the current period. The department calculates the cost incurred to complete the units in the beginning work in process inventory using the following formula: the number of whole units in the beginning work in process inventory x (100 percent – percentage of completion at the beginning of the period) x the cost per equivalent unit in the current period. The cost per equivalent unit multiplied by the units started and completed equals the cost of the units started and completed during the current period. The department calculates the ending balance in the work in process inventory in the same way as under the weighted average method. The cost per equivalent unit multiplied by the equivalent units in the ending work in process inventory equals the cost of the ending work in process inventory. Exhibit 6-8 illustrates a cost of production report using the FIFO method.

Cost assignment is easier under the weighted average method. The FIFO method, however, is more accurate and focuses on current period costs, which companies use to evaluate managerial performance. The FIFO method provides managers with better information for cost control.

In a process costing system, companies accumulate costs by each cost element (direct material, direct labor, and manufacturing overhead) in each production department. As a company transfers units from one department to another, it also transfers the related unit costs. At the end of production, the company has accumulated and assigned total production cost to all the units that flowed through that department during the period. Exhibit 6-9 shows process costing journal entries and T-accounts.

Most companies have more than one processing department. When one department completes its work, it transfers the units to the next department. The department must also transfer the costs incurred to the next department. The successor department calls these costs transferred-in costs or prior department costs. Transferred-in costs always have a completion factor of 100 percent. After the last department finishes its work, the department transfers the cost of completed production to finished goods. The demonstration problem at the end of the chapter in the textbook illustrates a cost of production report for a company with multiple departments.

A company can use a standard cost valuation method with a process costing system. If a company uses a standard process costing system, the calculation of equivalent units of production is the same as under the FIFO method. A company transfers units out of a department at standard cost. The use of a standard costing system allows a company to compute variances between actual costs and standard costs. A company that uses standard costs states its inventories at standard cost rather than at actual cost. Management can take remedial action where necessary to control the activities that cause costs.

Chapter 6: Process Costing

Exhibit 6-10 provides production and standard cost information the textbook uses to illustrate process costing with a standard cost valuation method. Exhibit 6-11 illustrates a cost of production report using standard cost information.

Using standard costs with process costing eliminates the need to distinguish the per-unit costs of units in the beginning work in process inventory and units started and completed during the current period. The reason is that under a standard cost valuation method, a company transfers all units out of a department at standard cost. Using standard costs simplifies recordkeeping, highlights variances from standard, and provides a useful tool for controlling costs. Managers should also compare costs to costs incurred by other companies.

Many companies are customizing goods that were previously mass-produced. In a production environment characterized by mass customization, neither job order costing nor process costing is well suited to determine product costs. Many companies are adopting a hybrid costing system suitable for their particular operations. A hybrid costing system contains characteristics of both job order costing and process costing. A hybrid costing system would be useful in a manufacturing operation that uses different raw materials but similar processing techniques for different product lines.

A hybrid costing system is suitable for companies that make products such as furniture, clothing, or jam. Hybrid costing systems enable accounting systems to compute product costs more accurately. The uses of hybrid costing systems will likely increase as companies install flexible manufacturing systems.

APPENDIX 1

The Appendix illustrates alternative calculations of equivalent units of production under the weighted average and FIFO methods. One of the most common methods to compute equivalent units under the weighted average method is as follows: units transferred + (units in ending work in process x percentage of completion). This alternative calculation is possible because the weighted average method assumes that all units in the beginning work in process inventory were started and completed in the current period. The accountant can compute the FIFO equivalent units of production as follows: weighted average equivalent units of production – (units in beginning work in process x percentage of completion at the beginning of the period).

The accountant can also compute the weighted average equivalent units of production using the following formula: total units to account for – (units in the ending work in process inventory x (100 percent – percentage of completion at the end of the period). The accountant can then compute the FIFO equivalent units of production by subtracting the equivalent units of production in the beginning work in process inventory.

APPENDIX 2

Although a company loses units at a specific point in a production process, the accounting

Chapter 6: Process Costing

treatment requires classification of the loss as continuous or discrete. Continuous losses occur evenly throughout the production process. Accountants usually treat a discrete loss as occurring at a specific point, like an inspection point, regardless of the point in the production process that the problem occurred. Management considers units that have passed an inspection point to be good units with respect to the attributes inspected. Units might be good, defective, or spoiled before they reach the inspection point.

The accounting treatment for the cost of lost units depends on whether the loss is normal or abnormal and whether it is continuous or discrete. Exhibit 6-12 describes the accounting for the cost of lost units. If the loss results from shrinkage that is an inherent part of the production process, treating the cost of lost units as an inventoriable cost would be appropriate.

Many companies are not aware of the actual cost of spoilage because they use the method of neglect to handle normal shrinkage losses and normal continuous losses. Under the method of neglect, the company simply excludes the spoiled units in computing the equivalent units of production. The method of neglect spreads the cost of the lost units proportionately over the good units transferred and the units that remain in Work in Process Inventory. The company assigns the cost of normal, discrete losses only to good units that have passed the inspection point. The cost of an abnormal discrete or continuous loss is a loss in the period incurred. This treatment is in accordance with the cost principle that provides that inventoriable costs should include only the costs necessary to make the inventory. All unnecessary costs are a loss in the period incurred. Abnormal losses are not necessary costs in the production of good units.

Exhibit 6-13 provides the basic production and cost data for the sample company in the textbook. Exhibit 6-14 illustrates a FIFO cost of production report that includes normal continuous shrinkage for the example company in the textbook. Accounting for normal continuous losses is the easiest of all the lost unit calculations. However, a theoretical problem occurs if a company uses this method and the weighted average method of computing the equivalent units of production. The problem is that units in the ending Work in Process Inventory have the cost of lost units assigned to them in the current period and will have the cost of lost units assigned again in the next period. Despite this flaw, treating normal continuous losses in this manner provides a reasonable measure of unit cost if the rate of spoilage is consistent over time.

Chapter 6: Process Costing

SELF TEST

<u>TRUE/FALSE</u>

1. T F Most companies have only one processing department.

2. T F In computing the cost per equivalent unit, the costs in the numerator under the weighted average method include current period production costs only.

3. T F Companies that make small quantities of custom products usually assign costs to products using process costing.

4. T F The two alternative methods that most companies usually use to compute unit costs in a process costing system are weighted average and LIFO.

5. T F The basic document in a process cost system is a job order cost sheet.

6. T F In process costing, a company must convert partially completed units to equivalent whole units through the use of equivalent units of production.

7. T F Material added at the beginning of the production process is 100 percent complete regardless of the percentage of completion of direct labor and manufacturing overhead.

8. T F The FIFO method of computing equivalent units of production treats partially completed units in the beginning work in process inventory as though the company started and completed them in the current period.

9. T F The weighted average method of process costing commingles units and costs of the prior period with those of the current period.

10. T F The FIFO method of computing equivalent units of production reflects more realistically the way that most goods flow through the production system.

11. T F Calculations for equivalent units of production for standard process costing are identical to those of FIFO costing.

12. T F A company using standard costs with its process costing system transfers all units out of a department at standard cost.

13. T F Hybrid costing is suitable for companies that make a variety of products using similar processing techniques but different materials.

APPENDIX

14. T F The weighted average units of production are equal to the units transferred plus the equivalent units in the ending work in process inventory.

15. T F The FIFO equivalent units of production are equal to the total units to account for minus the equivalent units of production to be completed next period.

MULTIPLE CHOICE

1. Which of the following would most likely use a process cost system?

    A. a company that builds custom computers
    B. a CPA firm
    C. a food processing company
    D. a law office

2. A process costing system is appropriate for a manufacturer of:

    A. small quantities of identical units.
    B. large quantities of identical units.
    C. small quantities of different units.
    D. large quantities of different units.

3. What are the two basic methods of calculating unit costs in a process costing system?

    A. weighted average and FIFO
    B. weighted average and LIFO
    C. FIFO and LIFO
    D. specific identification and LIFO

4. In a process costing system, which costs can a company easily trace to products?

    A. direct material and manufacturing overhead
    B. direct material and direct labor
    C. direct labor and manufacturing overhead
    D. direct material, direct labor, and manufacturing overhead

Chapter 6: Process Costing

5. Compared to the weighted average method of determining unit costs, the FIFO method is:

    A. less accurate and less complex.
    B. less accurate and more complex.
    C. more accurate and more complex.
    D. more accurate and less complex.

6. When can a company add materials to the production process?

    A. at the beginning
    B. during the production process
    C. at the end
    D. any of the above

7. The difference between the weighted average method and the FIFO method of calculating unit costs lies in the treatment of:

    A. ending work in process inventory.
    B. beginning work in process inventory.
    C. direct labor cost for the current period.
    D. manufacturing overhead cost for the current period.

8. In the FIFO method, the number of units started and completed equals:

    A. the total units completed during the period.
    B. the total units completed during the period minus the units in ending inventory.
    C. the total units completed during the period plus the units in the beginning inventory.
    D. the total units completed during the period minus the units in the beginning inventory.

9. The total costs to account for equal:

    A. the costs in the ending inventory plus current period costs.
    B. the costs in the beginning inventory plus current period costs.
    C. current period costs minus the costs in the beginning inventory.
    D. current period costs minus the costs in the ending inventory.

Chapter 6: Process Costing

10. What details all manufacturing quantities and costs, shows the computation of cost per equivalent unit, and indicates the cost assignment to goods produced during the period?

    A. cost of production report
    B. job order cost sheet
    C. work in process account
    D. general ledger

11. The only difference between the weighted average and FIFO methods of computing equivalent units of production (EUP) is that under FIFO:

    A. current period EUP does not include work done on partially completed units in the ending inventory.
    B. a company treats partially completed units in the beginning inventory as though the company started and completed them in the current period.
    C. EUP consists only of units started and completed in the current period.
    D. current period EUP does not include work done in the prior period on beginning inventory.

12. The computation of cost per equivalent unit under FIFO:

    A. ignores prior period costs and uses only costs incurred in the current period.
    B. includes prior period costs and costs incurred in the current period.
    C. includes costs of the prior period but excludes costs incurred in the current period.
    D. includes current period costs only in the denominator.

13. The number of equivalent units of production used to calculate the ending work in process inventory:

    A. will be greater under the FIFO method than under the weighted average method.
    B. will be greater under the weighted average method than under the FIFO method.
    C. will be the same whether a company uses FIFO or weighted average.
    D. may be greater under FIFO or under weighted average depending upon the circumstances.

14. Calculations for equivalent units of production for standard process costing are identical to those of:

    A. weighted average process costing.
    B. FIFO process costing.
    C. LIFO process costing.
    D. simple average process costing.

Chapter 6:   Process Costing

15. What will likely lead to an increase in the use of hybrid costing systems?

    A. an increase in the use of standard costs
    B. a decrease in manufacturing overhead costs
    C. an increase in the use of flexible manufacturing systems
    D. an increase in the mass production of items previously made to order

16. What does a company use in the numerator to calculate the cost per equivalent unit using the weighted average method?

    A. current period costs only
    B. current period costs plus beginning work in process
    C. current period costs minus beginning work in process
    D. current period costs minus ending work in process

17. Jefferson Company had beginning work in process of 40,000 units that were 70 percent complete. During the period, Jefferson started 250,000 units into production. The ending work in process consisted of 30,000 units that were 40 percent complete. How many units did Jefferson transfer to finished goods?

    A. 240,000
    B. 250,000
    C. 260,000
    D. 290,000

18. Jefferson Company had beginning work in process of 40,000 units that were 70 percent complete. During the period, Jefferson started 250,000 units into production. The ending work in process consisted of 30,000 units that were 40 percent complete. What were Jefferson's equivalent units of production using the weighted average method?

    A. 244,000
    B. 272,000
    C. 274,000
    D. 290,000

19. Jefferson Company had beginning work in process of 40,000 units that were 70 percent complete. During the period, Jefferson started 250,000 units into production. The ending work in process consisted of 30,000 units that were 40 percent complete. What were Jefferson's equivalent units of production using the FIFO method?

    A. 244,000
    B. 272,000
    C. 274,000
    D. 290,000

Chapter 6: Process Costing

20. Gray Company uses a weighted average process costing system. The cost per equivalent unit was $10.00. The beginning work in process inventory was $20,000. Costs added during the period were $350,000. What were the equivalent units of production?

    A. 33,000
    B. 35,000
    C. 37,000
    D. cannot be calculated from the information given

21. Bragg Company uses a FIFO process costing system. The cost per equivalent unit was $20.00. The beginning work in process inventory was $100,000. Costs added during the period were $500,000. What were the equivalent units of production?

    A. 20,000
    B. 25,000
    C. 30,000
    D. cannot be calculated from the information given

22. Harrigan Company uses the weighted average method of cost flows. The beginning balance in work in process was $271,000. Harrigan incurred $400,000 of production costs during the period. The beginning work in process inventory consisted of 30,000 units that were 80 percent complete. Harrigan completed 60,000 units during the period. The ending inventory consisted of 10,000 units that were 10 percent complete. What was the approximate cost per equivalent unit?

    A. $ 7.27
    B. $10.81
    C. $11.00
    D. $18.14

23. Harrigan Company uses the weighted average method of cost flows. The beginning balance in work in process was $271,000. Harrigan incurred $400,000 of production costs during the period. The beginning work in process inventory consisted of 30,000 units that were 80 percent complete. Harrigan completed 60,000 units during the period. The ending inventory consisted of 10,000 units that were 10 percent complete. What cost did Harrigan transfer to finished goods during the period?

    A. $400,000
    B. $407,000
    C. $660,000
    D. $671,000

24. Harrigan Company uses the weighted average method of cost flows. The beginning balance in work in process was $271,000. Harrigan incurred $400,000 of production costs during the period. The beginning work in process inventory consisted of 30,000 units that were 80 percent complete. Harrigan completed 60,000 units during the period. The ending inventory consisted of 10,000 units that were 10 percent complete. What is the cost of the ending work in process inventory?

    A. $10,810
    B. $11,000
    C. $97,290
    D. $99,000

25. Norris Company had 50,000 units that were 60 percent complete in its beginning work in process. New units started during the period were 450,000. Norris completed 420,000 units during the period. How many units remain in process at the end of the period?

    A. 50,000
    B. 60,000
    C. 80,000
    D. cannot be determined

26. Lopez Company has two processing departments. Lopez begins processing in Department 1 and completes production in Department 2. Department 2 had a beginning work in process balance of $40,000 and an ending balance of $50,900. The cost of goods transferred to finished goods during the period was $487,600. Department 2 added $375,000 in conversion costs but did not add any materials. What cost did Department 1 transfer to Department 2 during the period?

    A. $100,700
    B. $123,500
    C. $385,900
    D. $498,500

APPENDIX

27. When a company experiences a normal continuous loss, it:

    A. will always experience an abnormal loss in the same period.
    B. will never experience an abnormal loss in the same period.
    C. may or may not experience an abnormal loss in the same period.
    D. treats the amount of the loss as a loss of the period.

28. The method of neglect spreads the cost of the lost units:

   A. only over the units transferred to the next department.
   B. only over the units that remain in the Work in Process Inventory.
   C. only over the units sold.
   D. proportionately over the good units transferred and the units that remain in the WIP

29. Losses from shrinkage are:

   A. normal losses treated as a cost of the good units produced.
   B. normal losses treated as a loss of the period.
   C. abnormal losses treated as a cost of the good units produced.
   D. abnormal losses treated as a loss of the period.

30. If a process results in a continuous loss from defective or spoiled units, the company needs a quality control checkpoint for this loss at:

   A. the beginning of production.
   B. the middle of production.
   C. the end of production.
   D. no point in the production process.

QUESTIONS AND PROBLEMS

1. For which type of production system is process costing appropriate? Give some examples of the kinds of companies that use a process costing system.

Chapter 6:   Process Costing

2. What are the two primary differences between a job order costing system and a process costing system?

3. Under what conditions can a company use one percentage of completion estimate for direct labor and manufacturing overhead? Why is using one percentage of completion estimate for direct labor and manufacturing overhead becoming less common?

4. What are equivalent units of production? Why is calculating the equivalent units of production important?

Chapter 6: Process Costing 139

5. What are the two alternative methods of accounting for cost flows in process costing? How do these methods differ?

6. What is hybrid costing? For what type of companies is hybrid costing appropriate?

7. Explain how process costing using standard costs differs from process costing using actual costs.

8. Alexander Company has only one processing department. It adds all of the direct material at the very beginning of the production process. The production process is labor intensive. Alexander accumulates direct labor cost and overhead cost in one conversion cost pool.

Units:

Beginning inventory	30,000 (70% complete as to conversion cost)
Units started	170,000
	200,000
Ending inventory	20,000 (40% complete as to conversion cost)
Units completed	180,000

Costs:

	Material	Conversion Cost	Total
Beginning inventory	$ 210,000	$ 420,000	$ 630,000
Costs added in current period	1,200,000	3,509,200	4,709,200
Total costs	$1,410,000	$3,929,200	$5,339,200

Assume that Alexander Company uses a weighted average process costing system. Compute the equivalent units of production and the cost per equivalent unit for material and for conversion cost.

9. Alexander Company has only one processing department. It adds all of the direct material at the very beginning of the production process. The production process is labor intensive. Alexander accumulates direct labor cost and overhead cost in one conversion cost pool.

Units:

Beginning inventory	30,000 (70% complete as to conversion cost)
Units started	170,000
	200,000
Ending inventory	20,000 (40% complete as to conversion cost)
Units completed	180,000

Costs:

	Material	Conversion Cost	Total
Beginning inventory	$ 210,000	$ 420,000	$ 630,000
Costs added in current period	1,200,000	3,509,200	4,709,200
Total costs	$1,410,000	$3,929,200	$5,339,200

Assume that Alexander Company uses a weighted average process costing system. Compute the cost transferred to finished goods during the period and the cost of the ending work in process inventory.

10. Alexander Company has only one processing department. It adds all of the direct material at the very beginning of the production process. The production process is labor intensive. Alexander accumulates direct labor cost and overhead cost in one conversion cost pool.

Units:

Beginning inventory	30,000 (70% complete as to conversion cost)
Units started	170,000
	200,000
Ending inventory	20,000 (40% complete as to conversion cost)
Units completed	180,000

Costs:

	Material	Conversion Cost	Total
Beginning inventory	$ 210,000	$ 420,000	$ 630,000
Costs added in current period	1,200,000	3,509,200	4,709,200
Total costs	$1,410,000	$3,929,200	$5,339,200

Assume that Alexander Company uses the FIFO cost flow assumption in its process costing system. Compute the equivalent units of production and the cost per equivalent unit for material and for conversion cost.

11. Alexander Company has only one processing department. It adds all of the direct material at the very beginning of the production process. The production process is labor intensive. Alexander accumulates direct labor cost and overhead cost in one conversion cost pool.

Units:

Beginning inventory	30,000 (70% complete as to conversion cost)
Units started	170,000
	200,000
Ending inventory	20,000 (40% complete as to conversion cost)
Units completed	180,000

Costs:

	Material	Conversion Cost	Total
Beginning inventory	$ 210,000	$ 420,000	$ 630,000
Costs added in current period	1,200,000	3,509,200	4,709,200
Total costs	$1,410,000	$3,929,200	$5,339,200

Assume that Alexander Company uses the FIFO cost flow assumption in its process costing system. Compute the cost transferred to finished goods during the period and the cost of the ending work in process inventory.

12. Carter Company has two production departments: Cutting and Grinding. Carter adds all of the direct material in the Cutting Department. Carter adds conversion costs in both departments. Freeman first processes the direct material in the Cutting Department and then transfers it to the Grinding Department. After processing in the Grinding Department, Carter transfers the goods to finished goods. Carter Company uses the weighted average method of process costing. Carter Company provides you with the following information for the Grinding Department:

	Whole Units
Beginning inventory	1,000 (40% complete as to conversion cost in grinding)
Units transferred in	20,000
Units to account for	21,000
Beginning inventory completed	1,000
Units started and completed	16,000
Units completed	17,000
Ending inventory	4,000 (70% complete as to conversion cost in grinding)
	21,000

	Transferred-in	Conversion in Grinding	Total
Beginning inventory cost	$ 16,000	$10,000	$ 26,000
Current period costs	320,000	279,080	599,080
Total costs	$336,000	$289,080	$625,080

Compute the equivalent units of production for transferred-in cost and for conversion cost in the Grinding Department.

Chapter 6: Process Costing

13. Carter Company has two production departments: Cutting and Grinding. Carter adds all of the direct material in the Cutting Department. Carter adds conversion costs in both departments. Freeman first processes the direct material in the Cutting Department and then transfers it to the Grinding Department. After processing in the Grinding Department, Carter transfers the goods to finished goods. Carter Company uses the weighted average method of process costing. Carter Company provides you with the following information for the Grinding Department:

	Whole Units	
Beginning inventory	1,000	(40% complete as to conversion cost in grinding)
Units transferred in	20,000	
Units to account for	21,000	
Beginning inventory completed	1,000	
Units started and completed	16,000	
Units completed	17,000	
Ending inventory	4,000	(70% complete as to conversion cost in grinding)
	21,000	

	Transferred-in	Conversion in Grinding	Total
Beginning inventory cost	$ 16,000	$10,000	$ 26,000
Current period costs	320,000	279,080	599,080
Total costs	$336,000	$289,080	$625,080

Compute the cost per equivalent unit.

14. Carter Company has two production departments: Cutting and Grinding. Carter adds all of the direct material in the Cutting Department. Carter adds conversion costs in both departments. Freeman first processes the direct material in the Cutting Department and then transfers it to the Grinding Department. After processing in the Grinding Department, Carter transfers the goods to finished goods. Carter Company uses the weighted average method of process costing. Carter Company provides you with the following information for the Grinding Department:

	Whole Units
Beginning inventory	1,000 (40% complete as to conversion cost in grinding)
Units transferred in	20,000
Units to account for	21,000
Beginning inventory completed	1,000
Units started and completed	16,000
Units completed	17,000
Ending inventory	4,000 (70% complete as to conversion cost in grinding)
	21,000

	Transferred-in	Conversion in Grinding	Total
Beginning inventory cost	$ 16,000	$10,000	$ 26,000
Current period costs	320,000	279,080	599,080
Total costs	$336,000	$289,080	$625,080

Compute the cost transferred to finished goods.

15. Carter Company has two production departments: Cutting and Grinding. Carter adds all of the direct material in the Cutting Department. Carter adds conversion costs in both departments. Freeman first processes the direct material in the Cutting Department and then transfers it to the Grinding Department. After processing in the Grinding Department, Carter transfers the goods to finished goods. Carter Company uses the weighted average method of process costing. Carter Company provides you with the following information for the Grinding Department:

Whole Units

Beginning inventory	1,000 (40% complete as to conversion cost in grinding)
Units transferred in	20,000
Units to account for	21,000
Beginning inventory completed	1,000
Units started and completed	16,000
Units completed	17,000
Ending inventory	4,000 (70% complete as to conversion cost in grinding)
	21,000

	Transferred-in	Conversion in Grinding	Total
Beginning inventory cost	$ 16,000	$10,000	$ 26,000
Current period costs	320,000	279,080	599,080
Total costs	$336,000	$289,080	$625,080

Compute the cost of the ending work in process inventory in the Grinding Department.

Chapter 6: Process Costing

SELF TEST ANSWERS

TRUE/FALSE

1.	F	4.	F	7.	T	10.	T	13.	T
2.	F	5.	F	8.	F	11.	T	14.	T
3.	F	6.	T	9.	T	12.	T	15.	F

MULTIPLE CHOICE

1.	C	7.	B	13.	C	19.	A	25.	C
2.	B	8.	D	14.	B	20.	C	26.	B
3.	A	9.	B	15.	C	21.	B	27.	C
4.	B	10.	A	16.	B	22.	C	28.	D
5.	C	11.	D	17.	C	23.	C	29.	A
6.	D	12.	A	18.	B	24.	B	30.	C

QUESTIONS AND PROBLEMS

1.   A process costing system is appropriate for companies that make large quantities of homogeneous products. Many manufacturers use process costing. Examples include manufacturers of candy, bricks, food products, gasoline, and paper.

2.   The two primary differences between job order costing and process costing are (1) the quantity of production for which a company accumulates costs at any one time and (2) the cost object to which a company assigns those costs. A job order costing system accumulates costs for a relatively small quantity of production. A process costing system accumulates costs for a large quantity of production. A job order costing system assigns costs to a job and then to individual units. A process costing system assigns costs to departments and then to products.

3.   A company can use one percentage of completion estimate if it applies manufacturing overhead on the basis of direct labor hours or direct labor cost. In addition, a company could use one percentage of completion estimate for conversion costs if it adds direct labor and manufacturing overhead to the product at the same rate. The use of a single percentage of completion estimate for conversion costs is becoming less common because companies are using bases other than direct labor to apply manufacturing overhead costs to production. More companies are using multiple cost pools and activity-based costing to assign manufacturing overhead costs to production.

Chapter 6: Process Costing

4. Equivalent units of production represent the approximate number of complete units that a company could have produced from the actual materials, labor, and factory overhead used during the period. Companies must compute equivalent units of production to compute a proper unit cost for products. Using only completed units to compute unit cost would not reflect the work accomplished during the period.

5. The two alternative methods of accounting for cost flows in a process costing system are weighted average and first-in, first-out (FIFO). FIFO is more complex and more accurate. These two methods differ in the treatment of beginning work in process inventory in computing cost per equivalent unit of production. The weighted average method adds the cost of beginning work in process inventory to the production costs of the current period to compute the numerator. The FIFO method uses only costs incurred in the current period. To compute equivalent units of production, the weighted average method treats partially completed units in the beginning inventory as though the company started and completed them in the current period. The FIFO method considers only the work necessary to complete these units in computing equivalent units of production.

6. Hybrid costing is a costing system that contains characteristics of both job order costing and process costing. A hybrid costing system would be useful in a manufacturing operation that uses different raw materials but similar processing techniques for different product lines.

   A hybrid costing system is suitable for companies that make products such as furniture, clothing, or jam. Hybrid costing systems enable accounting systems to compute product costs more accurately. The uses of hybrid costing systems will likely increase as companies install flexible manufacturing systems.

7. Process costing using standard costing is simpler than using actual costing. In addition, the use of standard costs enables the company to compute variances from standard during the period. Actual costing requires the computation of a new production cost for each period. However, a company needs to review its standard costs at least annually. With standard costing, the computation of equivalent units of production is the same as under FIFO using actual costing.

8.

	Material	Conversion Cost
Units completed	180,000	180,000
Ending inventory 20,000 x 100% =	20,000	
Ending inventory 20,000 x 40% =		8,000
Equivalent units of production	200,000	188,000
Total costs	$1,410,000	$3,929,200
Divided by equivalent units of production	÷ 200,000	÷ 188,000
Cost per equivalent unit	$7.05	$20.90

Chapter 6: Process Costing

	Material	Conversion Cost
9.		
Units completed	180,000	180,000
Ending inventory 20,000 x 100% =	20,000	
Ending inventory 20,000 x 40% =		8,000
Equivalent units of production	200,000	188,000
Total costs	$1,410,000	$3,929,200
Divided by equivalent units of production	÷ 200,000	÷ 188,000
Cost per equivalent unit	$7.05	$20.90

Units completed	180,000
Times cost per equivalent unit ($7.05 + $20.90)	x $27.95
Cost transferred to finished goods	$5,031,000
Material 20,000 x $7.05 =	$141,000
Conversion cost 20,000 x 40% x $20.90 =	167,200
Ending work in process inventory	$308,200
Total costs reconciliation:	
Finished goods	$5,031,000
Ending work in process inventory	308,200
Total costs	$5,339,200

	Material	Conversion Cost
10.		
To complete beginning inventory:		
30,000 x (100% – 100%) =	0	
30,000 x (100% – 70%) =		9,000
Units started and completed:		
180,000 – 30,000 =	150,000	150,000
Ending inventory 20,000 x 100% =	20,000	
Ending inventory 20,000 x 40% =		8,000
Equivalent units of production	170,000	167,000
Costs added in current period	$1,200,000	$3,509,200
Divided by equivalent units of production	÷ 170,000	÷ 167,000
Cost per equivalent unit	$7.059	$21.013

Chapter 6: Process Costing

11.

	Material	Conversion Cost
To complete beginning inventory:		
30,000 x (100% – 100%) =	0	
30,000 x (100% – 70%) =		9,000
Units started and completed:		
180,000 – 30,000 =	150,000	150,000
Ending inventory 20,000 x 100% =	20,000	
Ending inventory 20,000 x 40% =		8,000
Equivalent units of production	170,000	167,000
Costs added in current period	$1,200,000	$3,509,200
Divided by equivalent units of production	÷ 170,000	÷ 167,000
Cost per equivalent unit	$7.059	$21.013

Beginning work in process inventory ($210,000 + $420,000)	$ 630,000
Cost to complete:	
Conversion cost [30,000 x (100% – 70%) x $21.013]	189,117
Total cost of units in beginning inventory transferred	$ 819,117
Units started and completed [150,000 x ($7.059 + $21.013)]	4,210,800
Cost transferred to finished goods	$5,029,917
Material 20,000 x $7.059 =	$141,180
Conversion cost 20,000 x 40% x $21.013 =	168,104
Ending work in process inventory	$309,284
Total costs reconciliation:	
Finished goods	$5,029,917
Ending work in process inventory	309,284
Total costs (off by $1 due to rounding)	$5,339,201

Chapter 6: Process Costing

12. Because all transferred-in units are 100 percent complete as to transferred-in costs, the equivalent units of production for transferred-in units are equal to the units in the beginning inventory plus the units transferred in during the current period. Thus, the equivalent units of production for the transferred-in units are 21,000 (1,000 + 20,000).

    Under the weighted average method, the equivalent units of production as to conversion cost are equal to the number of units completed plus the units in the ending inventory multiplied by the percentage of completion. The weighted average method treats the units in the beginning inventory as though the company started and completed them in the current period. Thus, the equivalent units of production as to conversion cost are computed as follows:

Units completed	17,000
Ending inventory (4,000 x 70%)	2,800
Equivalent units of production	19,800

13. Because all transferred-in units are 100 percent complete as to transferred-in costs, the equivalent units of production for transferred-in units are equal to the units in the beginning inventory plus the units transferred in during the current period. Thus, the equivalent units of production for the transferred-in units are 21,000 (1,000 + 20,000).

    Under the weighted average method, the equivalent units of production as to conversion cost are equal to the number of units completed plus the units in the ending inventory multiplied by the percentage of completion. The weighted average method treats the units in the beginning inventory as though the company started and completed them in the current period. Thus, the equivalent units of production as to conversion cost are computed as follows:

Units completed	17,000
Ending inventory (4,000 x 70%)	2,800
Equivalent units of production	19,800

	Transferred-in	Conversion in Grinding	Total
Beginning inventory cost	$ 16,000	$ 10,000	$ 26,000
Current period costs	320,000	279,080	599,080
Total costs	$336,000	$289,080	$625,080
Divided by EUP	÷ 21,000	÷ 19,800	
Cost per EUP	$16.00 +	$14.60 =	$30.60

14. Because all transferred-in units are 100 percent complete as to transferred-in costs, the equivalent units of production for transferred-in units are equal to the units in the beginning inventory plus the units transferred in during the current period. Thus, the equivalent units of production for the transferred-in units are 21,000 (1,000 + 20,000).

Under the weighted average method, the equivalent units of production as to conversion cost are equal to the number of units completed plus the units in the ending inventory multiplied by the percentage of completion. The weighted average method treats the units in the beginning inventory as though the company started and completed them in the current period. Thus, the equivalent units of production as to conversion cost are computed as follows:

Units completed	17,000
Ending inventory (4,000 x 70%)	2,800
Equivalent units of production	19,800

	Transferred-in	Conversion in Grinding	Total
Beginning inventory cost	$ 16,000	$ 10,000	$ 26,000
Current period costs	320,000	279,080	599,080
Total costs	$336,000	$289,080	$625,080
Divided by EUP	÷ 21,000	÷ 19,800	
Cost per EUP	$16.00 +	$14.60 =	$30.60

Units completed	17,000
Cost per EUP	x $30.60
Cost transferred to finished goods	$520,200

Chapter 6: Process Costing

15. Because all transferred-in units are 100 percent complete as to transferred-in costs, the equivalent units of production for transferred-in units are equal to the units in the beginning inventory plus the units transferred in during the current period. Thus, the equivalent units of production for the transferred-in units are 21,000 (1,000 + 20,000).

Under the weighted average method, the equivalent units of production as to conversion cost are equal to the number of units completed plus the units in the ending inventory multiplied by the percentage of completion. The weighted average method treats the units in the beginning inventory as though the company started and completed them in the current period. Thus, the equivalent units of production as to conversion cost are computed as follows:

Units completed	17,000
Ending inventory (4,000 x 70%)	2,800
Equivalent units of production	19,800

	Transferred-in	Conversion in Grinding		Total
Beginning inventory cost	$ 16,000	$ 10,000		$ 26,000
Current period costs	320,000	279,080		599,080
Total costs	$336,000	$289,080		$625,080
Divided by EUP	÷ 21,000	÷ 19,800		
Cost per EUP	$16.00 +	$14.60	=	$30.60

Units completed	17,000
Cost per EUP	x $30.60
Cost transferred to finished goods	$520,200

Transferred-in cost (4,000 x $16.00)	$ 64,000
Conversion cost (4,000 x 70% x $14.60)	40,880
Ending work in process inventory	$104,880

Total costs reconciliation:

Finished goods	$520,200
Ending work in process inventory	104,880
Total costs	$625,080

CHAPTER 7

STANDARD COSTING AND VARIANCE ANALYSIS

CHAPTER OVERVIEW

All kinds of organizations develop and use standards for many different tasks. No single performance measure is right for all situations. Some companies use standards for price but not for quantities. Service companies use labor rather than material standards.

This chapter discusses a traditional standard cost system that provides price and quantity standards for direct material, direct labor, and factory overhead. The differences between actual costs and standard costs are variances. This chapter discusses how a company develops standards, documents these standards, computes variances, and provides insight with detailed variance analysis. This chapter also illustrates the journal entries a company would make using standard costing. The Appendix covers mix and yield variances that can result from using multiple materials or groups of labor.

CHAPTER STUDY GUIDE

Manufacturing companies began the use of standard costs systems, but service and not-for-profit organizations can also use standard cost systems. An organization that uses a standard cost system records both standard costs and actual costs in the accounting system. The recording of both costs makes cost control easier because a company can easily compare actual results against the standard costs.

A standard cost is the estimated cost to make one unit of a product or to perform a single service. Developing standards requires judgment and practicality in deciding the types, quantities, and prices of materials and labor that a company will use. Management must also have a good understanding of the kinds and behavior of overhead costs.

An important objective in manufacturing a product is to reduce unit cost while achieving certain quality specifications. Companies can make almost any product with a variety of inputs to achieve the same output and quality level. Input choices affect the standards a company sets.

Chapter 7: Standard Costing and Variance Analysis

Management establishes the design and manufacturing process and decides the input resources that the company will use to make the desired products. Then, management develops quantity and price standards.

Representatives from the following areas should help develop the standards: cost accounting, industrial engineering, human resources (personnel), data processing, purchasing, and management. Managers should include subordinate managers and employees in the development of standards. This involvement helps to ensure that the standards are reasonable and helps to motivate the managers and employees to achieve the standards.

The first step in developing material standards is to identify and list the specific direct material used to make the product. If product specification sheets are not available, managers should seek the advice of material experts, engineers, cost accountants, marketing, human resources (personnel), and suppliers in making decisions about quality. Managers usually attempt to balance the relationships among cost, quality, and expected selling prices with the company's objectives. The tradeoffs between cost and quality affect the material mix, material yield, finished product quality and quantity, total product cost, and the company's ease in selling the product. Thus, the quality decision has a direct impact on cost and quantity estimates. Managers also base quantity estimates on engineering tests, opinions of managers and employees who use the materials, past material requisitions, and a review of the cost accounts.

Management must specify the type, quality, and quantity of materials needed to make a product and record the specifications on a bill of materials, shown in Exhibit 7-1. Even companies without a standard cost system will probably prepare a bill of materials for each of their products.

Next, the company must decide the standard prices for the materials. Prices should reflect the desired quality, quantity discounts, and freight and receiving costs. The purchasing agent should have input into the setting of material price standards. Managers multiply the standard prices by the standard quantities to compute the standard cost of each component. The sum of the standard costs for each component is the standard material cost for the product.

The development of labor standards is similar to the process for determining material standards. Managers identify each production operation employees perform. Companies often use time and motion studies to establish labor time standards. Other ways to set labor time standards include industrial engineering studies of various employee movements and the average time a company took to manufacture a product in the previous year. However, if a company bases labor time standards on past results, it can incorporate inefficiencies into the standards. Managers should exclude any unnecessary employee movements or inefficiencies in developing labor time standards. Therefore, managers might need to make subjective adjustments to preliminary standards. Exhibit 7-2 shows that a manufacturing worker performs productive work only about two-thirds of the day.

A company lists the labor tasks necessary to make a product and the standard time for each task on an operations flow document. Exhibit 7-3 illustrates an operations flow document.

Chapter 7: Standard Costing and Variance Analysis

For products the company can manufacture individually, the operations flow document lists the time necessary to make one unit. For products made only in a batch, the standard labor time per unit will be less accurate.

The labor rate standards should include the wages and fringe benefits paid to the employees doing the listed tasks. If the wage rate is different for different employees performing the same task, the company should use a weighted average labor rate.

Overhead standards are the same as the overhead application rates. A company can use a single overhead rate, separate overhead rates for fixed costs and variable costs, or multiple departmental overhead rates. Companies can use activity-based costing with multiple cost pools and cost drivers to compute standard overhead rates.

A standard cost card shows the standard costs and quantities needed to make one unit of product or to render a single unit of a service. The text uses an example of a company that makes bicycles to illustrate the development of standard costs. Exhibit 7-4 illustrates a standard cost card.

Companies use the standard costs and quantities to assign costs to inventory accounts. In most standard cost systems, companies charge standard costs instead of actual costs to Work in Process Inventory. Any difference between actual and standard costs is a variance.

The most basic variance calculation is the total variance. The total variance is the difference between the actual cost incurred and the standard cost applied to production during the period. A company also computes price and quantity variances for each component of product cost. A price variance reflects the difference between the price paid for inputs and the amount the company should have paid for the inputs. A quantity or usage variance shows the difference between the quantity of actual input and the quantity of standard input allowed for the actual output. The standard quantity allowed equals the standard quantity per unit multiplied by the number of units produced.

The price variance part of the total variance equals the difference between the actual price and the standard price multiplied by the actual quantity: (AP – SP)(AQ). The usage variance part of the total variance equals the difference between the actual quantity and the standard quantity multiplied by the standard price: (AQ – SQ)(SP). If a variance is positive, it is unfavorable (U) because the actual costs exceeded the standard costs. If a variance is negative, one drops the negative sign. The variance is favorable (F) because the actual costs were less than the standard costs. If variances are substantial, management will investigate to detect the causes and decide what corrective action to take.

One can also compute the total variance by adding the price variance and the quantity variance, taking negative signs, if any, into account. One can also compute the total variance using the following formula: (AP)(AQ) – (SP)(SQ). Exhibit 7-6 shows actual cost and standard cost data used to illustrate the calculation of variances.

Chapter 7: Standard Costing and Variance Analysis 158

The material price variance shows the money spent above or below the standard price for the quantity of materials purchased. The material price variance equals the difference between the actual price paid for material and the standard price of the material, multiplied by the actual quantity of materials.

The material quantity variance shows whether the actual quantity of material used was above or below the standard quantity allowed for the actual output. The material quantity variance equals the difference between the actual quantity of material used and the standard quantity allowed, multiplied by the standard price.

Usually, companies use the same quantities or hours to compute the price variance and the quantity variance. For material, however, the quantity purchased and the quantity used in production might be different. In such a case, a company should compute the material price variance on the quantities of material purchased using the point of purchase model. The cost accountant computes the material quantity variance on the quantities of material used in production. A company cannot derive any meaningful total material variance when it uses different quantities to compute the price variance and the quantity variance.

The price and usage elements of the total labor variance are the labor rate variance and the labor efficiency variance. The labor rate variance reveals the difference between the actual rate (or weighted average rate) paid to direct labor workers and the standard rate for the actual hours worked. The labor rate variance equals the difference between the actual rate and the standard rate, multiplied by the actual hours worked. The labor efficiency variance equals the difference between the actual hours and the standard hours allowed, multiplied by the standard rate.

In determining its overhead application rates, a company must select an operating level or capacity. Capacity means any measure of activity. A company can choose from theoretical, practical, normal, and expected capacity, which are defined in Chapter 3.

A flexible budget shows expected factory overhead costs at various activity levels within the relevant range. A flexible budget shows all costs as fixed costs or variable costs. To prepare a flexible budget, the cost accountant must separate mixed costs into their fixed and variable elements. Exhibit 7-7 illustrates a flexible overhead budget. Distinct fixed and variable overhead application rates allow a company to compute separate price and usage variances for each type of overhead. A four-way analysis of overhead variance provides managers with the most detail to use for control and performance evaluation.

The factory overhead variance includes the total variable overhead variance and the total fixed overhead variance. The total variable overhead variance is the difference between actual variable overhead costs and applied variable overhead. The total fixed overhead variance is the difference between total actual fixed overhead costs and applied fixed overhead.

The total variable overhead variance consists of the variable overhead spending variance and the variable overhead efficiency variance. The variable overhead spending (price) variance

Chapter 7: Standard Costing and Variance Analysis 159

is the difference between actual variable overhead and budgeted variable overhead based on actual output. The variable overhead efficiency (usage) variance is the difference between budgeted variable factory overhead at the actual input activity and budgeted variable factory overhead at the standard input allowed.

Price differences often cause a variable overhead spending variance. Such differences often happen because the standard rate does not reflect price changes. If managers cannot control prices, then a company should not hold the managers accountable for variances caused by such price changes. Rather, the company should adjust the standard rates. Waste or spoilage is another possible reason for an unfavorable variable overhead spending variance. A company should hold its managers accountable and encourage them to implement more effective controls to reduce waste.

The variable overhead efficiency variance shows the result of using more or less actual input than the standard allowed for the actual production. If the actual input exceeds the standard input allowed, managers consider the production operators to be inefficient. Excess input also shows that a company needs a larger variable overhead budget to support the additional input.

The total fixed overhead variance consists of the fixed overhead spending (price) variance and the fixed overhead volume (usage) variance. The fixed overhead spending variance is the difference between actual and budgeted fixed overhead. The fixed overhead spending variance depicts a variance in the costs of fixed overhead components or a mismanagement of resources.

The fixed overhead volume variance is the difference between budgeted and applied fixed overhead. The fixed overhead volume variance results from producing at a different level from that used to compute the predetermined overhead rate. Another term for the fixed overhead volume variance is noncontrollable variance. Managers have less control over capacity utilization in the short run, but managers should adjust and control capacity utilization to the extent possible. However, managers should not use capacity to produce excess inventory.

Managers can influence capacity utilization by changing work schedules, reducing obstructions or congestion in the production activities, and monitoring the movement of resources through the production process. Managers should take such actions before production begins to alter the capacity utilization for the upcoming period.

If a company does not account for fixed overhead and variable overhead costs separately, it cannot use the four-way analysis of overhead variance. A company that does not separate overhead costs according to their cost behaviors would begin the analysis of overhead costs by computing the total overhead variance. The total overhead variance is the difference between total actual overhead costs and total overhead applied to production.

The cost accountant can separate the total variance into a budget variance and a volume variance. The budget variance, also known as the controllable variance, is the difference between total actual overhead and budgeted overhead based on the standard quantity allowed for the actual output. The volume variance (noncontrollable variance) is the difference between total

Chapter 7: Standard Costing and Variance Analysis

applied overhead and the budgeted overhead based on the standard quantity.

A company can modify this two-way analysis of overhead variance by dividing the budget variance into a total overhead spending variance and an overhead efficiency variance. This modification results in three-way analysis of overhead variance. The total overhead spending variance is the difference between total actual overhead costs and total budgeted overhead at the actual activity level. The overhead efficiency variance relates only to variable overhead, and it equals the difference between total budgeted overhead at the actual activity level and total budgeted overhead at the standard activity level. This variance measures the approximate amount of variable overhead caused by using more or fewer inputs than standard for the actual output. The volume variance remains the same as in the two-way analysis of overhead variance. Exhibit 7-8 illustrates the relationships among the overhead variances.

Exhibit 7-9 illustrates the journal entries for a standard cost system. Unfavorable variances have debit balances, and favorable variances have credit balances. Standard costs are useful for internal use. They are not acceptable for external reporting unless they are substantially equivalent to actual costs. If a company uses standard costs in its financial reporting system, the company must adjust its accounts at the end of the period to approximate actual costs. If the variances are not significant, the company closes them to Cost of Goods Sold. On the other hand, the company closes significant variances to the ending inventories and to Cost of Goods Sold in proportion to their balances.

A standard cost system often requires less clerical time than does an actual cost system. Unit costs remain constant during the period. In an actual cost system, the cost accountant must recalculate unit costs continually.

Management can use standards to motivate employees. If a company rewards employees for achieving standards, the employees will strive to achieve the standards. The standards should require a reasonable effort on the part of the employees.

Standard costs also are helpful in the planning process. Managers can use current standards to estimate future quantities and costs. These estimates determine the need for material, staffing needs for labor, and capacity needs for overhead. In turn, these estimates affect the planning for cash flow. Standard costs aid in budgeting because a standard cost is a budgeted cost for one unit. A company can also use standard costs in cost-volume-profit analysis.

Standard costs are also useful in controlling operations because they establish a benchmark against which a company can compare actual costs. Variance analysis is the process of calculating the differences between actual costs and standard costs, deciding whether the variance is favorable or unfavorable, and searching for the reasons for such differences. Cost control and variance analysis should help managers learn who is responsible for the variance. If variances reflect poor performance, an early measurement system can help managers improve operational performance. Learning the cause of a variance becomes more difficult if the system delays reporting it.

Chapter 7: Standard Costing and Variance Analysis 161

Managers set upper and lower tolerance limits for variances. The setting of these tolerance limits allows managers to implement the management by exception concept. Exhibit 7-10 illustrates the management by exception concept. Managers can use different acceptable ranges to apply the management by exception principle, depending on the type of standard the company uses. Management by exception allows managers to investigate only the variances that are outside the tolerance limits. To discover the causes of variances, managers must examine problems through observation, inspection, and inquiry. Cost accountants and employees in operations are involved in investigating significant variances. Employees in operations should be aware of variances as they occur and record the reasons for the variances if known. The standard cost system should report variances timely so that management can improve operational performance quickly.

Standard costs are also helpful in decision making. Managers can compare standard costs to quote prices to decide whether to outsource production of a component or product. Standard costs help managers decide how much to bid on a contract.

Standard costs are also useful in performance evaluation because standard costs allow the calculation of variances. Variance reports highlight the performance of subordinate managers. Variance reports allow top management to learn what costs subordinate managers controlled or did not control. This information helps top management provide feedback to subordinate managers, investigate areas of special concern, and evaluate performance.

In setting standards, managers should consider the appropriateness and the attainability of the standards. Appropriateness refers to the basis on which managers developed the standards and the length of time they expect them to last. The attainability of the standards refers to the level of rigor required to achieve the standards.

A company should change its standards as its production process changes. To be useful, standards must reflect the current operating environment. Obsolete standards produce variances that do not help managers carry out their managerial functions.

Managers can set standards at three levels of attainability: expected, practical, or ideal. Expected standards are what a company expects to achieve in the current period. Practical standards are those standards that management expects employees to reach about 60 to 70 percent of the time. Practical standards allow for machine downtime and employee breaks. Traditionally, companies have viewed practical standards as the best type of standards for motivating employees. Ideal standards do not allow for any inefficiency or any operating delays. A company cannot attain ideal standards, and managers generally have thought that ideal standards would discourage employees. This belief, however, has begun to change.

To implement ideal standards, management must use a four-step migration process. The first step is to establish teams that will find the current problems and their causes. Second, use the answers to the previous question to determine what change is needed. For example, if the causes stem from equipment, the facility, or employees, management must take the second step by investing in plant and equipment and employee training. The third step is for management to give employees the authority to react to quality problems quickly. Fourth, management must recognize the employees' efforts and reward them for achievement.

A company that aspires to world-class status might want to use theoretical capacity in setting fixed overhead rates. Any underapplied overhead could indicate that the company had excess capacity it should use or eliminate. Another possibility is that the company has not fully developed the capabilities of its employees. If a company uses theoretical capacity, it should treat any underapplied overhead as a loss of the period rather than as a product cost. The loss should attract the attention of management to the inefficient or ineffective use of resources.

As business becomes more competitive, companies are more likely to set standards closer to the ideal level. If competitors use the highest possible standards, companies must also use such standards to compete on quality and cost objectives. Higher standards for efficiency reduce non-value-added activities and non-value-added costs.

Traditionally, a company has set standards after a thorough examination of various cost elements. The company often retained these standards for a year or longer. The current business environment changes so rapidly that a standard may not be useful for an entire year. Management needs to decide whether to change standards in a year of significant changes.

Ignoring the changes is a simplistic concept that means the company will use the same standards all year. This approach removes any opportunity to control costs or evaluate performance adequately. Changing the standards to reflect price or quantity changes makes some aspects of control and performance evaluation more effective and others more difficult. Changing the standards also causes a problem for record keeping and inventory valuation.

Management could use a hybrid approach by comparing plans made using original and new standards. Any variances would reflect changes in the business environment. Management could designate these variances as uncontrollable, internally initiated, or internally controllable. Variances between actual results and the revised standards should be more subject to control.

Although basing the material price variance on purchases rather than usage allows managers to see the effect of buying decisions quickly, such information is not as relevant in a just-in-time environment. Management should weigh the benefits of price savings against the additional inventory carrying costs.

As the proportion of product cost related to direct labor cost decreases, the need for calculating direct labor variances also decreases. A company might consider direct labor cost as a part of a conversion cost category. As a factory becomes more automated, employees' production activities become more indirect because employees spend most of their time watching over machines.

Conversion cost includes direct labor and manufacturing overhead. Traditionally, companies have separated product costs into three categories: direct material, direct labor, and manufacturing overhead. This treatment is appropriate in labor-intensive manufacturing

Chapter 7: Standard Costing and Variance Analysis 163

operations. In highly automated factories, direct labor cost is a small part of total product cost.

Many companies are changing their standard cost systems by combining direct labor cost with manufacturing overhead. The sum is conversion cost. This approach is appropriate for companies that have a highly automated production process with little direct labor cost. Companies are likely to separate conversion cost into its fixed and variable elements. Also, companies are likely to classify conversion costs as direct or indirect based on the ability to trace the costs to a machine rather than to a product. Companies might use a variety of cost drivers to apply conversion costs to products.

Variance analysis for conversion cost usually focuses on the following: (1) spending variances for overhead costs, (2) efficiency variances for machinery and production costs instead of labor costs, and (3) the traditional volume variance for production. Exhibit 7-11 illustrates the calculation of variances under the conversion cost approach.

APPENDIX

Most companies use a combination of numerous materials and classifications of direct labor to manufacture a product. When a company uses more than one material, one goal is to combine those materials to produce the highest quality product at the lowest possible cost. Sometimes a company can substitute one material for another without affecting quality. In other cases, the company can use only a specific material. A company can also combine labor in various ways to make the same product. Some combinations will be more efficient or more effective than other combinations.

A mix refers to each possible combination of materials or labor. Cost accountants use mix standards to calculate mix and yield variances for materials and labor. In product mix situations, a company assumes that it can substitute material and labor components in making a product. If this assumption is not valid, changing the mix will not improve the yield and might even be wasteful. In addition to mix and yield variances, the cost accountant still calculates price and rate variances for materials and labor, respectively. Exhibit 7-12 provides information for illustrating the materials mix and yield variances.

The material mix variance measures the impact of substituting a nonstandard mix of materials during the production process. The cost accountant computes the material mix variance using the following formula: (actual mix x actual quantity x standard price) – (standard mix x actual quantity x standard price). The material yield variance is the difference between the actual total quantity of input and the standard total quantity allowed based on output. This difference reflects the standard mix and standard prices. The cost accountant computes the material yield variance using the following formula: (standard mix x actual quantity x standard price) – (standard mix x standard quantity x standard price). The yield of a process is the quantity of output resulting from a quantity of input. The sum of the material mix variance and the material yield variance equals a material quantity variance. Exhibit 7-13 shows the computations needed for the material mix variance and the material yield variance.

Production variances are caused by the company paying workers other than the standard rate, workers not working in the standard mix on tasks, or workers not performing tasks in the standard time. A labor rate variance occurs when a company pays workers at rates other than standard rates. The labor mix variance is a consequence of changing the relative number of higher paid or lower paid workers in production. The cost accountant computes the labor mix variance using the following formula: (actual mix x actual hours x standard rate) – (standard mix x actual hours x standard rate). The labor yield variance reflects the effect of a different number of labor hours than the standard allowed. The cost accountant computes the labor yield variance using the following formula: (standard mix x actual hours x standard rate) – (standard mix x standard hours x standard rate). The sum of the labor mix variance and the labor yield variance is the labor efficiency variance. Exhibit 7-14 shows the computations needed for the labor mix variance and the labor yield variance.

Chapter 7: Standard Costing and Variance Analysis

SELF TEST

TRUE/FALSE

1. T F A bill of materials lists all operations necessary to make one unit of product.

2. T F In highly automated companies, the standard cost sytem may use fixed overhead rates based on theoretical capacity.

3. T F A static budget is a planning document that presents expected overhead costs at different activity levels.

4. T F In the current business environment, companies can usually use the same standards for five years or more.

5. T F Only cost accountants should be involved in setting price and quantity standards.

6. T F The estimated cost to manufacture one unit of a product is the standard cost.

7. T F The fixed overhead volume variance is also known as the noncontrollable variance.

8. T F In a standard cost system, a company debits Work in Process Inventory for the standard quantity of materials at the standard price, but credits Raw Material Inventory for the actual quantity of materials at the standard price.

9. T F If a material price variance is negative, it is a favorable variance.

10. T F The use of standard costs usually requires more clerical time and effort.

11. T F Under the management by exception principle, managers will investigate variances only if they fall outside of tolerance limits.

12. T F An extremely favorable variance is always a good variance.

13. T F The use of expected standards is an excellent tool for motivating employees.

14. T F The increase in automation often relegates labor to an indirect category.

APPENDIX

15. T F The yield of a process is the quantity of output produced from a specified input.

Chapter 7: Standard Costing and Variance Analysis

MULTIPLE CHOICE

1. Standards that provide for no inefficiency of any type are:

    A. normal standards.
    B. practical standards.
    C. expected standards.
    D. ideal standards.

2. The process of categorizing the nature of the differences between standard costs and actual costs and determining the reasons for the differences is:

    A. flexible budgeting.
    B. standard cost analysis.
    C. variance analysis.
    D. yield analysis.

3. What should companies consider in setting standards?

    A. appropriateness only
    B. attainability only
    C. appropriateness and attainability
    D. neither appropriateness nor attainability

4. The estimated cost to manufacture a single unit of product or perform a service is the:

    A. material yield.
    B. standard cost.
    C. normal cost.
    D. expected cost.

5. In setting the labor rate standard, what wage rate should a company use when it pays different wages to employees who perform the same tasks?

    A. the highest wage rate of those employees
    B. the lowest wage rate of those employees
    C. a simple average of the wage rates of those employees
    D. a weighted average of the wage rates of those employees

Chapter 7: Standard Costing and Variance Analysis

6. Which document summarizes the standard quantities and standard costs needed to make one unit of a product?

    A. flexible budget
    B. bill of materials
    C. standard cost card
    D. operations flow document

7. The difference between budgeted and applied fixed overhead is the:

    A. volume variance.
    B. budget variance.
    C. efficiency variance.
    D. total variance.

8. Which variance reflects capacity utilization?

    A. variable overhead spending variance
    B. variable overhead efficiency variance
    C. fixed overhead volume variance
    D. fixed overhead budget variance

9. Which management concept emphasizes the investigation of only significant differences between actual results and standards?

    A. management by objectives
    B. management by exception
    C. management by walking around
    D. span of control

10. Conversion cost consists of:

    A. direct material and direct labor.
    B. direct labor and manufacturing overhead.
    C. direct material and manufacturing overhead.
    D. direct material and indirect labor.

11. About how much the of the time spent on the job does a manufacturing worker spend in productive work?

    A. one-fourth
    B. one-third
    C. one-half
    D. two-thirds

Chapter 7: Standard Costing and Variance Analysis

12. Which document lists all operations necessary to make one unit of product?

    A. operations flow document
    B. flexible budget
    C. standard cost card
    D. bill of materials

13. What is a planning document that presents expected overhead costs at different activity levels?

    A. operations flow document
    B. flexible budget
    C. standard cost card
    D. bill of materials

14. At the end of the period, if the balances in the variance accounts are not significant, the company should close the variance accounts to:

    A. Work in Process Inventory.
    B. Cost of Goods Sold.
    C. Manufacturing Overhead.
    D. the ending inventories and to Cost of Goods Sold.

15. Ames Company had a $1,200 F labor rate variance and a $400 U total labor variance. What was the labor efficiency variance?

    A. $800 U
    B. $800 F
    C. $1,600 U
    D. $1,600 F

16. Davis Company's standard for raw material is 4 pounds per unit. The company produced 1,200 units and used 4,844 pounds of material. What was the standard quantity allowed?

    A. 300 pounds
    B. 1,211 pounds
    C. 4,800 pounds
    D. 4,844 pounds

Chapter 7: Standard Costing and Variance Analysis   169

17. Smith Company uses a labor-intensive manufacturing process. Smith applies variable overhead based on direct labor hours. Smith Company's standard variable costs are as follows: 20 pounds of materials at $15/pound, 8 hours of direct labor at $12/hour, and 8 hours of variable overhead at $6/hour. During the year, Smith produced 10,000 units. Smith purchased and used 209,000 pounds of material at an average price of $15.20 per pound. Smith used 83,000 direct labor hours. The total direct labor cost was $979,400. Actual variable overhead cost was $556,100. What was the material price variance?

   A. $41,800 F
   B. $41,800 U
   C. $135,000 F
   D. $135,000 U

18. Smith Company uses a labor-intensive manufacturing process. Smith applies variable overhead based on direct labor hours. Smith Company's standard variable costs are as follows: 20 pounds of materials at $15/pound, 8 hours of direct labor at $12/hour, and 8 hours of variable overhead at $6/hour. During the year, Smith produced 10,000 units. Smith purchased and used 209,000 pounds of material at an average price of $15.20 per pound. Smith used 83,000 direct labor hours. The total direct labor cost was $979,400. Actual variable overhead cost was $556,100. What was the material quantity variance?

   A. $41,800 F
   B. $41,800 U
   C. $135,000 F
   D. $135,000 U

19. Smith Company uses a labor-intensive manufacturing process. Smith applies variable overhead based on direct labor hours. Smith Company's standard variable costs are as follows: 20 pounds of materials at $15/pound, 8 hours of direct labor at $12/hour, and 8 hours of variable overhead at $6/hour. During the year, Smith produced 10,000 units. Smith purchased and used 209,000 pounds of material at an average price of $15.20 per pound. Smith used 83,000 direct labor hours. The total direct labor cost was $979,400. Actual variable overhead cost was $556,100. What was the total material variance?

   A. $41,800 F
   B. $135,000 U
   C. $176,800 F
   D. $176,800 U

Chapter 7: Standard Costing and Variance Analysis

20. Smith Company uses a labor-intensive manufacturing process. Smith applies variable overhead based on direct labor hours. Smith Company's standard variable costs are as follows: 20 pounds of materials at $15/pound, 8 hours of direct labor at $12/hour, and 8 hours of variable overhead at $6/hour. During the year, Smith produced 10,000 units. Smith purchased and used 209,000 pounds of material at an average price of $15.20 per pound. Smith used 83,000 direct labor hours. The total direct labor cost was $979,400. Actual variable overhead cost was $556,100. What was the labor rate variance?

    A. $16,600 F
    B. $16,600 U
    C. $36,000 F
    D. $36,000 U

21. Smith Company uses a labor-intensive manufacturing process. Smith applies variable overhead based on direct labor hours. Smith Company's standard variable costs are as follows: 20 pounds of materials at $15/pound, 8 hours of direct labor at $12/hour, and 8 hours of variable overhead at $6/hour. During the year, Smith produced 10,000 units. Smith purchased and used 209,000 pounds of material at an average price of $15.20 per pound. Smith used 83,000 direct labor hours. The total direct labor cost was $979,400. Actual variable overhead cost was $556,100. What was the labor efficiency variance?

    A. $16,600 F
    B. $16,600 U
    C. $36,000 F
    D. $36,000 U

22. Smith Company uses a labor-intensive manufacturing process. Smith applies variable overhead based on direct labor hours. Smith Company's standard variable costs are as follows: 20 pounds of materials at $15/pound, 8 hours of direct labor at $12/hour, and 8 hours of variable overhead at $6/hour. During the year, Smith produced 10,000 units. Smith purchased and used 209,000 pounds of material at an average price of $15.20 per pound. Smith used 83,000 direct labor hours. The total direct labor cost was $979,400. Actual variable overhead cost was $556,100. What was the total labor variance?

    A. $16,600 F
    B. $19,400 F
    C. $19,400 U
    D. $36,000 U

Chapter 7: Standard Costing and Variance Analysis

23. Smith Company uses a labor-intensive manufacturing process. Smith applies variable overhead based on direct labor hours. Smith Company's standard variable costs are as follows: 20 pounds of materials at $15/pound, 8 hours of direct labor at $12/hour, and 8 hours of variable overhead at $6/hour. During the year, Smith produced 10,000 units. Smith purchased and used 209,000 pounds of material at an average price of $15.20 per pound. Smith used 83,000 direct labor hours. The total direct labor cost was $979,400. Actual variable overhead cost was $556,100. What was the variable overhead spending variance?

A. $18,000 F
B. $18,000 U
C. $58,100 F
D. $58,100 U

24. Smith Company uses a labor-intensive manufacturing process. Smith applies variable overhead based on direct labor hours. Smith Company's standard variable costs are as follows: 20 pounds of materials at $15/pound, 8 hours of direct labor at $12/hour, and 8 hours of variable overhead at $6/hour. During the year, Smith produced 10,000 units. Smith purchased and used 209,000 pounds of material at an average price of $15.20 per pound. Smith used 83,000 direct labor hours. The total direct labor cost was $979,400. Actual variable overhead cost was $556,100. What was the variable overhead efficiency variance?

A. $18,000 F
B. $18,000 U
C. $58,100 F
D. $58,100 U

25. Smith Company uses a labor-intensive manufacturing process. Smith applies variable overhead based on direct labor hours. Smith Company's standard variable costs are as follows: 20 pounds of materials at $15/pound, 8 hours of direct labor at $12/hour, and 8 hours of variable overhead at $6/hour. During the year, Smith produced 10,000 units. Smith purchased and used 209,000 pounds of material at an average price of $15.20 per pound. Smith used 83,000 direct labor hours. The total direct labor cost was $979,400. Actual variable overhead cost was $556,100. What was the total variable overhead variance?

A. $18,000 F
B. $58,100 U
C. $76,100 F
D. $76,100 U

26. Carnes Company uses a fixed overhead application rate of $9 per machine hour. Actual machine hours were 70,000. Budgeted machine hours were 68,000. Actual fixed overhead cost was $565,800. The standard machine hours allowed were 74,000. What was the fixed overhead spending variance?

   A. $46,200 F
   B. $46,200 U
   C. $54,000 F
   D. $54,000 U

27. Carnes Company uses a fixed overhead application rate of $9 per machine hour. Actual machine hours were 70,000. Budgeted machine hours were 68,000. Actual fixed overhead cost was $565,800. The standard machine hours allowed were 74,000. Carnes Company uses a fixed overhead application rate of $9 per machine hour. Actual machine hours were 70,000. Budgeted machine hours were 68,000. Actual fixed overhead cost was $565,800. The standard machine hours allowed were 74,000. What was the fixed overhead volume variance?

   A. $46,200 F
   B. $46,200 U
   C. $54,000 F
   D. $54,000 U

28. Carnes Company uses a fixed overhead application rate of $9 per machine hour. Actual machine hours were 70,000. Budgeted machine hours were 68,000. Actual fixed overhead cost was $565,800. The standard machine hours allowed were 74,000. What was the fixed overhead total variance?

   A. $54,000 F
   B. $54,000 U
   C. $100,200 F
   D. $100,200 U

APPENDIX

29. The difference between the actual total quantity of input and the standard total quantity allowed based on output is the:

   A. material price variance.
   B. material mix variance.
   C. material yield variance.
   D. material total variance.

Chapter 7: Standard Costing and Variance Analysis

30. The financial effect associated with changing the relative number of higher or lower paid workers in production is the:

    A. labor mix variance.
    B. labor yield variance.
    C. labor efficiency variance.
    D. labor total variance.

QUESTIONS AND PROBLEMS

1. What steps must management take to implement ideal standards?

2. Who should be involved in setting standards?

Chapter 7: Standard Costing and Variance Analysis

3. What is variance analysis? How can variance analysis help management?

4. What does a company do with the balances in the variance accounts if the amounts are not significant? What does a company do with the balances in the variance accounts if the amounts are significant?

5. Explain how management uses standard cost systems to plan and control costs.

6. Define expected standards, practical standards, and ideal standards. Why are more companies that aspire to world-class status using ideal standards?

7. Why do accountants use standard cost systems?

8. How can managers control variable overhead resources?

9. What is a flexible budget?

10. Mullins Company's standard labor rate is $12 per hour. The company produced 3,000 units last month. The standard for labor hours is 5 hours per unit. The labor efficiency variance was $2,400 U. How many actual labor hours did Mullins Company use?

11. Scott Company applies fixed overhead based on machine hours. The fixed overhead application rate is $6 per machine hour. The budgeted fixed overhead cost was $30,000 based on expected capacity of 5,000 machine hours. The actual fixed overhead cost was $29,340. The company used 5,120 actual machine hours. The standard machine hours allowed were 4,900. Calculate the fixed overhead spending variance, the fixed overhead volume variance, and the total fixed overhead variance.

12. The standard variable cost per unit for a product of Hill Company is as follows:

	Quantity or Hours	Price or Rate	Total
Material	6 pounds	$ 7.00	$42.00
Direct labor	2 hours	9.50	19.00
Variable factory overhead	2 hours	15.00	30.00
			$91.00

During the month of September, Hill Company produced 2,000 units. The company used all of the material that it purchased in production. The quantity of material purchased was 12,800 pounds. The total cost of these materials was $88,320. The company used a total of 3,900 direct labor hours. The total direct labor cost was $39,000. The total variable overhead cost was $62,400. Hill Company applies variable overhead cost based on direct labor hours.

Calculate the material price variance, the material quantity variance, and the total material variance.

13. The standard variable cost per unit for a product of Hill Company is as follows:

	Quantity or Hours	Price or Rate	Total
Material	6 pounds	$7.00	$42.00
Direct labor	2 hours	9.50	19.00
Variable factory overhead	2 hours	15.00	30.00
			$91.00

During the month of September, Hill Company produced 2,000 units. The company used all of the material that it purchased in production. The quantity of material purchased was 12,800 pounds. The total cost of these materials was $88,320. The company used a total of 3,900 direct labor hours. The total direct labor cost was $39,000. The total variable overhead cost was $62,400. Hill Company applies variable overhead cost based on direct labor hours.

Calculate the labor rate variance, the labor efficiency variance, and the total labor variance.

14. The standard variable cost per unit for a product of Hill Company is as follows:

	Quantity or Hours	Price or Rate	Total
Material	6 pounds	$ 7.00	$42.00
Direct labor	2 hours	9.50	19.00
Variable factory overhead	2 hours	15.00	30.00
			$91.00

During the month of September, Hill Company produced 2,000 units. The company used all of the material that it purchased in production. The quantity of material purchased was 12,800 pounds. The total cost of these materials was $88,320. The company used a total of 3,900 direct labor hours. The total direct labor cost was $39,000. The total variable overhead cost was $62,400. Hill Company applies variable overhead cost based on direct labor hours. Calculate the variable overhead spending variance, the variable overhead efficiency variance, and the total variable overhead variance.

APPENDIX

15. Cook Company uses two materials in making 55,000 gallons of its product, the Super Duper Cleaner. The company can substitute one material for the other when necessary. The company does not expect any shrinkage in the production of the Super Duper Cleaner. The two materials and their standard quantities and prices are as follows:

Material	Mix	Total Gallons	Price	Cost
1	60%	55,000	$10	$330,000
2	40%	55,000	$12	$264,000
Total				$594,000

During the month of November, Cook produced 55,000 gallons of the Super Duper Cleaner. Cook used the following materials in making the 55,000 gallons of the Super Duper Cleaner:

Material	Total Gallons	Price	Cost
1	30,000	$11.20	$336,000
2	26,000	$11.50	$299,000
Total	56,000		$635,000

Calculate the material price variance, the material mix variance, and the material yield variance.

Chapter 7: Standard Costing and Variance Analysis

SELF TEST ANSWERS

TRUE/FALSE

1.	F	4.	F	7.	T	10.	F	13.	F
2.	T	5.	F	8.	T	11.	T	14.	T
3.	F	6.	T	9.	T	12.	F	15.	T

MULTIPLE CHOICE

1.	D	7.	A	13.	B	19.	D	25.	D
2.	C	8.	C	14.	B	20.	A	26.	A
3.	C	9.	B	15.	C	21.	D	27.	C
4.	B	10.	B	16.	C	22.	C	28.	C
5.	D	11.	D	17.	B	23.	D	29.	C
6.	C	12.	A	18.	D	24.	B	30.	A

QUESTIONS AND PROBLEMS

1. To implement ideal standards, management must prepare to use a four-step migration process. The first step is to establish teams that will find the current problems and their causes. If the causes stem from equipment, the facility, or employees, management must take the second step by investing in plant and equipment and employee training. The third step is for management to give employees the authority to react to quality problems quickly. Fourth, management must recognize the employees' efforts and reward them for achievement.

2. Management develops quantity and price standards. Representatives from the following areas, however, should help management develop the standards: management accounting, industrial engineering, human resources (personnel), data processing, purchasing, and production management. Managers should include subordinate managers and employees, whom the managers will evaluate by the standards, in the standards-setting process. This involvement helps to motivate these managers and employees to achieve the standards.

3. Variance analysis is the process of calculating the differences between actual costs and standard costs, deciding whether the variance is favorable or unfavorable, and searching for the reasons for such differences. The cost control and variance analysis should help managers learn who is responsible for the variance. If variances reflect poor performance, an early measurement system can help managers improve operational performance.

4. If the amounts in the variance accounts are not significant, the company should close them to Cost of Goods Sold. The company will credit the variance accounts with a debit balance for their balance. The company will then debit Cost of Goods Sold for the same amounts. The company will debit the variance accounts with a credit balance for their balance. The company will then credit Cost of Goods Sold for the same amounts.

Chapter 7:   Standard Costing and Variance Analysis

If the amounts in the variance accounts are significant, the company should close them to Cost of Goods Sold and to the inventory accounts. The company will credit the variance accounts with a debit balance for their balance. The company will then debit Cost of Goods Sold and the inventory accounts in a pro rata manner for the variance amounts. The company will debit the variance accounts with a credit balance for their balance. The company will then credit Cost of Goods Sold and the inventory accounts in a pro rata manner for the variance amounts.

5.   Management determines through research and analysis the standards or norms for the prices and quantities of material, the number of hours and the wage rate for labor, and the number of units and the price or rate of the variable(s) used to apply overhead. The variable(s) used to apply overhead could include various activities that drive overhead costs. Management uses these norms to plan what a product should cost to manufacture. Management can use the standards for the components of a single product to plan aggregate costs by simply multiplying the cost per unit by the number of units.

Management uses a standard cost system for control purposes by comparing the actual results with those predicted by the standards. If the variances are significant, management looks for the causes. Once management identifies the causes, it can take remedial action to reduce costs. Management could also decide that no remedial action is necessary and the company should revise its standards.

6.   Expected standards are the standards that reflect what a company expects to occur in the future period. They incorporate expected waste and inefficiencies. Practical standards are those standards that employees can achieve or slightly exceed 60 to 70 percent of the time. Practical standards allow for normal, unavoidable time problems or delays such as machine downtime. Ideal standards are rigorous standards that allow for no inefficiencies of any kind. They do not allow for normal operating delays or human limitations such as fatigue or boredom.

More companies are adopting ideal standards as part of their total quality management (TQM) and just-in-time (JIT) systems. Both TQM and JIT allow for zero defects, zero inefficiency, and zero downtime. Companies are improving quality to compete more effectively in the global economy.

7.   Accountants use standard cost systems for three main reasons: 1) A standard cost system allows management to plan for expected costs incurred in production or service activities, 2) the system collects information about standard costs incurred, and 3) the system allows management to control operations by comparing expected costs with actual costs and to evaluate performance based on size and explanation for the period's variances. The benefits derived from these activities include increases in appropriate 1) clerical efficiency, motivation, planning, controlling, decision-making, and performance evaluation.

8.   Managers control variable overhead resources by (1) watching and assessing their actual usage compared to standard usage, (2) quickly investigating any variances, and (3) adjusting resource usage when necessary. Managers must analyze each component of variable overhead rather than attempting to analyze and control total variable overhead.

Chapter 7: Standard Costing and Variance Analysis

9. A flexible budget shows expected factory overhead costs at various activity levels within the relevant range. A flexible budget shows all costs as fixed costs or variable costs. Therefore, the cost accountant must separate mixed costs into their fixed and variable elements.

10. The labor efficiency variance is (AH – SH)(SR). The standard hours allowed were 15,000 (3,000 units x 5 hours per unit). Mathematically, the $2,400 U variance is $2,400. Thus, the formula is (AH – 15,000)$12 = $2,400. One solves this equation with algebra as follows:

(AH – 15,000)$12
= $2,400
= $12AH – $180,000
= $2,400 = $12AH
= $182,400

AH = 15,200   The actual labor hours used were 15,200.

11. Fixed overhead spending variance
= Actual fixed overhead cost – Budgeted fixed overhead cost
= $29,340 – $6(5,000)
= $29,340 – $30,000
= –$660 = $660 F

Fixed overhead volume variance
= Budgeted fixed overhead cost – Applied fixed overhead cost
= $6(5,000) – $6(4,900)
= $30,000 – $29,400
= $600 = $600 U

Total fixed overhead variance
= Actual fixed overhead cost - Applied fixed overhead cost
= $29,340 – $6(4,900)
= $29,340 – $29,400
= –$60
= $60 F or –$660 + $600
= –$60 = $60 F

12. Compute the actual price: $88,320 ÷ 12,800 pounds = $6.90

Material price variance
= (AP – SP)(AQ)
= ($6.90 – $7.00)12,800
= –$1,280 = $1,280 F

Compute the standard quantity allowed: 2,000 units x 6 pounds per unit = 12,000 pounds

Chapter 7: Standard Costing and Variance Analysis

Material quantity variance = (AQ − SQ)(SP)
= (12,800 − 12,000)$7.00
= $5,600 U

Total material variance
= $1,280 F + $5,600 U
= $4,320 U or (AQ)(AP) − (SQ)(SP)
= (12,800)($6.90) − (12,000)($7.00)
= $4,320 U

13. Compute the actual rate: $39,000 ÷ 3,900 hours = $10.00

Labor rate variance
= (AR − SR)(AH)
= ($10.00 − $9.50)3,900
= $1,950 U

Compute the standard hours allowed: 2,000 units x 2 hours per unit = 4,000 hours

Labor efficiency variance
= (AH − SH)(SR)
= (3,900 − 4,000)$9.50
= −$950 = $950 F

Total labor variance

= $1,950 U + $950 F
= $1,000 U or (AH)(AR) − (SH)(SR)
= $10.00(3,900) − $9.50(4,000)
= $1,000 U

14. Compute the actual variable overhead rate:
$62,400 ÷ 3,900 hours
= $16.00 per hour

Variable overhead spending variance
= (AR − SR)(AH)
= ($16.00 − $15.00)3,900
= $3,900 U

Compute the standard hours allowed: 2,000 units x 2 hours per unit = 4,000 hours

Variable overhead efficiency variance = (AH − SH)(SR) = (3,900 − 4,000)$15.00
= −$1,500 = $1,500 F

Chapter 7: Standard Costing and Variance Analysis

Total variable overhead variance:

= $3,900 U + $1,500 F
= $2,400 U or (AH)(AR) – (SH)(SR)
= ($16.00)(3,900) – ($15.00)(4,000)
= $2,400 U

APPENDIX

15. Material price variance

= (actual mix x actual quantity x actual price) – (actual mix x actual quantity x standard price)

= [(30,000 x $11.20) + (26,000 x $11.50)] – [(30,000 x $10) + (26,000 x $12)]
= ($336,000 + $299,000) – ($300,000 + $312,000)
= $635,000 – $612,000
= $23,000 = $23,000 U

Material mix variance

= (actual mix x actual quantity x standard price) – (standard mix x actual quantity x standard price)
= [(30,000 x $10) + (26,000 x $12)] – [(60% x 56,000 x $10) + (40% x 56,000 x $12)]
= ($300,000 + $312,000) – ($336,000 + $268,800) = $612,000 – $604,800
= $7,200 = $7,200 U

Material yield variance

= (standard mix x actual quantity x standard price) – (standard mix x standard quantity x standard price)
= [(60% x 56,000 x $10) + (40% x 56,000 x $12)] – [(60% x 55,000 x $10) + (40% x $55,000 x $12) = ($336,000 + $268,800) – ($330,000 + $264,000)
= $604,800 – $594,000
= $10,800 = $10,800 U

CHAPTER 8

THE MASTER BUDGET

CHAPTER OVERVIEW

Budgeting is the process of formalizing plans and translating qualitative narratives into a documented quantitative format. Budgets are a set of predictions and assumptions about an organization's financial and nonfinancial goals as well as a communication tool for the organization. Before an organization begins any budget preparation, it should investigate the external environment and perform thorough strategic planning and tactical planning. Once the organization prepares the foundation for budgeting, then it begins the development of the master budget.

This chapter covers the budgeting process and the preparation of a master budget. The Appendix covers the budget manual. A master budget is the set of budgetary schedules and pro forma financial statements. A master budget consists of operating budgets and financial budgets. The capital budget is an important budget, but organizations do not include it in the master budget.

A company prepares the sales budget based on forecasted sales. Because the sales budget drives all the other budgets, a company prepares it first. Another critical budget is the cash budget. Other budgets include the production budget, the purchases budget, the direct labor budget, the manufacturing overhead budget, the selling, general, and administrative expenses budget, the cash budget, and the pro forma financial statements. This chapter illustrates each of these budgets.

After an organization implements a budget, the control phase of budgeting begins. The organization makes actual-to-budget comparisons, computes and investigates variances, takes corrective action, and provides feedback to management.

CHAPTER STUDY GUIDE

Managers engage in planning to sharpen the corporate vision. To survive in the constantly changing business environment, a company must isolate key variables that affect company performance and drive current conditions. The keys to planning involve translating goals into detailed quantitative goals. Planning includes qualitative descriptions of goals, objectives, and means of accomplishment.

Budgets are an integral part of planning. Budgeting is the process of formalizing plans and committing them to concise, written, financial terms. A budget is a financial plan based on a single level of activity. A budget is the quantitative expression of a company's commitment to planned activities and resource acquisition and use. A master budget is an organization's comprehensive set of budgetary schedules and the pro forma financial statements. Budgeting helps provide a focused direction or a path chosen from many alternatives.

Budgets should represent the road map leading to the achievement of corporate tactical and strategic plans. The budget provides specific quantitative criteria against which a company can compare performance using an accounting measure. Possible accounting measures include net income, earnings per share, and sales in dollars or units. Budgets are a type of standard against which a company can compute variances.

Exhibit 8-1 shows the relationships among the planning processes. Strategic and tactical planning are integrated with budgeting. Strategic planning first provides the vision for the tactical plans. An organization must then expand its tactical plans to financial terms. The objective of the expansion of tactical plans is to develop an allocation device with quantitative monetary constraints. The allocation device serves to control the activities and the resources of the organization for one year or less. That control device is the master budget.

Strategic planning is the process of developing a statement of long-range (5–10 years) goals for an organization and defining the strategies and policies that will help it achieve those goals. Key variables in strategic planning involve internal and external factors. The majority of time invested in planning involves the analysis of external factors. External factors include but are not limited to: competitor actions, market conditions, political and regulatory climate, emerging technologies, consumer trends and attitudes and demographics. Management seeks to balance controllable factors with uncontrollable factors to manage available resources. The proper or improper balance of critical factors will provide the means to achievement or non-achievement of organizational goals and objectives.

Once management has identified critical factors, management develops more specific plans. The development of these more specific plans is tactical planning. Tactical plans are the specific means or objectives by which the organization plans to achieve its strategic plans. Tactical plans are short-range in nature (usually 1–18 months). Tactical plans are single-use plans developed to address a given set of circumstances or a specific time frame. The annual budget is an example of a single-use tactical plan.

A well-prepared budget can effectively communicate objectives, constraints, and expectations to personnel throughout an organization. The budget becomes the basis for controlling activities and resource usage. The budget indicates the resource constraints under which managers must operate for the upcoming budget period.

Chapter 8: The Master Budget

Management should review the budget before implementing it to determine if the budget results appear acceptable. Once accepted, management adopts the master budget as a standard against which the organization can measure performance. The control phase involves actual-to-budget comparisons, calculating variances from the budget, investigating the causes of variances, taking necessary corrective action, and providing feedback to operating managers. Feedback, both positive and negative is essential to the control process and, to be useful, must be provided in a timely manner. The cyclical nature of the budgeting process is illustrated in Exhibit 8-2.

The master budget consists of both operating and financial budgets. An operating budget is a budget expressed in both units and dollars. A financial budget is a budget that aggregates monetary details from the operating budgets. Financial budgets include the cash budget, the capital expenditures budget, and the pro forma financial statements. Exhibit 8-3 lists the components of a master budget.

An organization prepares the master budget for a specific period. A master budget is static rather than flexible. The output level of sales or service quantities selected for use in the master budget affects all other organizational components. In an effective budget process, all the components will interact in a coordinated manner. The budgetary process begins with the sales department's estimates of the types, quantities, and timing of demand for the company's products. Exhibit 8-4 shows a flow chart of the budgetary process in a manufacturing organization. Exhibit 8-5 presents an overview of the master budget. A company must complete the sales budget first. The sales budget includes sales in units and in dollars. The sales dollars equal the sales in units multiplied by the product selling prices. Exhibit 8-7 illustrates a sales budget.

The cost accountant prepares the production budget next using the information from the sales budget regarding the type, quantity, and timing of units to be sold. The cost accountant combines sales information with information on beginning and ending inventories to calculate units to be produced. A current balance sheet, as illustrated in Exhibit 8-6, might include inventory information useful to production planning. Management specifies ending inventory policy. The desired ending inventory is usually a function of the quantity and timing of demand in the upcoming period related to the capacity and speed of production. Exhibit 8-8 contains an example of the production budget. Management might sometimes use a percentage of the expected sales for the next month as the desired ending inventory.

A company first states the purchases budget in whole units of finished products. Purchases include direct materials and indirect materials. The cost accountant later converts the purchases budget to individual direct material components. The cost accountant then converts the direct material requirements into the total product costs required for the period. Exhibit 8-9 illustrates a purchases budget.

The personnel budget requires coordination with the engineering and personnel departments to plan for the labor requirements for factory employees, sales staff, and office staff. The personnel budget provides information to compute the direct labor budget, the overhead budget, and the selling and administrative budget. The personnel budget shows labor

Chapter 8: The Master Budget 190

requirements in total number of people, specific number of types of people, and production hours needed for factory employees. The cost accountant calculates labor costs from such items as labor contracts, minimum wage laws, fringe benefit costs, payroll taxes, and bonus arrangements.

The direct labor budget calculation consists of direct labor cost estimates based on the standard hours of production needed to produce the number of units shown in the production budget. The direct labor budget builds on the production budget information. Exhibit 8-10 illustrates a direct labor budget. Normally, the allocated direct labor rate includes fringe benefit costs.

The overhead budget shows the estimated cost of each overhead item for each period. To estimate overhead costs, the cost accountant must specify all fixed and variable overhead costs and separate mixed costs into their fixed and variable components. Exhibit 8-11 illustrates an overhead budget.

The selling and administrative budget includes the estimated selling and administrative expenses for the period. The cost accountant allocates budgeted selling and administrative expenses using budgeted sales. As Exhibit 8-12 illustrates, the cost accountant must separate budgeted selling and administrative expenses into their fixed and variable components.

A company prepares the capital budget separately from the master budget. Capital budgeting affects the master budgeting process because it involves corporate resources. Capital budgeting examines the financial impact in the area of plant and equipment purchases and budgeting for long-term expenditures. Exhibit 8-13 shows a simple capital budget. Chapter 14 covers capital budgeting in greater detail.

A company prepares the cash budget after it develops all the preceding budgets. A company uses the cash budget to determine the timing of its financing needs. Cash flow problems can threaten the very survival of a company. Therefore, planning cash flows is crucial to the company as a whole. A company uses budgeted cash flows to predict seasonal fluctuations in cash flow, indicate needs for short-term borrowing, determine the availability of surplus cash, and measure the performance of the accounts receivable and accounts payable departments.

To begin the cash budget, management estimates the timing of sales receipts. Accountants analyze sales revenue information to determine the expected collection pattern of accounts receivable. Accountants consider the timing of payments received, discounts taken, and amounts uncollectible when determining an expected collection pattern. Accountants also consider the current balances of Accounts Receivable and the Allowance for Uncollectible Accounts. Accountants should project the balances of the Accounts Receivable and the Allowance for Uncollectible Accounts after they prepare a schedule of expected cash collections.

Consideration of the nature of receivables is important. Some customers take advantage of discounts allowed for early payment. Other customers take months to pay. Some customers pay by the due date or later, and some customers might not pay at all. Understanding the collection pattern for sales is critical to estimate cash receipts. Exhibit 8-14 shows a layered

Chapter 8: The Master Budget

collection pattern of total sales. Exhibit 8-15, and the related T-accounts in the textbook, illustrate cash collections based on a layered collection pattern.

Accountants prepare an estimated cash disbursement schedule for accounts payable using the purchases information prepared in the purchases budget. As illustrated in Exhibit 8-16, discounts on accounts payable and delayed payments significantly affect cash flows. The T-accounts in the textbook show how to work with accounts payable.

Accountants use cash receipts and disbursements information to prepare the cash budget. In addition to cash receipts from sales and cash disbursements from purchases, accountants should include the financing activities planned to cover cash flow shortfalls and cash flow excesses on the cash budget. Short-term borrowing and short-term investing are often part of the cash budget. Exhibit 8-17 provides an example of a cash budget with planned financing activities for excess cash flow.

When management handles cash flow properly, cash is available when needed and earns interest when not needed. Exhibit 8-18 lists 10 ways management can improve cash flow.

Upon completion of all the preceding budgets, the accountant prepares the budgeted financial statements. The budgeted financial statements reflect the expected results if the estimates and assumptions used for all previous budgets actually occur. The budgeted financial statements provide a financial picture for management to determine if the predicted results are acceptable. If the predicted results are not acceptable, management has the opportunity to change and adjust items before beginning the new period.

The cost accountant must prepare a schedule of cost of goods manufactured. Exhibit 8-19 provides an example of a pro forma cost of goods manufactured schedule. This schedule is necessary to compute budgeted cost of goods sold. The cost of goods manufactured schedule uses information from budgets prepared previously. The cost accountant uses expected cash disbursements, the direct labor budget, the factory overhead budget, and the purchasing budget in the calculation. The accountant then prepares the pro forma income statement.

As shown in Exhibit 8-20, the accountant relies on almost all of the information developed in the previous budgets to compute the revenues and expenses for the pro forma income statement for the period. The accountant prepares the pro forma balance sheet upon completion of the income statement. Exhibit 8-21 shows a pro forma balance sheet.

The accountant uses the information found in the pro forma income statement, the pro forma balance sheet, and the cash budget in preparing a pro forma statement of cash flows. The accountant may prepare the pro forma statement of cash flows using the direct method or the indirect method. The direct method uses the cash receipts and disbursement schedule as well as sources and uses of cash from financing and sources and uses of cash from investing activities. The indirect method starts with net income and adjusts it for items such as depreciation and changes in assets and liabilities. Either method will result in the same cash flow. Exhibit 8-22 illustrates a pro forma statement of cash flows.

Chapter 8: The Master Budget

A well-prepared budget provides the following benefits:

1. a guide to help managers align activities and resource allocations with company goals;
2. a vehicle to promote employee participation, cooperation, and departmental coordination;
3. a tool to enhance conduct of the managerial functions of planning, controlling, problem solving, and performance evaluating;
4. a basis to sharpen management responsiveness to changes in both internal and external factors; and
5. a model that provides a rigorous view of future performance of a company in time to consider alternative measures.

A company should forecast demand as accurately as possible because of its impact in the budgeting process. Sales forecasts should indicate the type and quantity of products the company expects to sell, the geographic locations of the sales, the types of buyers, and the times when company expects to make the sales. The sales forecast should be detailed because of the following reasons: (1) Different products require different production and distribution methods. (2) Different customers might have different credit terms and payment schedules. (3) Different seasons or months might require different shipping schedules or methods.

Management should estimate budgeted sales to the greatest degree of precision possible. Significant deviations from sales demand permeate the entire budgeting system. A significant deviation from actual sales might render the master budget useless. Managers must gather and use as much information as is available and use several estimation approaches in arriving at a valid prediction. The combining of prediction methods provides managers with a technique to confirm estimates and reduce uncertainty. Methods of estimating future demand include, canvassing sales personnel for a subjective consensus, making simple extrapolations of past trends, using market research, and employing statistical and other mathematical models.

Continuous budgeting is a process by which a company uses an ongoing 12-month budget. During a budget period, the company adds a new budget month as each current month expires. Managers must detect and often correct the causes of budget deviations. Managers sometimes revise the budget depending on the nature of the variances. Managers are more likely to change the budget when the actual performance is substantially better than expected. At other times, managers might not change the budget in order to highlight positive variances.

Budget slack is the intentional underestimation of revenues and/or overestimation of expenses. The presence of slack in the budget allows subordinate managers to achieve their objectives with less effort than would otherwise be necessary.

An imposed budget is a budget that top management develops with little or no input from operating personnel. Management informs operating personnel only of the budget objectives and constraints. However, a participatory budget involves joint decision-making.

Managers may expand their budget process to recognize activities and cost drivers consistent with activity-based management. Using this method, managers become aware of non-value-added activities and can take steps to reduce and eliminate them.

APPENDIX

A budget manual is a detailed set of documents that provide information and guidelines about the budgetary process. A budget manual should include the following:

1. statements of the budgetary purpose and its desired results
2. a listing of specific budgetary activities to be performed
3. a calendar of scheduled budgetary activities
4. sample budgetary forms
5. original, revised, and approved budgets

The use of a budget manual provides for more consistent budgeting across the organization. For example, budget forms in the manual facilitate a more consistent presentation of budget information.

Chapter 8: The Master Budget

SELF TEST

TRUE/FALSE

1. T F The budgeting activity plays an important role in organizational communication.

2. T F The cash budget is an example of a financial budget.

3. T F The financial budgets and operating budgets of an organization are independent of each other.

4. T F The master budget is flexible rather than static.

5. T F A master budget is a comprehensive set of all budgetary schedules and the pro forma financial statements of an organization.

6. T F The sales budget is the first budget a company prepares.

7. T F The production level is the activity level used in preparing the selling and administrative budget.

8. T F A company prepares the capital budget separately from the master budget.

9. T F The two acceptable formats for preparing the operating section of the statement of cash flows are the direct method and the indirect method.

10. T F Cash flow from operations and net income are required for continued business success.

11. T F A continuous budget adds a new month as each current month expires.

12. T F The intentional underestimation of revenues and/or overestimation of expenses is budget slack.

13. T F A budget prepared from the bottom up is a participatory budget.

14. T F An imposed budget is a budget that top management prepares with little or no input from operating personnel.

APPENDIX

15. T F A budget manual is a detailed set of information and guidelines about a budgetary process.

Chapter 8: The Master Budget

MULTIPLE CHOICE

1. A budget is:

    A. a qualitative expression of an organization's plans.
    B. always prepared to cover a period of one year.
    C. a quantitative expression of an organization's plans.
    D. useless in communicating management objectives.

2. Budgets are NOT an effective device to communicate:

    A. objectives.
    B. constraints.
    C. expectations to personnel.
    D. corporate strategies.

3. The set of operating budgets includes the:

    A. cash budget.
    B. purchases budget.
    C. capital expenditures budget.
    D. pro forma income statement.

4. The set of operating budgets does NOT include the:

    A. sales budget.
    B. cash budget.
    C. production budget.
    D. purchases budget.

5. The measure of activity used in preparing the selling and administrative budget is:

    A. sales.
    B. units produced.
    C. machine hours.
    D. direct labor hours.

6. Which budget does a company prepare first?

    A. production budget
    B. cash budget
    C. pro forma income statement
    D. sales budget

Chapter 8: The Master Budget

7. A pro forma income statement requires information from all of the following budgets except the:
8.
   A. cash budget.
   B. sales budget.
   C. direct labor budget.
   D. purchases budget.

8. Which of the following does the human resources (personnel) department prepare?

   A. factory overhead budget
   B. sales budget
   C. capital budget
   D. direct labor budget

9. An organization's pro forma financial statements represent:

   A. actual results of operations.
   B. a qualitative performance standard.
   C. results that the organization must achieve.
   D. budgeted results of operations.

10. An organization's pro forma balance sheet represents:

    A. budgeted assets, liabilities, and owners' equity.
    B. a qualitative performance standard.
    C. results that the organization must achieve.
    D. actual results of operations.

11. A very important role of the cash budget is to:

    A. determine how to finance dividend payments.
    B. plan for appropriate financing needs.
    C. determine the optimal source of financing for the organization's operations.
    D. help identify credit customers who might not pay.

12. The indirect method of preparing the operating section of the statement of cash flows begins with:
    A. net sales.
    B. net income.
    C. total cash collections.
    D. the ending cash balance.

Chapter 8:   The Master Budget   197

13. After an organization develops an imposed budget, the budget is:

    A. provided to operating personnel.
    B. flexible.
    C. not used for planning purposes.
    D. used to resolve all conflicts.

14. Slack in the operating budgets:

    A. will cause an organization to operate more efficiently.
    B. is rarely found if the budgets are imposed.
    C. results from unintentional managerial computational errors.
    D. will cause an organization to operate more effectively.

15. Whitehat Company prepared a production budget by month for the first quarter of the year (January, February, and March) and for the first quarter as a whole.. The ending inventory for the first quarter as a whole equals the:

    A. sum of the ending inventories for January, February, and March.
    B. ending inventory for March.
    C. beginning inventory for January.
    D. ending inventory for January.

16. Broshane Company prepared a production budget by month for the first quarter of the year (January, February, and March) and for the first quarter as a whole. The beginning inventory for the first quarter as a whole equals the:

    A. sum of the beginning inventories for January, February, and March.
    B. ending inventory for March.
    C. beginning inventory for January.
    D. ending inventory for January.

17. Courtney Company is preparing a cash budget by month for the fourth quarter of the year (October, November, and December) and for the fourth quarter as a whole. The beginning cash balance for the quarter as a whole equals the:

    A. sum of the beginning cash balances for October, November, and December.
    B. ending cash balance for December.
    C. beginning cash balance for December.
    D. beginning cash balance for October.

Chapter 8: The Master Budget

18. Stahl Company is preparing a cash budget by month for the fourth quarter of the year (October, November, and December) and for the fourth quarter as a whole. The ending cash balance for the quarter as a whole equals the:

   A. beginning cash balance for December.
   B. ending cash balance for December.
   C. the beginning cash balance for October.
   D. sum of the ending cash balances for October, November, and December.

19. Meadows Company makes all of its sales on account. Meadows collects its accounts as follows: 70 percent in the month of the sale, 25 percent in the month following sale, and 4 percent in the second month following sale. Uncollectible accounts are 1 percent of sales. Meadows expects sales for the first three months of the year to be as follows: January, $90,000; February, $95,000; and March, $100,000. How much cash should Meadows expect to collect in March?

   A. $70,000
   B. $97,350
   C. $99,000
   D. $100,000

20. Donald Company expects its purchases for June to be $130,000 and its purchases for July to be $124,000. Donald pays for 60 percent of its purchases in the month of purchase and receives a 2 percent discount. Donald pays for the remaining 40 percent for in the next month without any discount. For purchases only, what are the expected cash payments in July?

   A. $124,000
   B. $124,912
   C. $124,400
   D. $127,392

21. Wilson Company has a policy of maintaining an ending inventory of finished goods equal to 10 percent of the current month's sales. Wilson met this requirement for March. Sales for March were 4,800 units, and Wilson expects sales for April to be 6,000 units. How many units should Wilson produce in April?

   A. 5,880
   B. 6,120
   C. 6,600
   D. 7,080

Chapter 8:   The Master Budget

22. Henry Company plans to produce 640 units during September. Each unit takes 4 pounds of materials. Henry Company desires an ending raw materials inventory of 320 pounds. The raw materials inventory on September 1 contained 240 pounds. How many pounds of materials should Henry purchase in September?

   A. 2,480
   B. 2,460
   C. 2,640
   D. 2,880

23. Marker Company bases its manufacturing overhead budget on machine hours. Estimated machine hours are 10,000 for the quarter. Marker estimates its variable manufacturing overhead costs at $7.00 per machine hour. Marker projects its fixed manufacturing overhead costs for the quarter to be $16,000, including $5,000 in depreciation. By how much will manufacturing overhead costs affect the cash budget for the quarter?

   A. $70,000
   B. $75,000
   C. $81,000
   D. $86,000

24. Andy Company makes all of its sales on account. Andy collects its accounts as follows: 20 percent in the month of sale, 70 percent in the month following sale, and 10 percent in the second month following sale. Uncollectible accounts are so low as to be disregarded. Andy budgets sales for the first quarter of the year as follows: January, $17,600; February, $16,800; and March, $20,000. The accounts receivable balance on January 1 was $11,000 for sales made in November and December of the previous year. What is Andy's budgeted balance for accounts receivable at the end of March?

   A. $16,000
   B. $17,680
   C. $19,120
   D. $29,680

25. Sheets Company had a net income of $59,600 for the year. Depreciation expense was $8,000; accounts receivable increased $4,800; accounts payable decreased $3,800; and inventory decreased $1,200. What was the cash flow from operations?

   A. $51,600
   B. $59,000
   C. $59,600
   D. $60,200

Chapter 8: The Master Budget

26. Sherry Company makes all purchases of materials on account. Sherry pays for 60 percent of each month's purchases in the month of purchase taking a 2 percent discount. Sherry pays for the remaining 40 percent of each month's purchases in the month following purchase with no discount. Sherry budgets purchases for the second quarter as follows: April, $60,000; May, $68,000; and June, $70,000. The accounts payable balance for purchases was $50,000 on April 1 for purchases made in March. What are Sherry's expected cash payments for April?

   A. $35,280
   B. $50,000
   C. $85,280
   D. $86,000

27. Terry Company makes all purchases of materials on account. Terry pays for 60 percent of each month's purchases in the month of purchase taking a 2 percent discount. Terry pays for the remaining 40 percent of each month's purchases in the month following purchase with no discount. Terry budgets purchases for the second quarter as follows: April, $60,000; May, $68,000; and June, $70,000. The accounts payable balance for purchases was $125,000 on April 1 for purchases made in March. What is Terry's budgeted accounts payable balance on June 30?

   A. $28,000
   B. $42,000
   C. $53,000
   D. $67,000

28. Berry Company budgeted sales in units for the last quarter of the year as follows: October, 12,000; November, 14,000; and December, 16,000. The finished goods inventory on hand October 1 is 4,000 units. Berry desires an ending inventory on December 31 of 3,000 units. How many units should Berry produce for the last quarter?

   A. 41,000
   B. 43,000
   C. 45,000
   D. 49,000

29. Which of the following is an advantage of a continuous budget over the annual budget?

   A. The annual budget develops fiscal responsibility and budgetary skill in employees.
   B. The continuous budget includes specific resource requirements.
   C. The continuous budget is never realistic.
   D. The planning process is less sporadic.

Chapter 8: The Master Budget

30. Jerry Company expects cash collections during the year of $250,000. In addition, Jerry expects $25,000 in depreciation, $35,000 cash to be paid for direct labor, $2,000 to be paid for supplies, and $55,000 to be paid for raw materials. What is the budgeted net increase in cash for the year?

   A. $133,000
   B. $158,000
   C. $183,000
   D. $225,000

QUESTIONS AND PROBLEMS

1. Why is budgeting an important organization activity?

2. Define and explain operating budgets and financial budgets.

Chapter 8: The Master Budget

3. What must management do to components of manufacturing overhead costs before estimating total manufacturing overhead costs? What manufacturing overhead costs flow through to the cash budget?

4. Explain how the capital budget relates to the master budget.

5. What is the starting point in the budgeting process?

Chapter 8: The Master Budget 203

6. What is the purpose of the cash budget and why is it so important?

7. What are pro forma financial statements? What are their roles in the budgeting process?

8. What are the components of the master budget?

9. Which critical external factors do managers in the United States spend much of their time analyzing?

10. Why do managers make tactical plans? How long do these plans span and which type of manager makes these plans? Hint: See Exhibit 8-1.

11. Describe the cyclical nature of the budgeting process. Hint: See Exhibit 8-2.

Chapter 8: The Master Budget

12. What is the difference between a participatory budget and an imposed budget? Which budget is most often used?

13. What is a collection pattern? Why is developing a collection pattern important to company survival? Hint See Exhibit 8-14.

14. List ten ways to improve small business cash flow. (hint: see Exhibit 8-18)

Chapter 8:   The Master Budget

15. Pankey Company makes only one product. Its sales price is expected to be $82 per unit.

Actual sales:

November   6,200 units
December   6,800 units

Pankey's budgeted sales for the next six months are as follows:

January   5,400 units
February   5,200 units
March   5,500 units
April   5,000 units
May   5,800 units
June   6,000 units

All sales are on account. Pankey collects its accounts receivable as follows:

70 percent in the month of sale
20 percent in the month following sale
10 percent in the second month following sale

Uncollectible accounts are negligible and can be disregarded.

The beginning inventory on January 1 is 540 units. Pankey desires an ending finished goods inventory of 10 percent of the next month's budgeted sales.

Each unit of finished goods requires 4 pounds of raw materials that cost $3.00 a pound. Pankey desires an ending inventory of raw materials equal to 20 percent of the following month's production needs. Assume that Pankey met this requirement at the end of December of the previous year. Pankey makes all purchases on account on terms net 30. Pankey pays its accounts payable as follows: 60 percent in the month of sale and 40 percent in the month following sale. Purchases in December were $62,000.
Prepare or calculate the following:

(a) a sales budget by month for the first quarter and for the first quarter as a whole.
(b) a production budget by month for the 1st quarter and for the1st quarter as a whole.
(c) a purchases budget by month for the first quarter and for the first quarter as a whole.
(d) a schedule of cash collections from sales.
(e) a schedule of cash disbursements for accounts payable.
(f) the budgeted accounts receivable balance at March 31, 20XX.
(g) the budgeted accounts payable balance at March 31, 20XX.

Chapter 8: The Master Budget

Chapter 8: The Master Budget

SELF TEST ANSWERS

TRUE/FALSE

1.	T	4.	F	7.	F	10.	T	13.	T
2.	T	5.	T	8.	T	11.	T	14.	T
3.	F	6.	T	9.	T	12.	T	15.	T

MULTIPLE CHOICE

1.	C	7.	A	13.	A	19.	B	25.	D
2.	D	8.	D	14.	B	20.	B	26.	C
3.	B	9.	D	15.	B	21.	B	27.	A
4.	B	10.	A	16.	C	22.	C	28.	A
5.	A	11.	B	17.	D	23.	C	29.	D
6.	D	12.	B	18.	B	24.	B	30.	B

QUESTIONS AND PROBLEMS

1. Budgeting is important for several reasons. The budget is a quantitative expression of the goals and objectives of the organization. Because budgets are quantitative, they provide a concrete standard of performance. As performance standards, budgets are compared to actual results and become an important part of management control and performance evaluation. Because budgets are concise expressions of organizational objectives, they are useful in communicating the objectives to organizational members and coordinating the efforts of organizational members.

2. Management includes operating budgets and financial budgets in the master budget. Operating budgets contain information in units and possibly also in dollars. Financial budgets contain information in dollars but not in units. The financial budgets include the cash budget and the pro forma financial statements. The capital budget is also a financial budget, but management does not include it in the master budget. Accountants use the information in dollars from the operating budgets to help prepare the financial budgets.

3. Before a cost accountant can estimate total manufacturing overhead costs, the cost accountant must specify the component costs as fixed or variable. Some manufacturing overhead costs are fixed while other overhead costs vary with the number of units produced. The cost accountant must separate mixed costs into their fixed and variable components. The total manufacturing overhead costs minus depreciation flow through to the cash budget as cash payments for manufacturing overhead. Depreciation is a cost that does not require the outflow of cash.

4. The capital budget is not a part of the master budget, but the capital budget affects the master budget. Acquisitions of plant and equipment affect depreciation on the overhead budget and perhaps on the selling and administrative budget. Also, the capital budget affects the cash

budget because of the cash payments for plant and equipment or payments on loans used to acquire plant and equipment.

5. The budgeting process always begins with an estimate of the demand for the organizational output. The organization translates such an estimate into a budgeted level of output, which it then uses to compile budgets for the required inputs.

6. The cash budget identifies the timing of cash excesses and shortages. It is extremely important because cash is the medium of exchange for organizational inputs and outputs. If cash shortages exist, the organization cannot pay for its inputs and must make plans to obtain cash through borrowing, sales of assets, etc. If excess cash is available, the organization can plan to acquire investments.

7. The pro forma financial statements reflect budgeted operating and financial results. They are part of the master budget. A company uses them as performance standards and as bases for budget revision.

8. The master budget is simply the set of all budgets. The master budget consists of the operating budgets and the financial budgets. The operating budgets include the sales budget, the production budget, the purchases budget, the direct labor budget, the manufacturing overhead budget, and the selling and administrative budget. The financial budgets include the cash budget and the pro forma financial statements.

9. Managers spend the most time planning for the following critical external factors:

   1. competitor actions
   2. market conditions
   3. political and regulatory climates
   4. emerging technology issues
   5. consumer trends and attitudes
   6. demographics

10. Top management and middle management make tactical plans. The statement of organizational plans are short range, usually 1-18 months. Tactical plans provide direction for achievement of strategic plans; state plans in terms on which managers can act; and furnish a basis against which results can be measured.

11. The cyclical nature of budgeting process includes a comparison of actual performance to budgeted performance. Variances are then determined. Next feedback and discussion of causes takes place. Then changes, if necessary, are implemented. Then, once again, a comparison is made of actual to budgeted performance and the cycle begins again.

12. A participatory budget is developed through joint decision making by top management and operating personnel. Imposed budgets are prepared by top management with little or no input from operating personnel. In an imposed budget, operating personnel are informed of the

Chapter 8:   The Master Budget

budget goals and constraints. The budgeting process can be represented on a continuum with participatory on one end and imposed budgets on the other. Only rarely is a budget either purely participatory or purely imposed. The budget process in a particular company is usually defined by the degree to which the process is either participatory or imposed.

13. A collection pattern, as shown in Exhibit 8-14, shows the timing of collections and the amounts expected to be collected including discounts. Developing a collection pattern is important to company survival because management needs this information to plan cash flows. Without proper cash management, a company will likely fail.

14. Exhibit 8-18 illustrates ten ways to improve small business cash flow.

1. Establish sound credit practices.
2. Expedite fulfillment and shipping.
3. Bill promptly and accurately.
4. Offer discounts for prompt payments.
5. Aggressively follow up on past due accounts.
6. Deposit payments promptly.
7. Seek better payment terms from suppliers and banks.
8. Keep tight control on inventory.
9. Review and reduce expenses.
10. Pay bills on time, but never before they are due.

15 (a). Pankey Company

Sales Budget
For the First Quarter Ending March 31, 20XX

	January	February	March	First Quarter
Sales in units	5,400	5,200	5,500	16,100
Price per unit	$82	$82	$82	$82
Sales in dollars	$442,800	$426,400	$451,000	$1,320,200

Chapter 8: The Master Budget

15 (b).
Pankey Company
Production Budget
For the First Quarter Ending March 31, 20XX

	January	February	March	First Quarter
Sales in units	5,400	5,200	5,500	16,100
Add: Desired ending inventory	520	550	500*	500
Total needed	5,920	5,750	6,000	16,600
Less: Beginning inventory	540	520	550	540
Units to be produced	5,380	5,230	5,450	16,060

*April sales 5,000 x 10% = 500

15 (c).
Pankey Company
Purchases Budget
For the First Quarter Ending March 31, 20XX

	January	February	March	First Quarter
Units to be produced	5,380	5,230	5,450	16,060
Add: Ending inventory (units)	1,046	1,090	1,016**	1,016
Total units needed	6,426	6,320	6,466	17,076
Less: Beginning inventory (units)	1,076*	1,046	1,090	1,076
Purchases in whole units	5,350	5,274	5,376	16,000
x Pounds per unit	4	4	4	4
Total pounds to be purchased	21,400	21,096	21,504	64,000
x Price per pound	$3.00	$3.00	$3.00	$3.00
Total cost of materials	$64,200	$63,288	$64,512	$192,000

*The beginning inventory for January is the same as the ending inventory for December. The ending inventory of raw materials in terms of equivalent whole units for December met the 20 percent of the units to be produced for January: 5,380 x 20% = 1,076.

**Units to be produced in April = April sales 5,000 units + ending inventory (5,800 x 10%) – beginning inventory 500 = 5,000 + 580 – 500 = 5,080.

Desired ending inventory for March = 5,080 x 20% = 1,016.

Pankey Company

Chapter 8: The Master Budget

Schedule of Cash Collections
For the First Quarter Ending March 31, 20XX

	January	February	March	First Quarter
From:				
November:				
6,200($82)(10%)	$50,840			$50,840
December:				
6,800($82)(20%)	111,520			111,520
6,800($82)(10%)		$55,760		55,760
January:				
5,400($82)(70%)	309,960			309,960
5,400($82)(20%)		88,560		88,560
5,400($82)(10%)			$44,280	44,280
February:				
5,200($82)(70%)		298,480		298,480
5,200($82)(20%)			85,280	85,280
March:				
5,500($82)(70%)			315,700	315,700
Totals	$472,320	$442,800	$445,260	$1,360,380

15(e).

Pankey Company
Schedule of Cash Disbursements for Accounts Payable
For the First Quarter Ending March 31, 20XX

	January	February	March	First Quarter
From:				
December:				
$62,000(40%)	$24,800			$24,800
January:				
$64,200(60%)	38,520			38,520
$64,200(40%)		$25,680		25,680
February:				
$63,288(60%)		37,973		37,973
$63,288(40%)			$25,315	25,315
March:				
$64,512(60%)			38,707	38,707
Totals	$63,320	$63,653	$64,022	$190,995

Chapter 8: The Master Budget

15(f). Budgeted Accounts Receivable balance at March 31, 20XX:

From February sales: 5,200($82)(10%)= $42,640
From March sales: 5,500($82)(20%) =   90,200
Budgeted Accounts Receivable balance $132,840

15 (g). Budgeted Accounts Payable balance at March 31, 20XX:

From March purchases: $64,512 x 40% = $25,804.80

CHAPTER 9

BREAK-EVEN POINT AND COST-VOLUME-PROFIT ANALYSIS

CHAPTER OVERVIEW

This chapter discusses the usefulness of variable costing for break-even and cost-volume-profit analysis. Also discussed are the methods for determining the break-even point, the uses for cost-volume-profit analysis, and use of these methods in a multiproduct environment.

Variable costing allows a company to use models to calculate the break-even point, analyze cost-volume-profit relationships, and compute margin of safety and the degree of operating leverage. Managers should be aware of the assumptions upon which the break-even and cost-volume-profit models are based, because they limit the ability of these models to reflect reality.

CHAPTER STUDY GUIDE

Variable costing is more useful than absorption costing in determining break-even point and doing cost-volume-profit analysis because variable costing is more transparent. A useful starting point in understanding cost-volume-profit analysis is understanding the break-even point. At the break-even point, total revenues equal total costs resulting in a zero profit. The break-even point in units is the number of units that a company must sell to have a zero profit. The break-even point in sales revenue is the sales revenue in dollars that a company must generate to have a zero profit. Because managers seldom want to operate at a level that simply breaks even, CVP adds a profit element to break-even calculations so that managers can plan for volume levels that generate profits.

Five basic assumptions of CVP analysis are (1) that the company is operating within the relevant range. The relevant range is the range of activity for which cost and revenue behaviors are valid. (2) Within the relevant range, management assumes that revenue per unit remains constant. Managers must classify costs by how the costs behave when volume changes within the relevant range. Some costs are fixed, other costs are variable, and yet other costs are mixed. (3) Total variable costs increase proportionately with an increase in volume and decrease proportionately with a decrease in volume. Per-unit variable costs remain constant when volume changes. (4) Fixed costs remain constant in total when volume increases or decreases. However,

Chapter 9: Break-Even Point and Cost-Volume-Profit Analysis

per-unit fixed costs decrease when volume increases and increase when volume decreases. (5) Mixed costs have a fixed cost element and a variable cost element. Managers must separate mixed costs into their fixed and variable elements before using CVP analysis. Mixed costs increase in total when volume increases because of their variable cost element. Mixed costs decrease on a per-unit basis when volume increases because of their fixed cost element. Managers can use techniques such as regression analysis to separate mixed costs.

An important concept in CVP analysis is contribution margin, which is revenue minus variable costs. The cost accountant can compute contribution margin in total or on a per-unit basis. On a per-unit basis, contribution margin is constant because revenue and variable costs are constant on a per-unit basis. Product contribution margin differs from contribution margin in that product contribution margin is the difference between revenues and total variable production costs included in costs of goods sold.

The formula approach to break-even analysis uses an algebraic equation to compute the break-even point. The equation shows that the break-even point in units is equal to the fixed costs divided by the per-unit contribution margin. The break-even point in revenue equals the break-even point in units multiplied by the selling price. Exhibit 9-1 provides data for the example company used to illustrate the calculation of the break-even point and CVP analysis.

Another method for computing the break-even point in sales revenue involves the use of the contribution margin ratio. The contribution margin ratio is equal to the contribution margin divided by revenue. The variable cost ratio (VC) is equal to 100 percent less the contribution margin ratio. To compute the break-even point in revenue, the cost accountant divides the fixed costs by the contribution margin ratio. To compute the break-even point in units, the cost accountant divides the break-even point in revenue by the selling price.

Once a company reaches the break-even point, each dollar of contribution margin is a dollar of profit. To compute how many units the company must sell to achieve a target profit before tax, the cost accountant adds the target profit before tax to the fixed costs and divides this sum by the contribution margin per unit. To calculate the revenue the company must realize to achieve a target profit before tax, the cost accountant adds the target profit before tax to the fixed costs and divides this sum by the contribution margin ratio. Exhibit 9-2 illustrates CVP analysis with a target profit before tax.

The cost accountant can also compute the number of units the company must sell or the sales revenue that the company must realize to achieve a target profit after tax. To convert the target profit after tax to a target profit before tax, the cost accountant divides the target profit after tax by one minus the tax rate. Then the cost accountant uses the formulas for target profit before tax. Exhibit 9-3 illustrates CVP analysis with a target profit after tax.

A company might want to earn a specified per-unit profit. The cost accountant treats the desired per-unit profit before tax as an additional variable cost in the CVP formula. The number of units the company must sell to earn a desired per-unit profit before tax is equal to the fixed costs divided by the difference between the per-unit contribution margin and the desired per-unit

Chapter 9: Break-Even Point and Cost-Volume-Profit Analysis 217

profit before tax.

If a company wants profit before tax to be a specified percentage of sales, the specified percentage multiplied by the sales price equals the desired per-unit profit before tax. The cost accountant can calculate the amount of revenue the company must realize to earn a profit before tax equal to a specified percentage of revenue. To do so, the cost accountant divides the fixed costs by the difference between the contribution margin ratio and the desired profit before tax percentage. The desired profit before tax percentage must be less than the contribution margin ratio. Exhibit 9-4 illustrates the calculation of the number of units and the amount of sales revenue the example company must realize to earn a desired profit before tax as a percentage of sales revenue and per unit.

To calculate the number of units a company must sell to earn a desired per-unit profit after tax, the cost accountant must convert the per-unit profit after tax to a per-unit profit before tax. The cost accountant does so by dividing the per-unit profit after tax by one minus the tax rate. The cost accountant can compute the revenue the company must realize to earn a profit after tax equal to a specified percentage of revenue. The cost accountant must first convert the specified percentage of profit after tax to a specified percentage of profit before tax. Again, the cost accountant does so by dividing the desired percentage of profit after tax by one minus the tax rate. Exhibit 9-5 illustrates the calculation of the number of units and the amount of sales revenue the example company must realize to earn a set profit after tax.

The graph approach to break-even and cost-volume-profit analysis is more effective at conveying information to visually acute managers. Exhibit 9-6 presents each income statement item in Exhibit 9-1 in a visual representation. While these representations provide little useful information, the cost accountant can prepare a break-even chart. The break-even chart shows the break-even point as the intersection of two lines; one lines is total cost and the other is total revenue.

The cost accountant can use two approaches for break-even charts; the traditional or the cost-volume-profit approach. The focus of the traditional approach is the relationships of revenues, costs, and profits. Contribution margin is ignored. Exhibit 9-7 shows a graphical representation of fixed and total costs. The difference between these two lines is the variable cost. Using the traditional approach as illustrated in Exhibit 9-8, the cost accountant graphs the total revenue and total cost on one graph. The intersection of these two lines represents the break-even point.

The cost accountant can create a profit-volume graph that depicts the amount of profit or loss for each sales level. The accountant draws the line using two points on the graph: total fixed cost on the y-axis and the break-even point on the x-axis. Exhibit 9-9 illustrates the profit-volume graph for the example company.

The income statement approach to CVP analysis allows cost accountants to prepare budgeted income statements. The cost accountant can prove the solutions obtained using the formula approach with budgeted income statements. The solutions provided by break-even

Chapter 9: Break-Even Point and Cost-Volume-Profit Analysis

analysis or CVP analysis are valid only for the specified selling price and cost relationships. A change in the sales price, variable costs, or fixed costs, will cause a change in the break-even point and the sales required for a desired profit. A cost accountant can compute the effects of revenue and cost changes on a company's break-even point or sales volume using incremental analysis. Exhibit 9-10 proves each of the calculations made in Exhibits 9-1 through 9-5 for the example company.

Incremental analysis focuses only on factors that change from one decision to another. A cost accountant can use incremental analysis with CVP analysis to determine the feasibility of proposed changes without having to prepare a complete income statement. For example, a cost accountant can use incremental analysis to determine how many additional units a company must sell to cover an increase in fixed costs. To do so, the cost accountant divides the increase in fixed costs by the contribution margin per unit.

Although CVP analysis usually assumes that a company sells one product only, companies that sell multiple products can also use CVP analysis. Companies with multiple products must compute a weighted average contribution margin ratio assuming a constant sales mix. Then the cost accountant can compute the total revenue the company must realize to break even or earn a desired profit. The total revenue multiplied by the sales mix percentage equals the sales of a particular product. Exhibit 9-11 illustrates CVP analysis with multiple products.

The relative proportion of the quantities sold of a company's products is its sales mix. Factors that affect a company's sales mix include prices and advertising expenditures. If a company changes one or both factors, its sales mix could change also. Exhibit 9-12 illustrates that a shift toward a product with a lower contribution margin will cause a higher break-even point and a lower profit.

Managers often consider a company's margin of safety when making decisions about business opportunities and changes in the company's sales mix. Margin of safety is the difference between a company's sales and the break-even point. The cost accountant can compute margin of safety using actual sales or budgeted sales. In addition, the cost accountant can compute margin of safety using units or dollars of sales revenue. The margin of safety percentage equals the margin of safety divided by budgeted or actual sales. Exhibit 9-13 illustrates the calculation of the margin of safety and the margin of safety percentage. Margin of safety is a measure of risk. Margin of safety indicates how close to a danger level the company is operating.

Another measure closely related to the margin of safety is the company's degree of operating leverage. The degree of operating leverage measures how a percentage change in sales will affect profit. The degree of operating leverage equals contribution margin divided by profit before tax. The degree of operating leverage is also equal to one divided by the margin of safety percentage. This formula assumes that fixed costs remain constant when sales increase. A company's cost structure affects its degree of operating leverage. Cost structure is the relative proportions of fixed costs and variable costs. As a company's sales increase over the break-even point, the company's margin of safety increases and its degree of operating leverage decreases.

Chapter 9: Break-Even Point and Cost-Volume-Profit Analysis

Exhibit 9-14 illustrates the calculation of degree of operating leverage. Exhibit 9-15 illustrates the relationship between the margin of safety and the degree of operating leverage.

Seven assumptions underlie CVP analysis: (1) all revenue and variable cost behavior patterns are constant per unit and linear within the relevant range; (2) total contribution margin is linear within the relevant range and increases proportionally with volume; (3) total fixed costs are constant within the relevant range; (4) the cost accountant can separate mixed costs accurately into their fixed and variable elements; (5) sales and production are equal; (6) the sales mix remains constant for a multiproduct company; and (7) labor productivity, production technology, and market conditions do not change during the period.

Thus, CVP analysis is only as good as the validity of the underlying assumptions. In today's business world, many companies are discovering that many costs previously classified as fixed actually vary with activities other than volume. A company should specify the cost drivers of long-term variable costs and include them in the CVP formula. These adjustments to the CVP formula will force managers to take more of a long-run perspective of product opportunities.

Chapter 9: Break-Even Point and Cost-Volume-Profit Analysis

SELF TEST

TRUE/FALSE

1. T F At the break-even point, contribution margin equals variable costs.

2. T F Within the relevant range, per-unit variable costs remain constant.

3. T F The contribution margin ratio is equal to contribution margin divided by revenue.

4. T F Profit before tax plus fixed costs equals the contribution margin.

5. T F An important concept of break-even analysis is page margin.

6. T F A visual way to show break-even analysis is a break-even chart.

7. T F The two points located on a profit-volume graph are total fixed cost and the break-even point.

8. T F The margin of safety equals actual sales minus break-even sales.

9. T F The degree of operating leverage equals contribution margin divided by fixed costs.

10. T F As sales increase over the break-even point, the degree of operating leverage decreases.

11. T F Fixed costs are fixed forever.

12. T F Cost structure is the relative proportions of fixed costs and variable costs.

13. T F Per-unit contribution margin increases as the sales volume increases.

14. T F The contribution margin is readily apparent on the traditional break-even chart.

15. T F On a profit-volume graph, the horizontal axis represents sales volume.

MULTIPLE CHOICE

1. The relative proportion of the quantities sold of a company's products is its:

    A. cost structure.
    B. sales mix.
    C. margin of safety.
    D. degree of operating leverage.

Chapter 9: Break-Even Point and Cost-Volume-Profit Analysis

2. What costs must be separated into both variable and fixed elements before they are used in BEP or CVP analysis?

    A. mixed costs
    B. fixed costs
    C. variable costs
    D. relevant range costs

3. What is product contribution margin?

    A. sales minus all variable costs
    B. sales minus variable cost of goods sold
    C. sales minus all fixed costs
    D. sales minus fixed manufacturing overhead

4. Which costs are assumed to remain constant over a relevant range for BEP or CVP analysis?

    A. mixed costs
    B. fixed costs
    C. variable cost
    D. relevant range costs

5. What is gross margin?

    A. sales minus all variable costs.
    B. sales minus variable cost of goods sold
    C. sales minus cost of goods sold
    D. contribution margin minus fixed costs

6. Which of the following factors, in and of themselves, do NOT cause a company's profit to change?

    A. increase in selling prices and increase in advertising
    B. decrease in advertising and decrease in selling prices
    C. increase in total sales along with the same dollar increase in advertising
    D. change in the number of units sold.

7. Using CVP analysis, managers plan for sales volume levels that:

    A. exceed the break-even point.
    B. reach the break-even point.
    C. approach the break-even point.
    D. create a loss for the company.

Chapter 9: Break-Even Point and Cost-Volume-Profit Analysis

8. What are the three approaches to cost-volume-profit analysis?

    A. algebraic, graph, and income statement
    B. algebraic, traditional, and income statement
    C. formula, traditional, and income statement
    D. formula, graph, and income statement

9. Variable costs:

    A. are constant per unit.
    B. vary per unit.
    C. decrease per unit as volume increases.
    D. remain constant in total as volume increases.

10. Contribution margin is NOT equal to:

    A. revenue minus variable costs.
    B. fixed costs plus profit before tax.
    C. contribution margin per unit multiplied by the number of units sold.
    D. fixed costs minus variable costs.

11. Fixed costs:

    A. remain constant in total as volume changes.
    B. are fixed per unit as volume changes.
    C. increase per unit as volume increases.
    D. are always a product cost.

12. What decreases as a company's sales volume moves away from the break-even point?

    A. degree of operating leverage
    B. margin of safety
    C. contribution margin
    D. break-even point in dollars

13. Klein Company sells one product for $80. The variable costs are $16 per unit. Fixed costs are $240,000. How much sales revenue will Klein realize at the break-even point?

    A. $3,750
    B. $240,000
    C. $300,000
    D. $1,200,000

Chapter 9: Break-Even Point and Cost-Volume-Profit Analysis   223

14. Ellis Company sells one product for $200. Variable costs are $130 per unit. Fixed costs are $63,000. How many units will Ellis Company have to sell for profit before taxes to equal 10 percent of sales revenue?

   A. 90
   B. 700
   C. 900
   D. 1,260

15. Reynolds Company has a contribution margin ratio of 32 percent. Fixed costs are $90,000. What will the sales revenue be if profit before taxes equals 12 percent of sales?

   A. $ 54,000
   B. $144,000
   C. $200,000
   D. $450,000

16. Hawthorne Company sells one product for $8 per unit. Variable costs are $3 per unit. Fixed costs total $120,000. How many units must Hawthorne Company sell to break even?

   A. 15,000
   B. 24,000
   C. 40,000
   D. 600,000

17. Smyth Company sells one product for $12 per unit. Variable costs are $4 per unit. Fixed costs are $48,000. How many units must Smyth sell to have a $64,000 profit before taxes?

   A. 6,000
   B. 7,000
   C. 8,000
   D. 14,000

18. Decker Company has a contribution margin ratio of 80 percent. Variable costs are $4 per unit. At the break-even point, sales are $500,000. How many units would Decker sell if the profit before taxes is $80,000?

   A. 11,250
   B. 24,000
   C. 30,000
   D. 36,250

Chapter 9: Break-Even Point and Cost-Volume-Profit Analysis

19. Bosley Company sells one product for $90 per unit. Variable costs are $30 per unit. The marketing manager has proposed a new advertising campaign that would increase fixed costs by $360,000. How many more units must Bosley sell to pay for the advertising campaign?

    A. 3,000
    B. 4,000
    C. 6,000
    D. 12,000

20. Martin Company sells two products—widgets and gizmos. The company sells 3 widgets for every 2 gizmos. Widgets sell for $50 and have variable costs of $30. Gizmos sell for $40 and have variable costs of $12. Fixed costs are $1,450,000. How many units of widgets and gizmos would the company sell at the break-even point?

	Widgets	Gizmos
A.	25,000	37,500
B.	37,500	25,000
C.	25,000	62,500
D.	37,500	62,500

21. Brooks Company sells one product for $50 per unit. Variable costs are $20 per unit. Fixed costs total $839,000. The tax rate is 40 percent. How many units must Brooks sell to have a $780,000 profit after tax?

    A. 26,000
    B. 53,967
    C. 65,000
    D. 71,300

22. Travis Company had 5 degrees of operating leverage when its profit before tax was $200,000. If the company's sales increased by 10 percent, what is the company's profit before tax?

    A. $100,000
    B. $200,000
    C. $300,000
    D. $400,000

Chapter 9: Break-Even Point and Cost-Volume-Profit Analysis

23. Michaels Company sells one product for $100 per unit. Variable costs are $60 per unit. Fixed costs are $150,000. Michaels results of operations for the last year follow: Sales=$500,000, Variable costs=$300,000, Contribution margin=$200,000, Fixed costs=$150,000, Profit before tax=$50,000
What are the degrees of operating leverage for Michaels Company?

A. 1
B. 3
C. 4
D. 10

24. Michaels Company sells one product for $100 per unit. Variable costs are $60 per unit. Fixed costs are $150,000. Michaels results of operations for the last year follow: Sales=$500,000, Variable costs=$300,000, Contribution margin=$200,000, Fixed costs=$150,000, Profit before tax=$50,000
What is the margin of safety in sales revenue?

A. $125,000
B. $200,000
C. $375,000
D. $500,000

25. Michaels Company sells one product for $100 per unit. Variable costs are $60 per unit. Fixed costs are $150,000. Michaels results of operations for the last year follow: Sales=$500,000, Variable costs=$300,000, Contribution margin=$200,000, Fixed costs=$150,000, Profit before tax=$50,000
What is the margin of safety in units?

A. 1,250
B. 3,750
C. 3,000
D. 5,000

26. Michaels Company sells one product for $100 per unit. Variable costs are $60 per unit. Fixed costs are $150,000. Michaels results of operations for the last year follow: Sales=$500,000, Variable costs=$300,000, Contribution margin=$200,000, Fixed costs=$150,000, Profit before tax=$50,000
What is the margin of safety percentage?

A. 25%
B. 33%
C. 40%
D. 133%

Chapter 9: Break-Even Point and Cost-Volume-Profit Analysis

27. What are two approaches of creating break-even charts?

    A. traditional and world-style
    B. simple and traditional
    C. profit-volume and cost-profit-volume
    D. traditional and cost-profit-volume

28. Where are the y and x intercepts on volume-profit graphs?

    A. total fixed cost and break-even point
    B. simple and traditional
    C. variable cost and total revenue
    D. total cost and total revenue

29. On a profit-volume graph, the vertical axis represents:

    A. profit or loss.
    B. sales in units.
    C. sales in dollars.
    D. total costs.

30. The traditional approach to graphical break-even analysis focuses on:

    A. contribution margin.
    B. the precise break-even point.
    C. the relationships among revenues, costs, and profits.
    D. per-unit variable costs.

QUESTIONS AND PROBLEMS

1. Discuss the five basic assumptions that are the bases for break-even and cost-volume-profit analysis.

Chapter 9:   Break-Even Point and Cost-Volume-Profit Analysis   227

2. What are mixed costs? What must managers do to mixed costs before using them in CVP analysis?

3. Explain the graph approach of cost-volume-profit analysis and why it is used.

4. What is incremental analysis? How can a cost accountant use incremental analysis?

Chapter 9: Break-Even Point and Cost-Volume-Profit Analysis 228

5. What are all the underlying assumptions of cost-volume-profit analysis?

6. Explain why on a per-unit basis fixed costs vary and why on a per-unit basis variable costs are constant.

7. What is margin of safety? What does margin of safety indicate?

8. What is degree of operating leverage?

9. Wyatt Company sells one product for $25 per unit. Variable costs are $13 per unit. Fixed costs are $48,000.

(a) Compute the break-even point in units and in sales revenue.

(b) How many units would Wyatt have to sell to earn a profit before taxes of $150,000?

10. Norris Company produces one product that sells for $1,200. Variable costs are $840 per unit. Fixed costs are $720,000. The tax rate is 40 percent.

   (a) How much would the sales revenue have to be for Norris to have a profit after taxes of $1,080,000?

   (b) How many units would Norris have to sell to have a profit before taxes equal to 10 percent of sales revenue?

11. Upshaw Company sells one product for $4. The company's budgeted sales for the current period are 500,000 units. Break-even sales are 300,000 units.

   Calculate the margin of safety in units, the margin of safety in dollars of sales revenue, and the margin of safety percentage.

12. Vogle Company sells two products. The regular model has a selling price of $100 and per-unit variable costs of $68. The deluxe model has a selling price of $150 and per-unit variable costs of $90. Fixed costs are $168,000. The sales mix is a constant 75 percent regular model and 25 percent deluxe model in terms of the number of units sold.

   Calculate the sales in units for each model and in total if profit before taxes is $300,000.

13. The Hollinrake Refuse Engineer Club (HRE) has the following information: Monthly membership is $30 per member, monthly variable cost per member is $12, and monthly fixed cost is $1,800. Volunteers provide almost all services and supplies. Prepare a break-even chart for HRE.

Chapter 9: Break-Even Point and Cost-Volume-Profit Analysis   232

14. The Hollinrake Refuse Engineer Club (HRE) has the following information: Monthly membership is $30 per member, monthly variable cost per member is $12, and monthly fixed cost is $1,800. Volunteers provide almost all services and supplies. Prepare a profit-volume graph for HRE.

15. What are the steps that a cost accountant must take to prepare a break-even graph?

Chapter 9: Break-Even Point and Cost-Volume-Profit Analysis

SELF TEST ANSWERS

TRUE/FALSE

1. F
2. T
3. T
4. T
5. F
6. T
7. T
8. T
9. F
10. T
11. F
12. T
13. F
14. F
15. T

MULTIPLE CHOICE

1. B
2. A
3. B
4. B
5. C
6. C
7. A
8. D
9. A
10. D
11. A
12. A
13. C
14. D
15. D
16. B
17. D
18. C
19. C
20. B
21. D
22. C
23. C
24. A
25. A
26. A
27. C
28. A
29. A
30. C

QUESTIONS AND PROBLEMS

1. Five basic assumptions of CVP analysis are (1) that the company is operating within the relevant range. The relevant range is the range of activity for which cost and revenue behaviors are valid. (2) Within the relevant range, management assumes that revenue per unit remains constant. Managers must classify costs by how the costs behave when volume changes within the relevant range. Some costs are fixed, other costs are variable, and yet other costs are mixed. (3) Total variable costs increase proportionately with an increase in volume and decrease proportionately with a decrease in volume. Per-unit variable costs remain constant when volume changes. (4) Fixed costs remain constant in total when volume increases or decreases. However, per-unit fixed costs decrease when volume increases and increase when volume decreases. (5) Mixed costs have a fixed cost element and a variable cost element. Managers must separate mixed costs into their fixed and variable elements before using CVP analysis. Mixed costs increase in total when volume increases because of their variable cost element. Mixed costs decrease on a per-unit basis when volume increases because of their fixed cost element. Managers can use techniques such as regression analysis to separate mixed costs.

2. Mixed costs are costs that have a fixed cost element and a variable cost element. They increase in total when volume increases because of their variable cost element. Mixed costs per unit decrease when volume increases because of their fixed cost element. The cost accountant must separate mixed costs into their fixed and variable elements before using CVP analysis. Cost accountants can use techniques such as the high-low method or regression analysis to separate mixed costs.

Chapter 9: Break-Even Point and Cost-Volume-Profit Analysis 234

3. The cost account can use two approaches for break-even charts; the traditional or the cost-volume-profit approach. The focus of the traditional approach is the relationships of revenues, costs, and profits. Contribution margin is ignored. The difference between these two lines is the variable cost. Using the traditional approach, the cost accountant graphs the total revenue and total cost on one graph. The intersection of these two lines represents the break-even point. The cost accountant can create a profit-volume graph, which depicts the amount of profit or loss for each sales level. The account draws the line using two points on the graph: total fixed cost on the y-axis and the break-even point on the x-axis.

4. Incremental analysis focuses only on factors that change from one decision to another. A cost accountant can use incremental analysis with cost-volume-profit analysis to determine the feasibility of proposed changes without having to prepare a complete income statement. For example, a cost accountant can use incremental analysis to determine how many additional units a company must sell to cover an increase in fixed costs. To do so, the cost accountant divides the increase in fixed costs by the contribution margin per unit.

5. Seven assumptions for CVP analysis are: (1) all revenue and variable cost behavior patterns are constant per unit and linear within the relevant range; (2) total contribution margin is linear within the relevant range and increases proportionally with volume; (3) total fixed costs are constant within the relevant range; (4) the cost accountant can separate mixed costs accurately into their fixed and variable elements; (5) sales and production are equal; (6) the sales mix remains constant for a multiproduct company; and (7) labor productivity, production technology, and market conditions do not change during the period.

6. Fixed costs remain constant in total as the volume or level of activity changes. The per-unit fixed cost is equal to the fixed costs divided by the number of units. Because the numerator remains constant, a change in the denominator will cause the per-unit fixed cost to change or vary. Variable costs change in total in proportion to the change in volume or the activity level. Because the numerator (variable costs) changes in proportion to the denominator (the volume or activity level), per-unit variable costs remain constant.

7. Margin of safety is the difference between a company's budgeted or actual sales and the break-even point. One can calculate margin of safety using units or dollars of sales revenue. The margin of safety percentage equals the margin of safety divided by budgeted or actual sales. Margin of safety is a measure of risk. Margin of safety indicates how close to a danger level the company is operating.

8. The degree of operating leverage measures how a percentage change in sales will affect profit. The degree of operating leverage equals contribution margin divided by profit before tax. The degree of operating leverage is also equal to one divided by the margin of safety percentage. This formula assumes that fixed costs remain constant when sales increase. A company's cost structure affects its degree of operating leverage. Cost structure is the relative proportions of fixed costs and variable costs. As a company's sales increase over the break-even point, the company's margin of safety increases and its degree of operating leverage decreases.

Chapter 9: Break-Even Point and Cost-Volume-Profit Analysis

9. (a) The per-unit contribution margin is $12 ($25 – $13). The contribution margin ratio is 48% ($12 ÷ $25).

The break-even point in units equals the fixed costs divided by the per-unit contribution margin. Thus, one calculates the break-even point in units as follows: $48,000 ÷ $12 per unit = 4,000 units

The break-even point in sales revenue equals the fixed costs divided by the contribution margin ratio. Thus, one calculates the break-even point in sales revenue as follows:
$48,000 ÷ 48% = $100,000

Alternatively, one can calculate the break-even point in sales revenue by multiplying the break-even point in units by the selling price. Thus, one can calculate the break-even point in units as follows: 4,000 units x $25 per unit = $100,000

(b) To calculate the number of units that Wyatt must sell to earn a profit before taxes of $150,000, add the target profit to the fixed costs and divide the sum by the per-unit contribution margin. Thus, one calculates the number of units that Wyatt must sell to earn a profit before taxes of $150,000 as follows:

($48,000 + $150,000) ÷ $12 per unit = $198,000 ÷ $12 per unit = 16,500 units

10. (a) The per unit contribution margin is $360 ($1,200 – $840). The contribution margin ratio is 30% ($360 ÷ $1,200). To determine the sales revenue that Norris must realize to have a profit after taxes of $1,080,000, first convert the profit after tax to the profit before tax by dividing the profit after tax by one minus the tax rate.

Profit before tax = $1,080,000 ÷ (1 – 0.4) = $1,080,000 ÷ 0.6 = $1,800,000

Add the profit before tax to the fixed costs and divide by the contribution margin ratio:

($720,000 + $1,800,000) ÷ 30% = $2,520,000 ÷ 0.3 = $8,400,000

(b) If profit before taxes equals 10 percent of sales, the profit before taxes equals $120 ($1,200 x 10%) multiplied by the number of units sold. One can view this $120 as an additional variable cost, then use the break-even formula to solve for the number of units that Norris must sell.

Units = FC ÷ (CM – P_uBT)

= $720,000 ÷ ($360 – $120) per unit = $720,000 ÷ $240 per unit = 3,000 units

Chapter 9: Break-Even Point and Cost-Volume-Profit Analysis

11. Margin of safety in units = 500,000 − 300,000 = 200,000 units

    Margin of safety in dollars of sales revenue = 200,000 units x $4 per unit = $800,000

    Margin of safety percentage = 200,000 ÷ 500,000 = 40%

12. First compute the weighted average contribution margin.

	Regular Model	Deluxe Model
Selling price	$100	$150
Variable costs	68	90
Contribution margin	$ 32	$ 60
Sales mix	75%	25%

    Weighted average contribution margin = ($32 x 75%) + ($60 x 25%) = $24 + $15 = $39

    Add the target profit before taxes to the fixed costs and divide the sum by the weighted average contribution margin to determine the total number of units sold.

    ($168,000 + $300,000) ÷ $39 per unit = $468,000 ÷ $39 per unit = 12,000 units

    To determine the number of units of the regular model and the number of units of the deluxe model that Vogle must sell, multiply the number of total units by the sales mix %.

    Regular model   12,000 x 75% = 9,000 units
    Deluxe model   12,000 x 25% = 3,000 units

13. The total cost line would begin at the y-axis at $1,800 and increase $12 per each member. The formula for the total cost line would be y= 12(x) + 1,800. The total revenue line would start at the origin and increase by $30 per member. The formula for the total revenue line would be y= 30(x) + 0. We can verify the break-even point by setting these two equations equal to each other or 12(x) - y + 1,800 = 30(x) - y. Solving for x, we would get 1,800=18(x) or x=(1,800/18)= 100 or 100 members.

14. The two points that create the line on the profit-volume graph are the total fixed cost on the y-axis at -1,800 and the break-even point. The algebraic formula for profit-volume line is y=(30-12)(x) - 1,800. The break-even point is when y=0, therefore x=(1,800/18) or 100 or 100 members.

15. The first step is to draw the axes and label the x-axis as volume and the y-axis as dollars. Second, plot the variable cost line as a linear function with the slope equal to the variable cost per unit. Third, plot the revenue line with a slope equal to the sales price. The area between the variable cost line and the revenue line represents total contribution margin. Fourth, graph total cost with a line running parallel to the variable cost line. The distance between the total cost line and the variable cost line represents fixed cost. The break-even point is where the total revenue line intersects the total cost line.

CHAPTER 10

RELEVANT INFORMATION FOR DECISION MAKING

CHAPTER OVERVIEW

Managers must manage organizational resources effectively and efficiently to achieve the organization's goals and objectives. As a part of this responsibility, managers must make decisions about the use of organizational resources. Managers use cost information in making many types of decisions. Accountants provide information and expertise to managers to help them make decisions.

To be useful, cost information must be relevant. Relevant costs are the costs logically associated with a particular decision. Relevant costing involves the use of pertinent cost information and the careful omission of irrelevant data in the decision-making process. Managers must consider all relevant revenues and costs in the following common decision-making situations: (1) asset replacements, (2) outsourcing a product or part, (3) scarce resource allocations, (4) special price determinations, (5) sales mix distributions, and (6) retention or elimination of product lines. Besides the relevant costs, managers must consider the qualitative aspects of the decisions. Sunk costs, offshoring, and segment margins are additional related concepts discussed in this chapter

The Appendix introduces linear programming, a mathematical technique used to solve multiple resource allocation dilemmas. In an environment of multiple constraints, cost accountants use linear programming to find the optimal solution from the set of feasible solutions.

CHAPTER STUDY GUIDE

Relevant costing is a process that focuses managerial attention on a decision's pertinent facts. Information must be associated with a decision, important to the decision-maker, and connect to or bear on some future endeavor in order for the information to be relevant. Incremental or differential revenue is the amount of revenue that varies across decision alternatives. A differential cost or incremental cost is an amount of cost that differs across the various decision alternatives. Incremental costs can be either variable or fixed. Most variable costs are relevant, but most fixed costs are not relevant.

Chapter 10: Relevant Information for Decision Making

The difference between the incremental revenue and incremental costs of a particular alternative is the positive or negative incremental benefit of that course of action. Management can compare the incremental benefits of various alternatives to decide on the most profitable or least costly alternative or set of alternatives. Two reasons that such comparisons could be difficult are (1) the concept of relevance is often individually determined, and (2) the increasing amount of information available. The cost accountant can easily identify and quantify some relevant factors, such as sales commissions and prime product costs, because they are integral parts of the accounting system. However, the accounting system does not record opportunity costs. Opportunity costs represent the potential benefit foregone through the selection of one course of action over another.

The need for specific information depends on how important the information is relative to management objectives. Both past and present information can be relevant if the information pertains to a future decision. Management considers relevancy in the short run and/or the long run. However, the longer into the future a decision's time horizon, the more managers can control or avoid the costs. Only information that has a bearing on future events is relevant in decision-making.

Historical or past costs generally associated with the acquisition of assets or resources are sunk costs. The cost of a machine in prior years is an example of a sunk cost. Management cannot recover sunk costs through any decision made currently or in the future. Therefore, sunk costs are never relevant costs. However, while the original price of the machine is not relevant, costs to maintain the machine and the market value of the machine are relevant costs.

Exhibit 10-1 provides data used to illustrate the relevant costs involved in an asset-acquisition decision. Exhibit 10-2 shows the relevant costs from the data provided in Exhibit 10-1.

Managers must make decisions on alternative courses of action. These alternative actions should be feasible solutions to problems or feasible methods to use in the attainment of management objectives. To determine the best course of action, management compares all incremental revenues, costs, and benefits of each course of action to a baseline alternative. Managers should select the course of action that provides the highest incremental benefit with a comprehensive consideration of the monetary effects to the company. The chosen course of action should be one that will make the business better off in the future.

Sometimes management chooses the "change nothing" alternative as a baseline. The "change nothing" alternative has a zero incremental benefit because it represents current conditions. Management should use the "change nothing" alternative as a baseline only when management perceives it to be the best available alternative. When the current situation is serious enough to warrant a plant closure, such as a government injunction to stop polluting river water, the "change nothing" alternative does not exist.

The concept of outsourcing refers to the buying of a product or service from an outside supplier rather than making the product or performing the service within the company. Outsourcing outside the home country of the business is referred to as offshoring. Offshoring is

Chapter 10: Relevant Information for Decision Making

controversial within the United States due to the belief that offshoring sends away employment opportunities that should have been available to U.S. citizens.

An outsourcing decision, also known as a make-or-buy decision, involves a comparison of the cost of manufacturing a component with the cost of purchasing the same item from outside suppliers. Exhibit 10-3 gives the motivations to outsource. In the manufacturing environment, managers must ensure that the right quality components will be available at the right time and at a reasonable price. Companies often ensure part availability by manufacturing the part themselves. However, management must also consider the best use of the available facilities. As illustrated in the text, the balance between nonstrategic reasons and strategic reasons for outsourcing is weighted heavy on the nonstrategic side.

Relevant information for the make-or-buy or outsourcing decision includes both quantitative and qualitative factors. Exhibit 10-4 lists relevant quantitative and qualitative factors that managers should consider in an outsourcing decision. Companies can sometimes reduce costs and obtain better products and services through outsourcing. However, outsourcing involves more risk. Exhibit 10-5 illustrates the risks of outsourcing various services with a pyramid. Risk factors to consider include (1) whether the company considers the function as crucial to its viability, (2) the function is related to the company's core competency, and (3) unresolved unsatisfactory results of outsourcing the function. For instance, the strategic direction and unique core competencies of firm should never be outsourced.

Variable production costs and incremental fixed costs (the avoidable fixed costs) are relevant in the outsourcing decision. Exhibit 10-6 provides data for a decision regarding the outsourcing of keyboards. Exhibit 10-7 shows the relevant quantitative factors for the outsourcing decision concerning the keyboards.

The opportunity costs of the facilities used by the production of one component over another are also relevant. Another relevant opportunity cost would be the increased throughput arising from the component being bought rather than made. Opportunity costs include the effect of bottlenecks because of increased production. Bottlenecks slow production and reduce throughput.

A serious outsourcing risk is the financial failure of a sole supplier. Qualitative issues may suggest that a quantitatively beneficial decision is unwise. Thus, theoretically short-run decisions can have long-run effects. Another example is a company manufacturing a part for which it expects an increase in demand for over the next few years. The company may need to expand its capacity, which increases fixed costs. Fixed costs therefore are better termed long-run variable costs when used for decision-making. Outsourcing for service firms can include product and process design activities, accounting and legal services, utilities, engineering services, and employee health services.

A scarce resource is a resource essential to a production or service activity but available only in limited quantity. Constraints develop on producing goods or providing services with only limited machine hours, skilled labor hours, raw materials, production capacity and other inputs that create limitations on producing goods or services. Management might be able to obtain more of a scarce resource in the long run. However, management must make the best use of the scarce resources it has in the short run.

Management considers the best use of scarce resources while recognizing specific company objectives. If maximizing company profits is the objective, the company should produce and sell the product having the highest contribution margin per unit of the scarce resource, assuming only one scarce resource. Exhibit 10-8 illustrates the calculation of contribution margin per unit of one scarce resource. Manufacturing companies, however, rarely have only one scarce resource. Linear programming is a method of mathematical programming used to assist management in determining the best use of scarce resources with multiple limiting factors. The appendix covers linear programming.

Management cannot easily determine all qualitative and quantitative aspects of resource allocation. Limiting production to a single product can pose substantial business risk by severely limiting the customer base. Products infrequently purchased limit the amount of product the company can sell. Continued production of slow-moving products will result in the ultimate failure of the business. Further, management should consider whether the company must make and sell low-profit products to support its high-profit products. Some products are complementary, which means that the company sells one product as a part of a package. For example, a camera company might sell film. A company that makes printers might also sell cartridges and paper.

Sales mix is the relative combination of quantities of sales of the various products that make up the total sales of a company. Some important factors that affect the sales mix of a company are product selling prices, sales force compensation, and advertising expenditures. A change in any or all of these factors can cause a company's sales mix to shift. Exhibit 10-9 provides the selling price, variable expenses, and contribution margin for each of three products and the fixed costs associated with these products. These data are used to illustrate the effects of changes in various factors on the sales mix. Managers must constantly monitor the relative selling prices of a company's products, both in respect to each other as well as to competitors' prices. Price may be influenced by such factors as fluctuations in demand or production/distribution cost, economic conditions, and competition. Due to the economic law of demand elasticity with respect to price, any shift in the selling price of one product in a multiproduct firm normally causes a change in the sales mix.

To maximize profit, managers must maximize total contribution margin rather than the per-unit contribution margin of individual products. Exhibit 10-10 provides sales volume and contribution margin for a company that makes multiple products.

A clear understanding of marketing is essential to the development of a marketing mix. To this end, management must consider the law of demand elasticity. Market demand reacts sharply to price changes if the demand for the product is highly elastic with respect to price. For such a product, a slight increase in price results in a much lower quantity demanded. On the other hand, a slight decrease in price would significantly increase the quantity demanded. However, if the demand for the product is inelastic with respect to price, the market demand will change relatively little when price changes. Management must plan pricing and shift production

Chapter 10: Relevant Information for Decision Making 243

accordingly. Exhibit 10-11 illustrates the effect of a price increase when the demand for the product is relative inelastic with respect to price.

In making a decision to change prices, management must consider the following quantitative factors: (1) the new per-unit contribution margin of the product, (2) short-term and long-term changes in product demand and production volumes generated by the price change, and (3) the best use of the company's scarce resources. In addition, management should consider the following qualitative factors: (1) effect of changes on customer goodwill, (2) customer loyalty toward the products, and (3) competitors' responses.

Sales force compensation also fits into the marketing equation. Sales commissions based on gross sales generally increase sales of high-priced items. However, the sale of high-priced items might not generate higher profits for the company. When designing compensation plans to increase profits, management should consider increasing commissions on products and services with higher product contribution margins. Product contribution margin equals the selling price minus variable production costs. Using product contribution margin to determine sales commissions can quickly motivate a company's sales force to sell items that generate higher profits. Exhibit 10-12 illustrates the effect of basing sales commissions on product contribution margin.

Another factor that can cause shifts in sales mix involves either adjusting the advertising budgets for each of the company's products or increasing the total advertising budget. Increased advertising budgets on certain products will likely increase sales of that item and increase sales of any related items. However, any increase in the advertising budget must generate a sufficient increase in sales to cover the advertising costs and any other incremental fixed costs. Exhibit 10-13 illustrates the calculation of an incremental benefit for a proposed advertising campaign.

A special order decision is a situation that requires management to calculate a reasonable sales price for production or service jobs outside the company's normal realm of operations. The sales price quoted on a special order job typically should be high enough to cover the job's variable costs, incremental fixed costs, and provide the desired profit.

Management might price special order jobs with a low-ball bid. A low-ball bid barely covers costs and might actually be below cost. A company could use a low-ball bid to penetrate a certain market segment. However, the customer could develop the expectation that the low-ball price will be the price for future orders. The company might accept private-label orders during slack periods to use available capacity more effectively. A private-label order is where the buyer's name appears on the product label. Selling prices on private-label special orders are usually set high enough to cover variable costs and partially cover ongoing fixed costs. When the company makes a product to customer specifications, or when good production is limited to a one-time run, management may set special price options to cover unusual costs. Exhibit 10-14 presents information used to determine a bid.

Management must consider the Robinson-Patman Act. This law prohibits companies from charging different prices for the same products unless the different prices do reflect related cost differences. Management must keep detailed legal justification for price differences. An ad hoc discount is a price concession that relates to real (or imagined) competitive pressures rather than to location of the merchandising chain or volume purchased. Management needs little legal justification for an ad hoc discount because the company bases such discounts on a competitive market. Management must use caution to avoid charges of price discrimination. The only justification for pricing differences on stocked items is a difference in distribution costs.

When managers make pricing decisions, they analyze the marketing environment. Management often works with a disaggregated statement of operating results that shows income for each product lines. Exhibit 10-15 illustrates product line income statements. The income of a product line often reflects allocated common fixed costs. Management should eliminate the common fixed costs from full production costs because the allocated common fixed costs are not relevant costs. Management should classify costs into the following categories: (1) costs attributable to a particular product but avoidable if the company eliminates the product, (2) costs directly associated with a product but unavoidable, and (3) costs incurred for the benefit of the whole company and allocated to the product lines.

The cost accountant should isolate and classify common expenses or irrelevant costs from the information presented to management for decisions. The cost accountant must also separate unavoidable costs directly associated with particular products.

Segment margin represents the excess of revenues over direct variable expenses and avoidable fixed expenses. Thus, segment margin is the amount available to cover unavoidable direct fixed expenses and common expenses and to provide profits. Thus, segment margin is the appropriate measure on which managers should base product continuation or elimination decisions. Exhibit 10-16 illustrates segment margin income statements.

Many costs appear to be avoidable but they are in fact not. For example, a divisional manager's salary might not be avoidable if the company eliminated the division. If the manager had significant experience, the company might transfer the manager to another area rather than terminate the manager. Sometimes management considers a decision to terminate a segment based on segment margin. Before making such a decision, management should examine the costs to "turn the product line around" and all the possible long-term ramifications of such a decision. As in all decisions, managers should explore qualitative as well as quantitative. Managers should consider factors such as the effects of a reduction in market assortment available to customers.

APPENDIX

Mathematical programming refers to a variety of techniques used to allocate limited resources among activities to achieve a specific goal or purpose. Linear programming is a method of mathematical programming used to find the optimal allocation of scarce resources in a situation involving one objective and multiple limiting factors.

The objective function is the linear mathematical equation that specifies the objective of a linear programming problem. A common objective is to maximize contribution margin or to minimize cost. A constraint is any type of restriction that limits management's pursuit of the

Chapter 10: Relevant Information for Decision Making 245

objective. A nonnegativity constraint specifies that negative values of physical quantities are not possible. Exhibit 10-17 shows product information and constraints for two products.

A feasible solution is a solution to a linear programming problem that does not violate any problem constraints. Integer programming is a mathematical programming technique that restricts all solutions for variables to whole numbers. The optimal solution is the solution to a maximization or minimization goal that provides the best answer to the allocation problem.

A decision variable is an unknown item for which the linear programming problem is to be solved. A mathematical equation represents the decision information. Management must determine the objective function and each of the constraints. Often, the objective function is to find the solution that either maximizes contribution margin or minimizes variable costs.

The following are the basic objective function formats for maximization and minimization problems:

Maximization problem:

Objective function: MAX $CM = CM_1X_1 + CM_2X_2$

Minimization problem:

Objective function: MIN $VC = VC_1X_1 + VC_1X_1$

where:

CM = contribution margin

CM_1 = contribution margin per unit of the first product

CM_2 = contribution margin per unit of the second product

X_1 = number of units of the first product

X_2 = number of units of the second product
VC = variable cost

VC_1 = variable cost per unit of the first product

VC_2 = variable cost per unit of the second product

Resource constraints are normally expressed as inequalities, and the following is the general formula for a less-than-or-equal-to resource constraint:

Resource constraint (1): $A_1X_1 + A_1X_1 \leq$ Resource 1

where:

X_1 = number of units of the first product

X_2 = number of units of the second product

Input-output coefficients indicate the rate at which each decision variable uses up or depletes the scarce resource. The coefficients used above (A_1 and A_2) are input-output coefficients. Exhibit 10-18 shows the mathematical formulas for an objective function and five constraints.

The graphical method of solving linear programming problems is useful when only two decision variables exist and when a problem has few constraints or two constraints and few decision variables. Exhibit 12-19 illustrates the graphical method of solving a linear programming problem. The graphical method consists of five steps:

1. State the problem in terms of a linear objective function and linear constraints.
2. Graph the constraints and determine the feasible region. The feasible region is the graphical space contained within and on all of the constraint lines.
3. Determine the coordinates of each corner (vertex) of the feasible region. A vertex is a corner point produced by the intersection of lines on a graph.
4. Calculate the value of the objective function at each vertex.
5. Select the optimal solution to the allocation problem. The optimal solution for a maximization problem is the one with the highest objective function value; the optimal solution of a minimization problem is the one with the lowest objective function value.

The simplex method is an iterative (sequential) algorithm that solves multivariable, multiconstraint linear programming problems. An algorithm is a logical step-by-step problem-solving technique (generally requiring the use of a computer) that continuously searches for an improved solution from the one previously computed until it determines the best answer. The simplex method begins with a mathematical statement of the objective function and constraints. The simplex method expresses the inequalities in the constraints as equalities to solve the problems algebraically.

A slack variable is a variable used in a linear programming problem that represents the unused amount of a resource at any level of operation. Slack variables are associated with less-than-or-equal-to ($\leq$) constraints. A surplus variable is a variable used in a linear programming problem that represents overachievement of a minimum requirement and is associated with greater-than-or-equal-to ($\geq$) constraints. Solving a linear programming problem using the simplex method requires either the use of matrix algebra or a computer.

Chapter 10: Relevant Information for Decision Making

SELF TEST

TRUE/FALSE

1. T F Managers make efficient decisions based on an analysis of "relevant" costs.

2. T F In the analysis of a specific decision, a cost that can be avoided by taking one action rather than another is relevant.

3. T F Incremental costs are relevant costs.

4. T F The relevant costs in a special pricing situation may include some fixed costs.

5. T F In allocating scarce resources, allocate the scarce resource to the products that produce the highest contribution margin per product unit.

6. T F In setting prices on special orders, managers need to be mindful of the effect of the special order on their regular business.

7. T F The segment margin measures income after the deduction of all variable expenses and avoidable fixed expenses.

8. T F In equipment replacement decisions, the cost of the old equipment is relevant.

9. T F The purchase price of a new machine is a relevant cost.

APPENDIX

10. T F The simplex method requires the manager to manually calculate a solution to the linear programming problem.

11. T F A corner solution is one that occurs at the intersection of two constraint equations.

12. T F In linear programming, the objective function and the constraint equations are linear.

13. T F The linear programming problem can have one or more objective functions.

14. T F The solution to the linear programming problem must lie in the feasible region.

15. T F The solution to the linear programming problem is an expression in terms of the decision variables

Chapter 10: Relevant Information for Decision Making

MULTIPLE CHOICE

1. Relevant costs do not include:

    A. future costs.
    B. opportunity costs.
    C. incremental costs.
    D. sunk costs.

2. Managers can make the best use of a scarce resource by producing products with:

    A. a high contribution margin per unit.
    B. a high contribution margin ratio.
    C. a high contribution margin per unit of scarce resource.
    D. low variable costs.

3. If a cost has no influence on a decision, it:

    A. cannot be a future cost.
    B. is not a sunk cost.
    C. is not a relevant cost.
    D. is merely a differential cost.

4. In evaluating the profitability of a product line, a cost is not relevant if it is:

    A. allocated.
    B. fixed.
    C. variable.
    D. fixed and avoidable.

5. In deciding whether to accept a special order, price should be sufficient to cover all:

    A. variable production costs.
    B. incremental costs.
    C. variable costs.
    D. fixed costs.

6. A relevant cost is a cost that is:

    A. pertinent to a decision.
    B. important.
    C. optimal.
    D. effective.

Chapter 10: Relevant Information for Decision Making 249

7. When new technology becomes available, the potential cost savings from the new equipment represents:

   A. an irrelevant cost.
   B. a sunk cost.
   C. an opportunity cost of keeping the old equipment.
   D. a cost of acquiring the new technology.

8. In deciding whether to make a part or purchase it, management considers which opportunity cost?

   A. the effect of a bottleneck through production
   B. purchase price of the part
   C. variable costs to produce the part
   D. fixed costs to produce the part

9. An ad hoc sales discount is:

   A. based on sales volume.
   B. an allowance for the inferior quality of goods that are marketed.
   C. a quantity discount.
   D. a discount based on competitive pressure.

10. An example of a fixed cost that would be relevant in deciding whether a product line is maintained is:

    A. the cost of raw materials.
    B. an allocation of depreciation on corporate headquarters.
    C. the rental cost of production space acquired under a short-term lease.
    D. the depreciation on special-use equipment.

11. A company should base normal sales price on total:

    A. variable costs.
    B. costs plus profit.
    C. incremental production costs.
    D. incremental product and period costs.

12. The energy costs to operate an old machine are $40,000 per year. A new machine that performs the same task consumes $10,000 of energy per year. In an analysis of relevant costs, you would include energy costs of:

    A. $20,000.
    B. $50,000.
    C. $70,000.
    D. $30,000.

Chapter 10: Relevant Information for Decision Making 250

13. Jenkins Company acquired an expensive machine three years ago for $1,000,000. Annual depreciation on the machine is $100,000. The machine has a market value of $250,000, and annual property taxes on the machine run $12,000. Which of these amounts are relevant in deciding whether the company should sell the machine?

    A. the purchase cost and the property taxes
    B. the market value and the annual depreciation
    C. the purchase cost and the annual depreciation
    D. the market value and the property taxes

14. The objective of sales mix analysis is to maximize:

    A. total organizational contribution margin.
    B. total organizational gross margin.
    C. total organizational profit.
    D. segment margin.

15. On December 31, 2006, BB Company considers whether it should buy a particular machine. A short time later, the company purchases the machine. On January 8, 2007, BB Company sells the machine. Of the two dates mentioned, the purchase cost of the machine is a relevant consideration on:

    A. December 31, 2006, only.
    B. January 8, 2007, only.
    C. December 31, 2006 and January 8, 2007.
    D. a date before December 31, 2006.

16. All other things being equal, corporate profits will increase faster by selling those products that generate the most:

    A. segment margin per unit.
    B. contribution margin per unit.
    C. gross margin per unit.
    D. profit per unit.

17. Mathis Company can continue to manufacture a component or buy the component from an outside supplier and rent the firm's unused manufacturing facilities to another company. If the company continues to manufacture the component instead of buying it from an outside supplier, the rent the company would receive for its unused manufacturing facilities is a(n):

    A. sunk cost.
    B. avoidable cost.
    C. incremental cost.
    D. opportunity cost.

Chapter 10: Relevant Information for Decision Making

18. If a company is operating at maximum capacity, the minimum special order price must cover:

    A. variable costs and incremental fixed costs associated with the special order plus foregone contribution margin on regular units not produced.
    B. variable costs associated with the special order.
    C. variable and fixed manufacturing costs associated with the special order.
    D. variable and incremental fixed costs associated with the special order.

19. A company might have good reason to retain a segment if the segment's revenues exceed:

    A. segment variable costs.
    B. segment variable and fixed costs.
    C. avoidable costs associated with the segment.
    D. all costs recorded by the segment.

APPENDIX

20. A and B are two major ingredients used in the production of X and Y, two products manufactured by Janley Co. In a profit-maximizing linear programming model, A and B will be represented as:

    A. constraints.
    B. independent variables.
    C. dependent variables.
    D. surplus variables.

21. In a linear programming problem, the objective is to solve for the unknown quantities of:

    A. slack.
    B. the decision variables.
    C. the dependent variables.
    D. the shadow prices.

22. Nonnegativity constraints confine the feasible solution of the linear programming problem to the:

    A. upper left-hand quadrant.
    B. lower left-hand quadrant.
    C. middle left-hand quadrant.
    D. upper right-hand quadrant.

23. Consider the following three equations:

   1. Max Sales = $100 X + $35Y
      Subject to:
   2. $21X + 10Y \leq 2{,}300$
   3. $3X + Y \leq 492$

   In this set of equations, the objective function is:

   A. equation 1.
   B. equation 2.
   C. equation 3.
   D. equations 1 and 2.

24. In a profit maximization problem where all of the constraints are physical product inputs (materials), the optimal solution will not:

   A. be in a feasible region.
   B. be a corner solution.
   C. maximize the value of the objective function.
   D. minimize the value of the objective function.

25. Normally, a company would use inequalities to represent mathematically:

   A. the objective function.
   B. the nonnegativity constraints.
   C. the dependent variables.
   D. resource constraints.

26. The five steps in the graphical method of solving a linear programming problem include:

   A. determining the space outside of the constraint lines.
   B. selecting the suboptimal solution.
   C. calculating the objective function's value at each vertex.
   D. stating the problem in terms of a quadratic equation.

27. Assume that an optimal solution to a linear programming problem lies at a point where the X-axis intersects with exactly one constraint line. In this case:

   A. only two resource constraints are binding.
   B. less than three resource constraints are binding.
   C. only one resource constraint is binding.
   D. less than four resource constraints are binding.

Chapter 10: Relevant Information for Decision Making

28. A company must use linear programming to solve resource allocation problems when there are multiple:

    A. products.
    B. constraints.
    C. objective functions.
    D. decision variables.

29. Finding the graphical solution to a linear programming problem is not possible when there are more than two:

    A. products.
    B. constraints.
    C. objective functions.
    D. decision variables.

30. The term used to describe a factor that limits production is:

    A. objective function.
    B. limit.
    C. constraint.
    D. restriction.

QUESTIONS AND PROBLEMS

1. What is a relevant cost?

2. Why are sunk costs not relevant to decisions?

3. Are all relevant factors quantifiable? Explain.

4. Why should management evaluate the viability of a product line without regard to allocated fixed costs or certain direct fixed costs?

5. What are opportunity costs? Why are opportunity costs relevant costs?

6. The deluxe model of Byrd Company is not performing according to management's expectations. The income statement for the deluxe model for the previous year is as follows:

Sales	$850,000
Variable costs	450,000
Contribution margin	$400,000
Fixed costs	600,000
Net income (loss) before taxes	$(200,000)

The fixed costs include the $70,000 salary for the manager of the deluxe model. Byrd Company would terminate the manager if it no longer produced the deluxe model. Fixed costs also include other expenses of $150,000 associated with the deluxe model. Included in the $150,000 of these other fixed costs is $36,000 in depreciation on equipment that has no resale value. The remaining fixed costs represent corporate overhead costs that Byrd Company has allocated to the deluxe model based on relative sales.

The president wants to drop the deluxe model, but he wants to see an analysis first. Prepare an income statement in a more useful format for the deluxe model. What would be the effect on the net income before taxes if Byrd Company drops the deluxe model?

7. Abel Company has only 120,000 pounds of raw materials for the next month. Due to a shortage, Abel Company can purchase no more raw materials. Abel can make product A, product B, or a combination of each. Product A has a contribution margin of $42 per unit and used 6 pounds of raw materials. Product B has a contribution margin of $30 per unit and uses 3 pounds of raw materials. Abel Company can sell all of the output that it can produce. Calculate the number of units of product A and the number of units of product B that Abel Company should make if Abel Company wants to maximize its contribution margin.

8. The following cost information pertains to the Laptop Division of Real Computers Co. based on monthly demand and sales of 100 units:

Unit Costs

Variable production costs:	
Direct material	$100
Direct labor	125
Variable overhead	50
Fixed production costs:	
Factory depreciation	20
Factory rent	40
Other	10
Total product costs	$345
Variable selling expenses	20
Fixed operating expenses	30

(a) For this part only, assume that the Laptop Division does not exist, but is instead an aspect of Real Computers Co.'s future plans. Real Computers Co. will establish the Laptop Division if the relevant information indicates the division will be profitable. For this decision, which of the previous costs would be relevant?

(b) For this part only, assume that the Laptop Division is evaluating whether it will accept a special order for 10 Laptops at $305 per unit. For this purpose, which of the costs would be relevant?

(c) For this part only, assume that the original cost information pertains to five Laptops that have been produced this period. For purposes of setting a minimum sales price, which costs are relevant?

Chapter 10: Relevant Information for Decision Making 258

APPENDIX

9. Why are linear programming techniques not required for the optimal allocation of a single scarce resource?

10. Why would an optimal solution never lie in the interior of the feasible region?

11. How can one identify slack resources in a graphical presentation of the linear programming problem and solution?

12. Why is a graphical approach to the solution of a linear programming problem often infeasible?

13. Why are nonnegativity constraints an important part of the formulation of the linear programming problem?

14. What are the major components of a linear programming problem?

15. The Courtney Manufacturing Company is trying to determine which combination of products it should produce in the upcoming period. Two recent developments have created severe limitations on the availability of inputs that are crucial to the production of Courtney's two main products: inline skates and skateboards. Courtney produces both products from a plastic "pellet" derived from a petroleum by-product. Because of recent events in OPEC, petroleum-based products are in very limited supply. Courtney's main supplier has stated that it would guarantee Courtney only 10,000 pounds of the plastic pellets in the coming period. Another problem that Courtney is presently confronting involves its labor supply. A labor strike currently plagues Courtney's main factory. The factory is operating with managerial labor alone. Thus, the company estimates that in the coming period it will have no more than 8,000 direct labor hours. Other information on the two products produced by the company follows:

	Inline Skates	Skateboards
Expected unit sales price	$ 40	$ 30
Variable costs per unit (including materials and labor)	$ 15	$ 12
Estimated fixed costs for the coming period	$ 10,000	$ 15,000
Pounds of plastic pellets per unit	2	3
Direct labor hours per unit	3	2
Estimated demand in units for the coming period	5,000	4,000

(a) What is the objective function?

(b) What is the solution to the linear programming problem that maximizes the objective function you described in part A? Use any viable solution method.

Chapter 10: Relevant Information for Decision Making

SELF TEST ANSWERS

TRUE/FALSE

1.	T	4.	T	7.	F	10.	F	13.	F
2.	T	5.	F	8.	F	11.	T	14.	T
3.	T	6.	T	9.	T	12.	T	15.	T

MULTIPLE CHOICE

1.	D	7.	C	13.	D	19.	C	25.	D
2.	C	8.	A	14.	C	20.	A	26.	C
3.	C	9.	D	15.	A	21.	B	27.	C
4.	A	10.	C	16.	B	22.	D	28.	B
5.	B	11.	B	17.	D	23.	A	29.	D
6.	A	12.	D	18.	A	24.	D	30.	C

QUESTIONS AND PROBLEMS

1. Relevant costs are simply those costs that are pertinent to a decision. These costs are future costs that vary across the possible decision alternatives. The set of relevant costs includes opportunity costs.

2. Sunk costs are not relevant because no action that can be taken at the present time can influence them. They are not avoidable, and they do not differ among alternatives under consideration.

3. No. Some critically important factors are very difficult to quantify. These qualitative factors are important and relevant to decisions. For example, factors such as quality control, reliability of delivery schedules, and the type of production technology are important factors in the make/buy decision, but they are difficult to quantify. A firm would certainly not want to discontinue production of a crucial product component and purchase the part from a firm that rated low on these dimensions.

4. Allocated fixed costs are irrelevant because they do not differ among the alternatives under consideration: keep the product line/delete the product line. Some direct fixed costs are irrelevant for the same reason. For example, depreciation on production equipment can be a direct fixed cost of a product line, but irrelevant to the decision if it has no alternative use. In other words, there is no opportunity cost associated with the use of the equipment.

Chapter 10: Relevant Information for Decision Making

5. Opportunity costs are the benefits foregone when a company chooses one course of action over another. Companies do not record opportunity costs in the accounting records. Companies may not be able to quantify opportunity costs with precision. Nevertheless, opportunity costs are relevant costs that managers should take into account when making decisions. Opportunity costs relate to future endeavors and differ between alternatives. Thus, opportunity costs are relevant costs.

6.
Sales	$850,000
Variable costs	450,000
Product contribution margin	$400,000
Less: Avoidable fixed costs [$70,000 + ($150,000 − $36,000)]	184,000
Product margin	$216,000

The corporate overhead costs are common fixed costs and are not relevant. These common fixed costs will remain the same and be allocated to other products if Byrd Company drops the deluxe model. The depreciation expense of $36,000 is a direct fixed cost, but it is not relevant because it is an allocation of a sunk cost. Thus, Byrd Company's net income before taxes would be $216,000 lower if it drops the deluxe model.

7.
Product	A	B
Contribution margin per unit	$42	$30
Divided by pounds of raw materials used	÷ 6	÷ 3
Contribution margin per pound of raw materials	$ 7	$10

Abel should not produce any units of product A. Abel should produce 40,000 units of product B only to maximize its contribution margin. The contribution margin is $360,000 greater from producing product B rather than product A. Product A has a higher contribution margin per unit, but product B has a higher contribution margin per pound of raw materials.

$$\frac{120{,}000 \text{ pounds of raw materials}}{6 \text{ pounds of raw materials per unit of A}} = 20{,}000 \text{ units of product A}$$

20,000 units of A x $42 per unit = $840,000 contribution margin, or
120,000 pounds x $7 per pound = $840,000 contribution margin

$$\frac{120{,}000 \text{ pounds of raw materials}}{3 \text{ pounds of raw materials per unit of B}} = 40{,}000 \text{ units of product B}$$

40,000 units of B x $30 per unit = $1,200,000 contribution margin, or
120,000 pounds x $10 per pound = $1,200,000 contribution margin

Advantage of producing product B: $1,200,000 − $840,000 = $360,000,
or 120,000 pounds x ($10 − $7) per pound = $360,000

Chapter 10: Relevant Information for Decision Making 263

8. (a) All of the costs are relevant because the company can avoid all of the costs.

(b) The costs that are relevant are the ones that can be avoided by simply rejecting the special order offer. The avoidable costs would include the $275 of variable production costs and the $20 of variable selling expenses. All of the other costs are irrelevant. Thus, the company might accept the special order if it could obtain a sales price in excess of $295.

(c) Once the company has produced the laptops, none of the production costs is avoidable. The only cost that the company can avoid is the $20 per unit in variable selling expenses. All other costs are irrelevant.

APPENDIX

9. If a company has only one scarce resource, optimal allocation simply requires using the scarce resource in the way that maximizes the contribution margin per unit of the scarce resource. A company must consider tradeoffs that exist if it has multiple scarce resources. Thus, unlike a problem with only one scarce resource, a problem with multiple scarce resources has the potential for substitution. Linear programming is necessary to identify the optimal mix of scarce inputs.

10. The optimal solution would never lie in the interior of the feasible region because that would be tantamount to concluding that no resource is scarce (because the optimal solution required no resource to be 100 percent consumed). In other words, if several resources are scarce, the scarcest of those resources is going to be wholly consumed in an optimal allocation. Thus, if a company consumes all of one resource, the optimal solution must be a corner solution rather than an interior solution.

11. Slack will be associated with all resources that are not part of the intersection at the optimal solution's vertex. The optimal solution's vertex identifies those constraints that are wholly consumed in the optimal solution. All other constraints will have some slack.

12. A graphical approach has limited applicability for two reasons. The first reason stems from the obvious problems of graphing in four or more dimensions. Another practical reason is that computer programs are available to solve linear programming problems at a much quicker rate than a manual graphical approach.

13. The nonnegativity constraint prevents an unreal solution from emerging in the linear programming analysis. For example, a company cannot have negative labor hours, negative machine time, negative material inputs, or negative production. The nonnegativity constraint precludes all corner solutions that contain such unreal numbers.

14. The major components of a linear programming problem are (1) an objective function that is to be maximized or minimized, (2) a set of equations that constrain the organization's ability to maximize the objective function, and (3) an additional set of constraints (such as non-negativity constraints) that confine the solution set to solutions that a company can implement.

15. (a) Max CM = ($25 x Inline skates) + ($18 x Skateboards)

(b) This problem has three corner solutions to be evaluated:

	Inline skates	Skateboards
First corner solution	2,667	0
Second corner solution	0	3,333
Third corner solution	800	2,800

The first corner solution reflects the direct labor constraint; the second corner solution reflects the plastic pellet constraint; the third corner solution is the intersection of the two constraints. Courtney should base the decision as to which combination of products to produce on the value of the objective function at each corner solution:

First corner solution: ($25 x 2,667) + ($18 x 0) = $66,675

Second corner solution: ($25 x 0) + ($18 x 3,333) = $59,994

Third corner solution: ($25 x 800) + ($18 x 2,800) = $70,400

The third corner solution is computed as follows:
Let X = inline skates and Y = skateboards

Objective function: Max CM = 25X + 30Y

Constraints:

Express the inequalities in the constraints as equalities to solve the problem algebraically.

2X + 3Y = 10,000   plastic constraint

3X + 2Y = 8,000   labor constraint

The values of the two constraints can be determined when one function equals the other, which is where the functions intersect. Rewrite the equations so that they are equal to the same value.

By subtracting the constant from each side of each equation, both equations can be set to zero:

2X + 3Y − 10,000 = 0
3X + 2Y − 8,000 = 0

Chapter 10: Relevant Information for Decision Making 265

Because $0 = 0$, set the equations to equal each other:
$2X + 3Y - 10,000 = 3X + 2Y - 8,000$

Add 8,000 to each side: $2X + 3Y - 2,000 = 3X + 2Y$

Subtract 2Y from each side: $2X + Y - 2,000 = 3X$

Subtract 2X from each side: $Y - 2,000 = X$

Reverse the sides of the equation: $X = Y - 2,000$

Replace X with $Y - 2000$ in one of the constraint equations: $2(Y - 2,000) + 3Y = 10,000$

Combine terms:

$2Y - 4,000 + 3Y = 10,000$

Add 4,000 to each side: $2Y + 3Y = 14,000$

Combine terms: $5Y = 14,000$

Divide both sides by 5: $Y = 2,800$

Replace Y with 2,800 in one of the constraint equations:
$2X + 3(2,800) = 10,000$ $2X + 8,400 = 10,000$

Subtract 8,400 from each side: $2X = 1,600$

Divide both sides by 2: $X = 800$

Thus, the third corner solution is to produce 800 units of X (inline skates) and 2,800 units of Y (skateboards). This decision would maximize the objective function at an expected level of $70,400. At this level of production, the company would consume all of the available direct labor hours and plastic pellets.

CHAPTER 11

ALLOCATION OF JOINT COSTS AND ACCOUNTING FOR BY-PRODUCTS

CHAPTER OVERVIEW

A company might use a single process that generates various outputs simultaneously. A single process that results in various outputs is a joint process. Joint processes are common in the extractive, chemical, agricultural, and food industries. The costs incurred in a joint process are joint costs. This chapter explains the accounting treatment for the outputs of a joint process including joint products, by-products, scrap, and waste.

This chapter discusses joint processes, the outputs of joint processes, and accounting for joint costs. A company allocates joint costs to joint products only, using a physical measure or a monetary measure. These allocations are necessary for financial reporting purposes, but managers should generally disregard such allocations in making business decisions.

Service businesses and not-for-profit organizations also incur joint costs for such things as advertising with multiple purposes. The chapter describes the required allocation of joint costs for not-for-profit organizations for financial reporting purposes.

CHAPTER STUDY GUIDE

The products resulting from a joint process that have a sales value include joint products, by-products, and scrap. Joint products are the main products of a joint process. Joint products include different grades of the same basic product. Each joint product has substantial sales value. By-products and scrap are incidental outputs of a joint process. Although by-products and scrap have sales value, their sales value alone would not be enough to justify the production process. By-products have a higher sales value than scrap. Waste is a residual output of a joint process, but waste has no sales value. Exhibit 11-1 illustrates a joint process output for the processing of chicken.

Management classifies the outputs after considering their relative sales value. The classification of an output might change over time because of changes in technology, consumer demand, or ecological factors.

Chapter 11: Allocation of Joint Cost and Accounting for By-Products

The point at which a company can first identify the outputs of a joint process as individual products is the split-off point. A process may have more than one split-off point. A company may sell the outputs at the split-off point or process some or all of the outputs further.

A joint cost is the total of all costs (direct material, direct labor, and manufacturing overhead) incurred in a joint process up to the split-off point. A company allocates the joint cost at the split-off point to the joint products in accordance with the cost principle. The allocation of joint costs is necessary for financial accounting purposes. However, the allocation of joint costs is not relevant to managerial decisions because joint costs are sunk costs. A sunk cost is a cost incurred in the past that a company cannot change regardless of managerial decisions.

A company assigns any costs incurred after the split-off point to the separate products for which the company incurred the costs. Exhibit 11-2 shows a model of a joint process with multiple split-off points in which all of the output consists of joint products.

Management must make four decisions regarding a joint process. Before beginning production, management must compare the total expected revenues from the outputs of a joint process to the total expected costs of the joint process. The expected costs include the joint costs and any expected separate processing and selling costs. If the total expected revenues exceed the total expected costs, managers must then decide whether the expected net income from the joint process is greater than the net income of other potential uses of the company's resources. If the joint process is the best use of the company's resources, the next two decisions that managers face occur at the split-off point. The third decision is how to classify the outputs of the joint process. The fourth decision is whether to sell the outputs at the split-off point or process some or all of them further. In making the fourth decision, management should compare the additional revenues from further processing to the additional costs of further processing. Exhibit 11-3 shows a flowchart that illustrates the decision points in a joint production process. Managers must have a sound estimate of the selling price for each type of joint process output in order to make decisions at any potential point of sale. Managers should base expected selling prices on cost and market factors.

Exhibit 11-4 contains cost information for the example the textbook uses to illustrate allocation of joint costs. Physical measurement allocation and monetary measure techniques are two methods for allocating joint process cost. The monetary measure allocation technique includes the following methods: (1) sales value at split-off allocation, (2) net realizable value at split-off allocation, and (3) approximated net realizable value at split-off allocation.

A simple, objective way to allocate joint cost at the split-off point is by using a physical measure. Physical measurement allocation uses a common physical characteristic as the basis for allocating joint costs. This method treats each unit of measure as equally desirable and assigns the same per-unit cost to each. Physical measurement allocation, unlike monetary measure allocation, provides an unchanging yardstick of output. Physical measures are especially useful in allocating joint costs to products with volatile selling prices. Companies in some rate-regulated industries must use physical measurement allocation. A primary disadvantage of the method is that it ignores the revenue-generating ability of individual joint products. Exhibit 11-5

Chapter 11: Allocation of Joint Cost and Accounting for By-Products

illustrates joint cost allocation based on physical measurement.

Monetary measure allocation is more complex than physical measure allocation. Monetary measure allocation uses six steps to allocate joint costs to joint products. The first step is to choose a monetary allocation base. The second step is to list the values that constitute the base for each joint product. The third step is to sum these values in step to obtain a total value for the list. The fourth step is to divide each individual value by the total to obtain a numerical proportion for each value. The sum of these proportions should be 100 percent. The fifth step is to multiply the joint cost by each proportion to obtain the amount to be allocated to each product. The sixth step is to divide the prorated joint cost for each product by the number of equivalent units of production for each product to obtain a cost per equivalent unit of production for valuation purposes.

The main benefit of using monetary measure allocation over physical measure allocation is that monetary measure allocation considers the relative ability of each product to generate a profit. Changes in price levels are a potential problem in using monetary measure allocation, but this potential problem is not significant in times of relatively stable prices. Accountants usually ignore changes in price levels in the accounting system.

The sales value at split-off point allocation assigns joint cost to joint products based on their relative sales values at the split-off point. Before a company can use this method, all joint products must be marketable at the split-off point. Exhibit 11-6 illustrates sales value at split-off point allocation of joint cost.

The net realizable value at split-off allocation allocates joint cost to joint products based on sales value at the split-off point minus all costs necessary to prepare and dispose of the products. Before a company can use this method, all joint products must be salable at the split-off point. Exhibit 11-7 illustrates joint cost allocation using the net realizable value at split-off method.

Frequently, some joint products are not marketable at the split-off point. In these cases, companies cannot use the sales value at split-off or net realizable value at split-off methods to allocate joint costs. The approximated net realizable value at split-off allocation is a method of allocating joint cost using a simulated net realizable value at the split-off point. A company computes the approximated value by subtracting incremental separate costs from the final sales price. Incremental separate costs are all costs incurred for each joint product between the split-off point and the point of sale. An underlying assumption of this method is that the additional revenues from further processing equal or exceed the additional costs from further processing and selling. Exhibit 11-8 illustrates joint cost allocation using the approximated net realizable value at split-off method.

Each of the methods for allocating joint cost has advantages and disadvantages. For most companies, the approximated net realizable value at split-off method results in the best assignment of joint cost. This method is the most flexible because it does not require a common physical measure or marketable products at the split-off point. However, this method is more

Chapter 11: Allocation of Joint Cost and Accounting for By-Products

complex because the company must estimate additional revenues and processing costs. Exhibit 11-9, a diagram, illustrates further processing and selling costs as compared to sales price for the example product cost allocation in the text.

Allocating joint cost is necessary in computing inventory values for manufacturing companies. However, the net realizable values of by-products and scrap can affect the allocation process.

The difference between by-products and scrap is one of degree. The appropriate method of accounting for by-products and scrap depends on the amount of the net realizable value of the by-products and/or scrap and the need for further processing after the split-off point. The need for inventory recognition increases with the increase in the sales value of by-products and/or scrap. The two approaches for accounting for by-products and scrap are the net realizable value approach and the realized value approach. Exhibit 11-10 contains the basic cost information the textbook uses to illustrate the accounting for by-products and scrap.

The net realizable value approach treats the net realizable value of by-products or scrap as a reduction in the joint cost of producing the primary products. If the by-products and/or scrap generate a loss, the company adds the loss to the cost of the joint products. The inventory value of the by-products or scrap is equal to their selling prices minus costs of processing and disposal. A company records the net realizable value of the by-products or scrap by debiting Work in Process Inventory—By-Products and Scrap. The offsetting credit can go to one of two accounts.

When a company credits Cost of Goods Sold—Joint Products, it may result in a slight mismatching of revenues and costs if the company creates the by-products or scrap in a different period than it sells the joint products. In addition, this approach results in a slight overstatement of the inventory values of the joint products.

When the company credits Work in Process—Joint Products, it results in a reduction of the costs of the joint products for both costs of goods sold and inventory. The chief advantage of this approach is timing because the company reduces the cost of the joint products at the same time it generates the by-products or scrap. The disadvantage of this approach is that it is less conservative than waiting to record revenues until the company actually sells the by-products or scrap.

Reducing joint cost for the net realizable value of by-products or scrap is the traditional method for these outputs. However, this method is not necessarily the best method for managerial decision making. By-products could be a significant source of income. In such cases, the accounting methods should help managers monitor the processing of the by-products and make good decisions. Unfortunately, the net realizable value method does not show the revenues, expenses, or profits from the by-products. Thus, this method does not provide adequate information for managerial decision making.

Under the realized value (or other income) approach for accounting for by-products or scrap, under the first presentation method, a company does not recognize any value for these

Chapter 11: Allocation of Joint Cost and Accounting for By-Products

products until it sells them. A company can show the revenue from the sale of by-products or scrap as Other Revenue on the income statement. A company includes the additional processing or disposal costs of the by-products or scrap with the cost of producing the primary products. This approach provides management with little useful information because it does not match the cost of producing the by-products or scrap with the revenues they generate.

Another presentation of the realized value approach shows the by-products or scrap revenues on the income statement net of their additional costs of processing and disposal. This approach shows the sale of by-products or scrap as Other Income on the income statement in the period of sale. This method matches the revenues from the by-products or scrap with the related storage, further processing, transportation, and disposal costs. This method provides detailed information on financial responsibility and accountability, which may lead to better control and improved performance.

Alternative presentations include depicting the realized value from the sale of the by-product or scrap as an addition to gross margin, a reduction of the cost of goods manufactured, or a reduction of the cost of goods sold.

Regardless of the method a company uses to account for by-products and scrap, it should establish a specific method before allocating joint cost to the primary products. Exhibit 11-11 shows four comparative income statements for the different methods of accounting for by-products and scrap.

All types of businesses create by-products, scrap, and waste. Managers have begun to understand the need for more cost information on these secondary outputs. Many companies are realizing the potential value of scrap as a source of significant additional revenue.

Companies that use job order costing systems can also generate by-products and scrap. However, joint products are not common in companies with job order costing systems. A company using a job order costing system should credit the value of the by-products or scrap to Manufacturing Overhead if a significant proportion of all jobs undertaken creates by-products or scrap. However, if the company can identify the by-products or scrap with only a few a specific jobs, it should reduce the Work in Process Inventory of the specific jobs in process for the value of the by-products or scrap.

Service businesses and not-for-profit organizations incur joint costs for different product lines, locations, and types of activities. Service businesses and not-for-profit organizations might incur joint costs for advertising multiple products, printing multipurpose documents, or holding multipurpose events. Service businesses may allocate joint costs using either a physical or monetary base. Joint costs in service businesses often relate to advertisements than to processes.

While service businesses may decide that allocating joint costs is unnecessary, AICPA Statement of Position (SOP) 98-2 requires not-for-profit organizations to allocate joint costs among the activities of fundraising, accomplishing an organizational program, or conducting an administrative function. The SOP helps external users determine amounts spent for activities.

Chapter 11: Allocation of Joint Cost and Accounting for By-Products

SELF TEST

<u>TRUE/FALSE</u>

1. T F Joint products are common in companies using job order costing systems

2. T F Monetary measure allocation is more complex than physical measure allocation.

3. T F Only manufacturing companies create by-products, scrap, and waste.

4. T F Scrap generally has a higher sales value than by-products.

5. T F The approximated net realizable value at split-off method usually results in the best assignment of joint cost.

6. T F Monetary measure allocation of joint costs considers the relative ability of each product to generate a profit.

7. T F Under the realized value approach for accounting for by-products or scrap, a company does not recognize any value for these products until it sells them.

8. T F Before a company can use the sales value at split-off point allocation method for allocating joint cost, all joint products must be marketable at the split-off point.

9. T F Not-for-profit organizations must allocate joint costs for financial reporting purposes.

10. T F The net realizable value approach of accounting for by-products and scrap treats the net realizable value of these outputs as a reduction in the joint cost of producing the primary products.

11. T F Under all presentations of the net realizable value approach, a company credits Cost of Goods Sold—Joint Products for the net realizable value of by-products and scrap.

12. T F A primary advantage of the physical measure method of allocating joint cost is that it considers the revenue-generating ability of individual joint products.

13. T F A company using a job order costing system should credit the value of by-products or scrap to Manufacturing Overhead if a significant proportion of all jobs undertaken creates by-products or scrap.

14. T F Waste has a higher sales value than scrap.

15. T F Service businesses might decide that allocating joint costs is not necessary.

Chapter 11: Allocation of Joint Cost and Accounting for By-Products

MULTIPLE CHOICE

1. Which of the following outputs of a joint process has no sales value?

    A. joint products
    B. by-products
    C. waste
    D. scrap

2. In recording by-products or scrap under the net realizable value approach, a company would initially debit:

    A. Cost of Goods Sold—Joint Products.
    B. Cost of Goods Sold—By-Products and Scrap.
    C. Work in Process—Joint Products.
    D. Work in Process—By-Products and Scrap.

3. In recording by-products or scrap under the net realizable value approach, a company would initially credit:

    A. Cost of Goods Sold—Joint Products or Work in Process—Joint Products.
    B. Cost of Goods Sold—By-Products and Scrap.
    C. Other Income or Other Revenue.
    D. Work in Process—By-Products and Scrap.

4. In recording by-products or scrap under the net realizable value approach, to record a sale of by-product, a company may debit:

    A. Cost of Goods Sold—Joint Products or Work in Process—Joint Products.
    B. Cost of Goods Sold—By-Products or Work in-Process—By-Products.
    C. Finished Goods Inventory—By-Products.
    D. Cash or Accounts Receivable

5. In recording by-products or scrap under the net realizable value approach, to record a sale of by-product, a company may credit:

    A. Cost of Goods Sold—Joint Products or Work in Process—Joint Products.
    B. Cost of Goods Sold—By-Products and Scrap or Work in-Process—By-Products.
    C. Finished Goods Inventory—By-Products.
    D. Other Income or Other Revenue.

Chapter 11: Allocation of Joint Cost and Accounting for By-Products

6. If a company using a job order costing system creates by-products or scrap for only a few specific jobs, what account should it credit for the value of the by-products or scrap?

    A. Manufacturing Overhead
    B. Cost of Goods Sold
    C. Other Income
    D. Work in Process Inventory of the specific jobs

7. Which approach to accounting for by-products and scrap matches the cost of producing the by-products or scrap with the revenues they generate?

    A. Realized Value—Other Revenue Method
    B. Realized Value—Other Income Method
    C. Net Realizable Value—Work In Process Method
    D. Net Realizable Value—Cost of Goods Sold Method

8. Which type of output is not common in companies that use job order costing systems?

    A. Waste
    B. Scrap
    C. By-Products
    D. Joint products

9. Before a company can use the sales value at split-off method of allocating joint costs, all joint products must be:

    A. marketable at the split-off point.
    B. marketable after further processing.
    C. accompanied by by-products.
    D. accompanied by scrap.

10. Joint costs in service businesses often relate to:

    A. processes.
    B. advertisements.
    C. income taxes.
    D. direct labor.

11. Under the net realizable value approach to accounting for by-products and scrap, any loss generated by the by-products and scrap is:

    A. recognized as a period expense.
    B. added to the cost of the joint products.
    C. subtracted from the cost of the joint products.
    D. recognized as an extraordinary loss.

Chapter 11: Allocation of Joint Cost and Accounting for By-Products

12. Which of the following is NOT an acceptable method of presenting the realized value of by-products and scrap on the income statement?

    A. as Other Revenue
    B. as Other Income
    C. as an addition to gross margin
    D. as an addition to joint product revenues

13. AICPA Statement of Position 98-2 requires what type of organization to allocate joint costs?

    A. manufacturing companies
    B. retail companies
    C. not-for-profit organizations
    D. service businesses

14. If a service business incurs advertising as a joint cost, it cannot:

    A. allocate the joint cost using a physical measure.
    B. allocate the joint cost using a monetary measure.
    C. decide not to allocate the joint cost.
    D. allocate joint costs to inventory.

15. If a company using a job order costing system creates by-products or scrap for most of its jobs, what account should it credit for the value of the by-products or scrap?

    A. Manufacturing Overhead
    B. Work in Process Inventory
    C. Other Income
    D. Other Revenue

16. The primary advantage of using a monetary measure over a physical measure to allocate a joint cost is that it:

    A. is much simpler.
    B. recognizes the relative ability of each product to generate a profit.
    C. is not affected by changes in prices.
    D. never requires that products be marketable at the split-off point.

17. Which accounting principle requires joint cost allocation for inventory valuation for financial reporting purposes?

    A. materiality principle
    B. cost principle
    C. conservatism
    D. objectivity principle

Chapter 11: Allocation of Joint Cost and Accounting for By-Products

18. After the split-off point, joint cost is a(n):

    A. sunk cost.
    B. opportunity cost.
    C. period cost.
    D. relevant cost.

19. Any costs incurred after the split-off point are assigned to:

    A. Cost of Goods Sold.
    B. Manufacturing Overhead.
    C. the separate products for which those costs were incurred.
    D. a period expense.

20. A company should process a product further after the split-off point if:

    A. the additional revenues from further processing exceed the additional costs.
    B. the sales price of a product exceeds its total cost.
    C. the additional revenues from further processing exceed the product's total cost.
    D. the sales price of a product exceeds the additional costs.

21. A major advantage of physical measure allocation of joint cost is that it:

    A. is the only method that considers the ability of a product to generate a profit.
    B. is not affected by changing prices.
    C. requires that all joint products be marketable at the split-off point.
    D. provides a better matching of revenues and expenses.

22. Which method provides the best joint cost assignment for most companies?

    A. physical measure allocation
    B. sales value at split-off
    C. net realizable value
    D. approximated net realizable value

23. Which method of accounting for by-products and scrap provides the best information for managerial control?

    A. Realized Value—Other Revenue Method
    B. Realized Value—Other Income Method
    C. Net Realizable Value—Work In Process Method
    D. Net Realizable Value—Cost of Goods Sold Method

Chapter 11: Allocation of Joint Cost and Accounting for By-Products

24. Caster Company uses a joint process to produce two products—widgets and wonders. The joint cost was $400,000. The company produced 3,000 widgets and 5,000 wonders. Widgets sell for $50 per unit, and wonders sell for $90 per unit. The cost to dispose of the widgets is $10 per unit and the cost to dispose of the wonders is $14 per unit. What is the joint cost allocated to widgets using the sales value at split-off method?

A. $96,000
B. $100,000
C. $300,000
D. $304,000

25. Caster Company uses a joint process to produce two products—widgets and wonders. The joint cost was $400,000. The company produced 3,000 widgets and 5,000 wonders. Widgets sell for $50 per unit, and wonders sell for $90 per unit. The cost to dispose of the widgets is $10 per unit and the cost to dispose of the wonders is $14 per unit. What is the joint cost allocated to wonders using the sales value at split-off method?

A. $96,000
B. $100,000
C. $300,000
D. $304,000

26. Caster Company uses a joint process to produce two products—widgets and wonders. The joint cost was $400,000. The company produced 3,000 widgets and 5,000 wonders. Widgets sell for $50 per unit, and wonders sell for $90 per unit. The cost to dispose of the widgets is $10 per unit and the cost to dispose of the wonders is $14 per unit. What is the joint cost allocated to widgets using the net realizable value method?

A. $96,000
B. $100,000
C. $300,000
D. $304,000

27. Caster Company uses a joint process to produce two products—widgets and wonders. The joint cost was $400,000. The company produced 3,000 widgets and 5,000 wonders. Widgets sell for $50 per unit, and wonders sell for $90 per unit. The cost to dispose of the widgets is $10 per unit and the cost to dispose of the wonders is $14 per unit. What is the joint cost allocated to wonders using the net realizable value method?

A. $96,000
B. $100,000
C. $300,000
D. $304,000

Chapter 11: Allocation of Joint Cost and Accounting for By-Products

28. Wright Company produces three products. Wright can sell each of the three products at the split-off point or sell them for a higher price after further processing. Information about these three products follows:

Product	A	B	C
Sales value after further processing	$600,000	$350,000	$240,000
Sales value at split-off	500,000	300,000	200,000
Additional costs of further processing	60,000	180,000	55,000
Allocated joint cost	300,000	190,000	100,000

Which product(s) should Wright Company process further?

A. Product A
B. Product B
C. Product C
D. Products A and C

29. Jones Company produced 40,000 pounds of Product AZ and 10,000 pounds of Product XY in a joint process. The joint cost was $300,000. Product AZ sells for $10 per pound, and Product XY sells for $20 per pound. Using physical measure allocation, how much joint cost would be allocated to Product AZ?

A. $60,000
B. $100,000
C. $200,000
D. $240,000

30. Jones Company produced 40,000 pounds of Product AZ and 10,000 pounds of Product XY in a joint process. The joint cost was $300,000. Product AZ sells for $10 per pound, and Product XY sells for $20 per pound. Using physical measure allocation, how much joint cost would be allocated to Product XY?

A. $60,000
B. $100,000
C. $200,000
D. $240,000

Chapter 11: Allocation of Joint Cost and Accounting for By-Products

QUESTIONS AND PROBLEMS

1. What is a joint cost? Why must a company allocate joint costs? Why is the allocation of joint costs not relevant to managerial decisions?

2. What are the four decisions that management must make regarding a joint process?

3. What is physical measurement allocation of joint cost? What are the advantages and disadvantages of physical measurement allocation of joint cost?

Chapter 11: Allocation of Joint Cost and Accounting for By-Products

4. What are the six steps in allocating joint cost using a monetary measure allocation?

5. What is the main benefit of using monetary measure allocation of joint cost? What is a potential problem in using monetary measure allocation of joint cost?

6. How does a company allocate joint cost using the sales value at split-off method? What criterion must the joint products meet before a company can use this method?

Chapter 11: Allocation of Joint Cost and Accounting for By-Products

7. How does a company allocate joint cost using the net realizable value at split-off method? What criterion must the joint products meet before a company can use this method?

8. How does a company allocate joint cost using the approximated net realizable value at split-off method? What are the advantages and disadvantages of this method?

9. How does a company account for by-products and scrap using the net realizable value approach? What are the two methods that a company can use under this approach?

10. How does a company account for by-products and scrap using the realized value approach? What are the two methods that a company can use under this approach?

11. How does a company that uses a job order costing system account for by-products and scrap?

12. Parker Company uses a joint process to produce two chemicals—AC22 and SD14. The company produced 10,000 gallons of AC22 and 30,000 gallons of SD14. AC22 sells for $10 per gallon, and SD14 sells for $12 per gallon. The joint cost was $80,000. Compute the joint cost allocated to each product using physical measure allocation.

Chapter 11: Allocation of Joint Cost and Accounting for By-Products

13. Pillow Company uses a joint process to produce two chemicals—XB57 and JG42. The joint cost was $1,200,000. The company produced 20,000 barrels of XB57 and 25,000 barrels of JG42. Product XB57 sells for $40 per barrel, and Product JG42 sells for $48 per barrel. The cost to dispose of the XB57 is $8 per barrel, and the cost to dispose of the JG42 is $14 per barrel. Compute the joint cost allocated to each product using each of the following methods:

   (a) sales value at split-off method

   (b) net realizable value method

14. Collins Company produces two products—X59 and Z47—using a joint process. Collins Company produced 10,000 units of X59 and 8,000 units of Z47. Product X59 sells for $86 per unit after further processing. Further processing costs are $6 per unit and disposal costs are $20 per unit. Collins Company sells Product Z47 at the split-off point for $50 per unit. Disposal costs are $10 per unit. The joint cost was $640,000. Compute the joint cost allocated to each product using the approximated net realizable value method.

15. Cline Company uses a joint process that results in two joint products and one by-product J10. Cline produced 5,000 units of J10. By-product J10 sells for $20. The cost to dispose of J10 is $4 per unit. The joint cost for all products was $600,000. Prepare journal entries to record the cost of the by-products using each of the following methods:

(a) net realizable value approach, Work In Process method

(b) net realizable value approach, Cost of Goods Sold method

Chapter 11: Allocation of Joint Cost and Accounting for By-Products

SELF TEST ANSWERS

TRUE/FALSE

1.	F	4.	F	7.	T	10.	T	13.	T
2.	T	5.	T	8.	T	11.	F	14.	F
3.	F	6.	T	9.	T	12.	F	15.	T

MULTIPLE CHOICE

1.	C	7.	B	13.	C	19.	C	25.	C
2.	D	8.	D	14.	D	20.	A	26.	A
3.	A	9.	A	15.	A	21.	B	27.	D
4.	D	10.	B	16.	B	22.	D	28.	A
5.	C	11.	B	17.	B	23.	B	29.	D
6.	D	12.	D	18.	A	24.	B	30.	A

QUESTIONS AND PROBLEMS

1. A joint cost is the total of all costs (direct material, direct labor, and manufacturing overhead) incurred in a joint process up to the split-off point. A company allocates the joint cost at the split-off point to the joint products in accordance with the cost principle. The allocation of joint costs is necessary for inventory valuation for financial accounting purposes. The allocation of joint costs is not relevant to managerial decisions because joint costs are sunk costs. A sunk cost is a cost incurred in the past that a company cannot change regardless of managerial decisions.

2. The first decision is deciding whether to produce goods using the joint process. The second decision is deciding whether the expected net income from the joint process is greater than the net income of other potential uses of the company's resources. The third decision is how to classify the outputs of the joint process at the split-off point. The fourth decision is whether to sell the outputs at the split-off point or process some or all of them further.

3. Physical measurement allocation uses a common physical characteristic as the basis for allocating joint costs. This method treats each unit of measure as equally desirable and assigns the same per-unit cost to each. The advantages of physical measurement allocation are that it provides an unchanging yardstick of output, and it is especially useful in allocating joint costs to products with volatile selling prices. Companies in some rate-regulated industries must use physical measurement allocation. A primary disadvantage of the method is that it ignores the revenue-generating ability of individual joint products.

4. The first step is to choose a monetary allocation base. The second step is to list the values that constitute the base for each joint product. The third step is to sum these values in step to obtain a total value for the list. The fourth step is to divide each individual value by the total to obtain a numerical proportion for each value. The sum of these proportions should total 100

Chapter 11: Allocation of Joint Cost and Accounting for By-Products 286

percent. The fifth step is to multiply the joint cost by each proportion to obtain the amount to be allocated to each product. The sixth step is to divide the prorated joint cost for each product by the number of equivalent units of production for each product to obtain a cost per equivalent unit of production for valuation purposes.

5. The main benefit of using monetary measure allocation is that it considers the relative ability of each product to generate a profit. A potential problem in using monetary measure allocation is changes in price levels, but this potential problem is not significant in times of relatively stable prices. Accountants usually ignore changes in price levels in the accounting system.

6. The sales value at split-off point allocation assigns joint cost to joint products based on their relative sales values at the split-off point. Before a company can use this method, all joint products must be marketable at the split-off point.

7. The net realizable value at split-off allocation allocates joint cost to joint products based on sales value at the split-off point minus all costs necessary to prepare and dispose of the products. To use this method, all joint products must be salable at the split-off point.

8. The approximated net realizable value at split-off allocation is a method of allocating joint cost using a simulated net realizable value at the split-off point. A company computes the approximated value by subtracting incremental separate costs from the final sales price. Incremental separate costs are all costs incurred for each joint product between the split-off point and the point of sale. An underlying assumption of this method is that the additional revenues from further processing equal or exceed the additional costs from further processing and selling. An advantage of this method is that it is the most flexible because it does not require a common physical measure or marketable products at the split-off point. A disadvantage of this method is that it is more complex because the company must estimate additional revenues and processing costs.

9. The net realizable value approach treats the net realizable value of by-products or scrap as a reduction in the joint cost of producing the primary products. If the by-products and/or scrap generate a loss, the company adds the loss to the cost of the joint products. The inventory value of the by-products or scrap is equal to their selling prices minus costs of processing and disposal. A company records the net realizable value of the by-products or scrap by debiting Work in Process Inventory—By-Products and Scrap. The two methods of making the offsetting credit are the Cost of Goods Sold method and the Work in Process method. Under the Cost of Goods Sold method, a company credits Cost of Goods Sold—Joint Products. Under the Work in Process method, the company credits Work in Process—Joint Products.

10. The realized value approach for accounting for by-products or scrap does not recognize any value for these products until the company sells them. The two methods of recognizing the value of the by-products and scrap are the Other Revenue method and the Other Income method. Under the Other Revenue method, a company shows the revenue from the sale of by-products or scrap as Other Revenue on the income statement. Under the Other Revenue method, a company

Chapter 11: Allocation of Joint Cost and Accounting for By-Products 287

includes the additional processing or disposal costs of the by-products or scrap with the cost of producing the primary products. The Other Income method shows the by-products or scrap revenues on the income statement as Other Income. The Other Income is the revenue from the by-products and scrap net of their additional costs of processing and disposal.

11. A company using a job order costing system should credit the value of the by-products or scrap to Manufacturing Overhead if a significant proportion of all jobs undertaken creates by-products or scrap. However, if the company can identify the by-products or scrap with only a few specific jobs, it should reduce the Work in Process Inventory of the specific jobs in process for the value of the by-products or scrap.

12. Total Joint Cost Per Gallon = $80,000 ÷ 40,000 gallons = $2 per gallon

Product	Gallons	Cost per Gallon	Allocated Cost
AC22	10,000	$2	$20,000
SD14	30,000	2	60,000
	40,000		$80,000

13. (a) sales value at split-off method

Product	Barrels	Selling Price	Revenue	Decimal	Joint Cost	Allocated Cost
XB57	20,000	$40	$ 800,000	0.40	$1,200,000	$480,000
JG42	25,000	48	1,200,000	0.60	1,200,000	720,000
	45,000		$2,000,000			$1,200,000

(b) net realizable value method

Product	Barrels	Unit Net Realizable Value	Total Net Realizable Value	Decimal	Joint Cost	Allocated Cost
XB57	20,000	$32	$ 640,000	0.43	$1,200,000	$516,000
JG42	25,000	34	850,000	0.57	1,200,000	684,000
	45,000		$1,490,000			$1,200,000

14.

Product	Units	Approximate Unit Net Realizable Value	Approximated Total Net Realizable Value	Decimal	Joint Cost	Allocated Cost
X59	10,000	$60	$ 600,000	0.65	$640,000	$416,000
Z47	8,000	40	320,000	0.35	640,000	224,000
	18,000		$920,000			$640,000

15. (a) net realizable value approach, Cost of Goods Sold method

Work in Process Inventory—By-Products and Scrap   80,000
    Cost of Goods Sold—Joint Products   80,000

To recognize the net realizable value of by-product J10: [5,000 x ($20 – $4)] = 80,000

(b) net realizable value approach, Work In Process method

Work in Process Inventory—By-Products and Scrap   80,000
    Work in Process Inventory—Joint Products   80,000

To recognize the net realizable value of by-product J10: [5,000 x ($20 – $4)] = 80,000

CHAPTER 12

INTRODUCTION TO COST MANAGEMENT SYSTEMS

CHAPTER OVERVIEW

Managers are concerned about the impact their actions will have on costs incurred and benefits received. Financial experts, especially accountants are primarily responsible for providing measures of these costs and benefits.

Cost accounting information produced for financial reporting purposes is often of little value to managers. The information is historical and may be too highly aggregated to be useful for management's purposes. The cost information needed for management purposes must be current and relevant for a particular purpose.

The internal use of cost accounting information, especially for cost management purposes, is receiving increased attention as companies redesign their cost accounting systems. A cost management system is an integral part of an organization's overall management information and control systems. This chapter emphasizes the main factors that determine the structure and success of a cost management system, factors that affect the design of the system, and the elements of the system.

CHAPTER STUDY GUIDE

Managers need many kinds of information to manage an organization successfully. Exhibit 12-1 illustrates the types of information that managers need to perform their functions as well as requirements of external parties in performing their investment and credit granting functions. Organizations have management control systems in order to implement strategic and operating plans and the means to provide comparison to planned results for management control purposes. A management information system is a part of an organization's information and control system. A management information system consists of interrelated elements that collect, organize, and communicate information to managers so that they may perform their managerial functions. The management information system is computerized in most modern organizations. Managers can readily access information in computers and use it to predict outcomes of decision alternatives.

Chapter 12: Introduction to Cost Management Systems

The management information system is a part of the management control system. As Exhibit 12-2 illustrates, a control system has four primary components: (1) a detector or sensor, (2) an assessor, (3) an effector, and (4) a communications network. A detector or sensor identifies what is happening in the process being controlled. An assessor is a device that determines the significance of what is happening. An effector is a device that provides feedback for modifying behavior that the assessor determines to be necessary. A communications network transmits information between the detector and the assessor and between the assessor and the effector. Management uses these components to gather information about actual company occurrences, make comparisons against plans, make necessary changes and ensure communication among appropriate parties.

A management control system requires managerial judgment because the information is subject to different interpretations. As such, a managerial control system may also be referred to as a "black box" or an operation whose exact nature cannot be observed. A management control system should guide managers in the design and implementation of strategies to achieve organizational goals and objectives. Exhibit 12-3 shows the organizational role of cost management systems.

Control systems for a business might include a statistical control process to monitor and evaluate quality or procedures to screen potential suppliers.

A cost management system is an important part of the management information and control system. The cost management system consists of a set of formal methods developed for planning and controlling cost-generating activities relative to its short-term and long-term strategies. An effective cost management system should help managers achieve short-term profitability and maintain a long-term competitive position. Managers use a cost management system to manage core competencies, to exploit perceived opportunities and develop tactics and strategies to overcome threats. Managers use a cost management to link plans and strategies to actual performance. Managers achieve short-term profitability and long-term competitive advantage by using an effective cost management system.

Exhibit 12-4 lists the differences in the information needs for short-run success and long-run success. In the short run, profitability depends on controlling costs in relation to revenues, making efficient use of organizational resources. Managers need timely information about specific costs to make these operational decisions. Long-run survival requires the company to acquire the right inputs from the right suppliers, sell the right mix of products to the right customers, and use the most appropriate distribution channels. Managers need reasonably accurate information on a periodic basis to make these strategic decisions.

As Exhibit 12-5 illustrates, the information generated by the cost management system should benefit all functional areas of the company. A cost management system has six main goals: (1) develop reasonably accurate product costs, (2) assess product/service life-cycle performance, (3) improve understanding of processes and activities, (4) control costs, (5) measure performance, and (6) allow the pursuit of organizational strategies. Accurate product costs are of primary importance. However, costs do not have to be the most accurate possible because the benefits of the more accurate costs should exceed the costs of providing the increased accuracy. Improvements in technology such as bar coding and radio frequency identification have made tracing costs easier.

Management uses the product or service costs generated by the cost management system in managerial processes. These processes include planning, preparing financial statements, assessing product or service profitability, assessing overall profitability, setting prices for cost-plus contracts, and establishing a basis for performance measurements. Thus, if costs are not reasonably accurate, the output of these processes will not be suitable for purposes of control and decision-making.

The financial accounting system does not reflect life-cycle information. The cost management system should provide information about life-cycle performance. Managers need life-cycle information to relate costs incurred in one stage of the life cycle to costs and profits in other stages. A cost management system should help managers understand business processes and organizational activities. Managers need to understand these processes and activities to make cost-effective improvements in production and processing systems.

Cost control was the original purpose of a cost accounting system. In the global business environment, cost control remains an important function of a cost management system. Management can control a cost only when (1) management monitors the related activity, (2) management knows the cost driver, and (3) the information is available. The information produced by a cost management system should also help managers measure and evaluate performance, evaluate investment opportunities as well as human and equipment performance.

A cost management system should generate information necessary to define and implement organizational strategies. Strategy is the link between goals, objectives and operational activities. The information provided by the cost management system allows managers to perform strategic analysis on issues such as assessing core competencies and organizational constraints from a cost-benefit perspective. Management can also use the information to evaluate the positive and negative aspects of strategic and operational plans. Because managers must evaluate the tradeoffs between short-term costs and long-term benefits, the cost management system is vital to the generation of information for effective strategic resource management. Flexibility is essential. A cost management system must be dynamic and creative to adapt to management's changing information needs in developing competitive strategies especially in innovation and new business practice.

Managers and accountants must be aware of the unique characteristics of their organizations. Every organization needs a cost management system tailored to its circumstances. However, some factors are important in the design of any cost management system. Exhibit 12-6 illustrates a flowchart of these factors.

A company's legal nature reflects its organizational form. The selection of organizational form has a lasting influence on the organization. The organizational form affects the cost of

Chapter 12: Introduction to Cost Management Systems

raising capital, operating the business including taxation issues and litigation. A company may operate in the form of (1) a corporation, (2) a general partnership, (3) a limited partnership, (4) a limited liability partnership (LLP), or (5) a limited liability company (LLC). Most large companies operate as corporations. Smaller businesses or joint ventures between large businesses may operate as partnerships or limited liability companies. Limited liability partnerships and limited liability companies allow better control of legal costs by providing more protection for a partner's personal assets in the event of litigation than does a general partnership.

Organizational form also determines who has the legal authority to make decisions for the company. In a general partnership, each partner has the legal right to make business decisions. A corporation has centralized management because the shareholders act through a board of directors to manage the corporation. The board of directors hires professional managers to manage the company on a regular basis. A limited liability partnership and a limited liability company also have degrees of centralized management.

Top management is responsible for establishing an organizational structure to achieve the company's goals and objectives. Organizational structure refers to how top management distributes authority and responsibility for decision-making within the company. The current environment favors more decentralization. However, top management usually retains authority over operations that the company can perform more economically at a central location. Top management usually groups business segments geographically, by similar mission, or by natural product clusters. Grouping business segments in this manner allows for effective cost management because one manager can be responsible for cost control of the related segments. Notably, each life-cycle mission such as "build", "harvest" or "hold" requires different incentives and performance evaluation measures. Because different missions require different cost management tools, the potential for poor decisions would be increased if a manager were responsible for segments with different missions.

The extent of decentralization also affects who will be accountable for cost management and organizational control. An information system must provide relevant information to managers with responsibility for decisions with cost control implications. Also, a control system must exist to assess the quality of those decisions.

Organizational culture also affects the design of the cost management system. Organizational culture is the underlying set of assumptions about the organization and its shared goals, processes, practices, and values. The values of an organization are especially important in assessing the cost management system. The design of a cost management system is heavily influenced by organizational culture because the culture determines interaction and the extent of authority and responsibility for the firms outcomes. A cost management system provides the foundation for companies with an organizational culture emphasizing cost savings and continuous improvement.

Other important considerations in the design of a cost management system are the organization's mission and core competencies. The mission serves as a long-term goal and helps determine the desired information from the cost management system.

Chapter 12: Introduction to Cost Management Systems 293

External factors because of the nature and extent of competitive pressures and how the company competes also influence the design of a cost management system. A company may avoid competition by differentiation or by cost leadership strategy. In the current global business environment, many companies are finding avoiding competition to be difficult. Many companies are confronting competition by identifying and exploiting temporary opportunities for advantage. Companies still try to differentiate their products by introducing new features or developing a price leadership position. However, companies expect competitors to develop similar products or match prices.

Exhibit 12-7 shows how a company's strategy and the life-cycle stages of products affect what a company must do well to be successful at any point in time. Information needs of managers depend on the strategy and change over time with changes in the life cycle.

Because globalization has created many companies that are substantially identical, consumers often focus on price. Competition based on price changes a company's internal focus to costs.

A company can clarify its mission by identifying its core competencies. Core competencies are important aspects of operations that a company should always perform well. Five critical core competencies for most companies are as follows: (1) timeliness, (2) quality, (3) customer service, (4) efficiency and cost control, and (5) responsiveness to change. After management determines a company's core competencies, the company should design the cost management system to (1) gather information related to the measurement of the core competencies and (2) generate output about the core competencies in a useful format.

After management has devised strategies to achieve the company's mission, managers can assess internal specifics related to the design of a cost management system. The company's cost structure is a primary concern. Cost structure is a measure of how costs change with changes in production or sales volume. Companies' higher investments in infrastructure improvements and technology have decreased their ability to control costs by changing sales or production. Because costs are not as subject to short-run control, companies are directing more of their cost management efforts toward the long run. Managing costs is also becoming more of a matter of capacity utilization. However, while higher capacity utilization reduces per-unit costs, matching increased sales must follow. Also, companies now have less ability to take short-term cost control actions without long-term adverse consequences.

In pursuing either a differentiation or cost leadership strategy, the management of technology costs requires beating competitors to the market with new products. A company which is first to market a new product might be able to set the price low enough to penetrate the market. Thus, the company could obtain a large market share and become the cost leader in the industry. An alternative strategy is to set a high price for a new product to realize a substantial profit as long as the company sells an adequate number of units at an acceptable price before competitors enter the market.

Because product life cycles are shrinking in the high-tech industry, rapid time to market is critical to profitability because prices have been steadily falling. Reducing time to market is also a way to reduce costs. Exhibit 12-8 lists other actions to reduce product costs substantially. Many of these actions are associated with the development and design stage of the product life cycle. Thus, a good design and development process largely determines product profitability. However, getting products to market quickly often involves tradeoffs between product innovation and a superior design. A company may incur costs for marketing a product with flaws to reap the reward of getting the product to the market quickly. At the same time, managers need to consider the consequences such as product returns, warrantee work or "bad will" regarding the company's reputation when evaluating the benefits and costs of accelerated marketing.

Another important aspect of a company's operating environment is supplier relations. Strategic alliances with suppliers are often effective cost control mechanisms. By including suppliers in the design and development stage of new products, companies can achieve a better design for manufacturability. In addition, if the information systems of customers and suppliers are linked electronically, the company must consider the capabilities and functions of those systems in designing the cost management system.

The need to integrate an organization's current information systems is another operating environment consideration in the design of a cost management system. The company should evaluate existing "feeder" systems such as payroll, inventory valuation, budgeting, and costing and answer the following questions: (1) What data are being gathered and in what form? (2) What outputs are being generated and in what form? (3) How do the current systems interact with one another and how effective are those interactions? (4) Is the current chart of accounts appropriate for the cost management information desired? (5) What significant information issues (such as yield, spoilage, and cycle time) are not currently addressed and could those issues be integrated into the current feeder systems?

Management must then analyze the cost-benefit tradeoffs related to the design of the cost management system. A company needs a more sophisticated cost management system as its cost of producing and communicating information decreases, or as competition increases. A company also needs a more sophisticated cost management system as it focuses on customer satisfaction and the expansion of its product and service offerings. The cost management system must incorporate proper incentives and reporting systems for managers to make the appropriate decisions.

A cost management system consists of (1) motivational elements, (2) information elements, and (3) reporting elements. Exhibit 12-10 provides more details about each of these elements. The elements as a whole must be internally consistent and individual elements must be consistent with the strategies and missions of the subunits. A company may use different aspects of these elements for different purposes. For example, only certain performance measures will be suitable for specific purposes.

Motivational elements influence managers and employees to exert high effort and to act in the organizations best interest. Performance measures should be consistent with organizational goals and objectives and provide incentives for managers to achieve them. These

Chapter 12: Introduction to Cost Management Systems 295

measures can be (1) quantitative or nonquantitative, (2) financial or nonfinancial, and (3) short-term or long-term. A company can also design performance measures to help recruit and retain qualified employees.

In addition to performance measures, different rewards have different incentive effects. Long-term incentives encourage managers to take actions that benefit the company in the long run. Short-term incentives encourage managers to focus their attention on the short run. Cash is the most obvious reward for short-term performance. Stock options provide a more long-term incentive.

Rewards for top management usually include short-term and long-term incentives. Usually, one of the major incentives is tied to the company's stock price. Rewards for subunit managers depend on the specific subunit's mission. Product life-cycle changes the performance measure considerably. Managers of subunits with a build mission usually have long-term incentives such as stock options, but mangers of subunits with a harvest mission usually have short-term incentives like cash compensation and profit-sharing,. Profit sharing is a powerful incentive used in many industries.

Performance measures and rewards are important because managers evaluate decision alternatives based on how the outcomes may affect their measurements and rewards. The cost management system should generate performance measures and provide them to the appropriate individuals for evaluation. Managers usually compare performance measures to past results, to expected performance or relative to customer expectations.

The informational elements of a cost management system provide appropriate information to decision-making managers responsible for directing the effective and efficient operation of the organization. The accounting function should support managers in the areas of planning, controlling, performance evaluation, and decision-making. All of these roles converge in a cost management system. Budgets specify expected achievement and provide a benchmark against which to compare actual performance. The cost management system should be able to provide the financial information necessary for budget preparation. The cost management system should also disclose activity cost drivers so managers can better evaluate decision alternatives. The cost management system can also highlight activities with a poor cost-benefit relationship so that management can select these activities for reduction or elimination.

Companies must place greater emphasis on management of the product life cycle. Information on managing costs must focus on the design and development stage to be most effective. The life cycles of many products will become shorter as companies become more adept at copying competitors' products. Thus, in the future, a company's ability to adapt to changing competitive conditions will receive greater emphasis. In a highly competitive environment, flexibility will become a more important organizational attribute. Managers will also change the emphasis of control systems as shown in Exhibit 12-11.

The accounting information system must be able to relate resource consumption and its cost to alternative product and process designs. The resulting information should be relevant to product design and development. Computer simulation models are useful in such analysis. Capital spending decisions should also receive greater attention because new technology acquisitions affect a company's cost structure. To be relevant for control and decision-making purposes, the cost management system should provide cost information that has few distortions from improper or inaccurate cost allocations or from improper exclusions.

The information needed to support decisions relates back to the unique situational factors of the company and its subunits. The information system must be useful for decision makers to determine the impact of alternative courses of action and how they are used to measure performance. Managers regularly compare the cost of actions to the benefits received. Only data with a minimum distortion will result in valid cost-benefit analysis.

The reporting elements of a cost management system refer to methods of providing information to individuals in evaluative roles. The cost management system must also generate information for the financial statements including the cost of inventories and cost of sales. The "feeder" systems to the cost management system should be appropriately integrated and designed to minimize distortion in the "external" product or service costs. The reporting elements must also serve the needs of the responsibility accounting system.

A responsibility accounting system is a system that provides information to top management about the performance of organizational subunits. For each subunit, the responsibility accounting system separately tracks costs and, if appropriate, revenues.

Performance reports are useful only in comparison to measures of a meaningful baseline. The normal baseline is expected performance. Expected performance may be in financial terms or in nonfinancial terms. Nonfinancial measures include throughput, customer satisfaction, lead time, capacity utilization, and research and development activities. Top management links managerial rewards to the comparison of actual to expected performance

The movement toward decentralization has increased the importance of an effective reporting system. The reporting system is essential in aligning subunits with organizational goals. A cost management system is not designed to "cut " cost but to ensure satisfactory yield or revenue as a result of costs. The cost management systems provides information to assist management in the understanding of the nature of various costs. Some costs should provide immediate benefits, but other costs provide long-term benefits.

The cost management system should provide managers with information linking revenues and costs. Managers can understand the revenues realized from costs incurred only by linking costs to activities and activities to strategies. By breaking down operations into subunits, top management can assign responsibility and accountability and create proper incentives for subunit managers. As a result, top management more effectively encourages subunit managers to focus on costs and activities that relate more closely to the organizational mission.

Subunit managers must have relevant information to be effective in managing costs. Each manager requires different information because different subunits must make different decisions with various time horizons A reporting system provides a comparison of expected to actual performance or benchmark for each manager. Comparison is the key source of motivation for subunit managers.

Optimal organizational performance occurs only if there is consistency for each subunit across the elements of motivation, information, and reporting. Effective top management considers the product life cycle in determining incentives and rewards. Cost management systems should also involve the supply or "value"chain. Most cost management system design and implementation issues relate to modifications of the existing system.

After the company has assessed the subunits and determined the structure of the cost management system, management should evaluate the current information system(s). Gap analysis helps to identify and prioritize favorable changes to the cost management system and assesses differences in ideal and the existing cost management system. Gap analysis is a comparison of the differences or gaps between the information needed and the information available. All system gaps may be impossible to eliminate in the short run because of software or hardware capability or availability. Methods of reducing or eliminating gaps which include technical requirements and changes to existing feeder systems should be expressed qualitatively, quantitatively, in terms of cost and benefits and in detail. Top management may determine the differences to address and in which order to address them due to limited resources with a focus on cost as compared with benefits. Management must constantly evaluate and update the cost management system so that it will continue to meet user's informational needs.

Advances in technology have had a significant impact on the design of integrated cost management systems. For example, enterprise resource planning (ERP) systems enable companies to (1) standardize information systems and replace different "legacy" systems, (2) integrate information systems and automate the transfer data among systems, (3) improve the quality of information, including purchase preferences of customers; and (4) improve the timeliness of information by providing real-time, on-line reporting.   The ERP software often involves a large number of separate modules that collect data from individual processes in the company and assemble the data in a form accessible by all managers.

APPENDIX

In 1986, Computer Aided Manufacturing-International, Inc. (CAM-I) formed a consortium of progressive industrial organizations, accounting firms, and government agencies to define the role of cost management in the new advanced manufacturing environment. A conceptual framework of principles for designing a cost management system was one outcome of the consortium. Exhibit 12-12 lists principles for designing a cost management system.

The set of principles as a whole suggests a radical departure from traditional practices, even though it is compatible with existing accounting systems. The practices focus management attention on organizational activities, product life cycles, integrating cost management and performance measurement, and integrating investment management and strategic management.

Chapter 12: Introduction to Cost Management Systems

SELF TEST

TRUE/FALSE

1. T F Financial experts, especially accountants are primarily responsible for providing measures of organizational costs and benefits.

2. T F Cost accounting information produced for financial reporting purposes is also very useful in making strategic decisions.

3. T F The management information system is a part of the management control system.

4. T F The financial accounting system reflects life-cycle information.

5. T F Cost control was the original purpose of a cost accounting system.

6. T F Most large companies operate as limited liability companies (LLCs).

7. T F The degree of centralization affects who will be accountable for cost management.

8. T F Organizational culture has no effect on the design of the cost management system.

9. T F Competition based on price changes a company's internal focus to costs.

10. T F A cost management system helps managers measure and evaluate performance and evaluate investment opportunities.

11. T F Product life cycles are relatively long in high-tech industries.

12. T F Reducing time to market is one way to reduce costs.

13. T F Performance measures should be consistent with organizational goals and objectives.

14. T F Performance reports are useful only in comparison to measures of a meaningful baseline.

APPENDIX

15. T F A conceptual framework of principles for designing a cost management system was one outcome of the consortium formed by Computer Aided Manufacturing-International, Inc. (CAM-I).

Chapter 12: Introduction to Cost Management Systems

MULTIPLE CHOICE

1. The external operating environment does NOT include:

    A. Management
    B. Competition
    C. Suppliers
    D. Creditors

2. The management information system is a part of the:

    A. security system.
    B. financial accounting system.
    C. management control system.
    D. auditing system.

3. What identifies what is happening in a process being controlled?

    A. assessor
    B. detector
    C. effector
    D. communications network

4. What is a device that determines the significance of what is happening in a process being controlled?

    A. assessor
    B. detector
    C. effector
    D. communications network

5. What is a device that provides feedback for modifying behavior in a management control system?

    A. assessor
    B. detector
    C. effector
    D. communications network

6. What transmits information in a management control system between other components in the system?

    A. assessor
    B. detector
    C. effector
    D. communications network

Chapter 12:   Introduction to Cost Management Systems   300

7. In the short run, profitability depends on:

   A. controlling costs in relation to revenues.
   B. acquiring the right inputs from the right suppliers.
   C. selling the right mix of products to the right customers.
   D. using the most appropriate distribution channels.

8. Long-run survival does NOT require that a company:

   A. acquire the right inputs from the right suppliers.
   B. sell the right mix of products to the right customers.
   C. use the most appropriate distribution channels.
   D. minimize all current costs.

9. The original purpose of a cost accounting system was:

   A. cost control.
   B. computing cost of goods sold.
   C. computing inventory cost.
   D. to assist in budgeting.

10. Management may have difficulty controlling a cost when:

    A. management monitors the related activity.
    B. management knows the cost driver.
    C. the information is available.
    D. the information lacks integration.

11. Most large businesses operate as:

    A. general partnerships.
    B. limited liability partnerships.
    C. limited liability companies.
    D. corporations.

12. Who is responsible for establishing an organizational structure to achieve the company's goals and objectives?

    A. the controller
    B. the internal auditor
    C. subunit managers
    D. top management

Chapter 12: Introduction to Cost Management Systems

13. The information produced by a cost management system should NOT:

    A. help measure performance.
    B. assist in evaluating performance.
    C. help evaluate investment opportunities.
    D. make managerial decisions.

14. A company can clarify its mission by identifying its:

    A. legal form.
    B. organizational structure.
    C. core competencies.
    D. cost structure.

15. A cost management system does NOT include:

    A. motivational elements.
    B. information elements.
    C. reporting elements.
    D. management elements.

16. Strategic alliances with suppliers are often:

    A. a cause of unnecessary costs.
    B. effective cost control mechanisms.
    C. not very useful in the modern world.
    D. a cause of poor manufacturing designs.

17. What is an example of a long-term incentive?

    A. cash
    B. stock options
    C. profit sharing
    D. annual bonuses

18. Managers of a subunit with a build mission usually have:

    A. an annual bonus as the main incentive.
    B. a mix of various short-term incentives.
    C. long-term incentives.
    D. a cash prize as the main incentive.

Chapter 12: Introduction to Cost Management Systems

19. To be most effective, information on managing costs should focus on which stage of the product life cycle?

    A. design and development
    B. introduction
    C. growth
    D. maturity

20. What type of performance measure would not necessarily be very useful?

    A. quantitative
    B. qualitative
    C. financial
    D. popularity with top management

21. Effective rewards for top management usually are based on:

    A. short-term incentives.
    B. long-term incentives.
    C. fringe benefits.
    D. both short and long-term incentives.

22. In a cost management system, what are the methods of providing information to individuals in evaluative roles?

    A. assessors
    B. motivational elements
    C. information elements
    D. reporting elements

23. The cost management system should provide managers with information linking:

    A. revenues and costs.
    B. assets and liabilities.
    C. costs and liabilities.
    D. revenues and retained earnings.

24. Most cost management system design and implementation issues relate to:

    A. the audit of the existing system.
    B. the original design of the system.
    C. modifications of the existing system.
    D. the definition of product costs.

Chapter 12: Introduction to Cost Management Systems

25. Optimal organizational performance occurs only if there is a consistency for each subunit across the elements of:

    A. motivation and information.
    B. information and reporting.
    C. reporting and information.
    D. motivation, reporting and information.

26. Which of the following is NOT a nonfinancial performance measure?

    A. throughput
    B. lead time
    C. capacity utilization
    D. unit cost

27. A comparison of the differences between the information needed and the information available is called:

    A. cost structure.
    B. gap analysis.
    C. differentiation.
    D. responsibility accounting.

28. Enterprise resource planning (ERP) systems allow a company to:

    A. standardize information systems.
    B. improve timeliness of information
    C. improve quality of information
    D. segregate information systems.

29. Effective managers would NOT compare performance measures to:

    A. past results.
    B. expected performance.
    C. control systems.
    D. customer expectations

APPENDIX

30. The set of cost management system conceptual design principles developed by the CAM-I consortium:

      A. is incompatible with existing cost accounting systems.
      B. suggests a radical departure from traditional practices.
      C. simplifies cost management by disregarding product life cycles.
      D. disintegrates cost management for ease of understanding

QUESTIONS AND PROBLEMS

1. Name and describe the four primary components of a control system.

2. What must a company do to be profitable in the short run? What must a company do to ensure its long-term survival?

3. What are the six main goals of a cost management system?

4. Why do managers need life-cycle cost information?

5. What conditions must be satisfied before management can control a cost?

Chapter 12: Introduction to Cost Management Systems 306

6. Why is grouping business segments properly important for cost management?

7. What are the five critical core competencies for most companies?

8. What are the cost management implications of the shift in cost structure due to large investments in technology?

Chapter 12: Introduction to Cost Management Systems 307

9. What are the possible pricing strategies and related benefits for bringing a new product to the market?

10. What questions should a company answer as it evaluates existing systems before integrating them into the cost management system?

11. What are the three elements of a cost management system? What attributes should each element possess?

Chapter 12: Introduction to Cost Management Systems

12. What is a responsibility accounting system?

13. What is gap analysis? What should top management do following gap analysis?

14. What does an enterprise resource planning (ERP) system allow a company to do?

APPENDIX

15. What cost management practices should management focus on in the new manufacturing environment according to the CAM-I consortium?

Chapter 12: Introduction to Cost Management Systems

SELF TEST ANSWERS

TRUE/FALSE

1.	T	4.	F	7.	T	10.	T	13.	T
2.	F	5.	T	8.	F	11.	F	14.	T
3.	T	6.	F	9.	T	12.	T	15.	T

MULTIPLE CHOICE

1.	A	7.	A	13.	C	19.	A	25.	D
2.	C	8.	D	14.	C	20.	D	26.	D
3.	B	9.	A	15.	D	21.	C	27.	B
4.	A	10.	D	16.	B	22.	D	28.	D
5.	C	11.	D	17.	B	23.	A	29.	C
6.	D	12.	D	18.	C	24.	C	30.	B

QUESTIONS AND PROBLEMS

1. Four primary components of a control system are as follows: (1) a detector or sensor, (2) an assessor, (3) an effector, and (4) a communications network. A detector or sensor identifies what is happening in the process being controlled. An assessor is a device that determines the significance of what is happening. An effector is a device that provides feedback for modifying behavior that the assessor determines to be necessary. A communications network transmits information between the detector and the assessor and between the assessor and the effector.

2. To be profitable in the short run, a company must control costs in relation to revenues. Managers need timely information about specific costs to make these operational decisions. To ensure its long-term survival, a company must acquire the right inputs from the right suppliers, sell the right mix of products to the right customers, and use the most appropriate distribution channels. Managers need reasonably accurate information on a periodic basis to make these strategic decisions.

3. The six main goals of a cost management system are as follows: (1) develop reasonably accurate product costs, (2) assess product/service life-cycle performance, (3) improve understanding of processes and activities, (4) control costs, (5) measure performance, and (6) assist in pursuing organizational strategies.

4. Managers need life-cycle information to relate costs incurred in one stage of the life cycle to costs and profits in other stages. A cost management system should help managers understand business processes and organizational activities. Managers need to understand these processes and activities to make cost-effective improvements in production and processing systems.

Chapter 12: Introduction to Cost Management Systems 311

5. Management can control a cost only when the following conditions are satisfied: (1) management monitors the related activity, (2) management knows the cost driver, and (3) the information is available.

6. Grouping business segments properly allows for effective cost management because one manager can be responsible for cost control of the related segments. Top management usually groups business segments geographically, by similar mission, or by natural product clusters. Because different missions require different cost management tools, the potential for poor decisions would be increased if a manager were responsible for segments with different missions.

7. Five critical core competencies for most companies are as follows: (1) timeliness, (2) quality, (3) customer service, (4) efficiency and cost control, and (5) responsiveness to change.

8. The cost management implications of the shift in cost structure due to large investments in technology are significant. Because costs are not as subject to short-run control, companies are directing more of their cost management efforts toward the long run. Managing costs is also becoming more of a matter of capacity utilization. Higher capacity utilization reduces per-unit costs. However, matching increased sales must follow. Also, companies now have less ability to take short-term cost control actions without long-term adverse consequences.

9. In bringing a new product to the market, a company could set a low price to penetrate the market. The company would hope to obtain a large market share and become the cost leader in the industry. An alternative strategy is for the company to set a high price for the new product to realize a substantial profit before competitors can enter the market.

10. A company answers the following questions as it evaluates existing systems before integrating them into the cost management system: (1) What data are being gathered and in what form? (2) What outputs are being generated and in what form? (3) How do the current systems interact with one another and how effective are those interactions? (4) Is the current chart of accounts appropriate for the cost management information desired? (5) What significant information issues (such as yield, spoilage, and cycle time) are not currently addressed and could those issues be integrated into the current feeder systems?

11. The three elements of a cost management system are (1) motivational elements, (2) information elements, and (3) reporting elements. The elements as a whole must be internally consistent and individual elements must be consistent with the strategies and missions of the subunits.

12. A responsibility accounting system is a system that provides information to top management about the performance of organizational subunits. For each subunit, the responsibility accounting system separately tracks costs and, if appropriate, revenues. Performance reports about subunits are useful only in comparison to measures of a meaningful baseline. The normal baseline is expected performance. Expected performance may be in financial terms or in nonfinancial terms. Nonfinancial measures include throughput, customer

Chapter 12: Introduction to Cost Management Systems

satisfaction, lead time, capacity utilization, and research and development activities.

13. Gap analysis is a comparison of the differences or gaps between the information needed and the information available. Following gap analysis top management should determine the differences to address and in which order to address them due to limited resources. All system gaps may be impossible to eliminate in the short run because of software or hardware capability or availability. Management must constantly evaluate and update the cost management system so that it will continue to meet the company's needs.

14. An enterprise resource planning (ERP) system allows a company to (1) standardize information systems and replace different "legacy" systems, (2) integrate information systems and automate the transfer data among systems, (3) improve the quality of information, including purchase preferences of customers; and (4) improve the timeliness of information by providing real-time, on-line reporting. The ERP software often involves a large number of separate modules that collect data from individual processes in the company and assemble the data in a form accessible by all managers.

APPENDIX

15. According to the CAM-I consortium, management should focus on organizational activities, product life cycles, integrating cost management and performance measurement, and integrating investment management and strategic management.

CHAPTER 13

RESPONSIBILITY ACCOUNTING AND TRANSFER PRICING IN DECENTRALIZED ORGANIZATIONS

CHAPTER OVERVIEW

A company's organization structure often changes from highly centralized to highly decentralized as its goals, technology, and employees change. In a centralized organization, top management retains the majority of authority. On the other hand, a decentralized organization is one in which top management has delegated a great deal of decision-making authority to subunit managers.

This chapter describes the accounting methods of responsibility accounting, cost allocation and transfer pricing. Responsibility accounting is an accounting system that gives top management information about the performance of an operational unit in the organization. The four primary types of responsibility centers cover in this chapter are cost, revenue, profit and investment centers. Cost allocation involves the allocation of costs to other departments or departments rendered the service. Transfer pricing involves determining the appropriate price when subunits of decentralized companies exchange goods or services internally. Multinational companies have additional challenges when using transfer pricing.

CHAPTER STUDY GUIDE

The degree of decentralization in a company is a continuum from totally centralized to totally decentralized. In a totally centralized company, one individual makes all decisions and retains all authority for the company's activities. A completely decentralized company has almost no central authority, and each subunit acts as an independent unit. A transfer of authority, responsibility and decision-making rights from top management to lower management is called decentralization. Exhibit 13-1 lists some of the advantages and disadvantages to decentralization.

Top management evaluates managers of the various units based on the results of their subunit compared to the results of other subunits in the company. Managers in a decentralized company derive more satisfaction from their work and develop a feeling of importance to the company.

Chapter 13: Responsibility Accounting and Transfer Pricing in Decentralized Organizations

Decentralization is often more effective in achieving the company's goals and objectives because the unit manager has more knowledge of the local operating environment. This proximity to actual operations results in a reduction in time to make decisions. Decentralization also allows the use of the management by exception principle.

Although decentralization has many advantages, it also presents some disadvantages. The division of authority and responsibility among managers can result in lack of goal congruence. Goal congruence occurs when the personal and organizational goals of managers throughout a company are consistent and mutually supportive. Because of the competition inherent in a decentralized company, managers might make decisions that help their unit but hurt other units or the entire company.

A decentralized company must communicate plans, activities, and achievements effectively. Although top management delegates authority, it still has responsibility for the results of the decisions made at lower levels of management.

One possible roadblock to decentralization is that top management might have difficulty in giving up control or delegating effectively. Another disadvantage of decentralization is that it can be expensive. Companies incur costs in training lower-level managers. A company also faces the potential cost of poor decisions by those managers. A company also incurs costs because of the duplication of activities. Finally, a decentralized company incurs costs for its complex planning and reporting system, known as a responsibility accounting system.

One advantage is that decentralization allows managers to develop their abilities and provides an excellent training ground for aspiring leaders. Exhibit 13-2 shows Johnson & Johnson's i-Lead process model for enhancing employee leadership skills.

Neither a purely centralized company nor a purely decentralized company is desirable. Most companies have structures that function between these extremes. In Exhibit 13-3 are listed the factors that contribute to the degree of decentralization in an organization. A business segment that operates in a dynamic environment is likely to have a more decentralized structure so that it can respond to new problems quickly. A decentralized company must communicate plans, activities, and achievements effectively. Although top management delegates authority, it still has responsibility for the results of the decisions made at lower levels of management.

A responsibility accounting system is the key to making decentralization work effectively. It provides information about the performance, efficiency, and effectiveness of subunits and their managers. Information generated from the responsibility accounting system, including responsibility reports, helps top management evaluate the performance of organizational subunits. Exhibit 13-4 shows examples of information presented in responsibility reports. The responsibility reports might classify all costs incurred in a subunit as controllable or noncontrollable by the manager. Another possibility is to prepare separate reports for the unit and its manager. The report for the unit would include all costs, but the report for the manager would show only controllable costs.

A responsibility accounting system helps lower-level managers conduct the five basic control functions; (1) prepare a plan; (2) gather actual data; (3) monitor differences between actual and planned data at scheduled intervals; (4) exert managerial influence in response to significant differences; and (5) continue comparing and responding to data and then at the appropriate time, start the process again. A responsibility accounting system uses budgets to communicate expectations and spending authority. The responsibility accounting system should accumulate actual results in conformity with budgetary accounts. Top management will use comparisons of actual results to budgeted amounts to evaluate the performance of unit managers.

By the time top management receives these comparisons, the unit managers should have corrected the problems that resulted in significant variances. If the unit managers have not corrected the problems, the unit managers should offer explanations.

Responsibility reports for unit managers and their immediate supervisors usually compare actual results with amounts from the flexible budget. These comparisons are more effective for control purposes than comparisons of actual results to the master budget. However, top management normally receives comparisons of actual results to the master budget. These comparisons are more useful if accompanied by detailed variance analysis that identifies the effect of sales volume differences on segment performance.

The amount of detail in responsibility reports becomes less as subordinate managers prepare them for successively higher levels of management. Upper-level managers who want more specific information can review the prepared for their subordinates. Exhibit 13-5 illustrates a responsibility report. Responsibility accounting is not without disadvantage. Management should take care not to neglect important details or lower level variances at the top. Small variances in one center may impact others dramatically because centers are often interdependent.

Performance reports at lower levels list variances individually, so that managers act on significant variances to correct them. Detailed analysis alert operational managers to items that would be unexplainable to superiors. The manager who has control over a certain cost is the focus of responsibility accounting. Cost objects in a decentralized companies are organizational units called responsibility centers.

The four types of responsibility centers are (1) cost centers, (2) revenue centers, (3) profit centers, and (4) investment centers, as illustrated in Exhibit 13-6.

A manager of a cost center has control only over costs. Thus, the manager's evaluation depends on how well he or she controlled costs. A cost center can generate revenues, but they are either (1) not under the control of management, or (2) the outputs are not easily measurable. In a standard costing environment, the manager's focus is often on minimizing unfavorable variances. Management should investigate all significant variances, whether unfavorable or favorable, because unfavorable and favorable variances might be a function of each other.

Chapter 13: Responsibility Accounting and Transfer Pricing in Decentralized Organizations

In a revenue center, a manager has responsibility only for the generation of revenues, but has little control over costs. Thus, top management would evaluate the manager of a revenue center by the amount of revenue generated. A more appropriate term for such revenue centers is revenue and limited cost centers.

In a profit center, managers are responsible for generating revenues and controlling costs related to current activity. Top management evaluates managers of profit centers on the net income of their centers. Profit center managers should have the authority to acquire resources at the lowest prices and to sell products at the price that will generate the most revenue. Manufacturing companies, retail stores, and service firms all use profit centers.

A manager of an investment center is responsible for generating revenues, controlling costs, and managing plant assets. The goal of an investment center manager is to earn the highest possible rate of return on assets. Many investment centers are independent, freestanding divisions or subsidiaries of a firm. Thus, investment center managers make all kinds of decisions about their units, and top management evaluates them on the outcomes of those decisions.

One primary goal of any business is to generate profits. A company earns profits when it satisfies its critical success factors. If an organization consistently fails to satisfy its critical success factors, it will cease to exist. The following five critical success factors are common to most organizations: (1) quality, (2) customer service, (3) speed, (4) cost control, and (5) responsiveness to change. If an organization manages these five factors properly, the organization should be financially successful.

Suboptimization occurs when individual managers work toward goals and objectives that are in their own interest rather than in the company's best interest. Top management must be aware of possible suboptimal behavior and find ways to avoid it

Management allocates costs from service departments into other departments. Overhead costs include manufacturing costs and support costs. A company's support areas include service departments and administrative departments. A service department is an organizational unit (such as central purchasing, personnel, maintenance, engineering, security, and warehousing) that provides one or more specific functional tasks for other internal units. Administrative departments provide support for management activities that benefit the entire company. Generally, personnel, payroll, legal, insurance departments, and corporate headquarters are examples of administrative departments.

Costs incurred in service departments and administrative departments are called service department costs. A company allocates service department costs to production or service-rendering departments.

Allocation of service department costs has three objectives: full cost computation, managerial motivation, and managerial decision making. A company meets these objectives

Chapter 13: Responsibility Accounting and Transfer Pricing in Decentralized Organizations

when it allocates costs in a reasonable manner to revenue-producing departments. Exhibit 13-7 illustrates the three objectives and reasons for and the reasons against service department cost allocations.

The allocation base for service departments should meet four criteria. The first criterion is the need to consider the benefit received by the revenue-producing department. The second criterion emphasizes the causal relationship between factors in the revenue-producing department and the costs incurred in the service department. The third criterion is the actual fairness of the allocation or the equity of the allocations between or among the revenue-producing departments. The fourth criterion is the ability to bear the allocated costs. The benefit received and causal relationships criteria generally produce the most rational allocations. Exhibit 13-8 lists acceptable allocation bases for various types of service department costs.

Service department cost allocation involves pooling, allocating, repooling, and reallocating costs. The primary pools consist of all costs related both to the service departments and the revenue-producing departments. A company develops intermediate pools. The final layer of the intermediate pools includes only revenue-producing departments. The number of layers and the costs in the intermediate pools depend on the allocation method. A company then assigns costs to the final cost objects using cost drivers. Exhibit 13-9 shows primary cost pools or budgeted departmental and divisional costs the textbook uses to illustrate service department cost allocation. Exhibit 13-10 shows the service department allocation bases for the illustration in the textbook.

The three possible methods a company can use to allocate pooled service department costs to revenue-producing departments are the direct method, the step method, and the algebraic method. The direct method allocation allocates costs directly to revenue-producing departments using only one set of intermediate cost pools or allocations. Exhibit 13-11 and Exhibit 13-12 illustrate the direct method.

The step method of allocation considers the interrelationships of the service departments before assigning indirect costs to cost objects. Under the step method, a company ranks service departments based on benefits provided to other corporate areas. The ranking is referred to as "benefits-provided rankings." Then, the company allocates the costs of the service department that provides the largest amount of services. The company proceeds sequentially on down until the company allocates the costs of the service department that provides the least services. Once a company has allocated costs from a service department, it may not allocate any costs back to that department. Exhibit 13-13 illustrates the step method.

The algebraic method of allocating service department costs considers all departmental interrelationships simultaneously. While the algebraic method is the most complex of all the methods, it is most theoretically correct. In addition, the algebraic method eliminates the two disadvantages of the step method: (1) it recognizes all interrelationships among departments and (2) the company does not have to place service departments in a rank order. With proper

Chapter 13: Responsibility Accounting and Transfer Pricing in Decentralized Organizations

planning and consideration of relationships among departments, the algebraic method will provide the best allocation. Exhibit 13-14 illustrates developed interdepartmental proportional relationships for the illustration in the textbook. The algebraic method involves the substitution of algebraic equations to solve for cost allocations. Exhibit 13-15 illustrates the algebraic solutions to the service department costs, and Exhibit 13-16 provides the final determination of revenue-producing department overhead costs. The example in the textbook provides a comprehensive example of the algebraic method.

Responsibility centers of a company might sell products or services to another responsibility center of the company. The price charged is a transfer price. A company can base transfer prices on cost, the market price, or a price negotiated between the buying segment and the selling segment. Transfer pricing is useful for managerial purposes, but for external reporting, a company must eliminate profits on intracompany sales and show the cost at the producing segment's cost. A pseudo-profit center refers to when one responsibility center uses transfer prices to artificially sell goods or services to another responsibility center.

The appropriate transfer price should be one that ensures optimal resource allocation and promotes operating efficiency. A company can establish transfer prices to (1) promote goal congruence, (2) make performance evaluation among segments more comparable, and/or (3) transform a cost center into a profit center.

The maximum price should be no greater than the lowest market price at which the buying segment can acquire the goods or services externally. The minimum price should be no less than the sum of the selling segment's incremental costs associated with the goods or services plus the opportunity cost of the facilities used. Any transfer price set between the two limits is usually considered appropriate. The difference between these two limits is referred to as the corporate "profit." The transfer price acts to "divide the corporate profit" between the divisions, referred to as "divided profits."

The three traditional methods companies use for determining transfer prices are cost based, market-based, and negotiation listed in Exhibit 13-18. A cost-based transfer price is equal to total unit variable cost, absorption cost, or modified variable and/or absorption cost. A market-based transfer price is an objective measure of value and simulates the selling price that would exist if the segments were independent companies. A negotiated transfer price is an intracompany charge for goods or services set through a process of negotiation between the selling and purchasing unit managers.

In a dual pricing arrangement, a company uses a different transfer price for the buying segment and the selling segment. The selling division records the sale at the market price or negotiated market price. The buying division records the transfer based on cost.

Management decisions on transfer pricing systems should reflect the circumstances of the organizational units and the company's goals and objectives. No one method of transfer pricing is right in all instances. In addition, companies change transfer prices often to reflect changes in

Chapter 13: Responsibility Accounting and Transfer Pricing in Decentralized Organizations

costs, supply, demand, and competitive forces. These changes can encourage efficient use of divisional resources by stimulating internal consumption during downturns and reducing internal consumption during peak times.

A carefully set transfer price will provide the following advantages: (1) an appropriate basis for calculating and evaluating divisional performance, (2) the rational acquisition or use of goods and services between corporate divisions, (3) the flexibility to respond to changes in demand or market conditions, and (4) a means of motivating managers in decentralized operations.

Using transfer prices also has its disadvantages. First, the unit managers might disagree as to the appropriate transfer price. Second, implementing transfer prices in the accounting system requires additional time and money. Third, transfer prices might not work equally well for all types of service departments. Fourth, a transfer price could result in dysfunctional behavior among the organizational units. Fifth, tax regulation regarding transfers for multinational businesses are extremely complex.

Setting transfer prices can be difficult for companies engaged in multinational operations due to differences in tax systems, import/export regulations, and foreign exchange controls. Exhibit 13-19 shows the objectives of transfer pricing for multinational enterprises.

Multinational enterprises might use different transfer prices for the same product depending on which country transfers or receives the product. A company usually should not price transfers to a foreign subsidiary at a price that would transfer most of its costs to a subsidiary in the country with the highest tax rate. However, a company might use such a transfer price if it is reasonable and equitable to all subsidiaries. Usually, a company should price such transfers at an arm's length price.

Tax authorities in both the home and host countries are now carefully scrutinizing transfer prices by multinational enterprises. The U.S. Congress and the Internal Revenue Service (IRS) are concerned that companies could avoid paying U.S. income taxes by using misleading or inaccurate transfer prices. The IRS might be more likely to investigate U.S. subsidiaries that operate in low-tax countries or low-tax areas. Management can avoid much litigation by creating advance pricing agreements with national tax authorities. These agreements represent a binding contract that provide details about how transfer prices are set and establishes a basis for no penalty or adjustment if agreed-upon methodology is used. These agreements typically last three to five years and generally remain the same beyond if no significant changes occur.

Chapter 13: Responsibility Accounting and Transfer Pricing in Decentralized Organizations

SELF TEST

TRUE/FALSE

1. T F The direct method of allocating service department costs uses only one set of intermediate cost pools or allocations.

2. T F Suboptimization occurs when unit managers make decisions that are good for their units but detrimental to other units or the entire company.

3. T F Decentralization can be costly in terms of time and money.

4. T F A manager of a profit center is responsible for return on assets.

5. T F In a revenue center, managers are responsible for revenues and controlling all expenses.

6. T F Setting transfer prices in multinational operations can be difficult.

7. T F The division of authority and responsibility among managers in a decentralized organization might result in lack of goal congruence.

8. T F Management should ignore the favorable variances of a cost center.

9. T F Decentralization is often less effective in achieving the company's goals and objectives because top management usually has better knowledge of local operating environments.

10. T F The amount of detail in responsibility reports increases as subordinate managers prepare them for successively higher levels of management.

11. T F Managers of profit centers are responsible for generating revenues and controlling costs.

12. T F One way to reduce suboptimization is to communicate corporate goals to all organizational units.

13. T F For external financial reports, companies must eliminate profits on intracompany sales.

14. T F Corporate profits are the difference between the lowest price of buying externally and the cost of buying internally.

Chapter 13: Responsibility Accounting and Transfer Pricing in Decentralized Organizations

15. T F The step method of allocating service department costs considers the interrelationships of the service departments before assigning indirect costs to cost objects.

MULTIPLE CHOICE

1. The focus of responsibility accounting is on:

    A. overhead costs.
    B. selling costs.
    C. managers of responsibility centers.
    D. allocation methods.

2. The manager of a revenue center is responsible for:

    A. return on assets.
    B. cost containment.
    C. net income.
    D. revenue generation.

3. Responsibility reports reflect the:

    A. downward flow of information.
    B. diagonal flow of information.
    C. upward flow of information.
    D. horizontal flow of information.

4. What exists when the personal and organizational goals of managers throughout a company are consistent and mutually supportive?

    A. suboptimization
    B. management by exception
    C. goal congruence
    D. differential costs

5. What is NOT normally an important goal of a responsibility accounting system?

    A. performance
    B. efficiency
    C. effectiveness
    D. intracompany profits

Chapter 13: Responsibility Accounting and Transfer Pricing in Decentralized Organizations

6. What is a possible advantage of decentralization?

    A. the cost of poor decisions by subordinate managers
    B. the cost of training subordinate managers
    C. expensive duplication of activities
    D. use of management by exception

7. An internal charge established for the exchange of products or services between units of the same company is a(n):

    A. differential cost.
    B. fair-return price.
    C. transfer price.
    D. elastic price.

8. Which method is not used to allocate service department costs?

    A. step method
    B. direct method
    C. algebraic method
    D. arbitrary method

9. What is an advantage of using transfer prices?

    A. encourages development of new managerial talent
    B. no additional organizational costs are involved
    C. no dysfunctional behavior can occur
    D. no cost for training employees.

10. Five basic control functions of managers do NOT include

    A. communicating output expectations.
    B. monitoring differences between planned and actual data.
    C. exert managerial influence.
    D. management by exclusion.

11. The use of a different transfer price for the buying segment and the selling segment is:

    A. price fixing.
    B. a dual pricing arrangement.
    C. price discrimination.
    D. incremental transfer pricing.

Chapter 13: Responsibility Accounting and Transfer Pricing in Decentralized Organizations

12. An acceptable cost allocation base for research and development would be:

    A. square feet.
    B. pretax operating income.
    C. assets employed.
    D. payroll.

13. An acceptable cost allocation base for the purchasing function would be:

    A. estimated time of usage.
    B. pretax operating income.
    C. real estate valuation.
    D. payroll.

14. What is the key in making decentralization work effectively?

    A. transfer prices
    B. training for unit managers
    C. a responsibility accounting system
    D. top management intervention

15. A possible problem in instituting decentralization is that top management might:

    A. easily lose control.
    B. might recognize new talent.
    C. be unable to delegate effectively.
    D. begin using management by exception.

16. In addition to financial reports, many responsibility accounting systems now provide information on:

    A. personnel policies.
    B. critical nonmonetary performance measures.
    C. recent IRS rulings.
    D. recent laws passed by Congress.

17. When a company uses a different transfer price for the buying segment and the selling segment, the selling division records the transfer at:

    A. a cost-based amount.
    B. standard cost.
    C. a market or negotiated market price.
    D. the price dictated by top management.

Chapter 13: Responsibility Accounting and Transfer Pricing in Decentralized Organizations

18. Which of the following is an advantage of decentralization?

    A. It is usually very inexpensive.
    B. It may result in lack of goal congruence.
    C. It allows the use of management by exception.
    D. It requires more effective communication abilities.

19. Which method of allocating service department costs considers all interrelationships among service departments and reflects these relationships in simultaneous equations?

    A. direct method
    B. step method
    C. algebraic method
    D. redundant method

20. A company evaluates the manager of an investment center on the basis of:

    A. net income.
    B. product margin.
    C. cost control.
    D. return on assets.

21. Responsibility reports should:

    A. assist successively lower levels of management evaluate subordinate managers.
    B. be tailored to fit needs of subordinate managers.
    C. include only monetary information.
    D. NOT separately classify costs as controllable or noncontrollable.

22. An accounting system that provides information to top management about the performance of organizational units is:

    A. internal auditing.
    B. responsibility accounting.
    C. organizational accounting.
    D. authority accounting.

23. The objectives of allocating service department costs include:

    A. partial cost computation.
    B. managerial motivation.
    C. employee decision making.
    D. suboptimal behavior.

Chapter 13: Responsibility Accounting and Transfer Pricing in Decentralized Organizations 325

24. Considering the objective of computing full cost, a reason for allocating service department cost is that doing so:

   A. provides for cost recovery.
   B. provides relevant information in determining alternative courses of action.
   C. provides a best estimate of expected changes due to various courses of action.
   D. encourages use of certain services.

25. Considering the objective of motivating managers, a reason for allocating service department cost is that doing so:

   A. provides costs beyond the production manager's control.
   B. instills a consideration of support costs in production managers.
   C. meets regulations in some pricing instances.
   D. provides for cost recovery.

26. The direct method of allocating service department costs considers:

   A. the benefit-provided ranking system.
   B. interrelationships between departments.
   C. cost flows both in and out of all departments.
   D. only one set of intermediate cost pools.

27. The step method of allocating service department costs considers:

   A. the benefit-provided ranking system.
   B. simultaneous interrelationships between departments.
   C. complete cost flows both in and out of all departments.
   D. only one set of intermediate cost pools.

28. Consolidated Industries has two divisions—the Rock Division and the Sand Division. Sand makes a part that Rock is currently buying from an outside company for $91 per unit. Sand's variable production costs for this part are $35 per unit, variable selling costs are $10 per unit, and fixed factory overhead costs are $9 per unit. Sand will avoid $5 in variable selling costs on any sales to Rock. Sand normally charges $92 to outside companies for this part. Sand has enough idle capacity to make the 6,000 units of this part that Rock needs. What is the highest price that Rock would be willing to pay?

   A. $56
   B. $65
   C. $91
   D. $92

Chapter 13: Responsibility Accounting and Transfer Pricing in Decentralized Organizations

29. Consolidated Industries has two divisions—the Rock Division and the Sand Division. Sand makes a part that Rock is currently buying from an outside company for $91 per unit. Sand's variable production costs for this part are $35 per unit, variable selling costs are $10 per unit, and fixed factory overhead costs are $9 per unit. Sand will avoid $5 in variable selling costs on any sales to Rock. Sand normally charges $92 to outside companies for this part. Sand has enough idle capacity to make the 6,000 units of this part that Rock needs. What is the lowest transfer price that the Sand Division would accept?

   A. $35
   B. $40
   C. $45
   D. $54

30. Consolidated Industries has two divisions—the Rock Division and the Sand Division. Sand makes a part that Rock is currently buying from an outside company for $91 per unit. Sand's variable production costs for this part are $35 per unit, variable selling costs are $10 per unit, and fixed factory overhead costs are $9 per unit. Sand will avoid $5 in variable selling costs on any sales to Rock. Sand normally charges $92 to outside companies for this part. Sand has enough idle capacity to make the 6,000 units of this part that Rock needs. What is the potential increase or decrease in before-tax profit to Consolidated Industries if the Rock Division buys 6,000 units of this part from Sand rather than from an outside company?

   A. $6,000 decrease
   B. $252,000 increase
   C. $306,000 increase
   D. $336,000 increase

QUESTIONS AND PROBLEMS

1. What factors affect the degree of decentralization in a company?

Chapter 13: Responsibility Accounting and Transfer Pricing in Decentralized Organizations

2. What are the advantages of decentralization?

3. What are the disadvantages of decentralization?

4. Name the four types of responsibility centers, and explain how a company should evaluate each one.

5. Discuss the pros and cons of allocating service department costs.

6. What is suboptimization? What can top management do to limit suboptimization?

7. What difficulties would a company encounter in using cost-based transfer prices?

Chapter 13: Responsibility Accounting and Transfer Pricing in Decentralized Organizations

8. What are the advantages and disadvantages of using transfer prices for services?

9. Why is determining transfer prices for multinational enterprises difficult?

10. Why do tax authorities, such as the Internal Revenue Service, carefully scrutinize the transfer prices of multinational enterprises?

Chapter 13: Responsibility Accounting and Transfer Pricing in Decentralized Organizations

11. What characteristics must managers have for decentralization to be effective?

12. What are the advantages and disadvantages of using market-based transfer prices?

13. What benefits will a carefully set transfer price provide a company?

Chapter 13: Responsibility Accounting and Transfer Pricing in Decentralized Organizations

14. Jimenez Company has a computer networking business. The personnel department has one employee and incurs costs of $24,000. The payroll department has two employees and incurs costs of $42,000. Home Net is a revenue-producing department with 10 employees and incurs costs of $416,000. Office Net is a revenue-producing department with 20 employees and incurs costs of $832,000.

Allocate each department's personnel and payroll service costs using the step method. Assume that the payroll department provides the greater service benefit.

Chapter 13: Responsibility Accounting and Transfer Pricing in Decentralized Organizations

15. The Jay Division of Day Bird, Inc. is currently buying 6,500 units per year of a component at $78 per unit. The Robin Division of Day Bird Industries makes this component and usually sells it for $80 per unit. Robin's per-unit costs to make and sell this component are as follows:

Direct material	$24
Direct labor	9
Variable factory overhead	4
Fixed factory overhead	13
Variable selling and administrative costs	12
Total	$ 62

The fixed factory overhead costs are allocated and would not increase if Robin makes the 6,500 units for Jay. The variable selling and administrative costs would be reduced by $3 per unit on any sale to the Jay Division. The Robin Division has ample idle capacity to meet the demand for the components needed by the Jay Division. Robin has no alternative use for the idle capacity.

Calculate the following:

(a) the maximum transfer price that the Jay Division would pay.

(b) the minimum transfer price that the Robin Division would accept.

(c) the increase in before-tax profit to Day Bird Industries if the Jay Division buys the 6,500 units from the Robin Division rather than from an outside company.

Chapter 13: Responsibility Accounting and Transfer Pricing in Decentralized Organizations

SELF TEST ANSWERS

TRUE/FALSE

1.	T	4.	F	7.	T	10.	F	13.	T
2.	T	5.	F	8.	F	11.	T	14.	T
3.	T	6.	T	9.	F	12.	T	15.	T

MULTIPLE CHOICE

1.	C	7.	C	13.	A	19.	C	25.	B
2.	D	8.	D	14.	C	20.	D	26.	D
3.	C	9.	A	15.	C	21.	B	27.	A
4.	C	10.	D	16.	B	22.	B	28.	C
5.	D	11.	B	17.	C	23.	B	29.	B
6.	D	12.	C	18.	C	24.	A	30.	C

QUESTIONS AND PROBLEMS

1. The factors that affect the degree of decentralization in a company include the (1) company's age, (2) company's size, (3) stage of product development, (4) growth rate, (5) expected impact of poor decisions on profits, (6) confidence of top management in lower-level managers, (7) historical degree of control, (8) use of technology, and (9) rate of change in the company's market.

2. The advantages of decentralization include the following: (1) Managers can develop their abilities. (2) It provides an excellent training ground for aspiring managers. (3) Decentralization encourages healthy competition among managers. (4) Managers derive more satisfaction from their work and develop a feeling of importance to the company. (5) Top management can use the management by exception principle. (6) The company can achieve its goals and objectives more effectively. The last reason results in less time to make decisions, a reduction of difficulties in attempting to communicate problems through a chain of command, and faster perceptions of changes in the operating environment.

3. Decentralization has the following disadvantages: (1) possible lack of goal congruence; (2) suboptimization; (3) need for more effective communication of plans, activities, and performance measures; (4) the requirement of top management's continual awareness of the operations of the various units of the company; (5) the cost of training lower-level managers; (6) the potential cost of poor decisions by lower-level managers; (7) costly duplication of activities; (8) unwillingness of top management to give up control; (9) top management's inability to delegate effectively; and (10) the cost of developing and maintaining a complex planning and reporting system.

Chapter 13: Responsibility Accounting and Transfer Pricing in Decentralized Organizations

4. The four types of responsibility centers are (1) cost centers, (2) revenue centers, (3) profit centers, and (4) investment centers. A company evaluates a manager of a cost center on the basis of how well the manager controlled costs. Top management evaluates a manager of a revenue center based on the revenue generated. A company evaluates a manager of a profit center on the net income of their centers. A manager of an investment center is evaluated on return on assets.

5. Taken from Exhibit 13-7. The three objectives of allocating service department costs are (1) to compute full cost, (2) to motivate managers, and (3) to compare alternative courses of action. Pros for each: (1) Provide for cost recovery, instill consideration for service costs, reflect production's "fair share" in service costs; (2) instill consideration for service costs, relate profits of single production units to the company profit, reflect usage of services, encourage cooperation in controlling costs, and encourage usage of services; (3) provide relevant information, and provide best estimates. Cons for each: (1) includes costs outside a manager's control, arbitrary, and confusing to the pricing of products; (2) distort production profits, includes costs outside a manager's control, not material to profits, creates divisional ill will and is not cost beneficial; (3) unnecessary if changes do not change costs and presents distorted cash flows from alternative actions.

6. Suboptimization occurs when individual managers pursue goals and objectives that are in their own and/or their segment's best interest instead of in the company's best interest. Top management must first be aware of suboptimization. One way for top management to limit suboptimization is to communicate corporate goals to all organizational units.

7. Companies using cost-based transfer prices must decide how to define cost. Companies could define cost as variable cost or absorption cost. A company could define variable cost as variable production cost or as total variable cost. Another difficulty a company faces is deciding whether to use actual cost or standard cost. If a company uses actual cost, the selling division might not correct inefficiencies in production because the buying division will cover its cost. On the other hand, if a company uses standard cost and actual cost is less than standard, the buying division will be paying more than actual cost. Using cost-based transfer prices does not provide the selling division with the same income that it could earn by selling the products externally.

8. Advantages of using transfer prices for services are as follows: (1) More involvement occurs between user departments and service departments. (2) Managers become more cost conscious. (3) The resulting information is useful for performance evaluation. The disadvantages include the following: (1) User and provider departments might disagree on the transfer price. (2) Companies incur additional organizational costs and need more employee time to implement the transfer prices within the accounting system. (3) Transfer prices do not work equally well for all service departments. (4) Dysfunctional behavior could occur.

9. Differences in tax systems, customs duties, freight and insurance costs, import/export regulations, and foreign exchange controls make determining transfer prices for a multinational enterprise difficult. Also, the internal and external objectives of transfer pricing in multinational enterprises differ.

Chapter 13: Responsibility Accounting and Transfer Pricing in Decentralized Organizations

10. The Internal Revenue Service and tax authorities in other countries carefully scrutinize transfer prices for multinational enterprises because the transfer prices determine which country taxes the income from the transfer. Companies could reduce their tax liability by using misleading or inaccurate transfer prices. Companies do so by charging higher transfer prices to subsidiaries in countries with high tax rates. Thus, the income in the high-tax countries will be less, and the income in low-tax countries will be greater. The Internal Revenue Service and tax authorities in other countries want transfer prices to reflect market prices so that income will be taxed appropriately.

11. For decentralization to be effective, managers must be goal-oriented, assertive, decisive, and creative. Subordinate managers must be willing to accept the authority that top management gives them. They must be willing to have top management evaluate their performances by the results of their decisions.

12. An advantage of using market-based transfer prices is that a company avoids the problem in defining cost. Market-based transfer prices are objective and are similar to the prices that would be charged if the segments were independent companies. A disadvantage of using market-based transfer prices is that the products might not be exactly the same as products sold in external markets. Another problem with market-based transfer prices is that deciding on the appropriate market price is difficult if the market is depressed, especially if different sellers are quoting different prices to different buyers.

13. A carefully set transfer price will provide a company with the following benefits: (1) a means of encouraging what is best for the company as a whole, (2) an appropriate basis for calculating and evaluating divisional performance, (3) the rational acquisition or use of goods and services between corporate divisions, (4) the flexibility to respond to changes in demand or market conditions, and (5) a means of motivating managers in decentralized operations.

14. First level allocation of payroll to departments.

    Employees 31 (10 + 20 + 1)

Home Net (10 ÷ 31) x $42,000 =	$ 13,548
Office Net (20 ÷ 31) x $42,000 =	27,097
Personnel (1 ÷ 31) x $42,000 =	1,355 (carried below)
Total first allocation	$ 42,000

Second level allocation of personnel to departments. ($24,000 + $1,355 = $25,355)

    Employees 30 (10 + 20)

Home Net (10 ÷ 30) x $25,355 =	$ 8,452
Office Net (20 ÷ 30) x $25,355 =	16,903
Total second allocation	$ 25,355

Chapter 13: Responsibility Accounting and Transfer Pricing in Decentralized Organizations

Home Net	=	$13,548 + $8,452	= $22,000
Office Net	=	$27,097 + $16,903	= $44,000
Payroll	=	$42,000 − $1,355 − $13,548 − $27,097	= $0
Personnel	=	$24,000 + $1,355 − $8,452 − $16,903	= $0

15. (a) The maximum transfer price that the Jay Division would pay is $78 per unit. Jay will not pay Robin any more for the component than the price charged by the outside company.

(b)
Direct material	$ 24
Direct labor	9
Variable factory overhead	4
Variable selling and administrative costs ($12 − $3)	9
Minimum transfer price	$ 46

The fixed factory overhead costs are not relevant because they would not increase in total.

(c)
Maximum transfer price	$78
Less: Minimum transfer price	46
Per-unit increase in profit	$32

$32 per unit x 6,500 units = $208,000 increase in before-tax profit to Day Bird Industries, Inc.

CHAPTER 14

CAPITAL BUDGETING

CHAPTER OVERVIEW

The acquisition, operation, and disposition of capital assets involve a significant investment of resources over a long period. Companies invest in long-term assets to generate revenues or to reduce costs. Capital assets include plant, equipment, capital leases, and patents. Capital budgeting is the process of evaluating proposed investments in capital assets.

Capital budgeting provides the decision base for reaching strategic objectives. Capital budgeting represents an evaluation of long-range projects for allocating resources to capital assets. This chapter discusses commonly used financial techniques for evaluating capital projects. Managers rank capital projects through the use of these techniques. Common methods include the payback period, net present value, profitability index, and internal rate of return. Since each method has assumptions and limitations, managers need to evaluate the methods and determine which is most appropriate for project analysis. Most of these techniques involve an analysis of the amounts and timing of the project's cash flows. Management also considers the tax and depreciation impact on cash flows.

Analysis does not stop after the project starts. Management should conduct postinvestment audits of projects to determine continued viability and profitability. In addition, management often considers nonfinancial criteria. Exhibit 14-1 lists project evaluation criteria for research and development projects.

Appendix 1 discusses the time value of money, emphasizing future value and present value of single cash flow, ordinary annuity, and annuity due. Understanding the time value of money is vital to understanding the three discounted cash flow techniques for capital budgeting. Appendix 2 discusses the accounting rate of return.

CHAPTER STUDY GUIDE

Capital budgeting techniques include payback period, net present value, profitability index, internal rate of return, and accounting rate of return. All of these methods, except for accounting rate of return, focus on the amounts and timing of a project's cash flows.

Chapter 14: Capital Budgeting

The payback period is the length of time required to recover project costs through the cash inflows. If the payback period of a project is less than a predetermined maximum, the management considers the project viable. The payback period formula does not consider cash flows beyond the payback period. Unlike the payback period, the net present value, profitability index, and internal rate of return methods consider the time value of money. These methods discount a project's cash flows using a desired rate of return. Cost of capital should be the minimum discount rate.

Under the net present value method, the total present value of future cash flows minus the current investment equals net present value. If the net present value is equal to or greater than zero, the project provides a rate of return equal to or greater than the discount rate. A positive net present value is acceptable for investment, but a project with a negative net present value is unacceptable.

The profitability index is equal to the present value of net cash flows divided by the cost of the investment. Acceptable projects generally have a profitability index of 1.00 or more.

The internal rate of return calculates the rate of return expected on the investment project. The internal rate of return is equal to the discount rate at which the net present value of all cash flows equals zero. The project is acceptable if its internal rate of return is greater than the desired rate of return or hurdle rate.

By ranking projects in relationship to one another, management can select projects that best help to attain company objectives and provide the maximum return on investment. Because net present value, profitability index, and internal rate of return each have separate limitations, management often uses more than one method to rank projects. In certain situations, the net present value, profitability index, and internal rate of return methods generate different project rankings because of the timing of cash flows. Management should develop further analysis of project rankings when ranking differs. Because depreciation is deductible for tax purposes, depreciation expense and changes in income tax rates affect after-tax cash flows.

Management must consider any uncertainty about the expected cash flows or risk for each capital project as part of the ranking process. Cost accountants calculate project risk using a risk-adjusted hurdle rate. Management often uses judgment estimates to determine risk. Sensitivity analysis assists management in determining the effect on a project's outcome associated with a change in an estimate for any critical variables. Cost accountants use sensitivity analysis to compensate for risk by calculating an expected range for each of the variables used in the project ranking analysis.

A post-investment audit helps managers by assisting in the identification of problems that might exist. Early identification allows for possible correction. The post-investment audit could also provide insight to evaluate the accuracy of estimates used for the original investment decision to improve the forecasts of future investment projects.

Chapter 14: Capital Budgeting

Cash flows are the receipts or disbursements of cash. Cash flows in a capital budgeting context arise from the purchase, operation, and disposition of a capital asset. Management expects any investment to earn some type of return in the form of interest, cost savings, or operating income.

Management should evaluate all projects on an equivalent basis. Converting accrual-based income to cash flow information places all projects on a comparable basis.

A financing decision is based on an entity's ability to issue and service debt and equity securities. A financing decision evaluates the methods of raising funds used to make capital investments. An investment decision is a judgment about which capital investments to make. Cash flow generated from these two activities should not be combined in project evaluation. For example, the cash outflow for interest incurred in financing a project is not a factor that management should consider in the project selection process.

Because not all cash flows occur at the same time, a time line can be used to illustrate the points in time when cash flows are expected. Exhibit 14-2 provides information used to illustrate capital budgeting techniques. The time line below the exhibit shows cash inflows, cash outflows, and net cash flows at the end of each year. Positive net cash flows represent inflows, and negative cash flows represent outflows. Management often uses the end of the year or the beginning of the year for the timing of cash flows to simplify the calculation of cash flows.

The payback period is the time required to recover an original investment from a project's cash flows. An annuity is a series of equal cash flows each period. If the cash flows are an annuity, the payback period is computed as follows: payback period = investment ÷ annuity.

The payback method illustrated in the textbook uses the figures calculated in the time line example discussed previously. The underlying assumption of the payback period is the longer the time required to recover the initial investment, the greater the project's risk. The payback period for a project having unequal cash inflows is determined by accumulating cash flows until the company recovers the original investment. Management typically sets a maximum acceptable payback period as an initial evaluation technique for capital projects. The payback period has three limitations: (1) it ignores the cash inflows occurring after the payback period; (2) it does not consider the company's desired rate of return; and (3) it disregards the time value of money.

Money changes value over time. Appendix 1 covers the time value of money in more depth. The process of converting cash flows to be received in the future to their present values is discounting. Discounting removes the interest element and allows the cost accountant to state all cash flows in terms of their present values. Most capital budgeting techniques use discounted cash flows. The cost accountant does not discount current cash outlays because the present value of a current cash outlay is equal to itself. The cost accountant must discount cash flows across all project evaluations for comparability.

The discounting process requires estimates of a project's cash flows and the required rate of return used as the discount rate. The discount rate is the rate of return used to determine the imputed interest portion of future cash receipts and expenditures. The discount rate should equal or exceed a company's weighted average cost of capital. Cost of capital is the weighted average cost of the various sources of resources, such as debt and stock, which make up the company's financial structure.

A return on capital represents income and equals the discount rate multiplied by the investment amount. One hundred dollars invested in a project at 10 percent would return $110 to the investor after one year. The return on capital is $10, and the return of capital is $100.

The net present value method of capital budgeting uses discounted cash flows of a project to determine whether the rate of return on that project is equal to, higher than, or lower than the desired rate of return. Exhibit 14-3 and Exhibit 14-4 illustrate the calculation of the net present value for two different discount rates. The discount factors are contained in Appendix A of the textbook, and are based on the year in which each cash flow is received.

A project's net present value (NPV) is the difference between the present values of all cash inflows and cash outflows for an investment project. If the NPV is zero, the actual rate of return on the project is equal to the desired rate of return. If the NPV is positive, the actual rate of return on the project is greater than the desired rate of return. If the NPV is negative, the actual rate of return on the project is less than the desired rate of return.

Managers eliminate any projects with a negative net present value. Because the net present value method does not provide an actual rate of return, its use is not appropriate for projects with different initial investments. A greater investment will often yield a higher net present value, but the actual project return on capital invested could be much less. The net present values of projects with different initial investments are not comparable.

Management can overcome the comparability problem by using the profitability index. The cost accountant computes the profitability index by dividing the present value of the net future cash inflows by the net investment. The present value of the net cash inflows represents an output measure of the project's worth. The present value of the investment represents an input measure of the project's cost. The profitability index provides a measure of the company's efficiency of capital use. The higher the profitability index, the more efficient is the company's use of capital.

For the profitability index to provide better information than does the net present value method, the projects must be mutually exclusive or the availability of investment funds must be limited. The profitability index should be greater than or equal to 1.00 for a project to be acceptable.

The internal rate of return method calculates the rate of return earned on the project if the company reinvests all cash flows at the internal rate of return. The internal rate of return is the rate of return that when used as the discount rate causes the net present value to be zero.

Chapter 14: Capital Budgeting

A project's internal rate of return is the discount rate where the present value of the net cash inflows equals the present value of the net cash outflows using the project's expected rate of return. If the internal rate of return is used to determine the net present value of a project, the net present value will be zero.

If the cash flows an investment generates are equal per period for several periods, the cost accountant can calculate the internal rate of return using the table for present value factors of an ordinary annuity. Table 2 in Appendix A of the textbook provides the present value factors to calculate the present value of an annuity. The investment divided by the annuity equals a present value factor. Then, the cost accountant identifies the interest rate that matches the present value factor for that number of periods. That interest rate is the internal rate of return.

Exhibit 14-6 illustrates a chart that plots net present values for various discount rates. As this exhibit illustrates, as the discount rate goes up, the net present value goes down. If the cash flows are not equal, the cost accountant can solve the internal rate of return using a trial-and-error approach or using a financial calculator or computer.

Management compares the internal rate of return of a project with its discount rate or hurdle rate. The hurdle rate is the lowest rate of return acceptable to management, which is usually greater than or equal to the cost of capital. If the internal rate of return is greater than or equal to the hurdle rate, the investment is acceptable. If the internal rate of return is less than the hurdle rate, management should reject the investment.

Income taxes are a significant part of capital budgeting decisions. In evaluating potential investments, managers should use after-tax cash flows. Although depreciation is not a cash flow, it is a deductible expense for tax purposes. Depreciation acts as a tax shield to reduce taxable income. Thus, depreciation reduces the outflow of cash for income taxes. Cost accountants must consider the incremental cash outflows for income taxes in capital budgeting decisions. The tax benefit provided by depreciation is equal to the depreciation expense multiplied by the company's tax rate. Although the tax law might change regarding depreciation methods, a company may generally depreciate an asset using the method allowed when it placed the asset in service. Recent tax law allows many companies to deduct the entire cost of some assets in the year of acquisition In this case, a company realizes the entire tax benefit immediately. Exhibit 14-6 illustrates the effect of different tax rates on cash flows from an investment.

Managers should understand the basic similarities and differences of the various capital budgeting methods and use several techniques to evaluate a project. All of the methods have two similar limitations: (1) None of the methods provides a mechanism to include management preferences in regard to the timing of cash flows except to the extent that payback indicates the promptness of the investment recovery. (2) All the methods use single, deterministic measures of cash flow amounts rather than probabilities.

A company can compensate for the first limitation by subjectively favoring projects whose cash flow profiles better suit management's preferences, assuming other project factors are equal. A company can overcome the second limitation by using probability estimates of cash flows. Exhibit 14-7 summarizes the assumptions and limitations of the five capital budgeting techniques, including the accounting rate of return discussed in Appendix 2.

The investment decision must identify the best use of resources for a company to fulfill its goals and objectives. Proper identification requires addressing the following four questions: (1) Is the activity worthy of an investment? (2) Which assets can be used for the activity? (3) Of the available assets for each activity, which is the best investment? (4) Of the best investments for all worthwhile activities, in which ones should the company invest? Exhibit 14-9 illustrates a typical investment decision process for providing transportation for a sales force.

A company should invest in capital assets when the assets provide increased value in relation to company activity. Management considers cost-benefit analysis, often measured in monetary terms. However, management does not base all decisions solely on financial terms. Management should not exclude benefits from a capital budgeting analysis solely because they are difficult to quantify. The cost accountant can use surrogate quantifiable measures for hard-to-quantify benefits. In some worthy projects, monetary benefits might be less than the costs but the project is essential for other reasons. The determination of available and suitable assets is closely connected to the evaluation of the activity's value to a company.

To determine which assets a company can use for a particular activity, management must gather specific information. Management gathers the following information for each asset: (1) initial cost, (2) estimated life, (3) salvage value, (4) raw material and labor requirements, (5) operating costs (both fixed and variable), (6) output capability, (7) service availability and cost, (8) maintenance expectations, and (9) revenues to be generated (if any). Management must have both quantitative and qualitative information on each asset. Exhibit 14-8 illustrates the capital investment information needed for determining which assets to use in an activity.

Management should select the best asset from the possible candidates and exclude all others from consideration. A screening decision is the first decision made in evaluating capital projects. A screening decision determines whether a project is desirable based on some previously established minimum criterion or criteria. A preference decision is the second decision made in capital project evaluation. A preference decision involves ranking projects according to their impact on the achievement of company objectives.

Mutually exclusive investments accomplish the same task or function—if management selects one asset, it does not invest in the other assets under consideration. When a company is considering the replacement of an existing asset with a new asset, the assets are mutually exclusive. The company either keeps the existing asset or acquires the new asset and sells the old asset. Management can choose only one project and must exclude all others from further consideration.

If investments are independent, investing in one asset has no specific effect on the decision to invest in the other possible investments. Although limited resources might prevent the company from investing in all desirable investments, the investments themselves would not be mutually exclusive. Independent projects are investment projects that have no specific

Chapter 14: Capital Budgeting

bearing on one another.

Mutually inclusive projects consist of a set of related capital projects. Management must choose all projects if it chooses the primary project. If management rejects the primary investment, it must also reject the related investments.

All discounted cash flow techniques typically indicate the same decision alternative. The reinvestment assumption is a presumption made about the rates of return earned by intermediate cash flows from a capital project. The net present value method and the profitability index assume reinvestment at the discount rate. The internal rate of return method assumes reinvestment at the internal rate of return.

The three approaches to compensate for risk are the judgmental method, risk-adjusted discount rate method, and sensitivity analysis.

The judgmental method is an informal method of adjusting for risk. A manager uses judgment and personal experience along with a review of all available information such as payback period, net present value, profitability index, and internal rate of return. The manager then uses logic and reasoning to choose among projects.

The risk-adjusted discount rate method is a formal method of adjusting for risk. The cost accountant varies the rate used for discounting the future cash flows to compensate for increased risk. To reflect risk, management might discount some cash flows using a higher discount rate. For example, assume that management believes that the proceeds from the sale of a capital asset would be $600,000 in future years. However, based on economic trends, management feels that the asset might sell for a smaller amount. Management might adjust the discount rate from 9 percent to 15 percent for the selling price to compensate for the risk. In addition, if a risk exists that actual revenue could be less than the anticipated revenue, management might specify a higher discount rate for the cash inflows. While a company generally uses this method with net present value, a company could also use this method with the payback method or the accounting rate of return covered in Appendix 2. Exhibit 14-10 shows a product development evaluation illustrating the risk-adjusted discount rate method with both annual cash flows and a final cash inflow adjusted for increased risk.

Sensitivity analysis involves the determination of the amount of change that must occur in a variable before management would make a different decision. Management estimates a range of expected variables because of the use of estimates. All information used in capital budgeting is estimated except the initial purchase price. The use of estimates suggests the possibility of errors, and sensitivity analysis identifies an error range for the various estimated values over which the project would still be acceptable.

Management uses sensitivity analysis to determine what range in increases might occur in the estimated cost of capital and what range of decreases in cash inflows might occur while still maintaining an acceptable project. The textbook provides an example of the calculation of the range of the discount rate to recover an initial investment in a project. As long as the project's

Chapter 14: Capital Budgeting

internal rate of return is equal to or greater than the cost of capital, the project would be acceptable.

With sensitivity analysis, management must determine the possible range of the life of an asset expected from the project and compare it to the acceptable range of life in the asset. The textbook provides an example of the calculation of the range of the asset life in a project. As long as the asset's expected range of life is equal to or greater than the acceptable life of the asset, the project would be acceptable. Many factors affect asset life. Some factors are controllable while others are not. An error in the asset's estimated life will change the number of periods from which the company expects future cash flows. Significant differences in asset life could make a previously accepted project completely unacceptable.

Sensitivity analysis does not eliminate the uncertainty of the estimates of each variable. Rather, it provides management with a sense of tolerance for estimation errors by providing ranges with upper and lower limits for selected variables.

In a postinvestment audit, management compares the actual results of an investment to the expected results. The comparison should use the same techniques that management used to decide the acceptance of the project. The postinvestment audit serves as a financial control tool, provides feedback for future projects, and gives an incentive for more realistic future capital budgeting. A postinvestment audit becomes more crucial as the size of the capital expenditure increases.

Conducting a postinvestment audit is not easy for several reasons. The actual information might be in a different form from that of the original estimates. Some projects yield important benefits that are difficult to quantify. In addition, the returns on a project can vary over time. Despite the difficulties, postinvestment audits provide managers with information that can help them make better capital investment decisions.

APPENDIX 1

Appendix 1 covers the time value of money. Money to be received in the future is worth less than the same amount of money to be received today because one can invest money received today to earn interest. Present value is what a future amount of money is worth today at a given rate of interest. Future value is the amount that a sum of money would be worth at a specified time in the future if one invests it at a given rate of interest. Future value and present value depend on three things: (1) the amount of the cash flow, (2) the interest rate, and (3) the timing of the cash flow.

The discounted cash flow capital budgeting techniques generally assume compound interest. Compound interest means that the interest earned in prior periods adds to the investment so that the interest and principal earn interest. In contrast, simple interest means that only the principal earns interest.

A series of equal cash flows per period is an annuity. In an ordinary annuity, the cash flows occur at the end of the period. Cash flows from an annuity due occur at the beginning of the period. Each cash flow is a rent. Appendix 1 illustrates the calculation of the present value of a single amount and the present value of an annuity.

APPENDIX 2

Appendix 2 covers the accounting rate of return, which is another capital budgeting technique. The accounting rate of return measures the expected rate of earnings on the average capital investment over the investment's life. The accounting rate of return method uses accrual accounting net income rather than cash flows.

The formula to calculate the accounting rate of return is average annual profits from the project divided by the average investment in the project. The average investment is generally equal to one-half of the sum of the original investment and the sum of the salvage value and working capital released at the end of the project's useful life. Management compares a project's calculated accounting rate of return with a preestablished hurdle rate. This hurdle rate might be higher than the discount rate used in the net present value method because the accounting rate of return method does not include the time value of money.

Chapter 14: Capital Budgeting

SELF TEST

TRUE/FALSE

1. T F The payback method is based on net income rather than on cash flow.

2. T F The profitability index ignores the time value of money.

3. T F If the discount rate is zero, the future value and the present value of a cash flow are the same.

4. T F The payback method ignores all cash flows that occur after the payback period.

5. T F From a mutually exclusive set of capital projects, only one project will be chosen.

6. T F If a project's net present value equals zero, the project's internal rate of return has to also equal zero.

7. T F In a pretax analysis of cash flows, the cost accountant should ignore depreciation.

8. T F An after-tax cash flow equals the pretax cash flow multiplied by one minus the marginal tax rate.

9. T F Discounted cash flow techniques (such as net present value and internal rate of return) assume that cash inflows are not reinvested.

10. T F The profitability index is a ratio of the present value of all cash inflows to the present value of all organizational cash outflows.

11. T F A time line can be used to illustrate the points in time when cash flows are expected.

12. T F In a screening decision, the three project evaluation methods (internal rate of return, net present value, and profitability index) are likely to provide similar indications of which projects are acceptable.

13. T F The internal rate of return method assumes that all cash inflows are immediately reinvested at the internal rate of return.

APPENDIX 1

14. T F An annuity is a series of equal cash flows at equal intervals.

Chapter 14: Capital Budgeting 347

APPENDIX 2

15. T F The accounting rate of return does not consider depreciation in measuring the average annual investment profits.

MULTIPLE CHOICE

1. If a project has a positive net present value, the project's internal rate of return will be:

    A. less than the project's discount rate.
    B. greater than the project's discount rate.
    C. the same as the project's discount rate.
    D. less than the project's hurdle rate.

2. If a project has major cash inflows in the early years of its life and major cash outflows in the latter part of its life, it:

    A. might have multiple internal rates of return.
    B. must have a negative net present value.
    C. must have a positive net present value.
    D. must have a negative internal rate of return.

3. Which of the following capital budgeting techniques ignores the time value of money?

    A. internal rate of return
    B. net present value
    C. payback period method
    D. profitability index

4. In a comparison of two projects, a project would be considered less risky than the other if it has a lower:

    A. payback period.
    B. net present value.
    C. profitability index.
    D. accounting rate of return.

5. The net present value method implicitly assumes that a company reinvests all cash inflows over the life of the project at the:

    A. internal rate of return.
    B. profitability index.
    C. accounting rate of return.
    D. discount rate.

6. Interpolation is a mathematical procedure that might be required to determine a project's:

    A. internal rate of return.
    B. accounting rate of return.
    C. net present value.
    D. payback period.

7. A $100,000 investment in working capital would appear in a discounted cash flow analysis as a cash outflow:

    A. at time 0.
    B. at time 0 and a cash inflow in the terminal year of the project.
    C. in year 1 and a cash inflow in the terminal year of the project.
    D. in year 1.

8. A negative net present value indicates that the:

    A. profitability index is negative.
    B. project's internal rate of return is negative.
    C. project's accounting rate of return is negative.
    D. present value of all cash inflows is less than the present value of all cash outflows.

9. A net present value of zero is an indication that:

    A. the profitability index is zero.
    B. the return of capital is equal to the discount rate.
    C. the return on capital is equal to the discount rate.
    D. there is no return of capital.

10. An analyst might need to resort to a trial-and-error process to compute a project's:

    A. payback period.
    B. net present value.
    C. profitability index.
    D. internal rate of return.

11. Differences between actual investment cash flows and estimated investment cash flows are disclosed in the:

    A. variance analysis.
    B. postinvestment audit.
    C. responsibility center evaluations.
    D. published financial statements.

Chapter 14: Capital Budgeting

12. In a net present value analysis, if a company uses the internal rate of return as the discount rate, the net present value will be:

    A. negative.
    B. positive.
    C. either positive or negative.
    D. equal to zero.

13. A project's profitability is totally ignored by the:

    A. internal rate of return method.
    B. accounting rate of return method.
    C. payback period method.
    D. net present value method.

14. When managers are willing to consider all projects that have an internal rate of return that exceeds the cost of capital, the internal rate of return is being used as a:

    A. screening tool.
    B. judgmental tool.
    C. preference tool.
    D. performance measurement tool.

15. If a company can select only one project from a set of projects, the set is:

    A. discrete.
    B. indiscrete.
    C. mutually inclusive.
    D. mutually exclusive.

16. The presumption made about the rates of return earned by intermediate cash flows from a capital project is the:

    A. discount rate.
    B. reinvestment assumption .
    C. internal rate of return.
    D. accounting rate of return.

17. As the uncertainty about a future cash flow increases, so does the project's:

    A. discount rate.
    B. hurdle rate.
    C. risk.
    D. capital gain.

Chapter 14: Capital Budgeting

18. The minimal criterion for a project to be accepted is for the:

    A. net present value to be negative.
    B. profitability index to be less than one.
    C. payback period to be less than five.
    D. internal rate of return to be equal to or greater than the hurdle rate.

19. All other things remaining constant, a decrease in the marginal income tax rate will:

    A. increase the income tax benefit of the depreciation tax shield.
    B. decrease the income tax benefit of the depreciation tax shield.
    C. have no effect on the income tax benefit of the depreciation tax shield.
    D. increase the pretax depreciation cash flow.

20. In a pretax evaluation of a project, a net present value calculation would ignore all of the following except:

    A. a gain on the sale of an asset.
    B. a loss on the sale of an asset.
    C. the sales price of an asset.
    D. depreciation expense.

21. If the selection of one project in a set requires the selection of all other projects in the set, the projects are:

    A. complementary.
    B. mutually exclusive.
    C. mutually inclusive.
    D. replacements.

22. The pretax and after-tax cash flows would be different for:

    A. the initial cash outflow to purchase a machine.
    B. the initial cash investment in working capital.
    C. the annual rent payment on leased equipment.
    D. the initial cash outflow for purchase of stock.

23. The after-tax cash flow from the depreciation deduction equals the depreciation deduction multiplied by:

    A. the income tax rate.
    B. one minus the income tax rate.
    C. one times the income tax rate.
    D. one divided by the income tax rate.

Chapter 14: Capital Budgeting

24. Hatfield Company sells an asset with a book value of $20,000 for $40,000. If the company has an income tax rate of 50 percent, the after-tax cash flow from the sale of the asset will be:

    A. $30,000.
    B. greater than $40,000.
    C. greater than $10,000 but less than $20,000.
    D. $10,000.

APPENDIX 2

25. Which of the following capital budgeting techniques recognizes noncash revenues and noncash expenses?

    A. payback period
    B. net present value
    C. profitability index
    D. accounting rate of return

26. A change in the depreciation method for book purposes could affect a project's:

    A. accounting rate of return.
    B. payback period.
    C. internal rate of return.
    D. net present value.

27. The accounting rate of return is equal to:

    A. the average annual profit year divided by the initial investment.
    B. the profit in the first year divided by the average investment.
    C. the average annual profit divided by the average investment.
    D. the average annual cash flow divided by the average investment.

28. Which of the following is excluded in computing the average investment of a project?

    A. initial cost of the investment
    B. working capital needed for project support
    C. salvage value
    D. the payback period.

29. Which capital budgeting technique uses net income rather than cash flows?

    A. accounting rate of return
    B. payback period
    C. net present value
    D. internal rate of return

30. Carman Company bought a machine for $10,000. The machine will provide cash flows of $3,200 a year for each of the next five years. At the end of the five years, the machine will have no salvage value. Carman uses straight-line depreciation. What is the accounting rate of return?

    A. 12 percent
    B. 24 percent
    C. 32 percent
    D. 64 percent

QUESTIONS AND PROBLEMS

1. Under what conditions would a company prefer to use a slow rate of depreciation rather than an accelerated rate of depreciation?

2. What is the ultimate criterion in choosing one method over another to rank capital projects?

Chapter 14: Capital Budgeting

3. How can a cost accountant explicitly deal with greater uncertainty about the amount of one specific future cash inflow compared to all other cash inflows associated with a project?

4. What are the assumptions and limitations of the net present value? Hint See Exhibit 14-7.

5. What is the relationship between a project's internal rate of return and its net present value?

Chapter 14: Capital Budgeting

6. Under what circumstances is calculating the internal rate of return more difficult than using other capital budgeting techniques?

7. Why is using the payback period in conjunction with other techniques important in evaluating capital projects, rather than using it as the sole evaluation method?

8. What are the benefits of a postinvestment audit?

9. The LJ Company is considering an investment in a labor-saving machine that will have an initial cost of $3,000. The cost accountant expects the machine to reduce labor costs by $900 for each of the next five years. The company will depreciated the machine using the straight-line method with no salvage value. The company expects to sell the machine at the end of five years for $400. Assuming that the LJ Company has a marginal income tax rate of 25 percent, what is the after-tax payback period for the investment in the machine?

10. Sandy Enterprises is considering an investment in a new project. Management expects the investment to generate annual savings in cash operating costs of $10,000 for the next seven years. The project would require an initial cash outlay of $40,500, and the company would depreciate this cost over the project's life using the straight-line method. Management expects the project to have no salvage value at the end of the seven years. Sandy's cost of capital is 16 percent. What is the net present value of the proposed project?

11. Sandy Enterprises is considering an investment in a new project. Management expects the investment to generate annual savings in cash operating costs of $10,000 for the next seven years. The project would require an initial cash outlay of $40,500, and the company would depreciate this cost over the project's life using the straight-line method. Management expects the project to have no salvage value at the end of the seven years. Sandy's cost of capital is 16 percent. What is the internal rate of return of the proposed project?

12. Sandy Enterprises is considering an investment in a new project. Management expects the investment to generate annual savings in cash operating costs of $10,000 for the next seven years. The project would require an initial cash outlay of $40,500, and the company would depreciate this cost over the project's life using the straight-line method. Management expects the project to have no salvage value at the end of the seven years. Sandy's cost of capital is 16 percent. What is the payback period of the proposed investment?

13. Sandy Enterprises is considering an investment in a new project. Management expects the investment to generate annual savings in cash operating costs of $10,000 for the next seven years. The project would require an initial cash outlay of $40,500, and the company would depreciate this cost over the project's life using the straight-line method. Management expects the project to have no salvage value at the end of the seven years. Sandy's cost of capital is 16 percent. What is the profitability index of the proposed investment?

APPENDIX 1

14. What is the difference between simple interest and compound interest? What must the cost accountant do to compensate for interest compounded more often than annually?

APPENDIX 2

15. Brown, Inc. is considering an investment in the following project:

Required initial investment	$900,000
Net annual cash inflow	$150,000
Annual depreciation	$ 50,000
Estimated salvage value	$150,000
Life of the project in years	15

    Calculate the accounting rate of return of the proposed investment.

Chapter 14: Capital Budgeting

SELF TEST ANSWERS

TRUE/FALSE

1.	F	4.	T	7.	T	10.	F	13.	T
2.	F	5.	T	8.	T	11.	T	14.	T
3.	T	6.	F	9.	F	12.	T	15.	F

MULTIPLE CHOICE

1.	B	7.	B	13.	C	19.	B	25.	D
2.	A	8.	D	14.	A	20.	C	26.	A
3.	C	9.	C	15.	D	21.	C	27.	C
4.	A	10.	D	16.	B	22.	C	28.	D
5.	D	11.	B	17.	C	23.	A	29.	A
6.	A	12.	D	18.	D	24.	A	30.	B

QUESTIONS AND PROBLEMS

1. A firm would want to use a slow depreciation rate when it desires to preserve depreciation deductions for future periods. Motivation to preserve the deduction for future periods could come from an expectation of (a) rising future income tax rates or (b) increasing profitability in the future.

2. The ultimate criterion is to choose the method that will maximize the market value of the firm. The method that is the most consistent with this criterion is the one that should be used.

3. A cost accountant could do several things. In the interest of being conservative (and thereby not overestimating the present value of that risky future cash flow), the cost accountant could use a higher discount (risk-adjusted) rate for that one cash flow. Alternatively, if the cost accountant is uncertain about both the amount and the timing of the cash flow, he or she could increase the discount period. For example, move the cash flow to time period 10 from time period 7. Lastly, the cost accountant could experiment with a range of values for the cash flow (such as in a worst-case and best-case scenario situation) and examine the impact of these changes on the net present value of the project.

Chapter 14: Capital Budgeting 360

4. The assumptions of the net present value method are that:

   1. the discount rate used is valid,
   2. timing and size of cash flows are accurately predicted,
   3. the life of the project is accurately predicted, and
   4. if the shorter lived of two projects is selected, the proceeds of that project will continue to earn the discount rate of return through theoretical completion of the longer lived project.

   The limitations of the net present value method are that :

   1. cash flows and project life are treated as deterministic without explicit consideration of probabilities,
   2. alternate project rates of return are not known,
   3. cash flow pattern preferences are not explicitly recognized, and
   4. IRR on project is not reflected.

5. A project's net present value is determined based on a specific discount rate. When that specific discount rate happens to be the internal rate of return, the net present value of the project will be zero by definition. A lower discount rate will result in a positive net present value and a higher discount rate will result in a negative net present value.

6. Calculating the internal rate of return will be more difficult than other capital budgeting techniques if the cash flows are not in the form of an annuity. The internal rate of return must be calculated on a trial-and-error basis if all cash flows beyond period zero are not in the form of an annuity. A company can minimize the cost of the trial-and-error process in time and effort by using computer-based technology.

7. The payback period ignores all cash flows beyond the payback period. If two projects have similar payback periods, the cash flows beyond the payback period will be very important in determining which project management selects, but the payback period method does not consider these cash flows. If used in conjunction with discounted cash flow methods, the payback period method can provide information about relative risk, and the discounted cash flow methods can provide information about relative profitability.

8. The postinvestment audit serves as a financial control tool, provides feedback for future projects, and gives an incentive for more realistic future capital budgeting. A postinvestment audit becomes more crucial as the size of the capital expenditure increases.

9. The after tax cash flow from the annual savings in labor costs would be $675 ($900 x 0.75). The after-tax cash flow from the depreciation tax shield would be $150 [($3,000 ÷ 5) x 0.25]. The total annual after-tax cash flow would therefore be $825 ($675 + $150). This cash flow would provide a payback period of 3.64 years ($3,000 ÷ $825 per year).

Chapter 14: Capital Budgeting

10. The net present value is determined by deducting the initial outlay from the present value of the cash inflows. The present value of the cash inflows is $40,386 ($10,000 x 4.0386). The net present value of the project is therefore $(114) [$40,386 – $40,500].

11. The internal rate of return for the project is the discount rate that will yield a net present value of zero. Because the company's hurdle rate is 16 percent and yields a negative net present value, the internal rate of return must be less than 16 percent. In this instance, the internal rate of return is directly calculated without resorting to a trial-and-error approach. The initial investment divided by the net annual cash inflow equals the discount factor associated with the internal rate of return for an annuity lasting 7 years. That discount factor is 4.05 ($40,500 ÷ $10,000). From the annuity tables, the 4.05 discount factor lies between the discount factors associated with 15.5 percent and 16.0 percent. Using interpolation, the project has an internal rate of return of approximately 15.7 percent.

12. The payback period equals the initial investment divided by the net annual cash inflow: $40,500 ÷ $10,000 per year = 4.05 years.

13. The profitability index equals the present value of the future cash flows divided by the initial cost of the investment. The present value of the cash inflows is $40,386 ($10,000 x 4.0386). The profitability index is 0.997 ($40,386 ÷ $40,500).

14. Simple interest means that only the principal amount earns interest. Compound interest means that the interest earned in prior periods and the principal earns interest. If interest is compounded more often than annually, the cost accountant must multiply the number of years by the number of compounding periods per year and divide the annual interest rate by the number of compounding periods per year.

15.
15. The accounting rate of return equals the average annual profit divided by the average annual investment. The average annual profit is the net annual cash inflow minus depreciation: $150,000 – $50,000 = $100,000. The average annual investment is equal to the average book value of the investment: ($900,000 + $150,000) ÷ 2 = $525,000. The accounting rate of return = $100,000 ÷ $525,000 = 19.05 percent.

CHAPTER 15

MANAGING COSTS AND UNCERTAINTY

CHAPTER OVERVIEW

This chapter covers managing costs and uncertainty. The chapter illustrates how an effective cost control system controls cost prior and during the event causing the cost as well as feedback about performance after the event. Cost containment, cost avoidance and cost reductions are three generic approaches to cost control. Management uses primary fixed cost called committed and discretionary costs. Discretionary costs are more difficult to associate with specific benefits than are committed costs. Committed costs are long-run investments in plant assets or personnel and associated costs. Management maintains liquidity by managing cash. Technology plays a vital role as managers seek to reduce costs within supply chains through technology and integrated information. This chapter also covers the use of four generic strategies for dealing with uncertainty. Management faces more challenges with future uncertainty than past uncertainty.

CHAPTER STUDY GUIDE

A cost control system is a part of an organization's decision support system. The cost control system focuses on information within the organization and contains the detector, assessor, effector, and network components discussed in Chapter 12 A cost control system helps a company plan costs. In addition, a cost control system helps a company evaluate how well it managed costs during a period. As illustrated in Exhibit 15-1, an effective cost control system must perform at three points: (1) before an event, (2) during an event, and (3) after an event.

Exhibit 15-2 illustrates a general planning and control model. Control begins with planning. Management should plan operational objectives and targets to provide appropriate company direction.

Cost consciousness refers to a company-wide employee attitude concerning (1) cost understanding, (2) cost containment, (3) cost avoidance, and (4) cost reduction. Exhibit 15-3 illustrates the importance of cost consciousness in controlling costs.

Management first exercises cost control when it prepares the budget. However, management can properly prepare budgets only when management understands the reasons for periodic cost changes. Management can control costs only with an understanding of why costs might differ from the budgeted amounts.

Several reasons account for changes in costs. For example, total variable costs and mixed costs change with changes in the activity level. To compensate for differences between the budgeted activity level and the actual activity level, companies use flexible budgets. Flexible budgets provide expected costs at any activity level. Management can subsequently make valid budget-to-actual cost comparisons to determine if the company adequately controlled total costs.

Three other reasons for changes in costs are (1) inflation or deflation, (2) changes in supply or supplier cost adjustments, and (3) different-from-expected quantities purchased, Management should understand the reasons for a change in costs to control them effectively.

Inflation or deflation reflects changes in the general price level. Some companies, especially those with long production times, include provisions in contracts that increase prices to compensate for inflation before delivery. Fluctuations in the value of money are called general price-level changes, which cause the prices of goods and services to change. If all other factors are constant, general price-level changes affect almost all prices approximately equally and in the same direction. Management should examine inflation and deflation indexes by industry or commodity to obtain more accurate information about inflation/deflation effects on prices of particular inputs.

Changes in demand and technology may cause changes in supply or the price charged for specific goods. The relationship between the availability of a good or service and the demand for that item affect its selling price. Advances in technology also cause specific price-level changes. Alternatively, part of specific price-level changes are typically additional production or performance costs passed on by suppliers to their customers. The number of suppliers of a product or service can also affect selling prices. Changes in quantities purchased can affect unit costs because of changes in quantity discounts.

Sometimes, higher taxes or additional regulatory requirements cause cost increases. The companies can (1) pass along the costs to customers as price increases to maintain the same income level,(2) decrease other costs to maintain the same income level, or (3) experience a decline in net income.

Cost containment is the practice of minimizing period-by-period increases in per-unit variable and total fixed costs. Cost containment is not possible for changes resulting from (1) inflation, (2) tax and regulatory changes, and (3) supply and demand adjustments.

Costs are subject to cost containment activities if they rise because of (1) reduced competition, (2) seasonality, and (3) quantities purchased. A company should look for ways to limit increases in costs because of these factors. Purchasing agents can choose alternative suppliers that have lower prices. However, purchasing agents should consider other factors besides price.

If cost containment is not possible, a company might be able to control costs through cost avoidance. Cost avoidance is the practice of finding acceptable alternatives to high-cost items and/or not spending money for unnecessary goods or services. Avoiding one cost might require a company to incur a lower, alternative cost.

Cost reduction refers to the practice of lowering current costs, especially excessive costs. Cost reduction often focuses on the activities that cause a company to incur costs. Benchmarking is especially important to learn what costs are excessive.

Companies can also reduce costs by outsourcing certain activities or services instead of maintaining internal departments. Data processing, legal and financial functions, and distribution are good candidates for outsourcing.

Managers might adopt the following five-step method of implementing a cost control system shown in Exhibit 15 - 4

1. The organization must investigate and understand the types of costs incurred.
2. The company must communicate the need for cost consciousness to all employees for the control process to be effective.
3. The company must educate employees in cost control techniques, encourage them to provide ideas on how to control costs, and motivate them to embrace the concepts by some type of incentive.
4. Management generates reports that indicate actual results, budget-to-actual comparisons, and variances.
5. Management and employees view the cost control system as a long-run process, not a short-run solution.

Management categorizes all fixed costs (and the activities that create them) as either committed or discretionary. The difference between the two categories is primarily the period for which management binds itself to the activity and the cost. Committed costs are those costs associated with basic plant assets or with the personnel structure that a company needs to operate. Committed costs reflect long-term managerial decisions concerning the desired level of operations and organizational capacity. Management cannot easily change committed costs in the short run. Examples of committed costs include depreciation, property taxes, and lease payments.

Managers control committed costs before a company incurs the costs by comparing the costs of investing in plant assets or in human resources with the expected benefits. Managers can also control committed costs by comparing actual results to expected results from investments in plant assets.

Discretionary costs are costs management funds at a specified level for a specified period. Management periodically reviews discretionary costs to discover whether they are in line with management's ongoing policies. Examples of discretionary costs include advertising, employee travel, employee development programs, research and development, and maintenance.

Management often first cuts discretionary cost activities when profits are lagging because management cannot assess the benefits of these activities definitively. Thus, proper planning for discretionary activities and costs might be more important than subsequent control measures. Control measures after the planning stage often involve monitoring discretionary costs to assure that they conform to budget classifications and to prevent managers from spending over the budgeted amounts.

Budget appropriations (or rates for each budget item) serve as a basis for comparison of actual costs and budgeted costs. Management periodically compares actual costs to appropriated amounts for each category of expenditure. Before top management can address the issue of discretionary costs, it must translate company goals into specific objectives and policies that management believes will contribute to organizational success. Management budgets discretionary costs on the basis of three factors: (1) the related activity's perceived significance to the achievement of goals and objectives, (2) the expected level of operations in the upcoming period, and (3) managerial negotiations in the budgetary process.

Managers should expend the full amount of their appropriations within the specified time frame for certain discretionary costs. For example, preventive maintenance is a discretionary cost necessary for maintaining quality output. However, for other discretionary costs, the less cost incurred the better. Managers often view discretionary activities and costs as though they were committed costs, but such a viewpoint does not change the underlying discretionary nature of the costs.

Companies often assume that the benefits from discretionary activities are unimportant. However, many of these types of activities are vital to success in a world-class environment because they are necessary to produce quality products and services. Before reducing or eliminating discretionary costs in areas such as research and development and maintenance, managers should attempt to recognize and measure the benefits of these activities through surrogate, nonmonetary measures. Exhibit 15-5 gives some examples of discretionary- activities and surrogate measures of their results.

The comparison of input costs and output results determines a reasonable cost-benefit relationship between the two. Managers can judge this cost-benefit relationship by how efficiently the company used inputs and how effectively those resources achieved their purposes.

Efficiency is the process of performing tasks to produce the best yield at the lowest cost from the resources available. Efficiency is the degree to which a satisfactory relationship occurs when comparing outputs to inputs. Thus, efficiency is a yield concept and equals output divided by input. Management can calculate and compare planned efficiency and actual efficiency.

A reasonable measure of efficiency can exist only when (1) a company can match inputs and outputs in the same period, and (2) a causal relationship exists between inputs and outputs.

Thus, measuring the efficiency of discretionary activities is difficult. A time lag of several years is often necessary before the effects of discretionary activities become noticeable. Also, causal relationships between discretionary activities and results are difficult to detect.

Effectiveness is a measure of how well a company achieves its goals and objectives. Actual effectiveness equals actual output divided by planned output. Management can compare actual effectiveness to a preestablished standard. Effectiveness does not require the consideration of inputs. Measuring the effectiveness of discretionary costs is often a highly subjective process because a perfect causal relationship does not exist between discretionary activities and actual output.

Some discretionary activities are so repetitive that a company can develop standards for them. These discretionary activities result in engineered costs, which are costs that bear an observable and known relationship to a quantifiable activity base. A company usually ties engineered costs to a performance measure related to work accomplished.

For example, a company might consider quality control inspection cost to be an engineered cost. The company could compare actual inspection cost to standard cost for each period. To do so, the company must obtain a reasonably valid estimate of expected inspection costs based on a particular activity level. The activity base is the number of inspections performed.

Management can then analyze total inspection costs using the generalized cost analysis model for variance analysis illustrated in Chapter 7. According to this model, the price variance is the actual quantity multiplied by the difference between the actual price and the standard price. The efficiency variance is the standard price multiplied by the difference between the actual quantity and the standard quantity. The total inspection cost variance is the difference between actual total inspection cost and the standard quantity multiplied by the standard price. This analysis assumes that inspection cost is a variable cost.

If a company can hire inspectors only on a salary basis, the company might treat inspection cost as a discretionary fixed cost. In such a case, the company might prefer to analyze inspection cost using a fixed overhead variance analysis model.

In the fixed overhead variance analysis model, the spending variance is the difference between actual cost and budgeted fixed cost. The volume variance is the difference between budgeted fixed cost and standard hours allowed multiplied by the standard fixed rate. The total inspection cost variance is the difference between actual cost and standard hours allowed multiplied by the standard fixed rate.

Management controls discretionary costs through budget-to-actual comparisons. Management compares actual results to expected results and explains the variances. By recognizing and encouraging cost consciousness attitudes, management can often find explanations for variances.

Chapter 15: Managing Costs And Uncertainty 368

Before comparing budgeted costs to actual costs, management should ensure that the comparisons are appropriate. Because total variable costs change in direct proportion to changes in a related activity level, management should use a flexible budget for analyzing variances from expected variable costs. Comparing actual variable costs to the static master budget would not provide fair comparisons for control purposes. Exhibit 15-6 illustrates a condensed budget. Exhibit 15-7 gives actual results used in Exhibit 15-8 to compute variances from the budget.

Management of organizational cash resources is crucial to an organization's survival. Liquidity must be sufficient to cover retiring debt and current obligations. However, idle excess cash reduces a company's profitability.

Information used to determine the optimal level of cash includes the cash budget and the pro forma statement of cash flows. Depending on the volatility of cash flows in general, management assesses the level of cash needed. With predictable collection patterns, a company needs a lower cash reserve compared to a growing company with unpredictable cash flows.

A company generally has three sources of cash: (1) sale of equity, debt securities, and short-term instruments; (2) sale of assets; and (3) operations. Working capital equals current assets minus current liabilities. In the operating cycle, a company invests cash in material and conversion costs, then finished goods inventory, then in marketing and administrative costs, and finally in accounts receivable. The cash cycle is complete when the company collects its accounts receivable. Exhibit 15-9 shows the cash collection cycle.

To make up for unexpected changes in cash flows, managers can take measures to increase or decrease cash flows. By reducing inventory levels, cash flow increases. Discounts for early payment, the use of lock boxes, and factoring of accounts receivable can increase cash flows. Purchasing on credit and delaying payments can also increase the cash balance. Variables influencing the cost of carrying cash depend on the method used to increase cash. Borrowing and equity financing have costs. The opportunity cost of having too much cash is the loss due to the time value of money and the need for stockholders to receive higher yields than the current interest rates.

Managers rely on banks for much of their short-term liquidity, and long-term loans. In turn bankers rely on financial information from creditors to measure risk and determine eligibility for loans. Accounting and cash flow information are key determinants of loan eligibility, loan limits, and credit terms. Accountants must monitor the firms compliance with loan agreement covenants. If a covenant violation is unavoidable, accountants can work with the bank to negotiate a solution to the situation.

Competition in markets creates a greater dependency among firms and their suppliers. Exhibit 15-10 shows three important interactions and dependencies of the supply chain. Often, firms use electronic exchange of information and payments to reduce purchasing transaction cost. There are generally two types of exchange; (1) the acquisition of significant operating needs such as direct materials And (2) the purchase of indirect materials or non operating inputs. E-procurement systems are electronic B2B buy-side applications controlling the

Chapter 15: Managing Costs And Uncertainty

requisitioning, ordering, and payment functions for inputs.

The globe of influence of management and cost accountants is split into two hemispheres; the first is accounting for events and activities that have already occurred and the second is accounting for events and activities that may occur in the future. Uncertainty is doubt or lack of precision in specifying future outcomes. There are two sources of uncertainty: (1) a lack of understanding and identification of cost drivers, and (2) unforeseen events. When management plans for unforeseen events, it is impossible to know the severity of all contingencies that could occur. Random refers to the fact that some portion of the cost is not predictable based on the cost driver or the cost is conjecturally, rather than definitively related to the cost driver.

Management can use four generic strategies to manage costs in the realm of uncertainty. (1) Uncertainty can be explicitly factored into estimates of future costs. (2) Costs can be structured to automatically adjust to uncertain outcomes. (3) Options and forward contracts can be utilized to mitigate the effects of uncertainty. (4) Insurance can be purchased to reimburse the firm in the event of unexpected occurrences. When alternative independent variables exist, least squares regression can help select the independent variable that is the best predictor of the dependent variable. Coefficient of determination is the portion of the variance in the dependent variable explained by the variance in the independent variable. Exhibit 15-11 shows a hypothetical historical relationship between utility costs and alternative explanatory variables. Using the coefficient of determination as a tool to select the best among candidate predictor variables will reduce the uncertainty regarding estimated costs or revenues. All other things being equal, the higher the coefficient of determination, the lower the uncertainty regarding the resulting prediction or forecast. The alternative approach to explicitly considering the effects of uncertainty in cost estimates is to examine the sensitivity of costs and/or revenues to estimation errors.

If demand spikes, profits soar, and if demand falters, profits drop rapidly and quickly turn to losses. The greater the uncertainty about demand the greater the risk of allowing fixed costs to compare a high proportion of total costs. Exhibit 15-12 demonstrates the relationship between uncertainty and cost structure. Although in most companies, fixed and variable costs are not completely substitutable, most have many opportunities to change their cost structures.

Uncertainty of the cost of inputs arises from two sources: the quantity of the inputs consumed and the price per unit of those inputs. Options and forward contracts are agreements that give the holder the right to purchase a given quantity of a specific input at a specific price. Generally the use of these agreements to manage price risk is known as hedging. Forward contracts or options can be executed between a company and a specific vendor, or options can be purchased on organized exchanges. Exhibit 15-13 lists items commonly traded on the organized exchanges.

Insurance involves a contract in which one party in exchange for a payment agrees to reimburse a second party for the costs of certain occurrences. It is purchased to cope with uncertainty about occurrences of specific events.

Chapter 15: Managing Costs And Uncertainty

SELF TEST

TRUE/FALSE

1. T F The first exercise in cost control is the preparation of the budget.

2. T F Cost control requires the support and attention of management only.

3. T F The level of discretionary fixed costs is more difficult to adjust in the short-run than committed fixed costs.

4. T F Cost control may result in increases in efficiency.

5. T F Cost containment is difficult for changes resulting from inflation, supply and demand adjustments, and tax and regulatory changes.

6. T F One must consider inputs in measuring effectiveness but not in measuring efficiency.

7. T F Cost reduction often focuses on the activities that cause costs.

8. T F Management uses pro forma cash flow statements as a tool to control cash flows.

9. T F Measurement of efficiency requires the consideration of inputs.

10. T F Costs incurred because of the basic plant assets or personnel structure of a company are committed costs.

11. T F Depreciation and lease payments are examples of discretionary costs.

12. T F Management generally does not know the optimal amount of discretionary costs.

13. T F Management measures the effectiveness of an activity by comparing actual output results to desired results.

14. T F General price-level changes are the changes in the availability of goods and services due to fluctuations in the value of money.

15. T F Managers rely on financial institutions for remaining liquid on the short term.

Chapter 15: Managing Costs And Uncertainty

MULTIPLE CHOICE

1. Managers first exercise cost control when they:

    A. take corrective action.
    B. calculate actual costs.
    C. compute variances from the budget.
    D. prepare the budget.

2. What is the process of minimizing period-to-period increases in per-unit variable and total fixed costs?

    A. cost reduction
    B. cost avoidance
    C. cost containment
    D. cost utilization

3. An example of a committed fixed cost is:

    A. advertising contracts.
    B. supervisory salaries.
    C. periodic warehouse rent.
    D. long-term computer leases.

4. The costs associated with basic plant assets or with the personnel structure an organization must have to operate are:

    A. committed costs.
    B. discretionary costs.
    C. basic costs.
    D. structural costs.

5. Costs that management decides to fund at a specified amount for a specified period are:

    A. specified costs.
    B. funded costs.
    C. committed costs.
    D. discretionary costs.

6. Which of the following is an example of a committed cost?

    A. advertising
    B. research and development
    C. property taxes
    D. employee development programs

Chapter 15: Managing Costs And Uncertainty 372

7. Managers must consider inputs when measuring:

   A. efficiency.
   B. effectiveness.
   C. efficiency and effectiveness.
   D. machine ineffectiveness.

8. The degree to which a satisfactory relationship occurs when comparing outputs to inputs reflects the:

   A. cost of an activity.
   B. efficiency of an activity.
   C. effectiveness of an activity.
   D. importance of an activity.

9. Management achieves optimal control of a discretionary fixed cost when the cost is:

   A. minimized.
   B. optimal for the organization's goals and objectives.
   C. held at the same level as it was in the prior period.
   D. held below some threshold such as standard cost.

10. Why is cost control after an event important?

    A. to diagnose problems and guide future actions
    B. to correct problems as they occur
    C. to reflect planning
    D. to ensure that the event is pursued according to plans

11. Which of the following methods can management use to control costs before an event?

    A. responsibility reports
    B. variance analysis
    C. budgets and standards
    D. monitoring of ongoing activities

12. A company wide employee attitude about cost understanding, cost containment, cost avoidance, and cost reduction is:

    A. cost control.
    B. cost consciousness.
    C. cost efficiency.
    D. cost effectiveness.

13. Management generally bases discretionary cost appropriations on all of the following except:

    A. the activity's perceived importance to achieving goals and objectives.
    B. the upcoming period's expected level of operations.
    C. managerial negotiations during the budgetary process.
    D. liquidated transactions

14. What can compensate for differences between the budgeted activity level and the actual activity level by providing expected variable costs at the actual activity level?

    A. flexible budget
    B. master budget
    C. static budget
    D. program budget

15. As a general rule, if the technology of producing a good or service advances, the cost of that good or service:

    A. increases slightly.
    B. increases greatly.
    C. declines.
    D. does not change.

16. As taxes and the number of regulations increase, costs will:

    A. decline slightly.
    B. decline greatly.
    C. increase.
    D. not change.

17. Which of the following causes of changes in costs is subject to cost containment activities?

    A. quantities purchased
    B. inflation
    C. tax and regulatory changes
    D. supply and demand adjustments

18. Hedging is:

    A. removing authority from top-level management.
    B. the use of forward contracts and options to manage price risk.
    C. the relationship of uncertainty to cost structure.
    D. the sensitivity of costs and/or revenues to estimation errors.

Chapter 15: Managing Costs And Uncertainty   374

19. Management should view the cost control system as a:

    A. short-run solution to complex problems.
    B. long-run process, not a short-run solution.
    C. way to exert their authority over employees.
    D. way to satisfy government regulations.

20. Managers need to communicate the need for cost consciousness to employees so that the:

    A. company can receive favorable press reports.
    B. managers can receive a bonus.
    C. department will meet the budget.
    D. cost control process will be effective.

21. The difference between committed costs and discretionary costs is:

    A. committed costs are fixed and discretionary costs are variable.
    B. discretionary costs are fixed and committed costs are variable.
    C. the time horizon for which management binds itself to the activity and the cost.
    D. committed costs are easier to eliminate.

22. Companies that have fairly high contribution margins can withstand large increases in fixed costs as long as:

    A. revenues increase.
    B. variable costs increase.
    C. the contribution margin decreases.
    D. inflation remains low.

23. If a company treats a discretionary cost as an engineered cost, it can control it by using:
    A. program budgeting.
    B. static budgeting.
    C. budget appropriations.
    D. standards.

24. A reasonable measure of efficiency can exist only when:

    A. a company can measure inputs and outputs qualitatively.
    B. a company can measure inputs and outputs in different periods.
    C. a credible causal relationship exists between inputs and outputs.
    D. a company collects accounts receivable.

Chapter 15: Managing Costs And Uncertainty   375

25. Opportunities to reduce costs in an organization will increase if all employees are:

    A. cost conscious.
    B. temporary.
    C. permanent.
    D. required to meet cost budgets.

26. Budgeting the cost of repairs and maintenance at $3 per machine hour is an example of a discretionary cost being treated as a(n):

    A. fixed cost.
    B. mixed cost.
    C. programmed cost.
    D. engineered cost.

27. Managerial control of discretionary costs is NOT likely to rely on:

    A. periodical reviews..
    B. capital budgeting.
    C. program budgeting.
    D. budget-to-actual comparisons.

28. Joanne Enterprises budgeted inspection cost was $45,000 based on 30,000 budgeted inspections and 2,000 budgeted inspection hours. Thus, the budgeted average inspections per hour are 15, and the standard average pay rate for inspectors is $22.50 per hour. Actual inspection cost was $64,000. The actual inspections were 32,000, and actual inspection hours were 1,600. Inspection cost is a variable cost. What is Joanne Enterprises price (rate) variance for inspection cost?

    A. $12,000 U
    B. $12,000 F
    C. $28,000 U
    D. $28,000 F

29. The generic strategies for managing uncertainty do NOT include:

    A. uncertainty explicitly factored into future cost estimates.
    B. stock options used to mitigate effects of uncertainty
    C. costs that automatically adjust to unknown outcomes..
    D. insurance purchased to reimburse firm for unexpected event.

30. Cost changes resulting from supply cost adjustments include

    A. change caused by uncertainty of future events.
    B. cost controls that reduce purchased inputs.
    C. the reduction of the value of money.
    D. additional costs that are passed on to the customer.

QUESTIONS AND PROBLEMS

1. List the three functions of a cost control system and explain the reasons for each function.

2. Define cost containment. What causes of cost changes are subject to cost containment? What causes of cost changes are not subject to cost containment?

3. What is the difference between cost avoidance and cost reduction? On what does cost reduction focus?

4. Explain why participation by managers is important in cost reduction programs. What do managers need to communicate to their employees regarding cost consciousness?

5. What are the five steps that management should use in implementing a cost control system?

6. Define committed costs and discretionary costs and give examples of each. What is the primary difference between committed costs and discretionary costs?

7. Define efficiency and effectiveness. What does the determination of efficiency and effectiveness require?

8. Why is measuring the efficiency of discretionary activities often difficult?

9. Describe the strategies that managers can use for dealing with uncertainty.

10. How can management cover an unexpected shortfall in cash flows during a period?

11. What are the sources of a company's cash? Define working capital. How does cash management relate to the management of working capital?

12. Hollinrake Enterprises treats maintenance costs as a variable cost. Management expects that the total labor hours in maintenance to be 400 based on production of 200,000 units. Therefore, management expects that the company will use one maintenance hour for each 500 units produced (200,000 ÷ 400). The standard hourly pay rate for maintenance employees is $10 per hour. Thus, the total budgeted maintenance cost is $4,000 (400 x $10). During May, Hollinrake produced 192,000 units and used 380 maintenance hours at a total cost of $4,560.

(a) Calculate Hollinrake Enterprises total variance for maintenance cost.

(b) Calculate Hollinrake Enterprises rate variance.

(c) Calculate Hollinrake Enterprises efficiency variance.

13. Define uncertainty and its sources.

Chapter 15: Managing Costs And Uncertainty

14. Discuss the sources of uncertainty for inputs and the managing of the associated risks.

15. What is coefficient of determination and how can it be used as a tool to reduce the uncertainty of estimated costs and revenues?

Chapter 15: Managing Costs And Uncertainty

SELF TEST ANSWERS

TRUE/FALSE

1.	T	4.	T	7.	T	10.	T	13.	T
2.	F	5.	T	8.	T	11.	F	14.	F
3.	F	6.	F	9.	T	12.	T	15.	T

MULTIPLE CHOICE

1.	D	7.	A	13.	D	19.	B	25.	A
2.	C	8.	B	14.	A	20.	D	26.	D
3.	D	9.	B	15.	C	21.	C	27.	B
4.	A	10.	A	16.	C	22.	A	28.	C
5.	D	11.	C	17.	A	23.	D	29.	B
6.	C	12.	B	18.	B	24.	C	30.	D

QUESTIONS AND PROBLEMS

1. The three functions of a cost control system are (1) control before an event, (2) control during an event, and (3) control after an event. The reason for control before an event is to plan the costs a company expects to incur and to prevent unnecessary costs. The purpose for control during an event is to correct problems as they occur to minimize unnecessary costs. The reason for control after an event is to diagnose the causes of costs and to guide future actions to reduce non-value-added costs.

2. Cost containment is minimizing increases in per-unit variable costs and total fixed costs from one period to the next. Cost increases arising from reduced competition, seasonality, and quantities purchased are subject to cost containment. Cost changes arising from inflation, tax and regulatory changes, and supply and demand adjustments are not subject to cost containment. These changes are not subject to cost containment because they are due to factors outside the organization.

3. Cost avoidance is finding acceptable alternatives to high-cost items and not spending money for unnecessary goods or services. Cost reduction is similar to cost avoidance, but cost reduction means lowering current costs. Cost reduction efforts focus on reducing or eliminating non-value-added activities.

4. Managers provide important input on cost reduction efforts, and their attitude sets the tone for the entire department or organization. If managers are cost conscious, their employees are more likely to be cost conscious. Managers need to communicate the need for cost consciousness to their employees. Managers need to emphasize the benefits the employees will receive for engaging in cost control efforts. Employees do not mind participating in cost reduction efforts if managers reward their efforts.

Chapter 15: Managing Costs And Uncertainty 383

5. The five steps that management should use in implementing a cost control system are as follows: (1) investigate and understand the types of costs that the organization incurs, (2) communicate the need for cost consciousness to all employees, (3) motivate employees by education and incentives to engage in cost control, (4) generate reports that compare actual results to budget, and (5) view the cost control system as a long-run process not as a short-run solution.

6. Committed costs are the costs associated with basic plant assets or with the personnel structure an organization must have to operate. Long-run management decisions concerning the desired level of operations affect committed costs. Examples of committed costs are plant depreciation and property taxes. An organization incurs discretionary costs to fund an activity at a specified amount for a specified period. Management periodically reviews discretionary costs to decide whether their funding level is consistent with plans. Typical examples of discretionary costs are advertising, public relations, employee training and development, and research and development. The primary difference between committed costs and discretionary costs is the time horizon that management is committed to an activity and its corresponding costs.

7. Efficiency is the degree to which a satisfactory relationship occurs when comparing inputs to outputs. Efficiency is a yield concept and is measured by dividing input by output. Effectiveness is a measure of how well an organization achieved its goals and objectives. Management measures effectiveness by dividing actual output by planned output. A valid measure of output is required to calculate efficiency and effectiveness.

8. To measure efficiency the company must satisfy the following three conditions: (1) the company must measure inputs and outputs quantitatively; (2) the company must match inputs and outputs in the same time period; and (3) inputs and outputs must demonstrate a credible causal relationship. These three factors make measuring the efficiency of discretionary activities difficult. A time lag of several years might be necessary before the output of a discretionary activity becomes noticeable. Discretionary cost inputs might not have caused outputs of a discretionary activity.

9. Management can use four generic strategies that apply to cost management costs in the realm of uncertainty. (1) Uncertainty can be explicitly factored into estimates of future costs. (2) Costs can be structured to automatically adjust to uncertain outcomes. (3) Options and forward contracts can be utilized to mitigate the effects of uncertainty. (4) Insurance can be purchased to reimburse the firm in the event of unexpected occurrences.

10. Management might accelerate cash collection by sending invoices earlier. The purchasing department could delay purchases until the sales department receives orders. A company could pay selected accounts payable that allow a discount for early payment. Another option is to sell accounts receivables to intermediaries or factor accounts receivable. A company could delay payments on purchases by a few days more than usual. Management could decide to pay invoices by credit cards instead of cash. A company could request an installment plan from its creditors.

11. A company generally has three sources of cash: (1) sale of equity, debt securities, and short-term instruments; (2) sale of assets; and (3) operations. Working capital equals current assets minus current liabilities. In the operating cycle, a company invests cash in inventory, then in marketing and administrative costs, and finally in accounts receivable. The cash cycle is complete when the company collects its accounts receivable. Management of cash used by and generated from the operating cycle is integral to the management of working capital.

12.
(a) Actual cost $4,560
Standard rate $10
Standard hours: 192,000 ÷ 500 = 384   3,840
Total variance $ 720 U

(b) Actual rate ($4,560 ÷ 380 hours) $12
Standard rate   10
Difference in rate $ 2
Actual hours   380
Rate variance $ 760 U

(c) Actual hours   380
Standard hours: 192,000 ÷ 500 =   384
Difference in hours   (4)
Standard rate $10
Efficiency variance $40 F

13. Uncertainty is doubt or lack of precision in specifying future outcomes. There are two sources of uncertainty: (1) a lack of understanding and identification of cost drivers, and (2) unforeseen events. When management plans for unforeseen events, it is impossible to know the severity of all contingencies that could occur.

14. Uncertainty of the cost of inputs arises from two sources: the quantity of the inputs consumed and the price per unit of those inputs. Options and forward contracts are agreements that give the holder the right to purchase a given quantity of a specific input at a specific price. Generally the use of these agreements to manage price risk is know as hedging. Forward contracts or options can be executed between a company and a specific vendor, or options can be purchased on organized exchanges.

15. Coefficient of determination is the portion of the variance in the dependent variable explained by the variance in the independent variable. Using the coefficient of determination as a tool to select the best among candidate predictor variables will reduce the uncertainty regarding estimated costs or revenues. All other things being equal, the higher the coefficient of determination, the lower the uncertainty regarding the resulting prediction or forecast.

CHAPTER 16

IMPLEMENTING QUALITY CONCEPTS

CHAPTER OVERVIEW

Companies recognize that high quality is a fundamental strategy for success in the global economy. Companies are striving to attract more customers and to provide them with more choices for products and services. Customers are becoming increasingly aware of their product choices as to quality, price, service, and lead time. The Internet and advanced technology provide customers with expanded product and service options. Many companies have adopted a philosophy of improving the quality of their products, processes, and services continuously.

This chapter focuses on quality issues including benchmarking, total quality management (TQM), quality costs, quality cost measurement, balanced scorecard, and a cost management system that supports quality initiatives. Accountants must understand quality costs and the long-term tradeoffs involved between higher and lower product or service quality. Costs of quality improvement are an investment that will provide future returns. Accountants must provide management with information on quality costs and the results of quality improvement efforts. The Appendix discusses international quality standards, including the ISO 9000 series and European Foundation for Quality Management (EFQM.)

CHAPTER STUDY GUIDE

Quality consists of all the attributes of a product or service that affect its ability to meet the stated or implied needs of the person obtaining it.

Quality is an issue for the whole company because good quality is imperative for survival and profitability in today's competitive economy. The company should involve all of its processes in quality improvement efforts. Companies view quality from two perspectives. The first is the sum of the internal processes that produce a product or service. The second is customer satisfaction with that product or service.

Quality affects productivity because a company measures its productivity by dividing the number of good units of output by the specific inputs used to generate output during a period. Activities that stop or delay a production process do not add value to a product. These activities

Chapter 16: Implementing Quality Concepts 386

are non-value-added activities. Value-added activities, however, increase the value of the product in the eyes of the customer. A company should use activity analysis to target non-value-added activities for reduction or elimination.

Three important non-value-added activities are as follows: (1) storing products for which the company has little immediate demand, (2) moving materials unnecessarily, and (3) experiencing unscheduled production interruptions. Inspecting incoming components is another non-value-added activity. To minimize this activity, some companies require their suppliers to provide only zero-defect components. Companies may perform quality audits of their suppliers to ensure compliance.

Factors that cause non-value-added activities include the need to reprocess, rework, replace, and repair defective products. The factors that greatly affect the product's failure rate, useful life, and breakage tendencies include the quality of product design, materials used, and the production process. In addition, production process quality affects the amount of waste, rework, and scrap.

Production technology, employee skill and training, and management programs can help to control the production process quality. If companies can eliminate the causes of poor quality, higher quality products and productivity increases will follow. Some techniques that improve quality and increase productivity are as follows: (1) having suppliers to inspect materials for quality, (2) having employees monitor and be responsible for their own output, and (3) fitting machinery for error-free operations.

Quality control includes all attempts to reduce variability and defects in products. Quality control places the chief responsibility for the quality of the product on its maker. Some companies use statistical process control (SPC) procedures to analyze variations in a production process. Management views significant variations as errors or defects. Computer-integrated manufacturing systems often eliminate these variations. These systems have internal controls to evaluate variations and detect production problems.

Companies use control charts to analyze the variations. Exhibit 16-1 illustrates a control chart. These charts graph actual process results and show upper and lower control limits. These SPC charts are an application of the management by exception principle. The accountant must prepare these control charts consistently and accurately for analysis to be meaningful. The management accountant is personally involved in choosing the proper performance measures and assisting management in interpreting the charts.

The customer's view of quality is much broader than simply considering whether a particular product is defective. Customers see a product or service as having quality if it satisfies all specified needs. Exhibit 16-2 lists eight basic characteristics of product quality.

Important characteristics of service quality include assurance (knowledgeable, courteous and trustworthy employees), tangibles (clean-looking facilities, equipment and employees), and empathy (high degree of caring and attention). Some companies hire outside assessors to

Chapter 16: Implementing Quality Concepts

evaluate the quality of their services.

Grade refers to the addition or elimination of product or service characteristics to meet additional needs, especially price. Customers perceive that a product has value when it satisfies their needs at the lowest possible cost. Cost includes the cost of operating, maintaining, and disposing the product in addition to its purchase price.

Customers often compare products and services against an ideal rather than against similar products and services in the same industry. When a company formally uses this type of analysis, it is competitive benchmarking.

One way a company can improve its processes is through benchmarking. Benchmarking involves comparing a company's products, processes, or services to those of competitors or those that are the best in the class. A company cannot adopt all of the processes of another successful company. However, a company should develop a better understanding of its own strengths and weaknesses. A company can adopt better practices that are easily transferable.

When conducting competitive benchmarking, companies should adhere to accepted ethical standards. Codes of conduct have been established for benchmarking activities addressing the equal exchange of information, restricted use of learned data, avoidance of anti-trust issues and illegalities and interorganizational courtesy.

Three kinds of benchmarking are results, process and strategic. Exhibit 16-3 lists the reasons for benchmarking. Results benchmarking involves a comparison of the company's products or services to those of competitors. Results benchmarking uses reverse engineering to examine a competitor's products or services. Process benchmarking involves the comparison of specific characteristics to those of companies that are the best in that specific characteristic. The "best-in-class" process benchmarking is not necessarily a comparison to a competitor. Process benchmarking can include companies in different industries. Strategic benchmarking is identifying the winning strategies of highly successful companies. The implementation of benchmarking is illustrated in Exhibit 16-4.

Many companies have adopted the philosophy of total quality management (TQM) as the foundation for improving quality in all facets of their organization. TQM has four important characteristics: (1) an internal managerial system of planning, controlling, and decision making dedicated to continuous improvement, (2) participation by everyone in the organization, (3) a focus on improving goods and services from the customer's perspective, and (4) long-term partnerships with suppliers.

TQM requires a system that provides information about the quality of processes so that managers can carry out their function in the quest for continuous improvement. In the past, managers did not consider quality in the planning process. Rather, managers tolerated a certain level of defects. However, TQM emphasizes the prevention of defects, continuous improvement, and building quality into every process and product. In changing to TQM, managers should identify quality problems so that they can set goals and objectives for quality improvements. The system should also measure quality and provide feedback on quality improvements. The system should also foster teamwork in the quality improvement process.

TQM requires all levels in the organization to share in the responsibility for quality. Top management must be a part of the quality process and demonstrate a commitment to the TQM approach. Top management should provide feedback to lower-level managers about the need for quality improvements and recognize quality achievements. Managers should help employees to feel important in the quality improvement process. Managers should encourage employees and train them to perform multiple functions to improve efficiency and quality.

Under TQM, the external customer is the ultimate judge of quality. Companies must identify who their customers are. Some companies may need to eliminate some external customers if the costs to serve them exceed the revenues they generate.

Next, a company must understand what its customers want. Most customers want quality, value, and good service. The only difference between two companies is often their level of customer service. Poor service can result in a significant loss of customer goodwill. About 68 percent of customers that stop doing business with a company do so because of poor service.

Managers with a TQM philosophy are encouraged to review their entire supply chain and establish long relationships with preferred suppliers and see suppliers as a distinct part of their company's ability to satisfy customers. Managers need to be certain that they are working with suppliers that will enhance quality and customer satisfaction.

The Malcolm Baldrige National Quality Award (Baldrige Award) is given to companies that focus attention on management systems, processes, consumer satisfaction, and business results to achieve product and service excellence. The five categories of applicants are manufacturing, service, small business, education, and health-care organizations.

The Baldrige Award is given based on following seven qualities; (1) leadership, (2) strategic planning, (3) customer and market focus, (4) measurement, analysis, and knowledge management, (5) human resource focus, (6) process management, and (7) business results. Exhibit 16-5 illustrates the criteria for the Baldrige Award.

Some organizations putting TQM into practice find it costly due to the time needed for the philosophy and concepts to be incorporated throughout the company. However, most companies using TQM enjoy benefits and outcomes listed in Exhibit 16-6. A 2001study shown in Exhibit 16-7 shows that most companies do not fully realize the benefits of TQM until five years after implementing TQM.

A company can improve the quality of its products and services by investing in prevention costs, one type of quality cost. Prevention costs are the costs a company incurs to prevent defects because of poor processing. Examples of prevention costs include training, engineering, modeling, and better production equipment.

Chapter 16: Implementing Quality Concepts 389

Another category of quality costs is appraisal costs. Appraisal costs are the costs of monitoring the quality of a company's processes and products. A company incurs appraisal costs to help find defects that prevention efforts did not eliminate. Prevention costs and appraisal costs help to reduce failure costs from producing defective products.

Failure costs include internal failure costs and external failure costs. Internal failure costs are the costs a company incurs when it finds a defect before it ships the product to a customer. Examples are scrap and rework. External failure costs are the costs a company incurs after it ships a defective product to a customer. These costs include warranty costs, customer complaints, litigation, product recalls, and lost sales.

Total quality costs can also be classified into two broad categories: (1) the cost of compliance or assurance and (2) the cost of noncompliance or failure. The cost of compliance is equal to the sum of prevention cost and appraisal costs. Compliance cost expenditures are proactive action by managers to reduce present and future cost of failure. The cost of noncompliance is equal to the sum of internal and external failure costs. Exhibit 16-8 has specific examples of each type of quality cost.

Traditionally, accounting systems have not separately identified quality costs. Various general ledger accounts effectively bury and hide quality cost information. For example, Work in Process Inventory and Finished Goods Inventory contain costs for scrap, rework, preventive maintenance, and other overhead costs related to quality. For example, Marketing/Advertising Expense includes cost for product recalls and advertising campaigns to improve a company's image resulting from poor quality products. Because managers are not aware of the magnitude of quality costs, they do not actively seek to reduce them.

The management accountant must design the quality cost reporting system and identify the cost drivers of quality costs. The management accountant can use the quality cost information to help management make the best quality improvement decisions from a cost-benefit standpoint.

Exhibit 16-9 shows where in the production–sales cycle a company usually incurs a particular type of quality cost. A company should have an information feedback loop to connect the types and causes of failure costs to prevention costs that the company should incur. This loop facilitates continuous improvement.

In theory, if the company incurred enough prevention and appraisal costs, failure costs would drop to zero. However, in the real world failure costs are seldom, if ever, zero. Management needs to incur the prevention and appraisal costs that will yield the greatest reduction in failure costs.

Pareto analysis is a technique that management can use to decide where to spend money on prevention efforts. According to Pareto analysis, about 20 to 30 percent of items account for 70 to 80 percent of the cost of those items. Using this technique, management would classify the causes of process problems by their effect on an objective. Management should use Pareto

Chapter 16: Implementing Quality Concepts 390

analysis often enough to spot trends quickly to make prompt changes.

A company could expand its chart of accounts to handle either separate tracing or allocating quality costs to new accounts. Exhibit 16-10 provides some suggested accounts that could help management concentrate on quality costs. In addition, a company must estimate the opportunity costs of lost sales. Opportunity costs are important though a company does not record them in the accounts.

If the organization has a database management system, the organization could alternatively code transactions representing quality costs to produce the same information without expanding its chart of accounts. Such coding allows the company to reformat the information. With better quality cost information, a company can prepare a cost of quality report like the one illustrated in Exhibit 16-11.

Exhibit 16-12 gives formulas for calculating an organization's quality costs. Some of these amounts are, by necessity, estimates. The relevance of information is more important for managerial decisions than the absolute reliability of the information.

High quality helps a company to increase current profits through lower costs, higher prices, or both. Managers may want to focus on more strategic objectives, such as increasing market share, rather than on short-term profits. A company could combine the strategies of increasing quality and reducing prices to increase market share. Reducing costs and increasing productivity through better quality allows a company to reduce prices and increase the quantity demanded of its products. Thus, higher quality can result in greater market share, higher long-term profits, and possibly higher short-term profits.

The business strategy of focusing on customers and quality requires cost management to maintain a reasonable value-to-price relationship. Although the market sets prices, a company's costs influence its ability to supply the market at competitive prices. Companies that lack cost management skills will not succeed in the long run. Therefore, companies need to engage in strategic cost management.

Strategic cost management is the managerial use of management accounting information to formulate and communicate strategies, establish, implement and monitor methods for pursuing those strategies, and evaluate the degree of success in meeting the goals and objectives of those strategies. An organization's management accounting system should generate report information that measures the company's success in meeting customer needs and expectations and quality objectives.

A balanced scorecard (BSC) is one accounting tool managers use in implementing strategy. This tool is used to view the entire quality management strategy from four perspectives: (1) learning and growth, (2) internal business, (3) customers, and (4) finance. The accountant can integrate these perspectives with the seven categories of the MBNQA. For example, the learning and growth perspective of the BSC can be integrated into the human resource focus category of the MBNQA. The textbook provides an example of the potential use of a BSC in providing

Chapter 16: Implementing Quality Concepts

information on quality. Goals and measurements for the BSC perspectives are shown in Exhibit 16-13.

In designing a management accounting system, a company must consider cost accumulation and process measurement activities. The costs accumulated for the financial accounting system may not be adequate for management's needs. For example, a strategic cost management system would treat research and development costs as a product cost. The financial accounting system treats these costs as a period expense. A strategic cost management system would distinguish product costs that add value from product costs that add no value. By highlighting non-value-added costs, managers and employees can assess how effective they are at reducing such costs as a part of continuous improvement.

Many activities essential to success in the global economy are related to time, not money. Yet, the financial accounting system does not measure nonfinancial activities. A useful management accounting system includes nonfinancial performance measures.

The financial accounting system also has a short-term focus. However, an organization's goal of continuous improvement has a long-term focus. Thus, a strategic cost management system should report costs and benefits of activities in a form that will meet management's needs. Managers need to make informed assessments of the company's performance in the value chain, of its competitive advantage or disadvantage, and of its progress toward organizational goals. Having adequate information from the cost management system is vital to these judgments.

TQM and continuous improvement go together. The foundation for TQM is the behavior of management and employees. Top management must be committed to TQM for it to succeed. Management must provide an atmosphere of trust, and management should value ideas from everyone in the organization. Management must motivate employees by providing recognition for quality improvement efforts. If management treats employees well, employees are more likely to treat customers well.

The main idea behind TQM is doing the right things right the first time which means TQM emphasizes the concept of zero defects. Management must provide employees with the training, resources, and equipment necessary to meet this objective.

Exhibit 16-14 illustrates how a company progresses from having no quality system to achieving a world-class quality system. The first stage is quality conformance. In this stage, the company inspects products for conformance to standards or monitors employees to detect poor service. The company becomes quality conscious in the second stage and develops techniques for eliminating defective products or poor service. In the third stage, the company is quality competitive and competes against other organizations for quality awards. The company achieves world-class status in the fourth stage. In the fourth stage, quality becomes an integral part of the organizational culture. The world-class company sets tolerances for defective products or services at zero percent. However, a company does not stop pursuing better quality when it reaches world-class status. TQM is not a static concept but focuses on continuous improvement.

APPENDIX

Most large companies compete in international markets. To complete effectively in a global economy, a company must comply with a variety of international standards. International standards serve to assure customers in international markets that products and services provide the benefits the customers expected.

An international quality guideline is the ISO 9000 series. These standards are general in nature and prescribe the generic design, material procurement, production, quality control, and delivery procedures to assure quality. These standards are not product standards. Management decides how to meet the standards.

Some companies must meet ISO 9000 registration to sell regulated products in the European Union. No international organization administers the ISO 9000 registration process. Rather, national registrars such as Underwriters Laboratories and the British Standards Institution administer the program.

A company may apply for ISO 9000 registration after completing an internal review. To be registered, the company must first pass a quality audit conducted by a third-party reviewer. The quality audit involves a review of product design activities, manufacturing processes and controls, quality documentation and records, and management quality policy and philosophy. Quality audits are expensive. After registration, audit teams visit the company biannually to ensure compliance. Although the costs are high, many companies consider the benefits of ISO 9000 registration to outweigh the costs.

Although meeting ISO standards is not necessary to do business in the United States, companies may receive operational and competitive benefits from becoming ISO 9000 registered. If a company's competitors are ISO 9000 registered, good business sense would require the company to become ISO 9000 registered.

European Foundation for Quality Management (EFQM) was founded in 1988 by the presidents of 14 major European companies with the endorsement of the European Commission to develop a European framework for quality improvement similar to the U.S. MBNQA and Japan's Demig Prize. The EFQM Excellence Model shown in Exhibit 16-15 is based on the premise that leadership is delivered through people, policy and strategy, and partnerships and resources. The following concepts are the foundation, although subject to change, for the EFQM model: (1) result orientation, (2) customer focus, (3) leadership and constancy of purpose, (4) management by processes and facts, (5) people development and involvement, (6) continuous learning, innovation, and improvement, (7) partnership development, and (8) corporate social responsibility.

Chapter 16: Implementing Quality Concepts

SELF TEST

TRUE/FALSE

1. T F Quality control places the chief responsibility for the quality of a product on the quality control inspectors.

2. T F Computer-integrated manufacturing systems often eliminate variations in a production process.

3. T F Inspecting incoming components is a value-added activity.

4. T F Grade refers to the addition or elimination of product or service characteristics to meet additional needs including price.

5. T F Process benchmarking uses the technique of reverse engineering.

6. T F In TQM, the quality control inspector is the ultimate judge of quality.

7. T F Historically, companies have seriously considered quality in the planning process.

8. T F Traditionally, companies have not recognized quality costs separately in their accounting systems.

9. T F Scrap and rework are examples of internal failure costs.

10. T F The top award for TQM in the United States is the Malcolm Baldrige National Quality Award.

11. T F Costs accumulated for the financial accounting system are usually adequate to meet management's information needs for making strategic decisions.

12. T F A strategic cost management system would treat research and development costs as a product cost.

13. T F Many activities vital to success in the global economy involve time rather than money.

APPENDIX

14. T F To be ISO registered, a company must submit to a quality audit by an outside reviewer.

15. T F European guidelines for quality created in 1987 is the ISO 1000 series.

Chapter 16: Implementing Quality Concepts

MULTIPLE CHOICE

1. Management should view the costs of quality improvement efforts as:

    A. unnecessary expenses.
    B. prior period adjustments.
    C. recoverable investments.
    D. a loss of the period.

2. A company should view quality from the perspective of the:

    A. design engineer.
    B. management accountant.
    C. production manager.
    D. customer.

3. The addition or removal of product or service characteristics to satisfy additional consumer needs including price is:

    A. grade.
    B. statistical process control.
    C. continuous improvement.
    D. TQM.

4. Investigating, comparing, and evaluating a company's products, processes, and services against those of the best-in-class companies is:

    A. statistical process control.
    B. benchmarking.
    C. a quality audit.
    D. Pareto analysis.

5. Comparing specific characteristics to those of companies that are the best in that characteristic is:

    A. results benchmarking.
    B. process benchmarking.
    C. statistical process control.
    D. reverse engineering.

Chapter 16: Implementing Quality Concepts

6. Which of the following is NOT an important principle of TQM?

    A. The organization should have a managerial system of planning, controlling, and decision making.
    B. Everyone in the organization should participate.
    C. The organization should focus on improving goods and services from the customer's viewpoint.
    D. Management must provide an atmosphere of trust by taking credit for employees' ideas.

7. Total quality management directs management attention to the relationship between the internal production/service process and the:

    A. external customer.
    B. control charts.
    C. Malcolm Baldrige National Quality Award.
    D. financial statements.

8. TQM first requires that companies know who are their:

    A. stockholders.
    B. suppliers.
    C. customers.
    D. competitors.

9. Research indicates that about 68 percent of customers who stop doing business with a company do so because of:

    A. price.
    B. lack of product quality.
    C. lack of social responsibility.
    D. poor service.

10. Which of the following activities would result in a prevention cost?

    A. inspecting products before shipment
    B. reworking a defective unit
    C. handling a customer's complaint
    D. employee training

Chapter 16: Implementing Quality Concepts

11. Which of the following represents an internal failure cost?

    A. scrapping a defective product before shipment
    B. recalling a defective product after shipment
    C. monitoring products during production
    D. warranty costs

12. Which of the following quality costs are costs of compliance?

    A. prevention and appraisal
    B. internal failure and external failure
    C. appraisal and internal failure
    D. prevention, appraisal, and internal failure

13. Which of the following quality costs are costs of noncompliance?

    A. prevention and appraisal
    B. internal failure and external failure
    C. appraisal and internal failure
    D. appraisal, internal failure, and external failure

14. Theoretically, if a company prudently incurred prevention and appraisal costs, then failure costs would:

    A. equal the sum of prevention and appraisal costs.
    B. become zero.
    C. increase slightly.
    D. increase significantly.

15. Information about quality costs:

    A. historically has been a major section of the income statement.
    B. is required as footnotes to the financial statements by generally accepted accounting principles.
    C. is partially contained in the accounting records and supporting documentation.
    D. is of little benefit to management because the company has already incurred the costs.

16. When a company improves its quality through prevention and appraisal activities, noncompliance costs:

    A. decrease and productivity decreases.
    B. increase and productivity increases.
    C. decrease and productivity increases.
    D. increase and productivity decreases.

Chapter 16: Implementing Quality Concepts 397

17. The embodiment of TQM in the United States is the:

    A. Deming Prize.
    B. Malcolm Baldrige National Quality Award.
    C. ISO 9000 registration.
    D. Underwriters Laboratories certification.

18. TQM is inseparable from the concept of:

    A. process benchmarking.
    B. results benchmarking.
    C. management by exception.
    D. continuous improvement.

19. The heart of the foundational principle of TQM is:

    A. zero defects now and in the future.
    B. defective production not greater than one percent of total production.
    C. failure costs not greater than the sum of prevention and appraisal costs.
    D. failure costs less than two percent of sales.

20. A strategic cost management system would treat research and development costs as a(n):

    A. period expense.
    B. product cost.
    C. extraordinary loss.
    D. opportunity cost.

21. The first stage in a company's progress along the quality continuum is:

    A. quality competitive.
    B. quality conscious.
    C. world-class status.
    D. quality conformance.

22. A useful management accounting system would:

    A. include nonfinancial performance measures.
    B. treat research and development costs as a period expense.
    C. have a short-term focus.
    D. combine value-added costs and non-value-added costs.

Chapter 16: Implementing Quality Concepts

23. According to TQM, what is truly expensive?

    A. prevention costs.
    B. appraisal costs.
    C. lack of quality.
    D. process benchmarking.

24. Which of the following information would normally NOT obtained from a balanced scorecard?

    a. defect rates
    b. customer satisfaction levels
    c. on-time deliveries
    d. number of non-valued-added customers

25. The A Jay Company reworked 600 defective units discovered before shipment during August. The rework cost was $5 per unit. Customers returned 300 defective units. The rework cost per return was $8. The company also scrapped 100 defective units before shipment at a cost of $20 per unit. Prevention costs were $7,000, and appraisal costs were $6,000. What is the total amount of internal failure cost?

    A. $2,000
    B. $3,000
    C. $5,000
    D. $7,400

26. The A. Jay Company reworked 600 defective units discovered before shipment during August. The rework cost was $5 per unit. Customers returned 300 defective units. The rework cost per return was $8. The company also scrapped 100 defective units before shipment at a cost of $20 per unit. Prevention costs were $7,000, and appraisal costs were $6,000. What is the total amount of external failure cost?

    A. $2,400
    B. $4,400
    C. $5,400
    D. $7,400

APPENDIX

27. After ISO registration, how often do audit teams visit the company to monitor compliance?

    A. monthly.
    B. bimonthly.
    C. annually.
    D. biannually.

Chapter 16: Implementing Quality Concepts 399

28. The ISO 9000 series standards:

    A. are product standards.
    B. imply that companies using them have superior products.
    C. tell management exactly what to do to meet the standards.
    D. tell what a company must do to assure quality.

29. For some companies, ISO 9000 registration is required for regulated products to be sold in:

    A. the European Union.
    B. the United States.
    C. China.
    D. Canada.

30. To qualify for ISO registration, a company must first submit:

    A. to an independent audit of its financial statements.
    B. to a quality audit by a third-party reviewer.
    C. an approval by the Securities and Exchange Commission.
    D. a unanimous approval by its stockholders.

QUESTIONS AND PROBLEMS

1. What is quality? Who should be the ultimate judge of quality?

2. What is meant by a product's grade?

3. What is the difference between results benchmarking and process benchmarking?

4. What are the four main tenets of total quality management?

5. How does total quality management differ from the traditional view of quality?

6. Define each of the four categories of quality costs and give an example of each.

7. What should top management do to create an atmosphere that is conducive to total quality management?

8. Why is involving the management accountant essential in quality improvement efforts?

9. What is the Malcolm Baldrige National Quality Award? What are the criteria for receiving the award?

10. What is Pareto analysis? How can management use Pareto analysis to improve quality?

Chapter 16: Implementing Quality Concepts 403

11. What is strategic cost management? Why is strategic cost management important for long-term business success?

12. What are some important considerations in designing a strategic cost management system?

13. What are the four stages in the quality continuum?

Chapter 16: Implementing Quality Concepts

APPENDIX

14. Describe EFQM and the premise behind it.

15. What must a company do to become ISO 9000 registered?

Chapter 16: Implementing Quality Concepts

SELF TEST ANSWERS

TRUE/FALSE

1.	F	4.	T	7.	F	10.	T	13.	T
2.	T	5.	F	8.	T	11.	F	14.	T
3.	F	6.	F	9.	T	12.	T	15.	F

MULTIPLE CHOICE

1.	C	7.	A	13.	B	19.	A	25.	C
2.	D	8.	C	14.	B	20.	B	26.	A
3.	A	9.	D	15.	C	21.	D	27.	D
4.	B	10.	D	16.	C	22.	A	28.	D
5.	B	11.	A	17.	B	23.	C	29.	A
6.	D	12.	A	18.	D	24.	D	30.	B

QUESTIONS AND PROBLEMS

1. Quality consists of all the attributes of a product or service that affect its ability to meet the stated or implied needs of the person obtaining it. The customer should be the ultimate judge of quality. Companies should view quality from the customer's viewpoint as to performance and value of the product or service.

2. Grade refers to the addition or elimination of product or service characteristics to meet additional needs, especially price. All consumers cannot afford the same grade of product or service. Consumers perceive that a product has value when it satisfies their needs at the lowest possible cost. Cost includes the cost of operating, maintaining, and disposing the product as well as its purchase price.

3. Process benchmarking involves the comparison of specific characteristics to those of other companies that are the best in that specific characteristic. Results benchmarking involves a comparison of a company's products or services to those of competitors. Results benchmarking uses reverse engineering to examine a competitor's products or services. Results benchmarking helps determine which companies are the best in the class, and process benchmarking explains how those companies attained such a status.

4. Many companies have adopted the philosophy of total quality management (TQM) as the foundation for improving quality in all facets of their organization. TQM has four important characteristics: (1) an internal managerial system of planning, controlling, and decision making dedicated to continuous improvement, (2) participation by everyone in the organization, (3) a focus on improving goods and services from the customer's perspective, and (4) long-term partnerships with suppliers.

Chapter 16: Implementing Quality Concepts

5. In the past, managers did not consider quality in the planning process. Rather, managers tolerated a certain level of defects that reflected an acceptable view of quality. However, TQM emphasizes the prevention of defects, continuous improvement, and building quality into every process and product. TQM strives for zero defects.

6. Prevention costs are the costs a company incurs to prevent defects because of poor processing. Examples of prevention costs include training, engineering, modeling, and better production equipment. The second category of quality costs is appraisal costs. Appraisal costs are the costs of monitoring the quality of a company's processes and products. Internal failure costs are the third category of quality costs. A company incurs these costs when it finds a defect before it ships the product to a customer. Examples are scrap and rework. External failure costs are the fourth category of quality costs. A company incurs external failure costs because it delivered a defective product to a customer. These costs include warranty costs, customer complaints, litigation, product recalls, and lost sales.

7. Top management must be a part of the quality process and demonstrate a commitment to the TQM approach. Top management should provide reinforcement and recognition to lower-level managers and employees for quality improvements. Managers should help employees to feel important in the quality improvement process. Managers should encourage employees and train them to perform multiple functions. Top management should inspire and motivate all company employees until they are committed to exceeding customer expectations. Management should show appreciation for the employees' efforts in improving quality.

8. The management accountant should be involved in all activities relative to the accumulation and reporting of quality costs. Traditionally, accounting systems have not separately identified quality costs. The management accountant must design the quality cost reporting system and identify the cost drivers. The management accountant can use the quality cost information to help management make the best quality improvement decisions from a cost-benefit standpoint.

9. The hallmark of TQM in the United States is the Malcolm Baldrige National Quality Award. This award centers on management systems, processes, consumer satisfaction, and business results as the means to achieve product and service excellence. The five categories of applicants are manufacturing, service, small business, education, and health-care organizations. To receive the award, applicants must demonstrate excellence in the following seven categories: (1) leadership, (2) strategic planning, (3) customer and market focus, (4) measurement, analysis, and knowledge , (5) human resource focus, (6) process management, and (7) business results.

10. Pareto analysis means that about 20 to 30 percent of items account for 70 to 80 percent of the cost of those items. Management can use Pareto analysis to improve quality by learning where to spend money on prevention efforts. Using this technique, management could also classify the causes of process problems by their effect on an objective. Management should use Pareto analysis often enough to spot trends quickly to make prompt changes.

11. Strategic cost management is the managerial use of management accounting information to formulate and communicate strategies, establish, implement and monitor methods for pursuing those strategies, and evaluate the degree of success in meeting the goals and objectives of those strategies. Strategic cost management is important because the business strategy of focusing on customers and quality requires cost management to maintain a reasonable value-to-price relationship. Although the market sets prices, a company's costs influence its ability to supply the market at competitive prices. Companies that lack cost management skills will not succeed in the long run. Therefore, companies need to engage in strategic cost management.

12. In designing a strategic cost management system, a company must consider cost accumulation and process measurement activities. The costs accumulated for the financial accounting system may not be adequate for management's needs. For example, a strategic cost management system would treat research and development costs as a product cost. The financial accounting system treats these costs as a period expense. A strategic cost management system would distinguish product costs that add value from product costs that add no value. By highlighting non-value-added costs, managers and employees can assess how effective they are at reducing such costs as a part of continuous improvement.

A strategic cost management system should report costs and benefits of activities in a form that will meet management's needs. Managers need to make informed assessments of the company's performance in the value chain, of its competitive advantage or disadvantage, and of its progress toward organizational goals. Having adequate information from the strategic cost management system is essential to these judgments.

13. The first stage in the quality continuum is quality conformance. In this stage, a company inspects products for conformance to standards or monitors employees to detect poor service. The second stage is quality conscious. In this stage, a company develops techniques for eliminating defective products or poor service. The third stage is quality competitive. In this stage, a company competes against other organizations for quality awards. The fourth stage is world-class status. In this stage, quality becomes an integral part of the organizational culture. A world-class company sets tolerances for defective products or services at zero percent.

APPENDIX

14. The EFQM was founded in 1988 by 14 major European companies with the endorsement of the European Commission. The premise for this model is that leadership is delivered through people, policy and strategy, and partnerships and resources.

15. A company may apply for ISO 9000 registration after completing an internal review. To be registered, the company must first pass a quality audit conducted by a third-party reviewer. The quality audit involves a review of product design activities, manufacturing processes and controls, quality documentation and records, and management quality policy and philosophy. After registration, audit teams visit the company biannually to ensure compliance.

CHAPTER 17

INVENTORY AND PRODUCTION MANAGEMENT

CHAPTER OVERVIEW

Except for plant assets, inventory often represents a company's largest investment. Managing the costs of producing and carrying inventory is vital to a company's profitability. Inventory costs include purchase or production cost, ordering or setup cost, and carrying cost. A company should also consider stockout cost—the cost of not carrying adequate inventory.

This chapter discusses inventory and production management techniques a company can use to reduce the costs of producing and carrying inventory. These techniques include just-in-time (JIT) systems, flexible manufacturing systems (FMS), and computer-integrated manufacturing (CIM). Concepts of value chain, 'push' and 'pull' systems, product life cycle, and target costing are keys to these techniques. The Appendix covers the economic order quantity (EOQ) model, order point, safety stock, and Pareto inventory analysis.

CHAPTER STUDY GUIDE

The value chain consists of a company and its suppliers and customers. Real opportunities for improvement exist in quality, throughput, and cost efficiency through building improved cooperation, communication, and integration. Such integration allows a company to reduce non-value-added activities and enhance value-added activities.

Shared expertise and problem solving significantly enhance a company's effectiveness and efficiency. Opportunities for improvement include (1) enhanced communication of requirements and specifications; (2) greater clarity in requests for products or services; (3) better feedback regarding unsatisfactory products or services; (4) improvements in planning, controlling, and problem solving; and (5) shared managerial and technical expertise, supervision, and training. Employees can view customers and suppliers as extensions of themselves and work to take advantage of opportunities for improvement.

The value chain within a company provides similar opportunities. Within each company each employee or work center has an upstream supplier and a downstream customer. When

Chapter 17: Inventory and Production Management

employees see their internal suppliers and customers as extensions of themselves, they develop the spirit of teamwork to reduce defects, increase productivity, and reduce costs. All company stakeholders benefit from increased productivity through (1) reduced investment in inventory, (2) improved cash-to-cash cycle time, (3) higher asset turnover, (4) higher inventory turnover, and (5) reduced inventory risk.

If inventory levels meet the demand, reduced or minimized inventory investment increases profit margins. Raw material, work in process, finished goods, indirect material, supplies, or merchandise are all examples of inventory. Raw material purchases usually represent the most significant cash outflow for manufacturing companies. Merchandise purchased for resale usually represents the most significant cash outflow for retailers.

The three basic costs associated with inventory are (1) purchase or production, (2) ordering or setup, and (3) carrying or not carrying goods in stock. Exhibit 17-1 shows the elements of each of these costs. The cost accountant records purchasing/production costs in the appropriate inventory account (Raw Material Inventory, Work in Process Inventory, Finished Goods Inventory, or Merchandise Inventory).

Purchase costs include the contract purchase price and shipping charges, minus any discounts allowed. Production costs include costs for direct material, direct labor, traceable overhead, and allocated fixed overhead. Ordering costs are the incremental costs incurred for preparing, receiving, and paying for an order. Setup costs are the direct or indirect costs of preparing equipment for each new production run. Carrying costs include costs for storage, insurance, property taxes, handling, losses from obsolescence or theft, and the opportunity cost of capital invested in inventory. A manufacturing company's setup costs include labor, machine downtime, and other costs incurred to set up a production run.

The timing of inventory ordering depends on which production approach management uses—a push system or a pull system. A push system, as illustrated in Exhibit 17-2, is the traditional production system. In a push system, a company builds up inventory in anticipation of lead time or economic order requirements. A push system requires a company to store excess inventory until needed. A pull system, as illustrated in Exhibit 17-3, is a production system dictated by product sales and demand. In a pull system, a company delivers or produces inventory only as needed. Consequently, a pull system requires only minimal storage facilities.

The stages of the product life cycle are development, introduction, growth, maturity, and decline. Exhibit 17-4 shows a sales trend line through each of these stages. The product life cycle stage has a large impact on a product's sales, costs, and profits.

Decisions made during the development stage are especially important. They can affect the sales, design, costs, and quality of the product for the remainder of its life cycle. Studies indicate that decisions made before production begins determine 80 to 90 percent of a product's life-cycle costs.

The development stage of products has been greatly shortened due to technology and competition. Time spent in planning and development are critical to profitability over the entire life cycle by creating (1) lower production costs, (2) reduced time from design to manufacture stage, (3) higher quality, (4) greater flexibility, and (5) lower life cycle cost.

Virtual reality is a technology being increasingly used in the design stage. Virtual reality allows testing of a virtual prototype rather than a real one by creating a computer generated environment that gives the user the impression of navigating and manipulating real products that currently do not exist.

After the design of a new product, companies usually conduct market research to determine which features customers want. Some companies skip such market research to introduce products more quickly. Flexible manufacturing systems enable companies to make rapid changes to the product design if sales experience indicates that customers prefer different product features.

Following the design of a new product, companies have traditionally calculated production costs and selling prices based in part on costs. If the market will not bear the desired price, the company must accept a lower profit or attempt to reduce production costs.

A different approach to costing new products is the technique known as target costing. Target costing focuses on what the market will pay for a particular product. Through market research, a company determines the price that a product would command in the market. The company then subtracts its desired profit to give the target cost.

A company will make a product if it believes that the cost to make the product is less than or equal to the target cost. If the target cost is less than the expected cost of making the product, the company could (1) change the product design or production process to reduce costs, (2) accept a smaller profit margin, or (3) decide not to enter the market for that particular product at that time. Companies can apply target costing to services if the services are uniform enough to justify the effort.

Companies can use cost tables to determine how they can change the product design or production process. A cost table is a database that provides information on the effect on product cost of using different materials, manufacturing processes, and design specifications.

Management uses value engineering to search for various feasible combinations of resources that increase product functionality while reducing costs. Management considers the elements of reliability, conformance, durability, and cost reduction in its analysis.

Companies can use kaizen costing once production begins. Kaizen costing emphasizes continuous efforts to reduce product costs, to increase product quality, and to improve the production process. Exhibit 17-5 compares target costing to kaizen costing.

If a company designs its products well, the products should require few engineering changes after production begins. Each time a company makes an engineering change, it incurs additional costs due to one or more problems. These additional costs include having to reprint the productions documents, employees learning new tasks, changing machine setups, and parts in inventory becoming obsolete.

The product life cycle has a major impact on costs, prices, and profits. In the introduction stage of the product life cycle, sales are low and the prices of substitute products affect the price of the new product. A company incurs substantial costs for product design, market research, advertising, and promotion. The growth stage starts when the market accepts the product and sales begin to grow. Quality might improve because of competition, and prices are stable. The maturity stage reflects the period when sales are stable or slowly declining. In this stage, companies often compete on price. Costs could be lower in this stage resulting in high profits. This stage might last for a long time. In the decline stage, sales are shrinking. Companies might cut prices substantially to generate business. Unit cost typically increases because fewer units absorb the related fixed costs.

A just-in-time (JIT) system is a system in which a company purchases or produces inventory or performs an operation only as the company needs it. All kinds of organizations can use the JIT philosophy. The three primary goals of a JIT system are (1) elimination of production processes or operations that do not add value to the product or service, (2) continuous improvement in production or performance efficiency, and (3) reduction in the total cost of production or performance while increasing quality. Exhibit 17-6 lists the elements of the JIT philosophy.

A JIT manufacturing system is a production system that attempts to acquire components and produce inventory only as needed, to minimize product defects, and to reduce lead/setup times for acquisition and production. JIT systems originated in Japan where companies used a card or kanban to indicate a work center's need for additional components during a manufacturing process.

Implementation of a JIT system will expose defective products, excessive lead times, and setup times. Traditional push systems seek to maintain smooth production to maintain a steady workforce and continuous machine use. Smooth production often results in the accumulation of excess inventory. The inventory, however, can act as a buffer that prevents a company from discovering inefficiencies in the purchase and/or production process. Exhibit 17-7 compares traditional and JIT production philosophies and portrays these inefficiencies as rocks in high water. High water represents excess inventory. Once a company removes the excess inventory under the JIT system, the inefficiencies become visible and the company can correct them.

For a JIT system to be effective, a company must make certain changes in purchasing, supplier relationships, distribution, product design, product processing, and plant layout. Adequate time is necessary to realize the most benefits from a JIT system. A company normally receives the most benefits after the system has been in place for 5 to 10 years. In addition, a JIT implementation will not succeed without top management backing, commitment of resources, considerable retraining, and support from all levels of personnel.

Chapter 17: Inventory and Production Management

The optimal JIT situation would be to have only one vendor for any given item. However, having only one vendor would create the risk of not having alternative sources in the event of vendor production strikes, unfair pricing, or shipment delays. The realistic and feasible solution is to have a limited number of vendors that a company has certified as to quality and reliability. Other factors that management might consider in selecting vendors include responsiveness, ability to service, ability of vendor personnel, research and development strength, and production capacity.

Companies need to design products using the fewest number of parts and to reduce steps in production and potential risks. As much as possible, a company should use standardized parts. Parts standardization does not necessarily mean identical products. A company should design products for the desired quality and should require minimal engineering changes once the company releases the design for production. Changes in design must occur early for costs to be significantly reduced. Good product design should address all concerns of the intended consumers including the degree of recyclability of the product.

In a JIT system, one objective is to reduce setup time in the processing stage. Reducing setup time allows processing to shift more quickly among the different types of units and helps to make the manufacturing process more flexible. The savings resulting from reduced setup time are often much greater than the costs incurred.

A JIT system also emphasizes quality with a goal of zero defects. Companies using JIT assess quality continually rather than at quality checkpoints only. The first step is ensuring the quality of vendor's products at purchase point. Identifying defective units before a company performs additional work on them reduces costs. Important to any process is the standardization of procedures for workers to perform without variation, on time, and every time.

In a JIT system, a company arranges the physical plant in a manner conducive to the flow of goods, the organization of workers, and an increase in the value added per square foot of plant space. A company designs its plant layout to reduce lead time from one process to another. Often a company arranges machines in an S-shaped or U-shaped grouping known as manufacturing cells. Manufacturing cells improve materials handling and control, increase communication among workers, improve quality control, and increase use of machines. The cells can also reduce inventory storage. Exhibit 17-8 illustrates the flow of production and information in a manufacturing cell. A streamlined design allows a company to institute more visual controls for such problems as excess inventory, production defects, equipment malfunctions, and out-of-place tools.

Manufacturing cells provide a multiprocess environment for cross training employees. Cross training broadens employees' skills and increases their involvement in the workplace. Training results in a more highly skilled workforce. Employees often realize increased job satisfaction. As employees increase their understanding of a process as a whole, they can provide helpful suggestions for process improvement.

Multiprocess handling is the ability of a worker to monitor and operate several (or all)

Chapter 17:   Inventory and Production Management   414

machines in a manufacturing cell or perform all steps of a specific task. Exhibit 17-9 illustrates a factory floor redesign plan to facilitate multiprocess handling. Autonomation is the use of equipment that has been programmed to stop when sensing certain conditions.

Information technology, new support services, and new value chain relationships help logistics in a JIT environment. These advancements provide an efficient and effective means of providing overall support system direction.

The six-sigma method is a data-driven approach to solving business problems with four steps for successful application. First, a team using information technology determines important factors about customers and competitors. Second, planning provides the vision needed to assist the company in realizing its business goals. Third, personnel attend workshops to push improved performance by providing method and strategic integration. Fourth, team leaders learn the applications needed to implement JIT.

The Internet business model is changing the evaluation of costs and services across the corporate world. The Internet business model has few physical assets, little management hierarchy, and a direct pipeline to customers. Electronic commerce integrates the supply chain and provides cost savings.

Supply-chain management involves full integration of customers and vendors for enhanced corporate strategic planning, controlling, and problem solving. Three levels of business-to-business relationships within e-commerce are transactional, information-sharing, and collaboration.

Logistical support provided in the product design stage includes manufacturing simulation to develop production systems to improve financial performance. In addition, management can better serve the customer, minimize errors, and yield savings in labor, transportation, capital, and carrying costs through use of real-time information processing software for finished goods.

A focused factory arrangement is an arrangement in which a vendor agrees to provide a limited number of products according to specifications. A vendor could also agree to perform a limited number of unique services for a JIT company. A focused factory arrangement might involve relocation or plant modernization by the vendor. Financial assistance from the JIT manufacturer might be available to recover such investments. The vendor benefits from long-term supply contracts. Major reliance on a single customer can be difficult, especially for small companies.

Variance reporting and analysis in JIT systems virtually disappear because most variances first appear in a physical (rather than financial) fashion. A JIT system requires a company to recognize variances immediately, which allows a company to determine the causes of the variances and fix any problems rapidly. In a JIT system, a company trains its workers and expects workers to oversee quality and efficiency while production occurs.

Chapter 17: Inventory and Production Management 415

Under a JIT system, long-term agreements with vendors reduce material price variances. A company should design its JIT accounting system so that no one can prepare a purchase order at a price higher than the designated price without management approval. This feature allows management to know the variance amount and its cause in advance. It also helps to reduce unnecessary costs because the company can call the vendor to negotiate the price or obtain price quotations from other vendors.

Because a company selects its vendors based in part on the quality of their materials, material usage variances due to inferior materials should be rare. If usage standards are accurate, unfavorable material usage variances should be small. Under a JIT system, each production employee is responsible for maintaining quality and for spotting problems when they occur. When an employee finds a problem, that employee can stop production until the company solves the problem. Thus, employees detect unfavorable material usage promptly.

Engineering changes (ENCs) made to product specifications cause one type of usage variance. Exhibit 17-10 illustrates the calculation of a material quantity variance caused by an engineering change order. A JIT system has both an annual and a current comparison standard, and design modifications would change the current standard but not the annual one.

Labor variances should be small under a JIT system if the company has set standard rates and times appropriately. Redesigning the plant layout and reducing non-value-added activities should decrease labor time.

Some companies use a single conversion cost account to replace separate direct labor and overhead categories. Using a single conversion cost account simplifies the accounting procedures in a JIT system. A company with a JIT system no longer needs a Raw Materials Inventory account because materials go immediately into production. A company no longer needs a Work in Process account either. A new account called Raw and In Process (RIP) replaces the Raw Materials Inventory account and the Work in Process Inventory account.

Accounting in a JIT system focuses on output. All costs should be at standard because employees notice variations and correct them almost immediately. Daily accounting for the individual costs of production is not necessary. Companies allocate fewer costs arbitrarily to products. Companies can trace more costs directly to products by using manufacturing cells to make a particular product or family of products.

Backflush costing is a streamlined cost accounting method that speeds up and simplifies the accounting process. A company using backflush costing records purchases of raw materials and actual conversion costs. At the completion of production or upon the sale of the goods, the company makes a journal entry to allocate the total costs incurred to Cost of Goods Sold and to Finished Goods using standard production costs. Exhibit 17-11 illustrates backflush costing.

Four alternatives to the entries presented in Exhibit 17-11 due differences in the trigger point for journalizing transactions are included in the text. These four different scenarios are (1) raw materials are recorded at completion of finished goods, (2) completion of finished goods is recorded at the sale of goods, (3) entries made in A JIT system at the sale of goods, and (4) the backflush costing entries at the sale of goods. Companies implementing a JIT philosophy can significantly reduce cost and improve productivity.

Many companies have changed their basic manufacturing philosophy because of JIT, activity-based management, automated production equipment, and advances in computer technology. Traditional manufacturing systems encouraged long production runs to take advantage of economies of scale. Flexible manufacturing systems (FMSs) represent a new approach to manufacturing. An FMS is a network of robots and material conveyance devices monitored and controlled by computers. Two or more FMSs connected by a host computer and an information system constitute a computer integrated manufacturing (CIM) system. Companies usually use an FMS for short production runs, but many companies have begun to use CIM for long production runs also. Exhibit 17-12 compares a traditional manufacturing system to a flexible manufacturing system.

Companies using an FMS or CIM can quickly and inexpensively stop the production of one item and begin the production of another item. Such flexibility enables a company to produce many products while reducing costs, including direct labor cost. Remaining employees must be well trained and able to perform many tasks. A company must empower employees and give them the authority and responsibility to make quick decisions.

Manufacturing only those items that customers demand and without waste is lean manufacturing. Lean manufacturing companies put pressure on the entire value chain to minimize waste, maximize quality, eliminate activities that add costs but no value to products, and shorten the lead time for delivering products and services.

The theory of constraints can assist management in reducing cycle time. According to the theory of constraints, goods cannot flow through a production process any faster than the slowest bottleneck or constraint in the process.

Human constraints, machine constraints, and material constraints cause delays in the production process. A constraint is anything that restricts an individual's or machine's ability to perform a project or function. Human constraints often involve an inability to understand, react, or perform at a particular speed. Machine constraints or bottlenecks are slow points in a process that cause other processing mechanisms to endure idle time. Exhibit 17-13 illustrates a constraint in the production process. Machine constraints have implications for quality control. Companies should place quality control points before bottlenecks to reduce time spent on defective products.

Management should make the best use of the idle time caused by constraints. Management should specify the options available to minimize the limitations imposed by such constraints. These options include adding more machines and using different machines.

Chapter 17: Inventory and Production Management 417

APPENDIX

Once a company has selected its suppliers, the company can then use the economic order quantity (EOQ) model to calculate how many units to order each time. The EOQ equals the square root of [(2 x estimated annual quantity used in units x estimated cost of placing one order) ÷ estimated cost to carry one unit for one year]. The EOQ model minimizes the sum of ordering costs and carrying costs. Under the EOQ, this sum reaches a minimum when ordering costs equal carrying costs. A manufacturing company can change the EOQ model into an economic production run (EPR) formula by changing ordering costs to setup costs. An economic production run (EPR) is an estimate that reflects the production quantity that minimizes the total costs of setting up a production run and carrying a unit in stock for one year.

The order point is the inventory level at which the company places an order or produces more items. The rate of usage, the lead time, and the safety stock are the factors that affect the order point. Usage is the quantity of inventory used or sold each day. Lead time is the number of days from placing an order to receiving or producing the goods. If a company does not maintain a safety stock, the formula for the order point is as follows: average daily usage x lead time = order point. To allow for variations in the rate of usage and delays in receiving orders, companies might keep extra inventory as a buffer. This extra inventory is safety stock. A company should base the size of safety stock for a particular item on how critical the item is to the business, the cost of the item, and the uncertainty as to usage and lead time. When a company maintains a safety stock, the formula for the order point is as follows: (average daily usage x lead time) + safety stock = order point. The formula for maximum safety stock is as follows: (maximum daily usage – average daily usage) x lead time = maximum safety stock. Another way to compute the order point using a maximum safety stock is as follows: maximum daily usage x lead time = order point.

Pareto inventory analysis defines cost-benefit relationship for certain categories of inventory. In a typical environment, category A items represent about 20 percent of the inventory items, but they account for 80 percent of the cost or importance to a finished product. Category B items may represent about 30 percent of the inventory items, but they account for 10 percent of the cost or importance to a finished product. Category C items may represent about 50 percent of the inventory items, but they account for 10 percent of the cost or importance to a finished product. Handling of each inventory item depends on the category. Exhibit 17-14 illustrates the results of a Pareto inventory analysis.

Management might use simple techniques for managing items in the C category. Two such techniques are the two-bin system and the red-line system. Under a two-bin system, when the first bin or container for the item is empty, a company begins using the second bin and places an order or produces enough to fill the first container. Under the red-line system, a company uses a single container. A red line painted on the container shows the reorder point. When the inventory of the item drops below the red line, a company places an order or produces enough to fill the container.

Chapter 17: Inventory and Production Management

SELF TEST

TRUE/FALSE

1. T F Inventory carrying costs include costs for storage, insurance, property taxes, losses for obsolescence or theft, and the opportunity cost of capital invested in inventory.

2. T F The costs of preparing, receiving, and paying for an order are ordering costs.

3. T F A flexible manufacturing system emphasizes long production runs of identical products.

4. T F In backflush costing, daily accounting for the individual costs of production is extremely important.

5. T F Research indicates that decisions made before production often determine 80 to 90 percent of a product's life-cycle costs.

6. T F Just-in-time (JIT) manufacturing is a push system.

7. T F Kanban is the Japanese word for card.

8. T F In a push system of production, parts are delivered or made only as they are needed by the work center that requires them.

9. T F In a JIT system, the cost of scrap is buried in the cost of inventory.

10. T F The JIT philosophy was imported to the United States from Germany.

11. T F A stockout can lead to lost sales and lost customer goodwill.

APPENDIX

12. T F Two-bin and red-line systems are used to control the highest-cost production components.

13. T F In a Pareto inventory analysis system, management exerts the most control over category C items.

14. T F The economic order quantity (EOQ) includes purchase cost in the numerator.

15. T F One problem with the EOQ model is that it ignores relationships among inventory items.

Chapter 17: Inventory and Production Management

MULTIPLE CHOICE

1. What cost does a company record in its inventory account?

    A. carrying costs
    B. stockout costs
    C. ordering or setup costs
    D. purchase or production cost

2. Which costs would a manufacturing company incur instead of ordering costs?

    A. stockout costs
    B. carrying costs
    C. setup costs
    D. selling costs

3. The incremental, variable costs associated with preparing, receiving, and paying for an order are:

    A. stockout costs.
    B. carrying costs.
    C. setup costs.
    D. ordering costs.

4. In the development stage of the product life cycle:

    A. costs are low and revenues are high.
    B. costs are low and revenues are nonexistent.
    C. costs are high and revenues are nonexistent.
    D. costs are high and revenues are relatively low.

5. Carrying costs should include the:

    A. shipping charges on purchased items.
    B. cost of receiving an order.
    C. opportunity cost of capital invested in inventory.
    D. cost of lost customer goodwill.

6. One way to reduce cycle time in a plant is to establish S-shaped or U-shaped groupings of employees and machines known as:

    A. S- or U-control groups.
    B. manufacturing cells.
    C. ABC cells.
    D. a focused factory.

Chapter 17: Inventory and Production Management

7. In a JIT system:

    A. material price variances can be substantial.
    B. a company traces more costs directly to products.
    C. labor variances can be substantial.
    D. the Raw Material Inventory account becomes more important.

8. A traditional inventory system is:

    A. a pull system.
    B. very similar to JIT.
    C. a push system.
    D. not concerned with storing inventory.

9. Two or more flexible manufacturing systems connected through a host computer and an information networking system are usually referred to as:

    A. computer-assisted manufacturing (CAM).
    B. computer-integrated manufacturing (CIM).
    C. total quality management (TQM).
    D. just-in-time manufacturing (JIT).

10. Which of the following is NOT a primary goal of a just-in-time manufacturing system?

    A. elimination of non-value-added processes or operations
    B. continuous improvement in production efficiency
    C. reduction in the total cost of production
    D. elimination of stockouts due to long lead times.

11. Stockout cost is a(n):

    A. production cost.
    B. purchase cost.
    C. ordering cost.
    D. opportunity cost.

12. Kanban is the Japanese word for:

    A. inventory.
    B. card.
    C. production.
    D. work in process.

Chapter 17: Inventory and Production Management 421

13. Just-in-time manufacturing emphasizes:

    A. high quality.
    B. long lead times.
    C. many vendors.
    D. buying in large quantities.

14. When does a company using a JIT system assess quality?

    A. only at the completion of production
    B. only at quality control checkpoints
    C. on a continual basis
    D. only when the company receives materials

15. In a JIT system, what is the journal entry to record the purchase of $10,000 of raw materials?

    A. Raw and In Process Inventory   10,000
          Accounts Payable   10,000

    B. Raw Materials Inventory   10,000
          Accounts Payable   10,000

    C. Purchases   10,000
          Accounts Payable   10,000

    D. Conversion Costs   10,000
          Accounts Payable   10,000

16. The basic purpose of a JIT system is to eliminate:

    A. waste.
    B. inventory.
    C. the economic order quantity model.
    D. materials requirement planning.

17. Effective implementation of a JIT system requires employees to be:

    A. skilled at only one production task.
    B. quality conscious.
    C. unconcerned with operations.
    D. alert for ways to increase machine setup time.

Chapter 17: Inventory and Production Management 422

18. In a JIT system, a company can use a new account called:

    A. Raw Materials Inventory.
    B. Finished and In Process.
    C. Raw and Finished.
    D. Raw and In Process.

19. What type of costing focuses on output and works backwards through the system to allocate costs between Cost of Goods Sold and Inventory?

    A. backflush costing
    B. throughput costing
    C. backwards costing
    D. variance costing

APPENDIX

20. A company determines the optimal level of safety stock by considering the uncertainty between:

    A. carrying costs and ordering costs.
    B. lead time and daily usage.
    C. cost of a stockout and the carrying costs of safety stock.
    D. cost of a stockout and ordering costs of safety stock.

21. If a company were uncertain about the ability of a supplier to make a timely delivery of goods, it would:

    A. decrease the lead time.
    B. increase the lead time.
    C. decrease the EOQ.
    D. increase the EOQ.

22. What method of controlling inventory separates inventory into three groups based on relative cost-to-volume usage?

    A. Pareto inventory analysis
    B. red-line system
    C. two-bin system
    D. economic order quantity

Chapter 17: Inventory and Production Management

23. Which of the following affects the economic production run but not EOQ?

    A. estimated annual quantity used in units
    B. estimated annual quantity purchased in units
    C. estimated cost of placing one order
    D. estimated set up cost of one production run

24. The economic order quantity does not include the:

    A. cost of placing an order.
    B. estimated annual quantity needed in units.
    C. purchase cost.
    D. cost of carrying one unit in stock for one year.

25. The economic order quantity (EOQ) model assumes that when an order arrives, the inventory on hand will be equal to:

    A. zero.
    B. one-fourth of the order size.
    C. one-half of the order size.
    D. the order size.

26. The basic economic order quantity (EOQ) model does not consider:

    A. the annual cost of carrying an item for one year.
    B. relationships among inventory items.
    C. the estimated annual quantity needed in units.
    D. the cost to place one order.

27. The economic order quantity (EOQ) model computes the optimal balance between:

    A. ordering costs and carrying costs.
    B. purchase costs and stockout costs.
    C. ordering costs and stockout costs.
    D. carrying costs and stockout costs.

28. Wilson Company computed its economic order quantity to be 1,000 units. Wilson sells an average of 100 units a day. The lead time is 4 days and the desired safety stock is 200 units. What is the order point?

    A. 500 units
    B. 600 units
    C. 800 units
    D. 950 units

Chapter 17: Inventory and Production Management

29. Mosier Company sells a maximum of 300 units a day. The average sales are 260 units a day. The lead time is 6 days. What is the maximum safety stock that Mosier needs?

    A. 40 units
    B. 240 units
    C. 1,560 units
    D. 1,800 units

30. Nichols Company estimates that it will buy 9,000 units of a component each year. The cost to place an order is $20. The cost to carry one unit of the component in inventory for a year is $4. What is the economic order quantity (EOQ)?

    A. 80 units
    B. 300 units
    C. 2,000 units
    D. 2,250 units

QUESTIONS AND PROBLEMS

1. List and explain the elements of the three basic costs associated with inventory.

Chapter 17: Inventory and Production Management 425

2. Why is understanding the product life cycle important in controlling costs?

3. How do companies use virtual reality in product development?

4. What are the accounting implications of a JIT system?

5. What is the basic purpose of a just-in-time (JIT) system? What are the three primary goals of a JIT system?

6. How does a JIT system differ from a traditional inventory system?

7. Why is high quality so important to a successful JIT system? How does a company assure quality in a JIT system?

8. What is target costing? How do companies use target costing?

9. How is backflush costing a simplified cost system?

10. What are the three alternatives in recording costs in a backflush costing system?

APPENDIX

11. What is safety stock?

12. Why do managers use the Pareto inventory analysis?

13. What costs affect the calculation of the economic order quantity (EOQ) and the economic production run (EPR)?

14. Describe the two-bin system and red-line system for managing low-volume (category C) inventory items.

15. Hammer Company sells a maximum of 77 units per day. The average sales are 70 units per day. The lead time is 8 days. Calculate the following:

(a) the order point assuming no safety stock.

(b) the maximum safety stock.

(c) the order point assuming that Hammer carries the maximum safety stock.

Chapter 17: Inventory and Production Management 430

SELF TEST ANSWERS

TRUE/FALSE

1.	T	4.	F	7.	T	10.	F	13.	F
2.	T	5.	T	8.	F	11.	T	14.	F
3.	F	6.	F	9.	F	12.	F	15.	T

MULTIPLE CHOICE

1.	D	7.	B	13.	A	19.	A	25.	A
2.	C	8.	C	14.	C	20.	B	26.	B
3.	D	9.	B	15.	A	21.	B	27.	A
4.	C	10.	D	16.	A	22.	A	28.	B
5.	C	11.	D	17.	B	23.	D	29.	B
6.	B	12.	B	18.	D	24.	C	30.	B

QUESTIONS AND PROBLEMS

1. The three basic costs associated with inventory are (1) purchase or production costs, (2) ordering or setup costs, and (3) carrying costs, including costs of not carrying sufficient inventory (stockout costs). Purchase costs include the quoted price plus shipping costs minus discounts allowed. Production costs for a manufacturing company include direct material cost (taking shipping charges and discounts into account), direct labor, traceable overhead, and allocated overhead. Ordering costs include costs for invoice preparation, receiving and inspection reports, clerical processing, and payment. Setup costs for a manufacturing company include labor and machine downtime costs. Carrying costs are those costs incurred to carry inventory in stock, including storage, handling, insurance, property taxes, and losses from obsolescence, damage, and theft. They also include the opportunity costs of capital invested in inventory. Stockout costs include lost contribution margin from lost sales, lost customer goodwill, and increased ordering or setup costs for filling special orders.

2. The product life cycle is a major factor in executing a company's planning and control of costs. The stage in the product life cycle affects a product's sales volume, price, and unit production cost. Revenues and costs change as a product goes through the development, introduction, growth, maturity, and decline stages. Some products have short life cycles, and other products remain popular for many years.

3. Virtual reality is a technology being increasingly used in the design stage. Virtual reality allows testing of a virtual prototype rather than a real one by creating a computer generated environment that gives the user the impression of navigating and manipulating real products that currently do not exist.

Chapter 17: Inventory and Production Management

4. Under JIT, companies view variance analysis differently. Variances, if any, should be small. Long-term agreements with vendors reduce price variances. A company should design its JIT accounting system so that no one can prepare a purchase order at a price higher than the designated price without management approval. This feature allows management to know the variance amount and its cause in advance. Management can then reduce unnecessary costs because the company negotiates the price or obtains price quotations from other vendors. Because a company selects its vendors based in part on the quality of their materials, material usage variances caused by inferior materials should be rare. Labor variances should be small under a JIT system. Redesigning the plant layout and reducing non-value-added activities should decrease labor time. Some companies use a single conversion cost account to replace separate direct labor and overhead accounts. A new account called Raw and In Process (RIP) replaces the Raw Material Inventory account and the Work in Process Inventory account.

5. Although many people often regard a just-in-time (JIT) system as a system to eliminate inventory, the basic purpose of a JIT system is to eliminate or at least minimize wasted activities and excess costs. The three primary goals of a JIT system are (1) to eliminate any production process or operation that does not add value to products or services, (2) to strive for continuous improvement in production or performance efficiency, and (3) to reduce the total cost of production or performance.

6. A traditional inventory system maintains inventory not only to reduce stockout costs but also to act as a buffer when production problems arise. Inefficient operations often cause these production problems. A traditional inventory system is a push system that encourages smooth production. Traditional systems often create excess inventory and make detecting and correcting operating problems more difficult. A JIT system is a pull system in which parts are delivered only as a particular work center needs them. Forecasted sales are the variable that pulls production through a JIT system. Like a traditional system, JIT strives to maintain a steady production schedule. In JIT, the goal is to avoid accumulating unnecessary inventory. When the company does not need current production, production employees perform maintenance on the machines or receive additional training. Quality is much more important in a JIT system. Good relationships with suppliers and employees are essential to a successful JIT system.

7. Quality is important in a JIT system because little, if any, inventory is available to act as a buffer if the company has to rework or scrap defective units. Poor quality leads to higher costs in the form of downtime, rework, scrap, warranty costs, and lost sales. JIT assures quality by purchasing from only a small number of vendors that produce high-quality materials. A company chooses vendors based on quality, reliability, and other factors in addition to price. After a company chooses a vendor, the company monitors the vendor to ensure that the vendor maintains high quality. JIT also assures quality by assessing quality continually rather than at quality checkpoints only. A company finds defective units before it incurs additional costs. Thus, the company reduces the costs of poor quality.

Chapter 17: Inventory and Production Management

8. Target costing focuses on what the market will pay for a particular product. Through market research, a company determines the price that a product would command in the market. The company then subtracts its desired profit to give the target cost. A company uses target costing to decide to make a new product if it believes that the cost to make the product is less than or equal to the target cost. If the target cost is less than the expected cost of making the product, the company could (1) change the product design or production process to reduce costs, (2) accept a smaller profit margin, or (3) decide not to enter the market for that particular product at that time. Companies can apply target costing to services if the services are uniform enough to justify the effort.

9. Backflush costing focuses on output and works backward to allocate costs between cost of goods sold and inventory. Backflush costing is a streamlined cost accounting method that speeds up and simplifies the accounting process. A company using backflush costing records purchases of raw material and actual conversion costs. At the completion of production or upon sale of the goods, the company makes a journal entry to allocate the total costs incurred to Cost of Goods Sold and to Finished Goods using standard production costs.

10. If the production time is short, a company might not record raw material purchases until the completion of production. If a company ships goods to customers upon completion of production, the company could record the cost of goods sold and any unsold finished goods at the same time. A third alternative is to charge the accounts Raw and In Process Inventory, Finished Goods, and Cost of Goods Sold only at the end of the period.

11. Safety stock is the level of raw, in process, or finished goods inventory that protects a company from stockouts. Stockouts occur because of factors, such as (1) excess demand, (2) errors in estimating lead times, (3) actual production in excess of planned production during lead times, (4) excessive waste of materials, and (5) machinery breakdowns.

12. Management uses the Pareto inventory analysis to gain the most benefits from inventory control at the lowest cost. Pareto inventory analysis separates inventory into three groups based on annual cost-to-volume usage. Items with the highest dollar volume are A items, and items with the lowest dollar volume are C items. B items have a moderate dollar volume. A items receive the tightest controls, while C items receive the least control. Control for B items depends on management's judgment of the facts and circumstances for these items. Advances in technology, such as bar coding, have made controlling inventory easier and more cost effective.

13. A company determines the economic order quantity (EOQ) by considering inventory carrying costs (such as insurance, property taxes, and storage costs) and ordering costs. The EOQ equals the square root of [(2 x estimated annual quantity used in units x estimated cost of placing one order) ÷ estimated cost to carry one unit for one year]. The EOQ model minimizes the sum of ordering costs and carrying costs. Under the EOQ, this sum reaches a minimum when ordering costs equal carrying costs. A manufacturing company can change the EOQ model into an economic production run (EPR) formula by changing ordering costs to setup costs. An economic production run (EPR) is an estimate that reflects the production quantity that minimizes the total costs of setting up a production run and carrying a unit in stock for one year.

Chapter 17: Inventory and Production Management

14. Under a two-bin system, when the first bin or container for the item is empty, a company begins using the second bin and places an order or produces enough to fill the first container. Under the red-line system, a company uses a single container. A red line painted on the container shows the reorder point. When the inventory of the item drops below the red line, a company places an order or produces enough to fill the container.

15. (a) 70 units per day x 8 days = 560 units

    (b)
Maximum usage	77 units per day
Average usage	70 units per day
Difference	7 units per day
Lead time	x 8 days
Maximum safety stock	56 units

(c) 560 units + 56 units = 616 units, or 77 units per day x 8 days = 616 units

CHAPTER 18

EMERGING MANAGEMENT PRACTICES

CHAPTER OVERVIEW

This chapter examines recent changes and future trends in business practices. Global competition has been the driving force of many changes. Some of these changes include business process reengineering, downsizing, diversity, enterprise resource planning, strategic alliances, and open-book management. Management and control of environmental costs is also a growing concern of governments, citizens, investors and managers. Many of these changes result from new management practices and technological advancements.

The trend is to give more management authority and responsibility to individuals and teams. This trend has created opportunities and challenges for the accounting functions, because individuals must have the skills and information to be effective managers.

CHAPTER STUDY GUIDE

Business organizations have changed due to global competition and technological advancements. Managers seek immediate and gradual ways of organizational change to remain competitive. Exhibit 18-1 shows eight principles managers should follow when commencing change.

A major innovation companies use to achieve gains in effectiveness and efficiency is business process reengineering (BPR). BPR involves examining processes to identify and eliminate, reduce, or replace non-value-added activities. BPR focuses on discrete initiatives to improve specific processes. The goal of BPR is to cause radical changes in a company's operations. Downsizing, outsourcing, and technology acquisition often accompany BPR.

Three major trends are driving the increased use of BPR. The first trend is the advancement of technology. Technology makes electronic payments possible. Robots move and assemble components in manufacturing facilities. Neither of these functions was possible 50 years ago. BPR is a useful tool in automating processes that a company cannot eliminate. When technology changes, the feasibility of automating processes also changes.

The second driver of BPR is the pursuit of increased quality. Global competition allows consumers to buy products and services from the highest quality providers in the world. Quality has become a most important consideration in purchase decisions. BPR is a useful tool for increasing quality because it focuses on eliminating, replacing, or changing processes that contribute to poor quality.

The third driver of BPR is the increase in price competition due to global competition. To compete successfully on price, companies must find ways to reduce unit costs. BPR is one tool that companies can use to become more efficient. BPR can be a very effective tool for reducing costs when a company needs to reform a process or needs new technology to increase efficiency. Although BPR is a methodical way to transform business practices, creativity is an important part of BPR. Exhibit 18-2 lists the steps involved in BPR.

The objectives of a BPR project are to realize the potential benefits that a company expects to receive from reengineering. A company must obtain knowledge of all relevant technological innovations to identify all technological opportunities and constraints. Reengineering is much more profound than simply automating or upgrading existing processes. Creativity and vision are essential in designing a prototype of the reengineered process.

Accountants aid in the BPR process by providing baseline measurements, deciding the BPR objectives, and measuring the achieved performance of the redesigned process. Advances in technology can lead to BPR innovations. Accountants must be aware of potential applications for new software and hardware.

Keys to a successful implementation of BPR are (1) set 'stretch' goals for the process in appropriate terms; (2) make certain the efforts have a leader and top management supports him/her; (3) involve everyone that is in the value chain, if possible; (4) assign both authority and responsibility to a single person; and (5) use a pilot program to identify problems. The keys emphasize the importance of including customers and top-level managers in BPR implementation. Involving customers helps to ensure that the customer perspective drives the BPR project. Top managers stress the importance of the project and secure the necessary resources.

Downsizing is the commonly used term for management actions that reduce employment and restructure operations in response to competitive pressures. The results of a recent survey show that the strategic issues of greatest concern to managers were in three areas: (1) global competitiveness, (2) economic concerns including the need to reduce costs and improve profitability, and (3) core competency issues of quality, productivity, and customer service. Downsizing has been the most common response to these concerns. The reason the respondents cited most often for downsizing was the need to reduce costs and increase profits. Most firms in the survey made substantial investments in advanced technology along with downsizing.

Chapter 18: Emerging Management Practices

The risks and dangers of downsizing include the following: (1) depleting the company's talent pool, (2) breaching the level of trust between managers and employees, and (3) destroying corporate cultures in which lifetime employment has been a major factor in attracting employees. The reduction in employment eliminates middle-management positions that serve as training grounds for future top management.

Downsizing is an accounting issue because it affects financial reporting and cost management. Companies usually report losses in the year that they downsize. Companies incur losses from the sale of unprofitable assets and severance costs caused by layoffs.

From a cost management perspective, cost accountants must understand all the consequences of downsizing. Before recommending downsizing to improve efficiency, accountants should evaluate the potential impact on customer service, employee morale and loyalty, and future growth opportunities. Cost accountants should also perform a careful cost-analysis. Exhibit 18-3 provides the equation to evaluate when analyzing downsizing decisions. This exhibit shows that strategic decisions affect the way in which a company converts inputs into outputs for customers.

Downsizing puts more emphasis on automated-conversion processes and decreases the level of manual-conversion processes. Further, downsizing causes a change in the mix of inputs used to produce outputs. Downsizing emphasizes technology and outsourcing as substitutes for labor.

The financial analysis of the downsizing decision involves comparing future cost savings from reduced labor costs to a current expenditure for restructuring and acquiring additional technology. Analysts can use the capital budgeting methods discussed in Chapter 13 in performing this analysis. The capital budgeting model must include a comparison of the cash realized from any sale of assets and the net cash flows from those assets that the company will not receive in the future. The capital budgeting tools provide managers with the information about how downsizing will probably affect profitability and return on investment.

Many companies have expanded their operations geographically in the face of global competition. By doing business globally, companies can develop new markets, reduce input costs, and manage the effects of peaks and valleys in local economies. Such global expansion presents managers with unique opportunities and challenges.

With global operations, a company faces challenges in coordinating a diverse workforce of different races, values, cultures, and education levels. Corporate policies and information systems must adapt to the diverse workforce and greater diversity of operations. The greater diversity often requires that the accounting function play a larger role in managing operations. Although different languages and cultures can impair communication, accounting is an international technical language that can help to coordinate operations in a diverse company.

Managing a global business requires that management consider many factors including

Chapter 18:   Emerging Management Practices   438

differences in currency values, labor practices, political risks, tax rates, infrastructure, and commercial laws. These additional considerations require new systems and controls to manage risks and capitalize on opportunities. Exhibit 18-4 lists reasons for seeking a more diverse group of employees.

Increased use of personal computers and minicomputers has increased the need for integrated networks. Enterprise resource planning (ERP) systems are packaged software systems that companies use to (1) automate and integrate most of their business processes, (2) share common data and practices across the whole company, and (3) produce and access real-time information. To handle information management requirements, management uses ERP systems to integrate specific function capacities including financing, marketing, and manufacturing. Exhibit 18-5 illustrates the lack of information integration across the supply chain. In contrast, Exhibit 18-6 shows how an ERP system is a solution to the problem of non-integrated, decentralized information. The results of an integrated system include high-quality products and the best possible service.

ERP systems reduce or eliminate duplication of effort and data management. Data are entered into a central depository for all company data that flows through ERP modules. Exhibit 18-7 illustrates the typical modules in an ERP installation. To implement an ERP system, finance and system specialists must choose and install the software. Installation of an ERP system involves a significant investment in capital and labor hours. Finance specialists must analyze the data repository to support management decisions. Detailed analysis involves converting aggregate data to detailed data to discover the marketing opportunities and manage costs. Data mining uses statistical techniques to discover quality problems, determine marketing impact, and identify cost drivers. ERP systems include SAP, R/3, PeopleSoft, and Baan. These systems exponentially increase the ease of access to a global market thorough the Internet and strategic alliances.

In the ordinary value-chain structure, clear distinctions exist between supplier and customer firms. Sometimes companies have incentives to develop interorganizational agreements, known as strategic alliances, which go beyond traditional customer or supplier arrangements. A strategic alliance is an agreement involving two or more companies with complementary core competencies to contribute jointly to the value chain. A strategic alliance differs from a typical buyer or seller agreement in that the alliance produces output jointly and the allied companies split the rewards of the joint effort.

Often, a strategic alliance takes the form of a joint venture in which the allied companies create a separate legal entity to make and sell the joint output. Other possibilities include equity investment, licensing, joint R&D arrangements, technology swaps, exclusive buyer/seller arrangements, and exclusive buyer/seller agreements.

In a typical strategic alliance, the parties to the alliance create a new entity. The parties might contribute cash, human capital, technology, access to distribution channels, patents, and supply contracts. Strategic alliance agreements stipulate the risks for loss and rights to income.

Chapter 18: Emerging Management Practices

Alliance partners establish the structure needed in order to conduct business such as the composition of a governing board as well as the execution of agreements including control and rights in profits and losses. The interests of the parent organizations must align with the new entity's interest. Both parties must receive adequate consideration for their input. The parties involved must make complex decisions based on these expected inputs. The strategic alliance usually has as much complexity as establishing an entirely new organization.

<u>Open-book management</u> is a philosophy about increasing a company's performance by involving all employees and by assuring that they have access to all necessary operational and financial information for improving performance. This philosophy is appropriate for decentralized companies that have empowered employees to make decisions. Advocates of open-book management argue that it helps employees understand how their activities affect the company's revenues and costs. With this understanding, employees can adopt or modify work practices to either increase revenues or reduce costs.

Merely allowing employees to see the financial records will not necessarily solve any problems or improve performance. Most employees do not have any understanding of accounting concepts or the skills necessary to interpret financial information.

If financial information is the basis of employees' decisions, the company must organize the information with the level of understanding of the users in mind. Accountants must become more creative in the methods they use to compile and present financial information. Companies can use games to teach accounting and financial concepts to financially unsophisticated employees. Exhibit 18-9 lists 10 common principles of open-book management.

Games can simplify the learning of complex financial practices and make it enjoyable. Exhibit 18-10 is an example of data that employees could use to develop an understanding of the financial impact of decisions. The outcomes of the game must be easy to comprehend and must relate to the reason for establishing the game. These reasons could include maximizing profits, maximizing customer satisfaction, and maximizing shareholder value.

To take advantage of the financial information the company gives them, employees must be educated about ways to increase profits. The game of trying to increase profits motivates employees to learn about cost management and operational management techniques. Relating training to the game makes its relevance obvious to the employees. They will seek training to understand how to read a simple income statement and to identify methods that they can use to improve results.

Management cannot assume that employees are internally motivated to play games well. Upper management should provide the motivation for games. Management can do so by linking the employees' compensation to profits or to specific performance measures. Examples include profits above a target level, on-time delivery rates, defect rates, and output per labor hour. These measures should make employees aware of how their inputs and outputs affect other departments and financial outcomes. A company can include all critical dimensions of performance including costs, quality, and investment management in performance measurements.

Chapter 18: Emerging Management Practices 440

Once employees have become accustomed to receiving financial and operational information to manage their departments, a company can develop more elaborate information systems. For example, once employees understand direct material, direct labor, and quality costs, they can go on to evaluate overhead cost.

Implementing open-book management can be difficult. Characteristics of companies that are best suited to implement open-book management include small size, decentralized management, a history of employee empowerment, and a high level of trust between managers and employees.

Accountants face unique challenges in implementing open-book management in even the most favorable environments. One important obstacle to overcome in most companies is a history of closely guarding financial information. Even in publicly held companies, top managers have usually restricted employees' access to sensitive financial information. Accountants have seen themselves as those who guard such information rather than as those who dispense it. To implement open-book management successfully, accountants must develop an attitude about information sharing that is as intense as traditional attitudes of guarding information. They must be innovative in implementing open-book management and in conveying accounting information that users can understand. Accountants must assume roles as teachers as well as information providers. By teaching employees to become better users of accounting information, accountants foster better decision making.

Also, management must design performance measures that employees can understand. The measures should reflect the actual performance compared with the objectives of the segments and the company as a whole. The company and the segments may state the objectives in terms of competitors or industry norms. To specify these performance measures, accountants must develop information systems that focus on gathering quality types of information for an industry.

A major principle of open-book management is to involve all employees and to measure and reward performance of all employees. Accountants must devise performance measures that cause all segments and functional areas to work toward a common goal.

Governments, citizens, investors and managers are increasingly concerned about the environmental impact of business. Environmental management systems assist management in controlling environmental issues through all phases of operation. Social consciousness and risk reduction drive some companies to reduce pollutions voluntarily. Management might use one of three generic approaches to control environmental costs. First, management could use the end-of-pipe strategies that involve creating waste in the production process and then properly disposing of the waste. The second strategy involves process improvements that reduce, recycle, or produce no waste during the process. The third strategy involves pollution prevention, which means that a company does not produce pollutants in the first place.

Through research and development, companies develop processes and products. Management considers four things in the design of new products: (1) the types and quantities of materials to be produced, (2) the types and quantities of waste, scrap, and by-products to be produced, (3) the amount of energy used in the production process, and (4) the potential for gathering and recycling products when they reach obsolescence.

Exhibit 18-11 provides a checklist of things a financial professional should consider for environmental cost control, including cost management systems and cost reporting systems. The financial professional must include quantitative and non-quantitative data elements from both within and without the company.

Chapter 18: Emerging Management Practices

SELF TEST

TRUE/FALSE

1. T F Most employees are knowledgeable about how a company generates profits and measures performance in financial terms.

2. T F Companies can use games effectively to teach accounting concepts to employees.

3. T F Management should assume that assembly workers have a high degree of internal motivation to learn accounting concepts.

4. T F An advantage of open-book management is that it is easy to implement.

5. T F Business process reengineering is a management philosophy that deals with the ongoing management of an entire business.

6. T F The use of enterprise resource planning systems within the internal supply chain results in disjointed functions.

7. T F Enterprise resource planning systems use a decentralized location for data storage.

8. T F Modules in an enterprise resource planning system include finance, marketing, and manufacturing.

9. T F In implementing an environmental cost control system, the cost accountant considers cost management and cost reporting systems.

10. T F Often, a strategic alliance takes the form of a joint venture.

11. T F Data mining often uncovers quality problems.

12. T F In the development of new products, environmental management systems consider the potential for gathering and recycling obsolete products.

13. T F When companies become more efficient, they need fewer employees.

14. T F Downsizing has few risks.

15. T F Business process reengineering is a useful tool for improving quality.

Chapter 18: Emerging Management Practices 443

MULTIPLE CHOICE

1. Open-book management is a philosophy that deals with all except:

   A. increasing a company's performance.
   B. involving all employees.
   C. assuring that all employees have necessary information.
   D. limiting financial information to top management.

2. The increased use of business process reengineering is NOT driven by:

   A. advances in technology
   B. pursuit of increased quality
   C. increased price competition
   D. decreased reliance on machines

3. Business process reengineering is often associated with:

   A. technology sell-off.
   B. employee recruitment.
   C. outsourcing initiatives.
   D. increased middle management.

4. The first step in successful change management within a corporation is:

   A. educate all employees about the change.
   B. adopt only those innovations supporting current strategy.
   C. recognize the importance of organizational culture.
   D. dedicate equal time managing the human and technical aspects of change.

5. The last step in successful change management within a corporation is:

   A. adopt only those innovations supporting current strategy.
   B. educate all employees about the change.
   C. dedicate equal time managing the human and technical sides of change.
   D. make agreements as to when new systems will be online and old systems offline.

6. Steps to business process reengineering include all of the following except:

   A. develop the accounting systems for BPR implementation.
   B. identify the processes that are to be reengineered.
   C. determine the baseline for measuring the success of the BPR projects.
   D. define the objectives of the BPR project.

Chapter 18: Emerging Management Practices 444

7. Enterprise resource planning systems are packaged software that allow companies to do all of the following except:

    A. automate and integrate business processes.
    B. share common data and practices across the entity.
    C. produce and access information in real time.
    D. decentralize information.

8. Self-interested firms seek a diverse group of employees to do all of the following EXCEPT:

    A. decrease costs.
    B. increase productivity.
    C. increase market share.
    D. expand the accounting function.

9. Benefits of an enterprise resource planning system to a business include all of the following except:

    A. improved customer service.
    B. indirect access to systems.
    C. reduced overhead.
    D. better quality.

10. Enterprise resource planning systems software includes all of the following except:

    A. SAP.
    B. R/3.
    C. Quantum Integration
    D. PeopleSoft.

11. The term used for management actions that reduce employment and restructure operations as a response to competitive pressures is:

    A. outsourcing.
    B. target costing.
    C. constraints.
    D. downsizing.

12. The impact of a company on the environment is of increasing concern to:

    A. citizens and investors only.
    B. investors and government only.
    C. government and citizens only.
    D. citizens, government, management and investors.

Chapter 18:   Emerging Management Practices   445

13. The environmental management system concerned with the complete avoidance of pollution is called:

    A. end-of-pipe strategy.
    B. process improvements.
    C. pollution prevention.
    D. energy consumption planning.

14. The environmental management system concerned with cleaning up pollution after the production process is called:

    A. end-of-pipe strategy.
    B. process improvements.
    C. pollution prevention.
    D. energy consumption planning.

15. In environmental management systems, the design of a new product influences all of the following except:

    A. types and quantities of waste, scrap, and by-products produced.
    B. types and quantities of materials to be produced.
    C. amount of energy to be produced in the production process.
    D. potential for gathering and recycling obsolete products.

16. In open-book management, accountants must assume roles as information providers and:

    A. engineers.
    B. teachers.
    C. advertisers.
    D. purchasing agents.

17. Business process reengineering focuses on:

    A. value-added activities.
    B. the ongoing management of an entire business.
    C. discrete initiatives to improve specific processes.
    D. bottlenecks.

18. The application of open-book management is appropriate in:

    A. decentralized organizations that have empowered employees to make decisions.
    B. decentralized organizations that have not empowered employees to make decisions.
    C. large centralized organizations.
    D. small centralized organizations..

Chapter 18: Emerging Management Practices

19. Accountants assist in business process reengineering (BPR) by doing all of the following except:

    A. providing baseline measurements.
    B. deciding the BPR objectives.
    C. measuring the performance achieved with the redesigned process.
    D. redetermining corporate mission.

20. What is a question management should ask in considering cost management systems?

    A. Who receives reports on environmental costs in our company?
    B. Does our bonus plan explicitly consider environmental costs?
    C. How do we charge internal environmental costs to managers?
    D. How do we track compliance costs?

21. What is a question management should ask in considering cost reporting systems?

    A. Who receives reports on environmental costs in our company?
    B. Which divisions manage costs best?
    C. What kinds of waste do we produce?
    D. What are the proposed regulations that will affect our company?

22. A strategic alliance generally does not take the form of:

    A. licensing.
    B. non-exclusive seller agreements.
    C. equity investments.
    D. technology swaps.

23. The new strategic alliance entity generally does not require contributions of:

    A. human capital.
    B. stock.
    C. cash.
    D. patents.

24. Losses from downsizing often result from the:

    A. sale of unprofitable assets.
    B. excise tax imposed on downsizing.
    C. purchase of new advanced manufacturing equipment.
    D. purchase of new software.

Chapter 18: Emerging Management Practices 447

25. What techniques do analysts use in evaluating a downsizing decision?

    A. target costing
    B. value engineering
    C. throughput accounting
    D. capital budgeting

26. Agreements executed between parties involved in a strategic alliance include:

    A. unilateral sharing of losses.
    B. designing performance measures to evaluate team success.
    C. rights of the parties in sharing gains.
    D. keeping all data secret from the parties involved.

27. What is a common principle of open-book management?

    A. Show employees how their work influences financial results.
    B. Limit the books of account to only financial management on a need-to-know basis.
    C. Post success and results in upper management offices only for privacy.
    D. Link only financial measures to financial results.

28. The three generic strategies involved in environmental management systems include all of the following except:

    A. end-of-pipe strategy.
    B. process improvements strategy.
    C. pollution concealment strategy.
    D. pollution prevention strategy.

29. By sourcing and marketing globally, companies are rarely able to:

    A. develop new markets.
    B. reduce input costs.
    C. manage the effects of peaks and valleys in local economies.
    D. simplify labor practices.

30. In strategic planning for a global business, management considers:

    A. only currency values.
    B. only labor practices.
    C. only commercial laws.
    D. environmental factors too numerous to mention here.

Chapter 18: Emerging Management Practices 448

QUESTIONS AND PROBLEMS

1. Why will allowing employees to see financial records not necessarily solve problems and lead to improved performance?

2. What are the 10 common principles of open-book management?

3. What are the characteristics of companies that are best suited to implement open-book management?

Chapter 18: Emerging Management Practices

4. What are the five steps of business process reengineering?

5. What are the keys to successful use of business process reengineering?

6. What role do accountants play in business process reengineering?

Chapter 18: Emerging Management Practices

7. What are the risks and dangers of downsizing?

8. How does an enterprise resource planning system use computer software?

9. How does the installation process of an enterprise resource planning system affect the finance function?

Chapter 18: Emerging Management Practices 451

10. What are the many forms of strategic alliances and the expected terms of agreement between the parties involved?

11. What is the source and impact of environmental concerns on an organization?

12. How does the environmental management system consider new products and new processes?

Chapter 18: Emerging Management Practices

13. What are the three generic strategies involved in environmental management systems?

14. What are the eight managerial principles for successfully managing change?

15. Why do self-interested companies seek a diverse group of employees?

Chapter 18: Emerging Management Practices

SELF TEST ANSWERS

TRUE/FALSE

1.	F	4.	F	7.	F	10.	T	13.	T
2.	T	5.	F	8.	T	11.	T	14.	F
3.	F	6.	F	9.	T	12.	T	15.	T

MULTIPLE CHOICE

1.	D	7.	D	13.	C	19.	D	25.	D
2.	D	8.	D	14.	A	20.	D	26.	C
3.	C	9.	B	15.	C	21.	A	27.	A
4.	C	10.	C	16.	B	22.	B	28.	C
5.	D	11.	D	17.	C	23.	B	29.	D
6.	A	12.	D	18.	A	24.	A	30.	D

QUESTIONS AND PROBLEMS

1. Most employees do not have any understanding of accounting concepts or the skills necessary to interpret financial information. In addition, allowing employees to see financial information will have little effect if the company does not link the employees' compensation to financial performance measures.

2. The 10 common principles of open-book management are as follows: (1) Turn the management of a business into a game that employees can win. (2) Open the books and share financial and operating information with employees. (3) Teach the employees to understand the company's financial statements. (4) Show employees how their work influences financial results. (5) Link nonfinancial measures to financial results. (6) Target priority areas and empower employees to make improvements. (7) Review results together and keep employees accountable. Regularly hold performance review meetings. (8) Post results and celebrate successes. (9) Distribute bonus awards based on employee contributions to financial outcomes. (10) Share the ownership of the company with employees through employee stock ownership plans (ESOPs).

3. Characteristics of companies that are best suited to implement open-book management include small size, decentralized management, a history of employee empowerment, and a high level of trust between managers and other employees.

4. The five steps of business process reengineering are as follows: (1) Define the objectives of the project. (2) Identify the processes that are to be reengineered. (3) Determine a baseline for measuring the success of the project. (4) Identify the technology levers—the potential sources of innovation, increased quality, increased output, and decreased costs. (5) Develop initial prototypes of the reengineered processes, and then through subsequent iterations develop incremental improvements to the prototype until satisfactory results occur.

Chapter 18: Emerging Management Practices

5. Keys to a successful implementation of BPR are (1) set 'stretch' goals for the process in appropriate terms; (2) make certain the efforts have a leader and top management supports him/her; (3) involve everyone that is in the value chain, if possible; (4) assign both authority and responsibility to a single person; and (5) use a pilot program to identify problems.

6. Accountants aid in business process reengineering (BPR) by providing baseline measurements, deciding the BPR objectives, and measuring the achieved performance of the redesigned process. Because advancing technology can lead to BPR innovations, accountants must be aware of potential applications for new software and hardware.

7. The risks and dangers of downsizing include the following: (1) depleting the company's talent pool, (2) breaching the level of trust between managers and employees, and (3) destroying corporate cultures in which lifetime employment has been a major factor in attracting employees. Downsizing eliminates management positions that serve as training grounds for higher positions.

8. Companies manage data through a centralized depository through software systems such as SAP, R/3, PeopleSoft, and Baan. All data are accessible in an appropriate format in real time. Modules involve the subsets of the finance function, human resources management, manufacturing, and logistics. A complete enterprise resource planning system involves about 30 or more modules. The software facilitates the integration of customers to production and to suppliers. Customers can use the Internet to access information about orders. The information gathered through the software and data mining detects market opportunities and leads to better control of costs.

9. The installation of an enterprise resource planning (ERP) system affects the finance function in three significant ways. First, finance and system specialists must select and install software to implement an ERP system. The installation of a large system might involve millions of dollars in capital and thousands of hours of human capital. Second, financial specialists must analyze the data repository supporting management decisions. The specialist uses a process called drilling down to aggregate data properly into meaningful information. Finally, financial specialists need to maintain the integrity of the data repository. Cost accountants must monitor the ERP system modules to ensure that the system converts the raw data into a standardized format required for the main repository. The ERP system must properly integrate externally purchased data, such as industry sales data, with internally generated data.

10. Strategic alliances take many forms including the following: (1) exclusive buyer agreements, (2) exclusive seller agreements, (3) technology swaps, (4) joint research and development arrangements, (5) licensing, (6) equity investments, and (7) joint ventures. The parties execute agreements that provide the details about each party's share in gains and losses.

11. Governments, citizens, investors, and businesses are concerned with a company's environmental impact. Management should consider environmental cost in every aspect of operations. Significant environmental issues place the company at financial risk from the enforcement of governmental regulations. Investors evaluate a company's environmental track record before investing. Environmental issues span the entire value chain. From production to obsolescence, management should consider the environmental impact.

12. Through research and development, management identifies and develops new products and processes. The design influences the types and quantities of materials produced; the types and quantities of waste, scrap, and by-products; the energy consumed; and the potential gathering and recycling of obsolete products.

13. The three generic strategies for dealing with the environmental impact of operations are end-of-pipe, process improvements, and pollution prevention. The end-of-pipe strategy involves managing pollution after the production process creates it by finding a way to clean it up. Process improvement attempts to recycle waste internally, reduce the production of waste, or adopt processes that generate no waste. Pollution prevention involves avoidance of pollution by not producing pollutants in the first place.

14. From Exhibit 18-1, the eight managerial principles for successfully managing change are:

   1. Recognize the importance of organizational culture.
   2. Adopt only those innovations that support current strategies.
   3. Don't try to implement innovations during downsizing.
   4. Dedicate as much time in managing the human side of change as the technical side.
   5. Educate all employees about the change.
   6. Use medium- and long-term performance measure to gauge success.
   7. Generate useful and understandable reports to illustrate the effects of change.
   8. Make explicit agreements regarding when old information systems should be turned off once a new one is in place.

15. Companies seek a diverse group of employees for the following reasons: (1) to increase market share by greater market share connections; (2) to decrease costs through lower turnover, (3) increase productivity due to increased creativity; (4) to improve management quality through a diverse employee pool from which to draw talent; and (5) to improve recruiting efforts through expanded worker and talent pools.

CHAPTER 19

PERFORMANCE MEASUREMENT, BALANCED SCORECARDS, AND PERFORMANCE REWARDS

CHAPTER OVERVIEW

The most important factor affecting profitability in the global economy is attracting and satisfying customers. Historically, managers focused primarily on short-run financial performance, because companies used such measures to evaluate managers. Long-run and nonfinancial performance measures were often not available.

A mission statement guides the company to success. To compete effectively in the global marketplace, companies must use multiple types of performance measures. Multinational firms have more challenges than other organizations. The design of performance measures should include numerous short-run and long-run measures. A balanced scorecard measures performance by using various perspectives. Compensation strategy forms the underlying structure for compensation and determines what role compensation should play in the organization.

Managers are responsible for numerous functions. The primary managerial function is maximizing stockholder wealth. The design and implementation of employee performance measurement and reward system aligns performance with organizational goals. This chapter focuses on key tools in measurement and reward.

CHAPTER STUDY GUIDE

A mission statement describes a company's purposes and identifies how the company will meet its customers' needs. A company can also develop a values statement that reflects its organizational culture by stating the basic beliefs about what is important to the company. Values can be objective such as profitability or subjective such as ethical behavior.

The mission and values statements provide the foundation for setting organizational goals and objectives. Achieving short-term objectives is necessary for long-term survival, but a company must engage in long-term planning for short-term success to be meaningful.

To fulfill a company's mission, managers develop and implement strategies that apply

Chapter 19: Performance Measurement, Balanced Scorecards, and Performance Rewards

organizational resources to activities. Managers must also implement information systems to track how resources are applied. To assess effective and efficient management of resources, managers must define the terms *effective* and *efficient* and formulate performance measures consistent with those definitions. Managers can define these terms relative to historical performance, competitive benchmarking, or stakeholder expectations. Managers can evaluate performance by comparing measures of actual performance with defined performance goals.

Not setting performance measures in a critical area is tantamount to stating that the element is unimportant. Critical internal elements for performance measurement include production/performance and employees. Critical external elements for performance measurement include investors/creditors and customers. Critical elements are linked as high performance in one has an impact on the others. Exhibit 19-1 provides examples of critical elements for performance measures.

Internal measure focus on the efficiency and effectiveness of the production process. Internal measures must reflect concern for streamlined production, high quality, and minimized production complexity. A company can compete on the basis of price, quality, and/or product features. Superior performance in one or more of these areas can result in a competitive advantage for the company. Companies are searching for new ways to provide customers with more value at less cost. A company must develop an organizational culture that promotes learning, job satisfaction, and production efficiency. Each level of successive level of management establishes target measures for subordinates. Management uses measures to direct activities and make judgments about promotions and retentions. Managers can develop specific performance measures for each competitive dimension to identify different ways to take advantage of the company's competencies.

The organizational structure shows how a company assigns and coordinates people in implementing strategies. The company creates subunits and gives them specific responsibilities. Management should develop performance measures tailored to the role of each subunit. These performance measures reveal the extent to which each subunit is successful.

Performance measures should be appropriate for the type of responsibility assigned to a manager and the type of behavior desired. Performance measures should encourage managers to act in manners that will help the organization accomplish its missions. Top management should ask what behavior a specific performance measure will encourage.

Externally, performance measures must reflect the ability to satisfy customers better than rival firms do. Performance measures are not limited to financial areas. Product/service reliability, value and on-time delivery are examples of such measures. Meeting performance measures for customers increases the likelihood of meeting or exceeding the performance targets for creditors and investors.

A traditional area of performance measurement involves the effective and efficient use of capital. The financial accounting system provides financial reports to capital markets and other

Chapter 19: Performance Measurement, Balanced Scorecards, and Performance Rewards

external users. Companies must prepare these reports in accordance with generally accepted accounting principles (GAAP). These financial reports allow users to compare the performance of companies and decide which companies are worthy of investments. To obtain capital at competitive rates, managers must provide investors with an adequate return for the level of risk assumed. Stockholders are interested in performance measures that reveal the ability of the company to generate profits. However, considering the recent accounting scandals in the business community, management must take care that "good" financial performance should not be sought after by improper accounting.

Success in the global economy depends on the ability of a company to satisfy market segments better than any competitor. Profit is an important performance measure, but companies are developing additional performance measures for specific areas of market performance. Increased capital inflows, improved processes, more qualified employees and more satisfied customers should be the driving force of performance measures.

Since people tend to focus on things measured, management should set performance measures leading to corporate success. Management should consider five general criteria in developing a performance measurement system: (1) performance measures should assess progress toward organizational goals and objectives; (2) the persons being evaluated should have some input in developing the performance measures and be aware of them; (3) the persons being evaluated should have the necessary skills, equipment, information, and authority to be successful under the measurement system; (4) management should provide feedback about performance in a timely and useful manner; (5) the system should adapt to changes in the organizational environment. Exhibit 19-2 illustrates the criteria for designing a performance measurement system.

Because companies have a variety of goals and objectives, a single performance measure is unlikely to assess a company's progress toward all of its goals and objectives. A basic goal of any organization is to be financially viable. However, many companies now use nonfinancial performance measures along with financial performance measures. These nonfinancial performance measures include total customer satisfaction, zero defects, minimal lead time to market, and environmental and social responsibility. Companies can develop nonfinancial performance measures that show progress, or lack of it, toward achievement of these critical success factors for a world-class company.

Top management should establish high performance standards and communicate them to lower-level managers and employees. Performance measures should also encourage harmonious operations among all organizational units to prevent suboptimization. People usually act in accordance with how the company will measure and evaluate their performance.

If performance measures include comparisons of actual results to standard or budgeted results, people are more likely to support the process if they participated in setting the standards or budget. Participants should understand the standards and accept the reasonableness of the standards.

Chapter 19: Performance Measurement, Balanced Scorecards, and Performance Rewards

Management should place employees in jobs for which they are well suited. In addition, management should provide employees with the necessary equipment, information, authority, training, and support to perform their jobs in a manner consistent with the measurement process. Without the necessary tools, management cannot expect employees to accomplish their tasks.

In a decentralized company, top management has little opportunity to observe the actions of subunit managers. Thus, performance measures in a decentralized company should (1) directly relate to the subunit mission, (2) fairly reflect the subunit manager's performance, and (3) reflect performance under the subunit manager's control. Management establishes benchmarks against which it measures the performance of each subunit. The benchmarks can be monetary or nonmonetary.

Management should monitor the performance of employees and provide feedback on a continuous basis. This provides employees with time to make corrections and improve results before their performance review.

Traditionally, performance measures at the managerial level have included monetary measures such as profits, achievement of budget objectives, variances from budget or standard, and cash flow. Top management should evaluate managers of responsibility centers using measures related to their authority and responsibility. A manager of a cost center is responsible for costs incurred. The performance measures used to evaluate a manager of a cost center include variances from budgeted costs. A manager of a revenue center is responsible for revenues only. The primary performance measure for a manager of a revenue center is the difference between budgeted and actual revenues. Managers of profit and investment centers are responsible for revenues and expenses. Thus, various measures of income are appropriate for them. In addition, companies often evaluate managers of investment centers using return on investment, residual income, and economic value added.

Top management often evaluates managers of profit and investment centers based on segment margin. Segment margin equals sales revenue minus the sum of variable expenses and avoidable fixed expenses. Top management compares segment margin with the center's budgeted segment margin. Management also examines variances for specific revenues and expenses to learn where the center achieved or failed to achieve its objectives. Allocated common costs are not included in the calculation of segment margin.

However, managers can manipulate the components of segment margin through real or artificial means. Real manipulation includes accelerating or delaying discretionary expenses, shifting sales between periods, and delaying hiring of or terminating employees. Artificial manipulation is changing accounting methods or estimates to affect income. Manipulating segment margin to achieve budget expectations is not usually in the best long-run interest of the division or center. Such manipulations could also be improper accounting.

For a company or an investment center to succeed, it must achieve long-run profitability and always maintain liquidity. For external reporting purposes, companies must prepare a

Chapter 19: Performance Measurement, Balanced Scorecards, and Performance Rewards

Statement of Cash Flows. This statement shows the cash inflows and outflows for three categories: (1) operating, (2) investing, and (3) financing. The Statement of Cash Flows helps managers to assess the quality of the entity's earnings. Management uses financial ratios such as current ratio, quick ratio and number of days collection in accounts receivable with the cash flow statement to effectively conduct business. Combining statement of cash flows with budgets allows for meaningful analysis of cost reductions, collection policies, dividend payout, impact of capital projects and liquidity position.

Top management often evaluates managers of investment centers using return on investment (ROI) and residual income (RI). Return on investment is income divided by assets invested. However, management must define both terms specifically. Exhibit 19-3 lists questions and answers regarding return on investment definitions. Exhibit 19-4 provides data used to illustrate ROI calculations in Exhibit 19-5.

Companies often express ROI using the DuPont model. According to this formula, ROI equals profit margin multiplied by asset turnover. Asset turnover measures asset productivity and shows the number of sales dollars generated by each dollar of assets. Profit margin is income divided by sales, and asset turnover is sales divided by assets invested. Exhibit 19-6 illustrates the use of the DuPont model.

Managers can increase ROI by increasing sales, decreasing expenses, or decreasing the investment in assets. However, decisions that affect one element of the ROI formula will probably affect the other elements. Sales prices, volume and mix of products sold, expenses and capital asset acquisitions and disposals affect ROI. Management can increase ROI by 1) raising sales prices if demand is not impaired, 2) decreasing expenses and 3) decreasing dollars invested in assets, especially non-productive ones. Management should consider interrelationships between the elements that are used to calculate ROI before taking any actions. Thus, managers should make such decisions only after considering their dynamic effects. The elasticity of demand with respect to price is an important consideration regarding decisions about prices.

Management must compare the ROI to a benchmark used as a performance measure. Typically, the base of comparison could be expected ROI, prior ROI, or the ROI of similar companies or divisions. Using ROI as a performance measure discourages managers from investing in new assets whose projected rate of return is less than the current ROI. This reluctance sometimes is present even if the projected rate of return is greater than the target rate of return.

Management can also use residual income (RI) to evaluate the performance of investment center managers. Residual income is income minus the product of a target rate of return multiplied by the assets invested (asset base). Unlike ROI, residual income is a dollar amount rather than a percentage. Thus, managers have an incentive to invest in new assets if the projected ROI is greater than the target rate of return. Exhibit 19-7 illustrates the calculation of residual income.

Chapter 19: Performance Measurement, Balanced Scorecards, and Performance Rewards

A performance measure that is conceptually similar to residual income is economic value added (EVA). EVA attempts to align the interests of shareholders and managers. The major difference between EVA and RI is that EVA applies the target rate of return to the capital invested in the division or company while RI uses the book value of assets invested. Capital invested is the sum of the market value of total equity and total interest-bearing debt. The target rate is the weighted average cost of capital (%). In addition, EVA uses after-tax profits as the measure of income. Thus, EVA equals after-tax profits minus the product of capital invested and the weighted average cost of capital (%). Exhibit 19-4 provides data used to illustrate the economic value added calculations in Exhibit 19-8.

The more the divergence between the book value of capital and its market value, the greater is the difference between EVA and RI. Although EVA is a popular short-term performance measure, it cannot measure all dimensions of performance. EVA can discourage investments in long-term projects because such investments increase invested capital immediately, but they do not provide increased after-tax profits until some time in the future. Companies should supplement EVA with longer-term financial and nonfinancial performance measures.

Return on investment, residual income, and economic value added have three primary disadvantages: (1) three problems with income—managers can manipulate income, income depends on accounting methods, and income is based on accrual accounting, not cash flows; (2) three problems with assets invested—asset investment is difficult to measure, assets invested might reflect the decisions of previous managers, and if the company does not adjust assets and income for inflation, investment centers with older assets will have greater returns on investment; and (3) the use of these financial measures without relating them to company-wide objectives can motivate suboptimal behavior by managers.

Traditionally, companies have used only financial measures in performance evaluations. Financial measures are lagging indicators or reflections of the results of past decisions. Success requires that companies pay careful attention to the necessary steps to compete effectively in the global marketplace. Performance measures should track the leading indicators and occurrences of necessary steps to ensure profits. Exhibit 19-9 demonstrates examples of leading and lagging indicators.

Managers have often viewed managing for the long run as a series of short runs. This view is inappropriate when a company has not engaged in long-run technical and competitive improvements.

Short-run objectives usually focus on efficient and effective management of current operating, investing, and financing activities. Long-run objectives include resource investments and efforts to improve the company's competitive position. A company can improve its competitive position by improving customer satisfaction issues such as quality, delivery, cost, and service. Because several factors affect competitive position, a company must be able to identify the most important factors in achieving a long-run objective. In particular, a company

Chapter 19: Performance Measurement, Balanced Scorecards, and Performance Rewards

needs to know the underlying drivers of competitive position.

Managers might evaluate subordinates using quantitative and qualitative measures. Qualitative measures are often subjective. Examples of qualitative measures might be job skills or the need for supervision. However, managers are usually more comfortable with quantitative measures because they are more objective. Quantitative performance measures also are more effective in motivating employees because such measures provide a well-defined target. Quantitative measures can be either financial or nonfinancial.

Nonfinancial measures are appropriate under the following conditions: (1) if the company can clearly articulate them and define them, (2) if they are relevant to the objective, (3) if management can determine responsibility for the measures, (4) if the company can gather valid data, (5) if management can set target objectives, and (6) if management can establish internal and external benchmarks.

Nonfinancial measures include manufacturing cycle time, productivity, setup time, on-time delivery, and quality measures. Exhibit 19-10 lists advantages of nonfinancial performance measures over financial performance measures.

Before selecting nonfinancial performance measures, a company should identify its critical success factors. For each critical success factor, management should choose short-run and long-run nonfinancial performance measures.

After management selects performance measures, management should establish acceptable performance levels (benchmarks) against which to compare actual results. Management can develop these benchmarks internally or select them from external sources. Management should also install a system for monitoring and reporting comparative performance levels at regular intervals. Results from lower management should be monitored most frequently, such as continuously, daily, or weekly. Results from middle management are intermittently monitored, such as weekly, monthly, or annually. Results from upper management are least frequently monitored, such as monthly, quarterly, or annually.

A general model for measuring the relative success of an activity involves dividing the number of successes by total activity volume. For example, delivery success rate is equal to the number of on-time deliveries divided by total deliveries. A company could choose to measure a failure rate rather than a success rate. For example, the delivery failure rate is equal to the number of late deliveries divided by total deliveries. A benchmark for success could be 98% on-time deliveries.

Although internal measures are useful, ultimately customers are the judges of a company's performance. Good performance is providing a product or service that equals or exceeds a customer's expectations in terms of quality, price, and delivery. These expectations are unrelated to internal measures such as standard cost variances or capacity utilization. Therefore, nonfinancial measures that assess the level of customer satisfaction become more important.

Chapter 19: Performance Measurement, Balanced Scorecards, and Performance Rewards

Evaluating managers using external criteria of success should motivate the managers to implement concepts such as just-in-time inventory management, total quality management, and continuous improvement. The two common themes of these concepts are (1) to make the organization and its products and processes better and (2) to provide better value through lower costs.

Exhibit 19-11 lists ideas for evaluating managerial performance in four areas: (1) personnel, (2) market, (3) costs, and (4) returns (profitability). Management should monitor some of these measures for both short-run and long-run results. A specific set of performance measures reflects management's expectations and philosophies. As management's philosophy changes, performance measures will change also.

Throughput is the number of good units produced and sold within a particular period. The calculation of throughput involves three elements: (1) manufacturing cycle efficiency, (2) process productivity, and (3) process quality yield. The product of these three elements is the number of good units per hour of processing time. Thus, management should strive to increase throughput in terms of time and quality. Exhibit 19-12 shows an example of the throughput calculation.

Manufacturing cycle efficiency equals the value-added processing time divided by the total processing time. Process productivity equals the total units started during a period divided by the value-added processing time. Process quality yield is a measure of quality computed by dividing the number of good units by the total number of units. A company can increase throughput by decreasing non-value-added activities, increasing total production and sales, decreasing the per-unit processing time, or increasing the process quality yield. Improved throughput translates to quicker response to customer demand, production cost reduction and reduced inventory levels. Lower inventory results in lower non-value added costs such as moving and storage.

Companies operating in the global economy are concerned about providing high-quality products and services. These companies are developing nonfinancial quality measurements similar to the measures shown in Exhibit 19-13 to reduce the cost of poor quality.

One nonfinancial measure of service is lead time, which is how quickly customers receive their orders. Using lead time as a performance measure should motivate employees to reduce lead time by modifying the plant layout to ensure quicker work flow, increasing productivity, and reducing defects and rework. In addition, using fewer parts and more interchangeable parts after production begins will reduce lead time. Finally, managers should reduce non-value-added activities or constraints that create production, performance, or processing delays.

Some companies are adopting activity-based management (ABM) and activity-based costing (ABC). ABM emphasizes increasing throughput by decreasing non-value-added activities. ABC focuses on accurate cost measurement for long-term, strategic decisions. ABM and ABC can provide information on the effect of reengineered processes on overhead.

Chapter 19: Performance Measurement, Balanced Scorecards, and Performance Rewards

Management can use this information to increase efficiency and improve quality.

Companies are now beginning to use nonmonetary performance measures as part of a balanced scorecard to provide several perspectives of the performance for managers of responsibility centers. A balanced scorecard reflects the company's mission and strategies via performance measures from four perspectives: (1) financial, (2) internal business, (3) customer, and (4) learning, innovation and growth. Exhibit 19-14 illustrates a balanced scorecard.

Companies can use various performance measures in each of the four perspectives of the balanced scorecard. Management should design the financial measures of a balanced scorecard to reflect issues of interest to shareholders, such as profitability, stock price and growth. These measures (lag indicators of other perspectives) can include subunit operating income, overall net income, cash flow, change in market share, and return on assets. Balanced scorecard measures from the customer's perspective (lead indicators of financial measures) should show how well the company is doing relative to lead time, quality, service, and price. Internal measures should focus on vital internal processes for meeting customers' needs and expectations. These measures include process yields, manufacturing cycle efficiency, on-time delivery, and cost variances. Learning and growth measures should focus on the organization's intellectual capital. These measures include number of patent or copyright applications, percentage of research and development projects resulting in products eligible for patents, average time of research and development projects from conception to commercialization, and percentage of capital investments on high-tech projects.

The original purpose of a balanced scorecard was to provide top managers with a quick but comprehensive view of the business. However, some organizations now use a balanced scorecard at multiple levels of management. The balanced scorecard measurement system may be unique for each company and responsibility center.

Multinational segments require additional considerations in performance measurement and evaluation than do domestic operations. Using a single measure, such as net income, is even less appropriate for multinational segments than for domestic segments. In addition, when comparing the performances of multinational segments, management must consider differences in cultures, economies, accounting standards, and reporting practices. The required investment to create a business segment in different countries might vary significantly. Income comparisons between multinational units could be invalid because of differences in tariffs, income tax rates, currency fluctuations, and possible restrictions on the transfer of goods or currency.

Companies need flexible systems of evaluating profit performance for multinational profit centers and investment centers. The systems should recognize that factors such as accounting standards, economic conditions, and risk might be outside the manager's control. In such cases, qualitative performance measures such as increases in market share and quality improvements become more important.

No performance management system is suitable for all organizations or even for all

Chapter 19: Performance Measurement, Balanced Scorecards, and Performance Rewards

segments within an organization. Because people are unique, the performance measurement system should reflect the unique characteristics of the organization.

The compensation strategy provides a foundation for the compensation plan that addresses the role compensation should play in an organization. A rational compensation plan will closely link organizational goals and strategies with performance measures and employee rewards. Exhibit 19-15 provides a graphic illustration of the plan-performance-reward model. In this model, the board of directors and top management determine the strategic goals for the company. From these strategic goals, management identifies the company's critical success factors, defines its operational targets, identifies performance measures and rewards, measures performance, and determines rewards for achieving the targets.

The traditional compensation strategy has three basic employee groups: top management, middle management and workers. A company compensates each group differently. Top managers usually receive a salary with a possible bonus for exceeding financial objectives. A company often sets these objectives relative to net income or earnings per share. Middle managers receive salaries with the opportunity for raises usually based on financial performance measures such as segment income or divisional return on investment. Workers receive wages based on the number of hours worked with possible bonuses based on some quantitative measure.

Compensation plans should encourage greater levels of employee performance and loyalty, while reducing costs and increasing profits. Such plans must encourage behavior that is vital to achieving organizational goals and maximizing stockholder value. First, management must connect performance measures with the organization's operational targets. Otherwise, workers might earn incentive pay although the company does not achieve its objectives.

Second, performance measures must not focus too much on the short run. Maximizing shareholder wealth is inherently a long-run consideration. Short-run measures rarely promote long-run wealth maximization. Performance rewards should encourage workers to adopt a long-run viewpoint. Financial incentives often include common stock or stock options. When employees become stockholders of their employer company, they adopt the same long-run wealth maximization goals as other stockholders.

Each subunit of a company has a unique mission and possesses unique competencies. A company should develop its performance measurement and reward system with the subunit's mission in mind. Performance measures and rewards affect the focus of a subunit's employees. The focus of the employees should be on factors that determine the success of the subunit's operations. Exhibit 19-16 shows how a subunit's mission influences the form of reward.

Employee age is an important factor in designing employee incentive plans. Younger employees usually have a longer-term perspective than older employees who expect to retire within a few years. Management should consider this difference in perspective between younger and older employees in designing employee incentives.

Chapter 19: Performance Measurement, Balanced Scorecards, and Performance Rewards

Another consideration is balancing the incentives for groups (or teams) and individuals. Workers in automated production systems spend more time monitoring and controlling machinery rather than being involved in hands-on production. Incentives for small groups and individuals are often virtual substitutes. As the group grows larger, management should establish incentives for both the group and each individual. Group incentives are important, but some individual incentives are necessary to encourage all members of the group to perform rather than "free riding" on the efforts of others.

Once management knows the target objectives and compensation strategy, management can determine performance measures for individual employees or employee groups. Management should determine their compensation based on their required contributions to the operational plan. Performance measures should link individual actions with the basic business strategies.

Actual employee performance is a result of employee effort, employee skill, and random factors. Random factors include performance measurement error, co-worker problems or influences, illness, and weather related production problems. Determining which factors are under the employee's control may be impossible.

Workers' performance measures should be specific and short-term. Typically these measures are cost and/or quality control. Higher levels in the organization will have more measures of the company's success factors in correlation with their control and responsibility and these measures will become less specific and more long term.

Incentives should be mostly monetary and short-term at lower employee levels, and incentives should be mostly nonmonetary and long-term at higher levels. The system should provide a combination of rewards for all managers and employees. Such a two-fold compensation system provides lower-paid employees with more money to enrich their lifestyles, but still provides rewards (such as stock options) that cause them to take a long-run view of the company. Top managers should receive more rewards (such as stock and stock options) that should cause them to be more concerned about the company's long-term success rather than short-term personal gains.

Management monitors employees' performance as they perform their required tasks. Management must monitor individual and group effort and performance because teams rather than individuals perform many tasks. Both feedback loops shown in Exhibit 19-15 exist so that management can identify and correct any problems for future periods. The first feedback loop concerns the monitoring and measurement of performance, which management considers in setting targets for the following periods. The second feedback loop relates to the rewards given and the compensation strategy's effectiveness. Both loops are critically important to the managerial planning process.

Evolving management philosophies now emphasize the necessity for workers to perform in teams and groups. Workers are more detached from the production function and are more

Chapter 19: Performance Measurement, Balanced Scorecards, and Performance Rewards

involved with higher-technology tasks. The trend is to rely more on performance-based evaluation and less on direct supervision to control worker behavior.

Profit sharing provides incentive payments to employees. These current and/or deferred incentive payments are contingent on organizational performance and can be in the form of cash or stock. A company allocates the total profit sharing payment among individual employees on the basis of personal performance measurements, seniority, team performance, managerial judgment, or specified formulas.

The Employee Stock Ownership Plan (ESOP) is a popular profit-sharing compensation program in which employees receive the securities of the employer. An ESOP must conform to the tax law, but it offers both tax and employee incentive advantages. Under an ESOP, the employer makes tax-deductible payments of cash or stock to a trust fund. A trustee then uses any contributed cash to purchase shares of the employer's stock. The employees are the trust beneficiaries, and their wealth in the ESOP grows (or possibly diminishes) with both employer contributions and advances (or decreases) in the market price of the stock.

Management and supervisors can also motivate workers by nonfinancial incentives. Employees want nonmonetary rewards such as recognition, appreciation, and praise. Allowing subordinates to participate in decisions helps to make their employment more enjoyable.

One important consideration is the tax effect of each alternative reward provided by compensation packages. Differences in tax treatment are important because they affect the amount of after-tax income received by the employee and the after-tax cost of the pay plan to the employer. Three different tax treatments exist for employee compensation: (1) full and immediate taxation, (2) deferral of taxation, and (3) exemption from taxation. Tax deferral means that taxation occurs in the future. Tax-exempt income is never subject to taxation. Most forms of compensation are fully and currently taxable to the employee and fully and currently deductible by the employer.

Fringe benefits are compensation other than wages and salaries. Fringe benefits create extra costs for the employer and provide additional benefits for employees. Employee health insurance, child care, physical fitness facilities, and pension plans are common examples of fringe benefits. Certain employee fringe benefits, such as employer-provided accident and health insurance plans, are not taxable income to the employee but are fully and currently deductible by the employer.

A current debate centers on the disparity in pay between ordinary employees and top managers. CEOs often earn many times what ordinary employees earn. The greatest ethical dilemmas involve circumstances that place the welfare of employees against the welfare of stockholders or the welfare of managers against the welfare of workers. The organization will be capable of achieving the necessary efficiency to compete in global markets only if there is a perception of equity across the contributions and entitlements of labor, management, and capital.

Chapter 19: Performance Measurement, Balanced Scorecards, and Performance Rewards

With international operations increasing, companies must develop compensation plans that treat expatriate employees fairly and equitably. Expatriates are parent-company and third-country nationals assigned to a foreign subsidiary, or foreign nationals assigned to the parent company. A compensation package that is fair and equitable in one country might not be fair and equitable in another country.

Expatriates' compensation packages must reflect labor market factors, cost-of-living considerations, currency fluctuations, and tax consequences. Companies might pay expatriates in the currency where they live, in their home currency, or a combination of both.

Management usually builds in a price-level adjustment clause into the compensation system to counteract any local currency inflation or deflation. The fringe benefit related to retirement should align with the home country and consist of the home currency, regardless of the currency makeup of the pay package.

Chapter 19: Performance Measurement, Balanced Scorecards, and Performance Rewards

SELF TEST

TRUE/FALSE

1. T F Economic value added defines income as after-tax profits.

2. T F Return on investment is equal to assets invested divided by income.

3. T F Residual income is the income of an investment center minus the product of a target rate of return and the asset base.

4. T F Differences in cultures and economies are unimportant to performance measures.

5. T F The primary managerial function is maximizing stockholder wealth.

6. T F Throughput is a performance indicator that refers to the number of good units that a company manufactures and sells during a period.

7. T F Activity-based management is concerned with reducing non-value-added activities and increasing throughput.

8. T F Total units completed during a period divided by the value-added processing time equals process productivity.

9. T F Short-run objectives usually reflect a focus on the effective and efficient management of current operating, financing, and selling activities.

10. T F Retirement contributions for expatriates should be paid in their home currency and not in the currency of the country in which they are relocated.

11. T F Financial measures always predict the direction of future cash flows better than do nonfinancial measures.

12. T F The more the divergence between the book value of capital and its market value, the greater is the difference between economic value added and residual income.

13. T F Economic value added is a long-term performance measure.

14. T F To be successful in the global economy, a company must develop an organizational culture that promotes learning and innovation.

15. T F Tax deferral means that the employee will never have to pay tax on the benefit.

Chapter 19: Performance Measurement, Balanced Scorecards, and Performance Rewards

MULTIPLE CHOICE

1. Performance measurements should NOT:

    A. reflect organizational goals and objectives.
    B. be specific and understandable.
    C. cause harmonious relations among subunits.
    D. promote actions that hinder the organizational mission.

2. How does economic value added (EVA) define capital invested?

    A. the book value of equity
    B. the book value of equity and interest-bearing debt
    C. the market value of equity
    D. the market value of equity and interest-bearing debt

3. What is the preferred definition of income in determining an investment center's return on investment?

    A. operating income
    B. operating income less interest
    C. segment margin
    D. net income after taxes

4. Income comparisons among multinational units is usually NOT invalid because of:

    A. differences in tax rates and tariffs.
    B. currency fluctuations.
    C. possible restrictions on the transfer of goods or currency.
    D. differences in organizational goals.

5. Profit margin equals:

    A. income ÷ sales.
    B. income ÷ average assets.
    C. average assets ÷ income.
    D. sales ÷ income.

Chapter 19:   Performance Measurement, Balanced Scorecards, 472
and Performance Rewards

6. A problem with using income to measure performance is that the individual components used to derive income are:

   A. often variable with volume.
   B. not subject to precise measurement.
   C. subject to manipulation.
   D. not reported on a timely basis.

7. The total number of good units produced divided by the total value-added processing time during a period is:

   A. process productivity.
   B. throughput.
   C. process quality yield.
   D. not provided as an answer option.

8. Return on investment equals:

   A. asset turnover ÷ profit margin.
   B. average assets ÷ income.
   C. profit margin x asset turnover.
   D. income x assets.

9. The first step in the plan-performance-reward model is to set:

   A. strategic goals.
   B. operational targets.
   C. the compensation strategy.
   D. performance rewards.

10. What are the three sections of the Statement of Cash Flows?

    A. operating, investing, and financing
    B. assets, liabilities, and stockholders' equity
    C. revenues, expenses, and gains or losses
    D. sales, production, and financing

11. Managers can increase ROI by:

    A. decreasing the sales price if demand is inelastic with respect to price.
    B. increasing wasteful expenses.
    C. increasing unproductive assets.
    D. reducing what is invested in assets.

Chapter 19: Performance Measurement, Balanced Scorecards, and Performance Rewards

12. When designing pay-for-performance plans, management would not focus long on:

    A. correlating organizational goals and the appropriate time horizon.
    B. the subunit mission and employee ages.
    C. balancing group and individual benefits.
    D. short-term top management compensation.

13. What shows the manner in which a company assigns and coordinates people in implementing strategies?

    A. balanced scorecard
    B. organizational structure
    C. organizational culture
    D. organizational climate

14. A company's organizational culture should foster:

    A. learning, innovation and growth measures.
    B. internal process measures.
    C. financial measures.
    D. using the same performance measure for all subunits.

15. Which of the following is a nonfinancial performance measure?

    A. return on investment
    B. residual income
    C. lead time to market
    D. economic value added

16. Which of the following is an internal business perspective measure under the balanced scorecard approach?

    A. manufacturing cycle efficiency
    B. cash flow
    C. service
    D. number of patent applications

17. The primary performance measure for the manager of a revenue center is:

    A. return on investment.
    B. residual income.
    C. economic value added.
    D. the difference between budgeted and actual revenues.

Chapter 19:   Performance Measurement, Balanced Scorecards, and Performance Rewards

18. A company should NOT give overall compensation consideration for expatriates based on:

    A. the cost-of-living.
    B. currency fluctuations.
    C. taxes.
    D. psychological differences.

19. In calculating return on investment, which of the following is the most preferred way for a company to value plant assets in calculating the asset base?

    A. net book value
    B. current values
    C. original cost
    D. original cost adjusted for inflation

20. For higher-level managerial employees, more incentives should be:

    A. monetary and short term.
    B. nonmonetary and short term.
    C. monetary and long term.
    D. nonmonetary and long term.

21. How often should companies monitor performance and provide feedback?
    A. continuously
    B. monthly
    C. quarterly
    D. annually

22. The number of hours of quality related downtime is a nonfinancial measure of:

    A. prevention
    B. appraisal
    C. internal failure
    D. external failure

23. Gardner Company had a net income before tax of $500,000. The tax rate was 40 percent. The market value of debt and equity was $1,500,000, and the book value of debt and equity was $1,000,000. The weighted average cost of capital was 12 percent. What was the economic value added?

    A. $20,000
    B. $80,000
    C. $120,000
    D. $180,000

24. Hats Away Company presents you with the following information for the year:
    Total units processed   10,000
    Good units   9,500
    Value-added processing time   40,000 hours
    Total time   50,000 hours
    What was the manufacturing cycle efficiency?

    A. 20%
    B. 80%
    C. 95%
    D. 125%

25. Hats Away Company presents you with the following information for the year:
    Total units processed   10,000
    Good units   9,500
    Value-added processing time   40,000 hours
    Total time   50,000 hours
    What was the throughput?

    A. 0.19 units per hour
    B. 0.24 units per hour
    C. 0.95 units per hour
    D. 1.25 units per hour

26. Robbins Company had a profit margin of 10 percent, income of $50,000, and assets invested of $250,000. What was the turnover?

    A. 2
    B. 5
    C. 10
    D. 20

27. Knotts Division had the following results for the year:
    Net sales $300,000
    Income   36,000
    Average assets   150,000
    Target rate of return on average assets   9%
    What was the profit margin?

    A. 2%
    B. 9%
    C. 12%
    D. 24%

Chapter 19: Performance Measurement, Balanced Scorecards, and Performance Rewards

28. Knotts Division had the following results for the year:
    Net sales $300,000
    Income   36,000
    Average assets   150,000
    Target rate of return on average assets   9%
    What was the asset turnover?

    A. 2.00
    B. 8.33
    C. 12.00
    D. 24.00

29. Knotts Division had the following results for the year:
    Net sales $300,000
    Income   36,000
    Average assets   150,000
    Target rate of return on average assets   9%
    What was the return on investment?

    A. 2%
    B. 3%
    C. 12%
    D. 24%

30. Knotts Division had the following results for the year:
    Net sales $300,000
    Income   36,000
    Average assets   150,000
    Target rate of return on average assets   9%
    What was the residual income?

    A. $9,000
    B. $13,500
    C. $22,500
    D. $27,000

… **Chapter 19: Performance Measurement, Balanced Scorecards, and Performance Rewards**

QUESTIONS AND PROBLEMS

1. Why are financial measures inadequate to address new issues necessary for the survival of world-class companies?

2. Describe the plan-performance-reward model.

3. What are the three primary limitations of using return on investment, residual income, and economic value added as performance measures?

Chapter 19: Performance Measurement, Balanced Scorecards, and Performance Rewards

4. What are the general criteria for performance measurement?

5. What is a balanced scorecard and what purpose does it serve?

6. What is economic value added (EVA) and how does it differ from residual income?

Chapter 19: Performance Measurement, Balanced Scorecards, and Performance Rewards

7. Describe the impact of taxation on the design of a compensation plan.

8. What are the effects of linking performance measures to the managerial reward structure?

9. What are benchmarks? Why are benchmarks important in performance measurement?

Chapter 19: Performance Measurement, Balanced Scorecards, and Performance Rewards

10. Why is using original cost better than using net book value in the asset base in computing return on investment? What is the most preferred valuation method of plant assets in computing return on investment?

11. What is lead time? What are the benefits of measuring lead time?

12. Why do managers value the Statement of Cash Flows as an aid to performance measurement?

Chapter 19: Performance Measurement, Balanced Scorecards, and Performance Rewards

13. Describe and give examples of the internal and external critical elements for performance measurement.

14. Jennings Company worked 5,000 hours to produce 4,000 total units. Of the 5,000 hours worked, 4,000 hours were value-added processing time. Of the 4,000 units produced, 3,900 were good units. Compute the following:

(a) manufacturing cycle efficiency

(b) process productivity

(c) process quality yield

(d) throughput

15. The Northern Division of Brock Company had the following results for the year:

Sales	$2,500,000
Income	175,000
Average assets	1,250,000
Target return on average assets	11%

Calculate the following:

(a) profit margin

(b) asset turnover

(c) return on investment

(d) residual income

Chapter 19: Performance Measurement, Balanced Scorecards, and Performance Rewards

SELF TEST ANSWERS

TRUE/FALSE

1. T
2. F
3. T
4. F
5. T
6. T
7. T
8. T
9. T
10. T
11. F
12. T
13. F
14. T
15. F

MULTIPLE CHOICE

1. D
2. D
3. C
4. D
5. A
6. C
7. D
8. C
9. A
10. A
11. D
12. D
13. B
14. A
15. C
16. A
17. D
18. D
19. B
20. D
21. A
22. C
23. C
24. B
25. A
26. A
27. C
28. A
29. D
30. C

QUESTIONS AND PROBLEMS

1. Many companies have set goals of customer satisfaction, zero defects, minimal lead time to market, and social responsibility for the environment. Companies cannot measure these goals with monetary measures. Companies that make inferior goods, deliver products late, abuse the environment, or fail to satisfy customers will lose market share and eventually cease to exist. Companies can develop nonfinancial performance measures to track progress, or lack thereof, toward achievement of long-run critical success factors of world-class companies.

2. The plan-performance-reward model involves a continuous alignment of performance rewards with performance results. Management starts with strategic goals and then identifies critical success factors, operational targets, and compensation strategy. Management then identifies performance measures and sets performance rewards. Employees or employee groups then perform tasks. Management measures or monitors performance and determines rewards. The plan-performance-reward model has two feedback loops to correct problems in future periods. The first feedback loop relates to monitoring and performance measures. The second feedback loop concerns the rewards given and compensation strategy effectiveness.

3. Return on investment, residual income, and economic value added have three primary disadvantages: (1) three problems with income—managers can manipulate income, income depends on accounting methods, and income is based on accrual accounting, not cash flows; (2) three problems with assets invested—asset investment is difficult to measure, assets invested may reflect the decisions of previous managers, and if assets and income are not adjusted for inflation, investment centers with older assets will have greater returns on investment; and (3) the use of return on investment and residual income can cause suboptimal behavior.

Chapter 19: Performance Measurement, Balanced Scorecards, and Performance Rewards

4. Management should consider five general criteria in developing a performance measurement system: (1) performance measures should assess progress toward organizational goals and objectives; (2) the persons being evaluated should have some input in developing the performance measures and be aware of them; (3) persons being evaluated should have the necessary skills, equipment, information, and authority to be successful under the measurement system; (4) management should provide feedback about performance in a timely and useful manner; and (5) the system should adapt to changes in the organizational environment.

5. . A balanced scorecard is a set of financial and nonfinancial performance measures. It links all aspects of performance to a company's strategies. The balanced scorecard gives a comprehensive view of performance measures that reflect both the internal and external perspectives. The complexity of managing a company today requires that managers view performance in several areas simultaneously. A balanced scorecard enables managers to do so.

6. Economic value added (EVA) is a measure of profit produced above the cost of capital. EVA equals after-tax profits minus the product of capital invested and the weighted average cost of capital. Capital includes the market value of equity and interest-bearing debt. Residual income and EVA are similar. The major difference between EVA and residual income is that EVA uses the total market value of capital invested rather than the market value or book value of book assets.

7. The impact of taxes on the design of a compensation plan is profound. Creative ways to compensate employees through tax-deferred and tax-exempt benefits increase actual incentives for employees. Cafeteria plans contain a menu of tax-exempt or tax-deferred incentives to allow employees to choose the best incentives for themselves. By electing the benefits that they would use anyway, employees increase their after-tax income from their compensation. While federal income taxes play a significant role in the level of compensation, state and local taxes and payroll taxes also reduce the level of take-home pay of each individual.

8. By linking performance measures to rewards, managers have an incentive to improve performance in specific areas. The incentive should motivate managers to take desired actions to achieve the organization's mission. However, if performance measures do not capture the vital performance dimensions for accomplishing the missions, managers might have an incentive to act in manners contrary to the missions.

9. Benchmarks are standards against which management compares actual results to evaluate performance. Benchmarks can be monetary or nonmonetary. Benchmarks are important because they are performance standards that managers and employees should seek to achieve. Managers and employees should understand the benchmarks that management will use to evaluate their performance.

Chapter 19: Performance Measurement, Balanced Scorecards, and Performance Rewards

10. If a company used net book value in the asset base for computing return on investment, the asset base would decrease each year because of the increase in the accumulated depreciation. Thus, a manager could show a higher return on investment each year by earning the same amount of income. Using the original cost of plant assets is better because a manager would have to earn a higher income to show a higher return on investment. However, the most preferred valuation method of plant assets in computing return on investment is current values. Using current values measures the opportunity cost of using the plant assets. Current values are more difficult to obtain and are often very subjective estimates.

11. Lead time refers to how quickly customers receive their orders. Lead time is a nonfinancial measure of service. Measuring lead time should provide several benefits to a company. Customers should receive their orders more rapidly, which should build customer loyalty and goodwill. In addition, measuring lead time should motivate the company to reduce costs by using fewer parts and more interchangeable parts. The company might also be motivated to alter the plant layout to improve the work flow, increase productivity, and improve quality. Finally, managers should be motivated to reduce non-value-added activities and constraints that cause delays.

12. The Statement of Cash Flows provides managers with global view of the company's cash flows. The Statement of Cash Flows arranges cash flows by major activity. This arrangement allows managers to judge whether the anticipated cash flows are consistent with the company's strategic plans. In addition, the Statement of Cash Flows includes noncash investing and financing transactions in a separate schedule. Managers should be aware of major noncash investing and financing transactions to determine their potential effect on cash availability. By using the Statement of Cash Flows with budgets and other financial reports, managers can obtain information on the effects of cost reductions, collection policies, dividends, and capital projects on total cash flows and liquidity.

13. From Exhibit 19-1, internal critical elements for performance measurement are Production/Performance and Employees. Production/Performance organizational measures of performance include but are not limited to throughput, quality levels and reduction of product complexity. Employees organizational measures of performance include but are not limited to patents developed, days of training and retention. Also from Exhibit 19-1, external critical elements for performance measurement are Investors and Creditors and Customers. Investors and Creditors organizational measures of performance include but are not limited to profitability, stability and dividend payout. Customers organizational measures of performance include but are not limited to market share, rate of on-time shipments and referrals.

Chapter 19: Performance Measurement, Balanced Scorecards, and Performance Rewards

14. (a) manufacturing cycle efficiency = $\dfrac{\text{value-added processing time}}{\text{total time}}$

    $= \dfrac{4,000 \text{ hours}}{5,000 \text{ hours}} = 80\%$

    (b) process productivity = $\dfrac{\text{total units}}{\text{value-added processing time}}$

    $= \dfrac{4,000 \text{ units}}{4,000 \text{ hours}} = 1$ unit per value-added hour

    (c) process quality yield = $\dfrac{\text{good units}}{\text{total units}} = \dfrac{3,900 \text{ units}}{4,000 \text{ units}} = 97.5\%$

    (d) throughput = $\dfrac{\text{good units}}{\text{total time}}$

    $= \dfrac{3,900 \text{ units}}{5,000 \text{ hours}} = 0.78$ units per hour

15. (a) profit margin = $\dfrac{\text{income}}{\text{sales}} = \dfrac{\$175,000}{\$2,500,000} = 7.00\%$

    (b) asset turnover = $\dfrac{\text{sales}}{\text{average assets}} = \dfrac{\$2,500,000}{\$1,250,000} = 2.00$

    (c) return on investment = $\dfrac{\text{income}}{\text{average assets}} = \dfrac{\$175,000}{\$1,250,000} = 14.00\%$

    or return on investment = profit margin x asset turnover

    $= 7.00\% \times 2.00 = 14.00\%$

    (d)
income	$175,000
less: target income ($1,250,000 x 11%)	(137,500)
residual income	$37,500